Barcode on Back

MW01122406

# BLUES, FUNK, RHYTHM AND BLUES, SOUL, HIP HOP AND RAP

# ROUTLEDGE MUSIC BIBLIOGRAPHIES

## COMPOSERS

*Isaac Albéniz (1998)*
Walter A. Clark

*C. P. E. Bach (2002)*
Doris Bosworth Powers

*Samuel Barber, Second edition (2010)*
Wayne C. Wentzel

*Béla Bartók, Second edition (1997)*
Elliott Antokoletz

*Vincenzo Bellini, Second edition (2009)*
Stephen A. Willier

*Alban Berg, Second edition (2009)*
Bryan R. Simms

*Leonard Bernstein (2001)*
Paul F. Laird

*Johannes Brahms (2003)*
Heather Platt

*Benjamin Britten (1996)*
Peter J. Hodgson

*William Byrd, Second edition (2005)*
Richard Turbet

*Elliott Carter (2000)*
John L. Link

*Carlos Chávez (1998)*
Robert Parker

*Frédéric Chopin (1999)*
William Smialek

*Aaron Copland (2001)*
Marta Robertson and Robin Armstrong

*Frederick Delius, Second edition (2009)*
Mary L. Huisman

*Gaetano Donizetti, Second edition (2009)*
James P. Cassaro

*Edward Elgar (1993)*
Christopher Kent

*Gabriel Fauré (1999)*
Edward R. Phillips

*Alberto Ginastera, Second edition (2010)*
Deborah Schwartz-Kates

*Christoph Willibald Gluck, Second edition (2003)*
Patricia Howard

*Charles François Gounod (2009)*
Timothy S. Flynn

*G.F. Handel, Second edition (2004)*
Mary Ann Parker

*Paul Hindemith, Second edition (2009)*
Stephen Luttman

*Charles Ives, Second edition (2010)*
Gayle Sherwood

*Scott Joplin (1998)*
Nancy R. Ping-Robbins

*Zoltán Kodály (1998)*
Mícheál Houlahan and Philip Tacka

*Franz Liszt, Third edition (2009)*
Michael Saffle

*Guillaume de Machaut (1995)*
Lawrence Earp

*Gustav and Alma Mahler (2008)*
Susan M. Filler

*Felix Mendelssohn Bartholdy (2001)*
John Michael Cooper

*Olivier Messiaen (2008)*
Vincent P. Benitez

*Giovanni Pierluigi da Palestrina (2001)*
Clara Marvin

*Giacomo Puccini (1999)*
Linda B. Fairtile

*Maurice Ravel (2004)*
Stephen Zank

*Gioachino Rossini, Second edition (2010)*
Denise P. Gallo

*Camille Saint-Saëns (2003)*
Timothy S. Flynn

*Alessandro and Domenico Scarlatti (1993)*
Carole F. Vidali

*Heinrich Schenker (2003)*
Benjamin Ayotte

*Alexander Scriabin (2004)*
Ellon D. Carpenter

*Jean Sibelius (1998)*
Glenda D. Goss

*Giuseppe Verdi (1998)*
Gregory Harwood

*Tomás Luis de Victoria (1998)*
Eugene Casjen Cramer

*Richard Wagner, Second edition (2010)*
Michael Saffle

*Adrian Willaert (2004)*
David Michael Kidger

## GENRES

*American Music Librarianship (2005)*
Carol June Bradley

*Blues, Funk, R&B, Soul, Hip-Hop, and Rap (2010)*
Eddie S. Meadows

*Chamber Music, Third edition (2010)*
John H. Baron

*Church and Worship Music (2005)*
Avery T. Sharp and James Michael Floyd

*Concerto (2006)*
Stephen D. Lindeman

*Ethnomusicology (2003)*
Jennifer C. Post

*Jazz Scholarship and Pedagogy, Third edition (2005)*
Eddie S. Meadows

*The Musical (2004)*
William A. Everett

*North American Indian Music (1997)*
Richard Keeling

*Opera, Second edition (2001)*
Guy Marco

*Piano Pedagogy (2009)*
Gilles Comeau

*The Recorder, Second edition (2003)*
Richard Griscom and David Lasocki

*Serial Music and Serialism (2001)*
John D. Vander Weg

*String Quartets, Second edition (2009)*
Mara E. Parker

*The Violin (2006)*
Mark Katz

*Women in Music, Second edition (2010)*
Karin Pendle

# Blues, Funk, Rhythm and Blues, Soul, Hip Hop and Rap

## A Research and Information Guide

Eddie S. Meadows

ROUTLEDGE MUSIC BIBLIOGRAPHIES

Routledge
Taylor & Francis Group

NEW YORK AND LONDON

First published 2010
By Routledge
270 Madison Ave, New York, NY 10016

Simultaneously published in the UK
by Routledge
2 Park Square, Milton Park, Abingdon, Oxon OX14 4RN

*Routledge is an imprint of the Taylor & Francis Group, an informa business*

© 2010 Taylor & Francis

Typeset in Times New Roman by
Taylor & Francis Books

*Library of Congress Cataloging in Publication Data*
Meadows, Eddie S.
   Blues, funk, rhythm and blues, soul, hip hop, and rap : a research and information guide / Eddie S. Meadows.
      p. cm. – (Routledge music bibliographies)
   Includes bibliographical references and index.
   1. Blues (Music)–Bibliography. 2. Funk (Music)–Bibliography. 3. Rhythm and blues music–Bibliography. 4. Soul music–Bibliography. 5. Rap (Music)–Bibliography. I. Title.
   ML128.P63M43 2010
   016.78164–dc22
            2009042239

ISBN10: 0-415-97319-8 (hbk)
ISBN10: 0-203-85472-1 (ebk)

ISBN13: 978-0-415-97319-9 (hbk)
ISBN13: 978-0-203-85472-3 (ebk)

*Dedication*
*To J.J., the light at the end of the tunnel.*

# Contents

# About the author

Eddie S. Meadows is Professor Emeritus of Ethnomusicology and Jazz Studies and former Graduate Advisor of the School of Music and Dance at San Diego State University (SDSU). He received the BS degree in Music from Tennessee State University, the MS degree in Music from the University of Illinois, and the PhD in Music Education from Michigan State University. In addition, he did postdoctoral work in Ethnomusicology at the University of California, Los Angeles (UCLA), specializing in African music, and studied *Atenteben* and Ewe drumming at the University of Ghana, Legon (West Africa). He has held Visiting Professorships at the University of Ghana, Michigan State University (Martin Luther King Visiting Scholar), UCLA and the University of California, Berkeley. From January to June 2007, Dr Meadows was a Visiting Professor of Jazz at the University of Southern California (USC), and served as Adjunct Professor of Jazz from Fall 2007 to 2009.

His publications include the following books: *Jazz Scholarship and Pedagogy: A Research and Information Guide* (Routledge, 2006), *Bebop to Cool: Context, Ideology, and Musical Identity* (Praeger, 2003; named a *Choice Outstanding Academic Title of 2004*), *California Soul: Music of African Americans in the West* (co-edited with Jacqueline Cogdell DjeDje, University of California Press, 1998), *Jazz Research and Performance Materials: A Select Annotated Bibliography* (Garland, 1995), and *Jazz Reference and Research Materials* (Garland, 1981). Other publications include numerous articles, encyclopedia entries and reprints, and book/record reviews. In addition to his publications, Dr Meadows has given papers and lectures at colleges, universities and meetings of scholarly societies.

# Introduction

Few would argue the well-deserved place of jazz studies in most institutions of higher learning, or question scholars who have produced a myriad of studies, including reference works, to enhance the serious teaching and research of jazz. The same is not true, however, of other African American musical styles. With the exception of blues, there are few reference materials (e.g. bibliographies, dictionaries and encyclopedias) on funk, rhythm and blues, soul, hip hop and rap. Given the significant increase in scholarly research in these musical styles, and the fact that no single annotated bibliography exists on the above-mentioned musical genres, my primary objective is twofold: to provide the first annotated sampling of research on funk, rhythm and blues, soul, hip hop and rap; and to provide a reference tool that will increase the quality and quantity of scholarly research in these musical traditions.

This bibliography comprises primarily English language sources: books, theses and dissertations and, to a lesser degree, articles published in North America between the 1920s and 2008. The literature was accessed via catalogues, library holdings (primarily UCLA and UC Berkeley), online databases like ProQuest and stores like Amazon.com. Some online sources are also included. The sources were selected based on availability, importance of an artist or topic, and whether any new ideas or issues were raised. This bibliography differs from those of Floyd and Reisser, Ford, Haggerty, Hart/ Eagles/Howorth, McCoy, and Price in several ways: 1) it is fully annotated; 2) it combines the literature of several different musical genres into one annotated source; and 3) it includes articles, books, theses, dissertations and online sources. Although not complete, this bibliography is the first annotated compilation of literature available on the aforementioned cultural and musical genres.

The majority of the works cited herein are in English. However, there are a few entries in foreign languages. These have been included because of the unusual or unique topic or perspectives presented. When including foreign language sources, I relied on various translators, in many cases the authors themselves, who are familiar with the topics.

The book contains more than 1,300 annotations and is divided into three primary areas: 1) blues; 2) funk, rhythm and blues, and soul; and 3) hip hop and rap, with each section containing multiple subcategories. Although the emphasis herein is on longer works, articles have been added, primarily as the result of a lack of book-length scholarly studies on certain individuals and topics, especially early hip hop and rap artists, producers and topics.

These styles emerged in the early 1970s, at a time when books were rarely published on those associated with creating, marketing and producing of hip hop culture in general, and rap music in particular. Instead, I looked to more popularly oriented print sources for significant contemporary writings on hip hop and rap. I include citations from trade publications like *Billboard, Melody Maker,* and *Spin,* and other respected music publications like *Rolling Stone.* In such cases, the information is often limited to interviews and seeking artists' opinions on a wide variety of musical, political and social issues. Selected articles are also annotated for the blues, funk, rhythm and blues, and soul music sections.

Another group of entries may be considered quite unusual for a scholarly work such as this: works for younger readers. I have chosen to include selected works aimed at middle school and high school students because in some cases, especially in the areas of rap and hip hop, there are very few books, in-depth articles, or scholarly writings published on particular artists. Although the works included are necessarily more simplistic, some of them include information or a perspective that is not found elsewhere.

Another special feature of this reference book is the number of Masters theses and doctoral dissertations that are included. Hip hop and rap are heavily represented in theses and dissertations, proof of their status as the most popular contemporary style for African American cultural and musical research. Most bibliographies avoid including Masters theses, but I feel they offer an important contribution. Like dissertations, the research is guided and approved by faculty before publication, and these works often include important, very specialized, narrowly focused information, frequently illuminating previously unresearched topics. I have included all known theses and dissertations that, in my opinion, add to the scholarly discourse on the topics.

General coverage of entries is divided into subcategories, including autobiographies and biographies; reference materials; discography and listening guides; gender; historical surveys, regional and global studies; photography; religion; and literature. Some categories include coverage of issues unique to that musical style. For example, among the most important elements in hip hop and rap are B-boying, DJing and MCing, each represented in the literature. Although my primary purpose is to cover the aforementioned styles, because of their importance and relevance to the main subject I have also included selected entries on disco queens Gloria Gaynor and Donna Summer, rock and roll icons Chuck Berry, Bo Diddley, Jimi Hendrix and Little Richard, and neo-soul pioneers Erykah Badu and Lauryn Hill.

The appendices cover four areas: 1) web sources and periodicals for blues; 2) web sources for funk, rhythm and blues, and soul music; 3) web sources for hip hop and rap; and 4) web sources covering the broader African American range of music.

When compiling an annotated bibliography of the breadth and depth of this book, the love and support of family is extremely important. A special thanks to Jacqueline Cogdell DjeDje, my wife, and to Dominique and Eddie, Jr, our children, for their love and support. I also thank Gail Ryan for assisting in collecting materials, Dr Karin Patterson for compiling the web sources and periodicals, and Dr Wanda Bryant for her expert editing.

I assume full responsibility for any errors or misconceptions contained in this book.

## REFERENCES

Floyd, Jr, Samuel A. and Marsha J. Reisser. *Black Music in the United States*. Millwood, New York: Krause International Publishers, 1983.

Ford, Robert. *A Blues Bibliography*. New York: Routledge, 2007.

Haggerty, Gary. *A Guide to Popular Music Reference Books: An Annotated Bibliography*. Westport, CT: Greenwood Press, 1995.

Hart, Mary L., Brenda M. Eagles and Lisa A. Howorth. *The Blues: A Bibliographic Guide*. New York: Garland, 1989.

McCoy, Judy. *Rap Music in the 1980s: A Reference Guide*. Metuchen, NJ: Scarecrow Press, 1992.

Price, Emmett G. *Hip Hop Culture*. Santa Barbara: ABC Clio, 2006.

# Research trends: Blues, funk, R&B, soul, hip hop and rap

In the course of preparing this bibliography, I discovered that although many studies have been published on African American popular music, this subject did not receive serious scholarly interest until the 1970s, when researchers began producing works on blues. Responding to social and political events in black culture in the 1970s, researchers began documenting the many different musical expressions of blacks. Several scholarly writings on both rhythm and blues (R&B) and soul music were produced during the 1970s. Yet everything changed in the 1990s when the proliferation of research in all areas of African American popular music increased dramatically, with studies on hip hop culture and rap music leading the way.

This introductory essay provides a limited appraisal of the trends in musical research on blues, funk, R&B, soul, hip hop and rap, with special focus on works published during the 1990s and later, when popular music studies blossomed. Two cursory observations emerge from these categories of study. First, research in the 1990s was no longer limited to topics on music and musical analyses, but expanded into autobiographies, biographies, histories and beyond. Second, by the 1990s researchers from a variety of disciplines displayed interest in issues more diverse, such as gender, identity, representation, and regional and global perspectives. In this essay, I highlight selected works that demonstrate major trends in popular music studies of African American musical genres.

## BLUES

Although autobiographical, biographical and historical studies continued to be published in the last decade of the twentieth century, researchers used both well established and newer, different methodologies to discuss the musical lives and contributions of blues musicians. Works by Barrow-Pryor (2005) and Richardson (1987) are similar to earlier studies. Barrow-Pryor's biography provides insight about Handy's life, career, music and influences on musicians such as Linda Hopkins. Richardson's penetrating assessment of B.B. King focuses on King's life, career, music and guitar style. Taking a more innovative approach, Moore's (2000) biography of W.C. Handy uses the Bantu-centered philosophical and intercultural origins of *Uraeus Mi* to document the blues musician's life, career and pioneering contributions to the world.

Collective biographies (publications that focus on two or more musicians) are popular formats in which to present information about music and musicians. For example, Samuel Charters' *The Blues Makers* (1991) contains the reprints of both *The Bluesmen and Sweet as the Showers of Rain*, two sources that are permeated with biographical information on bluesmen. David Dicaire's *Blues Singers: Biographies of 50 Legendary Artists of the Early 20th Century* (1999) is another important source of information on a myriad of blues musicians.

Some of the more groundbreaking works concern issues of gender. For example, Davis' (1999) examination of how African American women became economically independent, in a culture that had not previously allowed such achievements, explores meanings behind the performances of Billie Holiday, Ma Rainey and Bessie Smith. Harrison's two publications (1988, 2006) cover several issues germane to women and blues. She discusses the role and function of African American females in blues, especially the cultural and social impact of 1920s blues, by deconstructing selected texts of Alberta Hunter, Victoria Spivey, Sippie Wallace and Edith Wilson. She places the performers' activities within historical context and investigates a myriad of issues regarding gender which provide new insights about the performers and connect ideology in African American literature to the blues text. Wright's (1997) use of Frances Beale's theory of double jeopardy to ascertain whether a relationship exists between African American female blues performers and the music they perform, is one of the more recent collective studies to deal with gender and other issues. Burns' (1977) assessment of blues lyrics offers insight into meaning, themes and categories, and Dougan's (2001) discussion of blues criticism, blues discourse and the codification of a blues canon also represents an important addition to blues research.

No less important are studies that mediate issues of blues and religious music. Examples of these include Cone's (1972) classic work on the similarities, uses and functions of blues and spirituals, and Spencer's (1993) use of Theomusicology to ascertain the relationship between blues, mythology and religion.

Among the many scholarly discourses on regional blues history and styles are those by Evans (1982) and Titon (1977). Evans focuses on the blues tradition and compositional features used in Drew, Mississippi, while Titon explores downhome blues in the wider African American culture during the first part of the twentieth century. To the list of regional studies, one must add Keil's (1966) classic work on urban blues which examines the 1960s blues scene in Chicago and Ferris' (1970) study which is a continuation of traditional Delta Blues scholarship. However, research such as Govenar's (2008) exploration of Texas blues and Bastin's (1995) discussion of blues in the southeast United States demonstrate that blues research has expanded beyond its original almost exclusive focus on the Delta to include rural and urban issues, to include different geographical areas, and to discuss the role, function and impact of artists outside the Delta on the history and evolution of blues.

## FUNK, RHYTHM AND BLUES, AND SOUL MUSIC

Although immensely popular among listeners, fewer studies have been published on funk, R&B and soul music topics as compared with publications on blues, hip hop and rap music. Nevertheless, several scholars have made significant contributions. Davis' (2006) work is important because he researches the etymology of funk from the 1950s to 1979. In Vincent's (1996) examination of funk, he discusses its African roots, the disenfranchisement of African Americans, and his belief that the genre has been considerably free of industry greed. In addition, he presents an in-depth analysis of the music of James Brown, George Clinton, Miles Davis and the Ohio Players. George's (2003, 2004) works are significant because he focuses on multiple topics, including his belief that the 1980s represent a departure from both the gains of the Civil Rights era and the music of James Brown, and the rise and fall of "race" music and its eventual transformation into R&B and crossover music. Other studies include Kamin's (1976) argument regarding the appropriation of African American R&B by white musicians and Neal's (1999, 2003) discussions of formal and informal black institutions, black cultural production, mass consumerism, and the belief that contemporary African American musicians use a cultural memory to build on the musical traditions of the past. Maultsby's (2006a, 2006b, 2006c) works on the history, artists, trends and developments in R&B, funk and soul music are pioneering because no one had previously presented such a comprehensive and thorough discussion of the topic.

Other major contributions include works by Haralambos (1975, 1985), Herbert (2000), Meadows (1983), Ripani (2006), and Shaw (1970, 1978, 1986). Haralambos discusses the roots and transformation of soul music from its earliest style to the mid-1980s. Herbert argues that the themes used in R&B between 1968 and 1972 are aligned with those espoused by the Black Power Movement during the same period. Meadows discusses the musical characteristics, cover records and instrumentation of many early R&B groups; and Ripani explains how African American influences in the melodies, rhythms, harmonies and form of R&B songs reflect connections between blues, country, gospel, jazz, and rock and roll. Long a champion of R&B, funk and soul, Shaw espouses that American popular music can best be understood from a black perspective; he incorporates numerous conversations with musicians and discussions of the stylistic elements of various blues, funk, R&B and soul artists.

Numerous regionally-based works have focused on funk, R&B and soul in various cities and regions of the US, including Detroit, Houston, Los Angeles, Memphis, New Orleans and Philadelphia. While Sykes' (2006) history of Motown includes information on Berry Gordy and selected artists, Smith's (2001) work provides a scholarly discussion of Motown and the cultural politics of Detroit. Govenar (1990) presents the history and evolution of

R&B in Houston and information about local performers. Otis' (1993) regional study of Los Angeles and California include insider perspectives on his associations with noted R&B artists (e.g. Little Easter Phillips, Big Mama Thornton, Wynonie Harris, T-Bone Walker) and jazz musicians (e.g. Count Basie and Lester Young). Otis also comments on musical activities of Central Avenue in Los Angeles and discusses the works of other scholars who have written about music in California. In addition, Eastman's (1989, 1998) works detail the venues, contributions of musicians, and activities that transpired on Central Avenue in Los Angeles, while Collins (1998) critiques R&B recordings made in California between 1942 and 1972.

The role of Memphis, New Orleans and Philadelphia as important incubators of funk, R&B and soul music has been addressed by several scholars, including Bowman's (1993, 1997, 2006) work on Stax records, Guralnick's (1986) research of the history of R&B and soul music, and factors that contributed to their development, Helper's (1997) use of Memphis as a site to discuss the history and evolution of R&B and rock and roll, and Ryan's (2008) discussion of the schism between R&B and blues musicians, and their faith. Broven (1974) focuses on the importance of New Orleans and Philadelphia in the development of R&B, and provides insight into important contributors of the early 1970s, including Fats Domino and Allan Toussaint. Jackson (2004, 2006) gives an in-depth assessment of Philadelphia International Records and the contributions of Leon Huff and Kenneth Gamble.

Several studies chronicle African American influences in rock and roll. Redd (1972) makes a strong argument that rock and roll is in fact rhythm and blues, and discusses the role and function of the disc jockey, radio, motion pictures and television in disseminating both genres, enhanced by interviews with Jerry Butler, Dave Clark, Arthur "Big Boy" Crudup, B.B. King, Brownie McGhee and Jerry Whitaker. Mahon (1997, 2004, 2006) examines African American involvement in rock and roll in a groundbreaking study on the Black Rock Coalition in New York and Los Angeles, and discusses the power dynamics of rock and the goals of the coalition.

Although regional studies on R&B, funk and soul music outnumber global studies, research by Browne (2005) and Wright (2007) provides new information on the diffusion and influence of these genres internationally. While Browne discusses the emergence and popularity of the Northern Soul scene among England's working class, Wright illuminates the influence of Boney M's 1978 disco performances on the culture and musicians of Russia.

## HIP HOP AND RAP

According to my research, since the 1990s hip hop and rap have become the most prevalent topics for African American popular music research, surpassing the number of studies on blues and jazz. The majority of studies are autobiographical and biographical profiles, histories and surveys, and works focusing on regional and global perspectives, and the intersection of hip hop and rap. However, many interesting studies also have developed from a variety of disciplines and issues, including literature, music, history, sociology and politics, with significant emphasis on issues of gender, identity and representation.

Because few scholarly works were published on the pioneers of hip hop culture or rap music before the 1990s, selected articles on these topics from more popular print media are included throughout the bibliography. Most articles are concise and focus on the life, career and controversies surrounding an artist or group. Their inclusion enables scholars to ascertain the research methods and topics most important to early observers of hip hop culture and rap music.

The studies on hip hop and rap are very diverse in approach and discipline. Some of the more interesting include Boyd's (2003) discourse on hip hop and American culture; Kitwana's (2005) investigation of why white kids love hip hop; Ramsey's (2003) discussion of how music, including rap, works as racial discourse and practice; and Rose's (1993) exploration of cultural, social and political issues endemic in hip hop culture and rap music. Spencer's (1991) collection of essays is among the first studies to examine the emergence of rap and its importance in understanding some of the complex intercultural issues in modern society.

The continuing expansion of hip hop culture and rap musical research has led to several reference resources. Among these include Bynoe's (2005) encyclopedia of rap music and hip hop culture; McCoy's (1992) reference guide on rap music in the 1980s; Price's (2006) discussion and annotated bibliography of hip hop culture; and Stancell's (1996) comprehensive collection of information on rap artists and social issues.

Studies on communication, language, poetry and text in hip hop and rap music have increased since the 1990s. While Griffin's (1998) study focuses on images and offenses portrayed in gangsta rap lyrics, Kitwana (1995) examines the use of lyrics to reveal insights into oral histories and political and social issues pertinent to hip hop culture. Williams' (1995) discussion of rap music as an innovative linguistic form of African American oral culture offers new perspectives on the subject.

Gender studies about hip hop culture and rap music cover numerous topics, including issues of representation, black nationalism, black males and Chicano/a participation. The most provocative works include Anderson's (1999) examination of sex roles and stereotypes in music videos; Celious' (2002) analysis of lyrics used by black women to determine if they are empowering or destructive; Burton's (2005) discussion of class, gender and racial representations in media and society; and Cheney's (1999, 2005) examinations of rap music's influence on discussions about the politics of black nationalism, gender and masculinity. Additional studies include Durham's (2007) exploration of black women identified with the hip hop or post-Civil Rights generation; Horton-Stallings' (2002) assessment that conversations on hermeneutics, black literature, and folk and oral studies tend to complicate discussions of class, gender and sexuality; Jeffries' (2008) investigation on "objectionable" themes performed by black male hip hop artists; McFarland's (2008) discussion of Chicano/a participation in hip hop culture and rap music; Turner's (2004) use of counterpublic discourses in African American folklore, literature, film and popular music to investigate the negative masculine identities imposed upon African American males and publics; and White's (2005) investigation of the black body, racial attitudes, black masculinity, personal and social identities.

Historical studies that trace hip hop culture and rap music's origins and evolution, in whole or part, to the South Bronx are common (e.g. Chang 2005; Forman and Neal 2004; Light 1999; Marshall 2007; Mook 2007; and Ogg and Upshal 2001). Studies that cover hip hop and rap music history from general, regional and global perspectives have also proliferated. For example, Patricia Rose (1993) explores some of the complex cultural, social and political issues in rap music and hip hop culture, Cheryl Keyes (2002) used theoretical paradigms from cultural studies, ethnomusicology and folklore to present an assessment of the urban youth movement that emerged in the South Bronx in the late 1970s, and Ian Condry (2006) provides deep insight into issues of gender, prosody and race in Japanese hip hop.

Regional assessments of hip hop and rap music history include Cross's (1993) discourse on rap, race and resistance in Los Angeles, and Ginwright's (2004) investigation of multicultural educational reform in Oakland, California. Washington, DC is the locus of Hopkinson's (2007) investigation of *go-go*, an African American musical genre and counter-discourse to hip hop. Many studies focus on New York. Baker (1993) uses the South Bronx to contextualize the history of rap from its roots, while Keyes' (2002) discussion is more expansive, including rap's origins in the West African bardic tradition, African and Jamaican influences on rap, aesthetics, social control, politics, ethnicity, and the use of rap as a means of attaining socioeconomic mobility. In addition to New York City and Washington, DC, other regional studies focus on rap in Chicago, Compton, Los Angeles, Miami, Seattle and the Mississippi Delta, including the influences and participation of American artists of Jamaican, Mexican, Puerto Rican and Samoan heritage.

Just as regional studies have expanded, so has the global dissemination and research of hip hop culture and rap outside North America. In addition to specific studies on Brazil, Canada, Cuba, Colombia, Ghana, Japan, Malawi and the Province of Nova Scotia, global studies range from Kelly's (2006) collection of insightful perspectives from a variety of scholars, to Mitchell's (2001) essays on the history, status and style of rap in countries like Australia, Bulgaria, Canada, Germany, Italy, Japan, South Korea, the United Kingdom and New Zealand.

Studies focusing on Africa and the Middle East include Jabbaar-Gyambrah's (2007) provocative and informative work on women's roles and representations in American hip hop and Ghanaian hip life; Mapuranga's (2006) discussion of gangsta rap's influences on the singing of gospel music in Harare, Zimbabwe, and Fenn's (2004) investigation of rap and reggae in the social lives of Malawi youth. McDonald (2006), in his powerful discussion of music, nationalism and resistance among Palestinians in Israel, the occupied territories and Jordan, incorporates several musical genres, including rap, as part of his methodology.

The Caribbean, Central America and South America are also represented in global hip hop and rap musical research. Rivierre (2005) documents the cultural diffusion of hip hop's four elements (i.e. DJing, MCing, B-boying/B-girling and graffiti art) in Cuba and Puerto Rico. Flores (2000) challenges the belief that hip hop culture is the sole creation of African Americans. Other works include Marc Perry's (2004b) examination of the emergent Movimiento de Hip Hop (Cuban Hip Hop Movement); Baker's (2005) exploration of how and why Cuba has become amenable to rap music; and Dennis' (2006) use of hip hop to ascertain the attitudes of young Afro-Colombians toward the challenges of globalization. Laurie's (2000) examination of the ways in which new identities compete with prioritized Brazilian identities is another important study.

Studies on Canada and Europe include Alook's (2005) discussion of the hip hop community in Edmonton, Alberta, Canada; Chennault's (2007) analysis of the relationship between French rap lyrics and violence; and Green's (2007) research into young African Nova Scotian women's responses to images of black female bodies in three popular hip hop videos. Works from Asia are represented by Condry's (1999, 2006) pioneering studies of capitalism, gender, prosody, race, and rap's rise to transnational popularity in Japan.

Political issues are dominant themes in the current research on hip hop culture and rap. Among these are Boyd's (2002) assertion that hip hop has both rejected and replaced Civil Rights as the defining issue of blackness; Bynoe's (2004) plea to replace ineffective black leaders with "citizen leaders" who are engaged in a policy-centered relationship with the white power structure, and Forman's (1996, 2002) examination of the spiritual dimension of hip hop and rap, geo-cultural expansion, and the integration of localized musical scenes, transnational media and musical industries. Other studies include George's (1998) discourse on the business, culture and politics of hip hop; Kitwana's (2002) look at social issues and challenges endemic to African American youth who embrace hip hop attitudes and values; and Perkinson's (2005) collection of essays that deal with American identity, white privilege and entitlement, and black disenfranchisement. Imani Perry's (2004a) discussion of rap's African American origins and hybridity is indicative of the wide array of politically oriented topics that have emerged in hip hop culture and rap musical research since the late 1990s.

In addition to politics, some recent studies focus on the connection and interaction between rap and religion. Davlatzai's (2003) research involved rap's role in cinema, television and sports as well as its relationship to cultural identity, nation, race and Islam. Dyson's (1992, 1997) works center on testimonials, lessons, celebrations and values in rap culture; Nelson (1992) posits that a theology exists in African American folk and popular musical traditions, especially rap, while Pinn (2003) points, instead, to rap music's connection to Christianity, Islam and secular humanism.

Works by Demers (2002) and Schloss (2000) focus on the art of sampling in hip hop. In addition to tracing the history of sampling and its uses in the construction of African American identity, Demers identifies sampling's distinctive features and argues that hip hop can be recontextualized in humorous, ironic and respectable ways through sampling. Schloss discusses the phenomenon of "making beats", specifically, how producers conceive vocal elements of hip hop, and how raw conceptualizations are informed by a variety of artistic, social and practical concerns.

The abovementioned studies are a small sampling of the literature included in this bibliography. In addition to works on stylistic developments and histories, issues of gender, identity, meaning, politics and representation permeate the studies and provide new insights into the cultural and musical uses and functions of these different musical genres. The breadth and depth of the research is reflective of a global interest in African American popular music.

## REFERENCES

Alook, Angela. "An Ethnographic Study of the Edmonton Hip Hop Community: Anti-Racist Cultural Identities." Masters thesis, University of Alberta, 2005.

Anderson, Darnell. "The Portrayal of African American Women in Rap Music Videos." PhD dissertation, Wayne State University, 1999.

Baker, Geoffrey. "Hip Hop Revolucion Nationalizing Rap in Cuba!" *Ethnomusicology* 49(3) (2005): 368–403.

Baker, Jr, Houston A. *Black Studies, Rap and the Academy.* Chicago: University of Chicago Press, 1993.

Barrow-Pryor, Erany. "Motherin' The Blues: Linda Hopkins; The Continuing Legacy of the Blues Woman." PhD dissertation, University of California, Los Angeles, 2005.

Bastin, Bruce. *Red River Blues: The Blues in the Southwest.* Urbana: University of Illinois Press, 1995.

Battle, J. *Culture-free Self-esteem Inventories,* Second edn. Austin, TX: Pro-Ed, 1992.

Bowman, Robert Maxwell James. "Stax." In *African American Music: An Introduction,* eds Mellonee V. Burnim and Portia Maultsby, pp. 452–70. New York: Routledge Publishing, 2006.

——*Soulsville USA: The Story of Stax Records.* New York: Schirmer Books, 1997.

——"Stax Records: A Historical and Musicological Study." PhD dissertation, Memphis State University, 1993.

Boyd, Todd. *Young, Black, Rich and Famous: The Rise of the NBA, The Hip Hop Invasion and the Transformation of American Culture.* New York: Doubleday, 2003.
——*The New H.N.I.C. (Head Niggas in Charge): The Death of Civil Rights and the Reign of Hip Hop.* New York: New York University Press, 2002.
Broven, John. *Rhythm and Blues in New Orleans.* Gretna, LA: Pelican, 1974.
Browne, Kimasi Lionel John. "'Soul or Nothing:' The Formation of Cultural Identity on the British Northern Soul Scene." PhD dissertation, University of California, Los Angeles, 2005.
Burns, Loretta Susie. "A Stylistic Analysis of Blues Lyrics." PhD dissertation, University of Michigan, 1977.
Burton, Nsenga. "Traveling Without Moving: Hypervisibility and Black Female Rappers." PhD dissertation, University of Southern California, 2005.
Bynoe, Yvonne. *Encyclopedia of Rap and Hip-Hop Culture.* Westport, CT: Greenwood Press, 2005.
——*Stand and Deliver: Political Activism, Leadership, and Hip Hop Culture.* Brooklyn: Soft Skull Press, 2004.
Celious, Aaron Kabir. "Blaxploitation Blues: How Black Women Identify With and Are Empowered by Female Performers of Hip Hop Music." PhD dissertation, University of Michigan, 2002.
Chang, Jeff. *Can't Stop Won't Stop: A History of the Hip-Hop Generation.* New York: St Martin's, 2005.
Charters, Samuel. *The Blues Makers: Containing Reprints of Two Titles: The Bluesmen and Sweet as the Showers of Rain.* New York: Da Capo Press, 1991.
Cheney, Charise L. *Phallic/ies and Hi(s)tories: Masculinity and The Black Nationalist Tradition, From Slave Spirituals to Rap Music.* Urbana-Champaign: University of Illinois Press, 1999.
——*Brothers Gonna Work it Out: Sexual Politics in the Golden Age of Rap Nationalism.* New York: New York University Press, 2005.
Chennault, Schyler. "Je Vis Donc Je Vois, Donc Je Dis: Banlieue Violence in French Rap." Bachelors thesis, Brigham Young University, 2007.
Collins, Willie. "California Rhythm and Blues Recordings, 1942–72: A Diversity of Styles." In *California Soul: Music of African Americans in the West*, eds Jacqueline C. DjeDje and Eddie S. Meadows, pp. 213–44. Berkeley: University of California Press, 1998.
Condry, Ian. *Hip-Hop Japan: Rap and the Paths of Cultural Globalization.* Durham: Duke University Press, 2006.
——"Japanese Rap Music: An Ethnography of Globalization in Popular Culture." PhD dissertation, Yale University, 1999.
Cone, James H. *The Spirituals and The Blues.* New York: Seabury, 1972.
Cross, Brian. *It's Not About Salary: Rap, Race, and Resistance in Los Angeles.* London and New York: Verso, 1993.
Davis, Angela Y. *Blues Legacies and the Black Feminism: Gertrude "Ma" Rainey, Bessie Smith, and Billie Holiday.* New York: Vintage, 1999.
Davis, Robert. "Who Got the Funk? An Etymophony of Funk Music from 1950s to 1979." PhD dissertation, University of Montreal, 2006.
Davlatzai, Solail. "Prophets of Rage: Race, Nation, Islam, and the Cultural Politics of Identity." PhD dissertation, University of Southern California, 2003.
Demers, Joanna Teresa. "Sampling as Lineage in Hip-Hop." PhD dissertation, Princeton University, 2002.

Dennis, Christopher Charles. "Afro-Colombian Hip-Hop: Globalization, Popular Music, and Ethnic Identities." PhD dissertation, Ohio State University, 2006.

Dougan, John M. "Two Steps From the Blues: Creating Discourse and Constructing Canons in Blues Criticism." PhD dissertation, The College of William and Mary, 2000.

——*Two Steps From The Blues: Creating Discourse and Constructing Canons in Blues Criticism.* Williamsburg: The College of William and Mary, 2001.

Durham, Aisha S. "Homegirl Going Home: Hip Hop Feminism and the Representational Politics of Location." PhD dissertation, University of Illinois, 2007.

Dyson, Michael Eric. *Between God and Gangsta Rap: Bearing Witness to Black Culture.* New York: Oxford University Press, 1997.

——"Rap Culture, The Church and American Society." *Sacred Music of the Secular City: From Blues to Rap.* A special edition of *Black Sacred Music: A Journal of Theomusicology* 6(1) (Spring 1992): 268–74, ed. Jon Michael Spencer. Durham: Duke University Press, 1992.

Eastman, Ralph. "Pitchin' Up a Boogie: African-American Musicians, Nightlife, and Music Venues in Los Angeles, 1930–45." In *California Soul: Music of African Americans in the West,* eds Jacqueline C. DjeDje and Eddie S. Meadows, pp. 79–104. Berkeley: University of California Press, 1998.

——"Central Avenue Blues: The Making of Los Angeles Rhythm and Blues, 1942–47." *Black Music Research Journal* 9(1) (Spring 1989): 19–35.

Evans, David. *Big Road Blues: Tradition and Creativity in the Folk Blues.* Berkeley: University of California Press, 1982.

Fenn III, John Bennett. "Rap and Regga Musical Cultures, Life Styles, and Performances in Malawi." PhD dissertation, Indiana University, 2004.

Ferris, William R. *Blues From the Delta.* London: Studio Vista, 1970.

Flores, Juan. *From Bomba to Hip-Hop: Puerto Rican Culture and Latino Identity.* New York: Columbia University Press, 2000.

Forman, Murray Webster. *The "Hood" Comes First: Race, Space, and Place in Pop and Hip-Hop Musical Culture.* Hanover: Wesleyan University Press, 2002.

——*The "Hood" Comes First: Race, Space, and Place in Pop Music and Hip-Hop, 1978–1996.* PhD dissertation, University of Montreal, 1996.

Forman, Murray Webster and Mark Anthony Neal. *That's the Joint: The Hip-Hop Studies Reader.* New York: Routledge, 2004.

George, Nelson. *Post-Soul Nation: The Explosive, Contradictory, Triumphant, and Tragic 1980s as Experienced by African American Musicians.* New York: Viking Press, 2004.

——*The Death of Rhythm and Blues.* New York: Penguin Press, 2003.

——*Hip Hop America.* New York: Viking, 1998.

Ginwright, Shawn A. *Black in School: Afrocentric Reform, Urban Youth, and the Promise of Hip-Hop Culture.* New York: Teachers College Press (Columbia University), 2004.

Govenar, Alan. *Living Texas Blues: The Rise of Contemporary Sound.* College Station: Texas A&M University Press, 2008.

——*The Early Years of Rhythm and Blues; Focus on Houston.* Houston: Rice University Press, 1990.

——*Sweet Soul Music: Rhythm and Blues and the Southern Dream of Freedom.* New York: Harper and Row, 1986.

Green, Alecia. "Whose Revolution is Televised?: Young African Nova Scotian Women Respond to Sexual Politics in Hip Hop Culture and Everyday Life." Masters thesis, Saint Mary's University (Halifax, Nova Scotia), 2007.

Griffin, Monica Denise. "The Rap on Rap Music: The Social Construction of African American Identity." PhD dissertation, University of Virginia, 1998.

Guralnick, Peter. *Sweet Soul Music: Rhythm and Blues and the Southern Dream of Freedom*. New York: Harper and Row, 1986.

Haralambos, Michael. *Soul Music: The Birth of a Sound in Black America*. New York: Da Capo, 1985.

——*Right On: From Blues to Soul Music in Black America*. New York: Drake, 1975.

Harrison, Daphne Duval. "Blues." In *African American Music: An Introduction,* eds Mellonee V. Burnim and Portia Maultsby, pp. 508–28. New York: Routledge, 2006.

——*Black Pearls: Blues Queens of the 1920s*. New Brunswick: Rutgers University Press, 1988.

Helper, Laura. "Whole Lot of Shakin' Going On: An Ethnography of Race Relations and Crossover Audiences For Rhythm and Blues in 1950s Memphis." PhD dissertation, Rice University, 1997.

Herbert, Sharmine S. "Rhythm and Blues, 1968–72: An African-Centered Rhetorical Analysis." PhD dissertation, Howard University, 2000.

Hopkinson, Natalie Adele. "Go-Go Live: Washington, D.C.'s Cultural Information Network, Drumming the News, Knitting Communities, and Guarding a Black Public Sphere." PhD dissertation, University of Maryland, 2007.

Horton-Stallings, LaMonda. "Trickster-Troping on Black Culture: Revised Readings of Gender and Sexuality." PhD dissertation, Michigan State University, 2002.

Jabbaar-Gyambrah, Tara Aminah. "Hip-Hop, Hip Life: Global Sistahs." PhD dissertation, State University of New York at Buffalo, 2007.

Jackson, John A. "Philadelphia International." In *African American Music: An Introduction*, eds Mellonee V. Burnim and Portia Maultsby, pp. 470–91. New York: Routledge, 2006.

——*A House on Fire: The Rise and Fall of Philadelphia Soul*. New York: Oxford University Press, 2004.

Jeffries, Michael. "Thug Life: Race, Gender, and the Meaning of Hip-Hop." PhD dissertation, Harvard University, 2008.

Kamin, Jonathan L. "Rhythm and Blues in White America: Rock and Roll as Acculturation and Perceptual Learning." PhD dissertation, Princeton University, 1976.

Keil, Charles. *Urban Blues*. Chicago: University of Chicago Press, 1966.

Kelly, Robin D.G., ed. *The Vinyl Ain't Final: Hip-Hop and The Globalisation of Black Popular Culture*. New York: Pluto Press, 2006.

——*Race Rebels: Culture, Politics, and the Black Working Class*. New York: Free Press, 1994.

Keyes, Cheryl. *Rap Music and Street Consciousness*. Urbana: University of Illinois Press, 2002.

Kitwana, Bakari. *Why White Kids Love Hip Hop: Wangstas, Wiggers, Wannabes, and the New Reality of Race in America*. New York: Civitas, 2005.

——*The Hip Hop Generation: Young Blacks and the Crisis in African American Culture*. New York: Basic Civitas Publishers, 2002.

——*The Rap on Gangsta Rap: Who Runs It? Gangsta Rap and Visions of Black Violence*. Chicago: Third World Press, 1995.

Laurie, Shoshanna Kira. "Funk and Hip-Hop Transculture in the 'Divided' Brazilian City." PhD dissertation, Stanford University, 2000.

Light, Alan. *The Vibe History of Hip Hop*. New York: Three Rivers Press, 1999.

McCoy, Judith. *Rap Music in the 1980s: A Reference Guide*. Metuchen, NJ: Scarecrow Press, 1992.

McDonald, David A. "My Voice is My Weapon: Music, Nationalism, and The Poetics of Palestinian Resistance." PhD dissertation, University of Illinois, 2006.

McFarland, Pancho. *Chicano Rap: Gender and Violence in the Postindustrial Barrio*. Austin: University of Texas Press, 2008.

Mahon, Maureen. "Rap, Race, Gender, and Genre: The Power Dynamics of Rock." In *African American Music: An Introduction*, eds Mellonee V. Burnim and Portia Maultsby, pp. 558–85. New York: Routledge, 2006.

——*Right to Rock: The Black Rock Coalition and the Cultural Politics of Race*. Durham: Duke University Press, 2004.

——"The Black Rock Coalition and the Cultural Politics of Race in the United States." PhD dissertation, New York University, 1997.

Mapuranga, Tapiwa Praise. "Gangsters For Christ: Youth Identity in Gospel, Rap and Hip-Hop Music in Harare." Masters thesis, University of Zimbabwe, 2006.

Marshall, Wayne Glenn. "Routes, Rap, Reggae: Hearing the Histories of Hip-Hop and Reggae Together." PhD dissertation, University of Wisconsin, 2007.

Maultsby, Portia. "Funk." In *African American Music: An Introduction*, eds Mellonee V. Burnim and Portia Maultsby, pp. 245–71. New York: Routledge, 2006a.

——"Rhythm and Blues." In *African American Music: An Introduction*, eds Mellonee V. Burnim and Portia Maultsby, pp. 271–93. New York: Routledge, 2006b.

——"Soul." In *African American Music: An Introduction*, eds Mellonee V. Burnim and Portia Maultsby, pp. 293–315. New York: Routledge, 2006c.

Meadows, Eddie S. "A Preliminary Analysis of Early Rhythm and Blues Musical Practices." *Western Journal of Black Studies* 7(3) (Fall 1983): 172–83.

Mitchell, Tony, ed. *Global Noise: Rap and Hip-Hop Music Outside the USA*. Hanover and Middletown: Wesleyan University Press, 2001.

Mook, Richard. *Rap Music and Hip Hop Culture: A Critical Reader*. Dubuque, IA: Kendall Hunt, 2007.

Moore, Charles Eugene. "William Christopher Handy and Uraeus Mi: A Bantu-Centered Philosophical and Intracultural Assessment." PhD dissertation, University of California, Los Angeles, 2000.

Neal, Mark Anthony. *Songs in the Key of Black Life: A Rhythm and Blues Nation*. New York: Routledge, 2003.

——*Soul Babies: Black Popular Culture and the Post-Soul Aesthetic*. New York: Routledge, 2002.

——*What the Music Said: Black Popular Music and Black Public Culture*. New York: Routledge, 1999.

Nelson, Angela Marie Spence. "A Theomusicological Approach to Rap: A Model for the Study of African American Popular and Folk Musics." PhD dissertation, Bowling Green State University, 1992.

Ogg, Alex and David Upshal. *The Hip Hop Years: A History of Rap*. New York: Fromm International, 2001.

Otis, Johnny. *Upside Your Head: Rhythm and Blues on Central Avenue*. Hanover and London: Wesleyan University Press/ University Press of New England, 1993.

Perkinson, James W. *Shamanism, Racism, and Hip Hop Culture: Essays on White Supremacy and Black Subversion.* New York: Palgrave Macmillan, 2005.

Perry, Imani. *Prophets of the Hood: Poetics and Politics of Hip Hop.* Durham: Duke University Press, 2004.

Perry, Marc. "Los Rappers: Rap, Race, Ethnicity, and the Performance of Diasporic Identities." PhD dissertation, University of Texas, 2004.

Pinn, Anthony B., ed. *Noise and Spirit: The Religious and Spiritual Sensibilities of Rap Music.* New York: New York University Press, 2003.

Price, Emmett. *Hip Hop Culture.* Santa Barbara: ABC CLIO, 2006.

Ramsey, Guthrie. *Race Music: Black Cultures From Bebop to Hip-Hop.* Berkeley: University of California Press, 2003.

Redd, Lawrence N. *Rock is Rhythm and Blues: The Impact of Mass Media.* East Lansing: Michigan State University Press, 1972.

Richardson, Jerry Scott. "The Blues Guitar Style of B.B. King." PhD dissertation, Memphis State University, 1987.

Ripani, Richard J. *The New Blue Music: Changes in Rhythm and Blues, 1950–1999.* Jackson: University Press of Mississippi, 2006.

——"The New Blue Music: Changes in Melody, Harmony, Rhythm, and Form in Rhythm and Blues, 1950–99." PhD dissertation, University of Memphis, 2004.

Rivierre, Melisa. "Son Dos Alas: The Cultural Diffusion of Hip-Hop en Cuba and Puerto Rico." PhD dissertation, University of Minnesota, 2005.

Rose, Patricia L. "Black Noise: Rap Music and Black Cultural Resistance in Contemporary American Popular Culture." PhD dissertation, Brown University, 1993.

Ryan, Jennifer. "Can I Get A Witness?: Soul and Salvation in Memphis Music." PhD dissertation, University of Pennsylvania, 2008.

Schloss, Joseph G. "Making Beats: The Art of Sample-Based Hip-Hop." PhD dissertation, University of Washington, 2000.

Shaw, Arnold. *Black Popular Music in America: From the Spirituals, Minstrels, and Ragtime to Soul, Disco, and Hip-Hop.* New York: Schirmer Books/ London: Collier Macmillan, 1986.

——*Honkers and Shouters: The Golden Years of Rhythm and Blues.* New York: Macmillan, 1978.

——*The World of Soul: Black America's Contributions to the Pop Music Scene.* New York: Cowles Book Co., 1970.

Smith, Suzanne. *Dancing in the Streets: Motown and the Cultural Politics of Detroit.* Cambridge, MA: Harvard University Press, 2001.

Spencer, Jon Michael. *Blues and Evil.* Knoxville: University of Tennessee Press, 1993.

——ed. *Sacred Music of the Secular City: From Blues to Rap.* A special edition of *Black Sacred Music: A Journal of Theomusicology* 6(1) (Spring). Durham: Duke University Press, 1992.

——ed. *The Emergence of Black and The Emergence of Rap.* A special edition of *Black Sacred Music: A Journal of Theomusicology* 5(1). Durham: Duke University Press, 1991.

Stancell, Steven. *Rap Whoz Who: The World of Rap Music: Performers and Promoters.* New York: Schirmer, 1996.

Sykes, Charles. "Motown." In *African American Music: An Introduction*, eds Mellonee V. Burnim and Portia Maultsby, pp. 431–52. New York: Routledge, 2006.

Titon, Jeff Todd. *Early Downhome Blues: A Musical and Cultural Analysis*. Urbana: University of Illinois Press, 1977.

Turner, Jr, Albert Uriah Anthony. "Bad Niggers, Real Niggas, and the Shaping of African American Counterpublic Discourses." PhD dissertation, University of Massachusetts, 2004.

Vincent, Rickey. *Funk: The Music, The People, and the Rhythm of One*. New York: St Martin's Press, 1996.

White, Miles. "We Some Killaz: Affect, Representation and the Performance of Black Masculinity in Hip-Hop Music." PhD dissertation, University of Washington, 2005.

Williams, Frank Douglas. "Rap Music in Society." PhD dissertation, University of Florida, 1995.

Wright, Delane Elizabeth. "Poppin' Their Thang: African American Blueswomen and Multiple Jeopardy." Masters thesis, University of North Texas, 1997.

Wright, Jeffrey Marsh. "Russia's Greatest Living Machine: Disco, Exoticism, and Subversion." Masters thesis, University of North Carolina, Chapel Hill, 2007.

# I

# Blues resources

**GENERAL**

1. Abbot, Lynn and Doug Seroff. *Ragged But Right: Black Traveling Shows, "Coon Songs," and the Dark Pathway to Blues and Jazz.* Jackson: University Press of Mississippi, 2007.

   A pioneering study of coon songs and ragtime performed in black musical comedies, circus sideshows and tented minstrel shows. Examines African American performers in Buffalo Bill's Wild West shows. The authors chronicle the trials and tribulations of the performers, segregation in the tent shows and how "Coon Shouters" like Ma Rainey and Bessie Smith prepared the way for the evolution of blues and jazz.

2. ——. *Out of Sight: The Rise of African American Popular Music, 1889–1895.* Jackson: University Press of Mississippi, 2003.

   A comprehensive and detailed coverage of the sociocultural factors that led to the development of genres like blues and jazz. The authors present concrete insight into the cultural dynamics that engendered the development of twentieth-century popular music as an outgrowth of African American culture.

3. Baraka, Imamu Amiri [LeRoi Jones]. *Blues People: Negro Music in White America.* New York: Harper Perennial, 1999.

   Beginning with the music of African American slaves through the musical scene of the 1960s, Baraka (born LeRoi Jones) traces the influence of African American music on white America in both the musical and popular culture contexts, and discusses the values and perspectives transmitted through the music. Poet, playwright, novelist, critic and political activist, the author discusses the place of blues in American social, musical, economic and cultural history. He uses music brilliantly to illustrate how African Americans have impacted American history and culture.

4. Burnim, Mellonee V. and Portia Maultsby, eds. *African American Music: An Introduction*. New York: Routledge, 2006.

A comprehensive and thorough discussion of all genres, past and present, that are deemed African American music. Essays by Bob Bowman on Stax records, David Evans and Daphne Duval Harrison on blues, John Jackson on Philadelphia International Records, Charles Sykes on Motown, and Dawn Norfleet on hip hop/rap. Editor Maultsby contributes excellent essays on R&B, funk and soul music. This is the most scholarly text to date on the topic.

5. Carney, George O., ed. *The Sounds of People and Places: A Geography of American Music from Country to Classical and Blues to Bop*. Fourth edn. New York: Rowman & Littlefield Publishers, 2003.

First published in 1978, this edition compiles fifteen essays, about half of which were previously published and one-third of which were written by editor Carney. Includes assessments of people like Stephen Foster and Woody Guthrie, essays on American Indian music, analysis of numerous songs recorded between the 1920s through the 1990s, a detailed look at the geographical origins of rap groups, the bebop revolution in jazz, and an exploration of urban blues in Chicago. A rap terminology index is also included.

6. DjeDje, Jacqueline Cogdell and Eddie S. Meadows, eds. *California Soul: Music of African Americans in the West*. Berkeley: University of California Press, 1998.

The first book to explore the rich cultural and musical creativity of African Americans in California. The focus is on blues, jazz, gospel music, R&B and soul music. The essays cover topics like Oakland blues, California rhythm and blues, and jazz in San Diego and Los Angeles, and individuals like Al Bell, Lora Bryant, Bob Geddins and Brenda Holloway. Contains an extensive bibliography of source materials and guides to African American musicians and culture in California.

7. Evans, David, ed. *Ramblin' On My Mind: New Perspectives on the Blues*. Urbana: University of Illinois Press, 2008.

Essays from anthropologists, folklorists and musicologists examine blues as literature, music, personal expression and cultural product. In addition, there are essays on artists like Ella Fitzgerald, Son House, Robert Johnson, and on topics like the styles of vaudeville, Zydeco, blues and African music, and more.

8. Garabedian, Steven Patrick. "Reds, Whites, and the Blues: Blues Music, White Scholarship, and American Cultural Studies." PhD dissertation, University of Minnesota, 2004.

   An interdisciplinary study of white scholarship on African American blues music. Specifically, explores the content and character of consensus blues research and interpretations from the turn of the century until World War II. Garabedian asserts that from the early 1920s, blues historiography cast black vernacular music in terms of Negro pathology, blight and victimization; in the 1930s and 1940s folk song revival created new perspectives and new priorities, and the music was often perceived as revolutionary. Studies the rise and fall of this competitive discourse on blues politics and protest.

9. Garon, Paul. *Blues and the Poetic Spirit.* New York: City Lights Books, 1996.

   Explores the meaning of blues from a literary and psychological perspective. Specifically, investigates the social and political phenomena that have influenced the history and evolution of blues over the last few decades, and as a "psychopoetic" contribution to both American music and history. Includes rare photographs of blues artists and their milieu.

10. Hansen, Barry and B.B. King. *Rhino's Cruise Through the Blues.* San Francisco: Miller Freeman Books, 2000.

    Explores the history of blues from the Delta by focusing on musicians, recordings and historical events. Covers artists like Leadbelly, Bessie Smith, Robert Johnson, Muddy Waters, B.B. King, Stevie Ray Vaughan and many more. Also discusses cultural and social mores, blues impact on American history, blues influence and the immoral character of blues. Photographs, album covers and record labels are also included.

11. Keith, Laura Jessena Johnson. "Eileen Southern, *The Black Perspective in Music*: Documentation of Black Music History." PhD dissertation, University of South Carolina, 2008.

    Investigates the role of the journal *The Black Perspective in Music* in documenting black musical history. The author focuses on which musical genres are documented in the journal, the sociopolitical context surrounding each genre, the authors and their topics, and the relationship of the journal to music education. In addition, the author develops and categorizes the journal's articles into four large areas of focus, including blues/ragtime, jazz, art music and music education.

12. Lynn, Kwaku. "American Afrikan Music: A Study in Musical Change." PhD dissertation, University of California, Los Angeles, 1987.

    Examines musical change, viewing music industry personnel as the main purveyors of musical change. Although traditional concepts and terms such as acculturation, assimilation, syncretism and other theoretical perspectives are alluded to throughout the study, new terms and new definitions of standard terms were developed and utilized in the study. Although historical, sociological and political events coupled with acculturation, assimilation, syncretism and other processes have been active participants in shaping American Afrikan music, other factors such as conceptual change, crossover, creative control, computers and synthesizers, black radio and other variables must also be considered in any discussion on contemporary musical change.

13. Martin, Waldo E. *No Coward Soldiers: Black Cultural Politics and Postwar America*. Cambridge: Harvard University Press, 2005.

    Based on three lectures given by Martin as the Nathan I. Huggins Lecturer at Harvard University. Situated in the lived experience and historical memory of the Civil Rights movement, he discusses and contextualizes his theory of blacks embracing themselves by fighting through tangled duality to imagine, realize and transcend new identities in a changing culture and society. He argues that this new identity resonated with both authenticity and representation in African American musical genres from jazz to Motown to hip hop. Draws upon the provocative works of Hazel Carby, Vincent Harding, Cornell West and others.

14. Maxilla, Horace Joseph, Jr. "Say What? Topics, Signs, and Signification in African-American Music." PhD dissertation, Louisiana State University and Agricultural and Mechanical College, 2001.

    The theories of Kofi Agawu and Samuel A. Floyd are the basis for a discussion on expressivity in African American music. Uses Agawu's expansion of the semiotic theory of topics to form a union of musical expression and formal design. Concepts from Floyd's *Power of Black Music* are used to seek richer interpretations of the expressive power of selected works of African American composers. Identifies cultural and musical traditions like call and response, signifyin(g), the spiritual/supernatural blues, and jazz in selected works of David Baker, Charles Mingus, Hale Smith and William Grant Still.

15. Melnick, Jeffrey. *A Right to Sing the Blues: African Americans, Jews and American Popular Song*. Cambridge, MA: Harvard University Press, 1999.

   The author's primary assumption is that more than anything else, "Black-Jewish relations is a ritualistic pattern of discussion" (p. 3), and that "Black-Jewish relations needs to be approached—not exclusively, but still significantly—as a story told *by* Jews *about* interracial relations" (pp. 3–4). Contends that the subject "blacks and Jews" is more a rhetorical construct than a sociopolitical description, supported by the publication of several thematically related books in the late 1990s and 2000 (e.g. Billig. *Rock 'N' Roll Jews.* 2009). He focuses primarily on the 1920s and 1930s when Jewish musicians like Al Jolson, Eddie Cantor, Sophie Tucker, George and Ira Gershwin, Irving Berlin and Jerome Kern were using black cultural content to produce a transformation in American music. Explores how some Jews exploited both African American music and selected musicians to enhance their assimilation into American culture.

16. Murray, Albert. *Stomping the Blues.* New York: Da Capo, 1986.

   An insightful and provocative discussion of the sources, styles and mythologies of blues. He discusses blues aesthetics, the manner in which they originated in African American communities, and how they reflect ritual responses to life. Situates the role and function of blues within African American culture, and devotes a chapter to correcting misconceptions and illuminating the true meaning of blues in American culture.

17. Ottenheimer, Harriet. "Emotional Release in Blues Singing: A Case Study." PhD dissertation, Tulane University, 1973.

   In this case study, blues texts serve as a mechanism for understanding catharsis, the psychological release of emotion. Author's research methodology focused on interviews with two singers and analysis of numerous performances by them. In the interviews, she allows the singers to describe their songs as blues or non-blues, divides the songs into lines to analyze for topical issues, and then uses a form of content analysis to analyze the data. Interestingly, the topic of "women" is prominent in the songs of the two singers.

18. Pyne, Rochelle. "The Blues: An Interdisciplinary Curricular Design." EdD dissertation, New York: Teachers College, Columbia University, 2006.

   Aimed at facilitating high school teachers' development of interdisciplinary units of study with blues as an organizing center of the curriculum. Examines interdisciplinary instructional methods that would enable students to explore connections across disciplines, to help teachers to design lessons that highlight why the blues emerged as a musical genre, and to assist participants in developing units of study with embedded instructional activities.

19. Roberts, John Storm. *The Latin Tinge: The Impact of Latin American Music on the United States.* New York: Oxford University Press, 1999.

   Presents evidence that blues, rock, jazz, rhythm and blues, and country have been influenced throughout their development by musical idioms from Brazil, Cuba, Mexico and other Latin American countries. The influences can be found in the rhythmic structures, musical forms and specific musical genres like the Cuban *mambo, rumba* and *son*; the Puerto Rican *bomba* and *plena*; the Argentinean *tango*; and the Brazilian *samba*. His specific interest is in processes of influence, transformation and reinterpretation.

20. ——. *Black Music of Two Worlds: African, Caribbean, Latin, and African-American Traditions.* Second edn. New York: Schirmer Books, 1998.

   Covers the influences of African musical traditions on diasporic musical cultures. His coverage begins with a study of African roots music and how those traditions were either preserved, transformed, or reinterpreted in the Caribbean, South and Central America, and in North America in black music like blues, jazz, spirituals and rap. Includes a CD with many of the examples from the book.

21. Rublowsky, John. *Popular Music.* New York: Basic Books, 1967.

   Focuses on the process used to create a "hit" record, from recording studio to international exploitation. Explains why styles like blues, country, Tin Pan Alley, show business and soul music attract dedicated audiences. Acknowledges the influence of African Americans, and traces the evolution of American popular music from the roots of black musical genres.

22. Smith, Christopher John. "'I Can Show it to You Better Than I can Explain it to You': Analyzing Procedural Cues in African-American Musical Improvisations." PhD dissertation, Indiana University, 1999.

   Argues that improvised musical performances are made possible by participants' understanding of sophisticated cues that communicate directions, goals and intent. He surveys the literature on the analysis of improvisation, and using performance studies theories from folklore and cultural anthropology, analyzes performances and performance vocabularies of James Brown (funk), Miles Davis (jazz), Screamin'

Jay Hawkins (R&B), Big Bill Broonzy (country blues), and Fela Anikulapo-Kuti (Afro-Beat). His research, which combines sound and video transcription with contextual analysis and references to a wide variety of methodologies, reveals how the participants use cues to communicate musical perceptions and to direct musical behavior.

23. Sobol, John. *Digitopia*. Toronto: Banff Centre Press, 2002.

Examines both oral and literate cultures in the United States, combining African American stories of revolution and power in music (specifically blues, jazz, rock and roll, rap and hip hop) with those of literate poets who struggle to transcend the printed page to embrace the body, music and public speech. Discusses the implication of oral and literate values of rave, Napster, and the digital divide in North American culture.

24. Southern, Eileen. *The Music of Black Americans: A History*. Third edn. New York: W.W. Norton and Co., 1997.

Thorough coverage of the history and evolution of African American musical traditions from their African legacy to contemporary times. In addition to music of the slave era, and genres like ragtime, concert music and composers, opera, spirituals and gospel, discusses blues and jazz, and presents a concise overview of popular music, including rap.

25. Starr, Larry and Christopher Waterman. *American Popular Music: From Minstrelsy to MTV*. New York: Oxford University Press, 2002.

An overview of the major styles of popular music, including the relationship between music and American culture from the late nineteenth century to the early 1990s. Organized by themes, including the development of critical learning skills, the multicultural roots of popular styles, music and social identity, and the influence of technology on music. In addition to coverage of genres like blues, rhythm and blues, soul, hip hop and rap, the book contains numerous musical examples, boxed inserts, sidebars, biographical sketches, listening charts and lyrics.

26. Stewart, Earl L. *African-American Music: An Introduction*. New York: Schirmer Books, 1998.

An introduction to the richness and diversity of African American musical styles with a special emphasis on distinctive musical characteristics and the development of genres like blues, gospel, jazz, ragtime, spirituals, rhythm and blues, and classical music. He provides new insights and uses musical analysis throughout to support the validity of his conclusions regarding musical styles, form and structures.

27. Stoia, Nicholas. "The Musical Frameworks of Five Blues Schemes." PhD dissertation, City University of New York, 2008.

Illustrates ways in which harmony, melody, rhythm and text interact in five blues schemes: "John Henry," "Alabama Bound," "How Long," "Trouble in Mind," and "Sitting on Top of the World." The tunes, analyzed from recordings made between the early 1920s and the early 1940s, were chosen because they are eight to ten bars long. Overall, the author concludes that his project may be viewed as five case studies of different types of musical frameworks because the use and function of the musical components varied from scheme to scheme.

## REFERENCES

28. Anderson, Tom and Bradley Shank. *Exploring the Blues*. Milwaukee: Hal Leonard, 2001.

A 56-page resource that covers topics like birth of the blues (with information on important figures like W.C. Handy), early blues guitarists (Robert Johnson, Charley Patton and others), women and the blues (Ma Rainey, Dinah Washington, Aretha Franklin and others), and now and then. The author discusses the role and function of artists like Chuck Berry, Eric Clapton and Elvis Presley, and blues greats like B.B. King, John Lee Hooker and Bessie Smith.

29. Bird, Christiane. *The Da Capo Jazz and Blues Lover's Guide to the United States*. New York: Da Capo Press, 2001.

A comprehensive guide to live blues and jazz venues, from national clubs to lesser known local and regional venues. The book covers clubs in 25 cities and the Mississippi Delta with current listings for festivals, historical theaters, record stores, radio stations and more.

30. Bogaert, Karel. *Blues Lexicon: Blues, Cajun, Boogie Woogie, Gospel*. Antwerp, Belgium: Standard Vitgeverij, 1972.

In Flemish. A biographical dictionary of blues and related genres. Each entry includes dates, a career summary and a concise discography. Entries on styles and places are also included. Data gathered by personal interviews and correspondence with artists and recording companies. Translation and coverage by Karel Bogaert.

31. Cateforis, Theo, ed. *The Rock History Reader*. New York: Routledge, 2006.

Numerous essays by fanzine writers, media critics, musicologists and rock critics detail the contentious issues, conflicts and creative tensions that have characterized the rise and popularity of rock music: censorship, copyright, feminism, race relations, youth subculture and the meaning of musical value in blues, R&B and hip hop. Contributions from and material related to artists like Chuck Berry and Ronnie Specter.

32. Clark, William. *Temples of Sound: Inside the Great Recording Studios.* San Francisco: Chronicle Books, 2005.

   Recounts the stories of the legendary studios where great music was recorded, including blues, funk, jazz, country, soul and pop styles. Profiles 15 studios, including Chess Capital, Motown, Stax, Philadelphia International and others.

33. Clifford, Mike. *The Illustrated Encyclopedia of Black Music.* New York: Harmony Books, 1982.

   Numerous biographies and photographs of African American popular music artists, from the 1940s to the early 1980s. The entries are arranged by decade; each section contains a concise history of each decade, followed by an alphabetical listing of the artists prominent during that decade, with a concise biography, a photograph and a discography for each.

34. DeSalvo, Debra. *The Language of the Blues: From Alcorub to Zulu.* New York: Billboard Books, 2006.

   A thoroughly researched dictionary of blues slang. The author claims that blues artists nicked words and phrases from drag queens, hookers, numbers runners, junkies, pimps and others. She presents the origins of phrases, the ongoing history of phrases, and current applications of words and concepts.

35. Ferris, William. *Mississippi Black Folklore: A Research Bibliography.* Hattiesburg: University and College Press of Mississippi, 1971.

   A compilation of rural black culture in Mississippi with special emphasis on the blues. The listings are divided into the following categories: general, social and historical background, Negro life in Mississippi, the blues, folk songs (including collections), prose narrative, literature and field techniques. A discography of Microgroove issues (including label, names and catalog numbers) is divided into four categories: traditional singers, traditional blues singers, urban blues and pop singers. A discography of gospel music and list of films is also included.

36. Floyd, Jr, Samuel A. and Marsha J. Reisser. "On Researching Black Music in California: A Preliminary Report About Sources and Resources." *Black Music Research Journal* 9(1) (Spring 1989): 109–17.

A concise narrative that cites sources and issues that one can use to conduct African American musical research in California.

37.    ——. *Black Music Biography: An Annotated Bibliography.* Millwood, NY: Kraus International, 1987.

This bibliography of books written about African American musicians includes concise biographical information, discographies, and information on musical genres, autobiographies, blues, jazz and other genres. The information is divided into sections by subject, including general guides, bibliographies, periodical literature, black musical histories, collective biographies, anthologies and more.

38.    ——. *Black Music in the United States.* Millwood, NY: Krause International, 1983.

An annotated listing of archival and research materials related to African American musical research. The book is divided into subject categories, and contains concise annotations of general guides, bibliographies, periodical literature, black music histories, collective biographies, anthologies and repertoires, and archival materials.

39.    Ford, Robert. *A Blues Bibliography.* Second edn. New York: Routledge, 2007.

Updated version of the 1999 edition contains mostly books and journal articles. Includes some record liner notes, newspaper articles, unpublished theses, and other publications that were published between 1999 and 2005. The entries are divided into categories like history and background, instruments, record labels, reference sources, regional variations, and lyric transcriptions and musical analysis. Numerous biographical citations; entries are not annotated.

40.    Gillette, Charlie, Greil Marcus, Bill Miller and Greg Shaw, eds. *Encyclopedia of Rock.* New York: Schirmer Books, 1987.

The entries are wide ranging and summarize the careers of numerous artists, record producers, session musicians, songwriters and more. Among the numerous artists/groups covered are James Brown, Aretha Franklin, Major Lance, Leadbelly, The Manhattans, The Staple Singers, and The Stylistics.

41.    Haggerty, Gary. *A Guide to Popular Music Reference Books: An Annotated Bibliography.* Westport, CT: Greenwood Press, 1995.

The 427 entries, ranging from 50–250 words, cover blues, big bands, country, jazz, pop, rock, heavy metal and rap. The annotations include content, format and sources of reviews; appendices contain discographies of individual performers, bibliographies of performers and electronic sources for music.

42. Hardy, Phil and Dave Laing, eds. *The Encyclopedia of Rock*. 3 vols. New York: St Albans and Panther, 1976.

   The three volumes of this encyclopedia include Volume 1: *The Age of Rock 'n' Roll*, Volume 2: *From Liverpool to San Francisco*, and Volume 3: *The Sounds of the Seventies*. The coverage is good but is limited primarily to artists and issues related to rock and roll, including artists like James Brown, Fats Domino, Aretha Franklin and other R&B and soul artists.

43. Harris, Sheldon. *Blues Who's Who: A Biographical Dictionary of Blues Singers*. New York: Da Capo, 1981.

   Lists numerous known and obscure bluesmen, blues women, and rhythm and blues artists. The amount of information provided varies with each performer, with the better-known artists' careers detailed with dates, places and more. In some cases, the author offers critical assessments, cites performers who influenced him and lists some of the songs that are identified with the artist.

44. Hart, Mary L., Brenda M. Eagles and Lisa N. Howorth. *The Blues: A Bibliographic Guide*. Music Research and Information Guides, Vol. 7. Introduction by William Ferris. New York: Garland, 1989.

   A comprehensive (but not annotated) bibliography organized into the following categories: background (black history and folklore); music of the blues; blues in American literature; blues interviews and biographies; blues in Great Britain; blues in Europe; how to play; discographies; and filmography. Each of the twelve chapters includes a bibliography arranged alphabetically and is introduced by a blues scholar. The one exception to this is the chapter "Biographies of Blues Musicians," in which the entries are arranged by artist. The bibliography contains books, book reviews, films, journal articles, liner notes, newspaper articles, dissertations, and record liner notes in Dutch, English, French, German and Swedish.

45. Helander, Brock. *Rock's Who's Who: A Biographical Dictionary and Critical Discography Including Rhythm-And-Blues, Soul, Rockabilly, Folk, Country, Easy Listening, Punk, and New Wave*. New York: Schirmer, 1982; London: Collier Macmillan, 1986.

   Although the coverage is broad, the entries on R&B and soul are useful for scholars. Includes critical comments on recordings from artists of each musical style.

46. Herzhaft, Gerald. *Encyclopedia of the Blues*. Translated by Brigitte Debord. Fayetteville: University of Arkansas Press, 1992.

Primarily a biographical sourcebook with topics relating to blues, festivals, instruments and styles, and East Coast blues. The biographical section includes information on dates, achievements, influences, performance and styles. Also includes a bibliography, annotated discography (including recorded anthologies), list of standards, and a directory of musicians organized by instrument.

47. Hine, Darlene Clark, ed., Elsa Barkley and Rosalyn Terborg-Penn, assoc. eds. *Black Women in America: An Historical Encyclopedia.* Brooklyn, NY: Carlson Publishing, 1993.

A comprehensive assessment of African American women in North America from the seventeenth century until the early 1990s. Entries focus on women who overcame adversity and worked to change their world. The blues/jazz entry includes information on rhythm and blues, and on noted singers on Lavern Baker, Cleopatra Brown, Ruth Brown, Aretha Franklin, Ma Rainey, Bessie Smith, Dinah Washington and others.

48. Hoffmann, Frank. *Chronology of American Popular Music, 1900–2000.* New York: Routledge, 2007.

A basic reference that includes biographical information, styles and an overall comprehensive view of the subject. Includes information on blues, hip hop, jazz, rhythm and blues, rock and roll, soul music and more.

49. Horn, David, Dave Lang, Paul Oliver, John Shepherd and Peter Wicke, eds. *Continuum Encyclopedia of Popular Music of the World.* London and New York: Continuum, 2003.

This encyclopedia originated with the *International Associations for the Study of Popular Music* (IASPM) in the mid 1980s. Designed as a comprehensive and reliable reference book for scholars, researchers, students, information and media professionals. Divided into two primary sections: "social and cultural dimensions" (covering topics like class, deviance, fashion, gender and sexuality), and "the industry" (includes topics like broadcasting, copyright, deals and contracts, and publishing).

50. Iwaschkin, Roman. *Popular Music: A Reference Guide.* New York and London: Garland, 1986.

The book contains over 5,000 entries (not annotated), arranged into categories like folk, country, Cajun and black music. They are further divided into subcategories like biographies, music education and appreciation, and more. Includes listings on blues, jazz, rhythm and blues, soul, rap and hip hop, Caribbean music and other traditions.

51. Komara, Edward, ed. *Encyclopedia of the Blues.* 12 vols. New York: Routledge, 2005.

    The 2,100 entries written by 140 scholars cover the blues as a cultural, historical and musical form. Arranged alphabetically, thematically, and by person and subject, with a song-title index. Most of the entries are biographical, of historians, label owners and performers; each contains a bibliography and discography. Entries focus on different aspects of business, record labels, instruments, geographical regions, styles and numerous other under-researched topics.

52. Koskoff, Ellen, ed. *The United States and Canada: The Garland Encyclopedia of World Music.* Vol. 3. New York: Garland, 2001.

    The section on African American music, pp. 503–717, contains scholarly essays and insights from scholars like David Evans on blues, Portia Maultsby on funk, rhythm and blues, and soul music, and Dawn Norfleet on hip hop/rap.

53. Larkin, Colin, ed. *The Encyclopedia of Popular Music.* Third edn. London: Muze, 1998.

    This encyclopedia was originally published in four volumes in 1992. Includes numerous entries and an album rating system. Does not list artists by genre but includes categories which are based on a band or artist's primary area of music. The encyclopedia includes numerous American artists and groups like Fontella Bass, Brenda and the Tabulations, James Brown, Ruth Brown, Ray Charles, Graham Central Station and Stevie Wonder, as well as some popular international groups. An essay on blues is also included.

54. ——. *The Virgin Encyclopedia of the Blues.* London: Virgin, 1998.

    Includes biographies of the numerous artists associated with Delta, Chicago and other blues styles, and biographical information on British blues artists like Mike Bloomfield, Eric Clapton and the Rolling Stones.

55. ——. *The Guinness Who's Who of Blues.* Enfield and New York: Guinness, 1995.

    Thorough coverage of performers and topics from Delta blues, Chicago blues, and later blues traditions and performers. Among the numerous artists covered are Robert Johnson, Charley Patton, Big Bill Broonzy, B.B. King, Albert King, The Mississippi Sheiks and many more.

56. Leadbitter, Mike, ed. *Nothing but the Blues.* London: Hanover Books, 1971.

A collection of notable articles on blues and blues musicians, most of which were reprinted from the first 50 issues of *Blues Unlimited*. The focus is on biographical information, and the book does include some previously unpublished articles. The articles are categorized by geographical area, and identify the author and date of publication. No table of contents or index.

57. Mandel, Howard, ed. *The Billboard Illustrated Encyclopedia of Jazz and Blues*. New York: Billboard Books, 2005.

Permeated with photographs of jazz and blues artists from the past to the present, this chronological survey includes profiles and biographical sketches of key artists in both genres. The book is organized by decade, and each chapter begins with an overview of the history and evolution of jazz and blues of the specific time period. The first part of each chapter is devoted to blues and the second part to jazz, followed by the biographical entries of the major and lesser known artists of the time.

58. Martinelli, David. "Source Materials and Guide to African-American Music, Musicians, and Culture in California." In *California Soul: Music of African Americans in the West*, eds Jacqueline C. DjeDje and Eddie S. Meadows, pp. 353–449. Berkeley: University of California Press, 1998.

A comprehensive bibliography that covers music, musicians and venues associated with the performance of blues, jazz, gospel music, rhythm and blues, and soul music. The listings are not annotated, but it is very thorough.

59. Napier, Simon A., compiler. *Backwoods Blues: Selected Reprints from* Blues Unlimited Magazine *and Elsewhere*. Bexhill-on-Sea, UK: Blues Unlimited, 1968.

A concise fifty-five-page anthology with fourteen articles from 1962–68, on lesser known artists like Jaybird Coleman, Arthur Spires, Henry Spires and Babe Stovall. Includes autobiographical entries from Rev. Jack Harp and Fred McDowell, and biographies on Texas Alexander, Snooks, Eaglin, Hattie Hart, Son House, Bull City Red and Allan Shaw are included. Includes an article on Cajun music, the Archive of American Folk Song at the Library of Congress, and a memoir of Muddy Waters by Paul Oliver. Other authors include David Evans, Paul Garon, Charlie Gillette, Simon Napier, Gayle Dean Wardlow and Peter Welding.

60. Obrecht, Jas, ed. *Blues Guitar: The Men Who Made the Music From the Pages of* Guitar Player Magazine. Second edn. San Francisco: GPI Books (Miller Freeman Books), 1993.

A collection of the best blues articles published in *Guitar Player Magazine* between 1974 and 1993. The articles, based on interviews, are divided into two sections: country roots and prime movers. The focus is on performers who have spent most of their careers as blues musicians, thus Eric Clapton, Stevie Ray Vaughan and others are not included. However, this is not a definitive collection of articles because blues artists like Blind Blake, Earl Hooker, Lightin' Hopkins, Blind Lemon Jefferson, Leadbelly, Blind Willie Johnson, Son House, Charley Patton and T-Bone Walker are omitted.

61. Oliver, Paul. "Blues." In *New Grove Dictionary of Music*, Vol. 1, eds Stanley Sadie and H. Wiley Hitchcock, pp. 36–168. New York: Macmillan, 1986.

An extensive entry on blues history from its roots to its realization in the Mississippi Delta, Chicago and elsewhere. This very thorough article covers issues like southern blues in the 1930s, post-war blues on the West Coast, white blues and much more. Other volumes of the *New Grove Dictionary* contain numerous entries on artists of blues and other popular African American musical styles. For a listing of those articles, see entry 63 by Marsha Reissner.

62. Pendergast, Tom and Sara Pendergast. *St James Encyclopedia of Popular Culture*. Detroit: St James Press, 2000.

Contains numerous references to blues, hip hop, rhythm and blues, and soul music and performers. The performers are covered from the early years of blues to the late 1990s.

63. Reissner, Marsha. *Black Music and Musicians in the New Grove Dictionary of American Music and the New Harvard Dictionary of Music*. Chicago: Columbia College Press, 1989.

A list of entries relating to African American musicians and genres in both the *New Grove* and *Harvard* dictionaries. The book is divided into three sections: individuals, ensembles and organizations; subjects; and authors. The sections are organized internally alphabetically by artist's last name.

64. Robins, Wayne. *A Brief History of Rock, Off the Record*. New York: Routledge, 2007.

Traces the history and evolution of rock from Chuck Berry to the Beatles, punk rock and to hip hop. The discussions are authoritative, concise and informative, and span from the end of World War II until the rise of disco and the impact of hip hop on rock. Of special note is the discussion of the musical roots of rock, individual contributors, and the sociopolitical developments that birthed the new provocative teenage music of the 1950s.

65. Salzman, Kack, David L. Smith and Cornel West. *Encyclopedia of African-American Culture and History*. 6 vols. New York: Macmillan, 1995.

The six-volume set contains numerous references to musical styles, artists, producers and related information. Information on music is found in volume one, which covers blues styles, explores the origins of blues from its roots in field songs to its transformation into Mississippi Delta blues, Chicago blues and other styles. The editors also cover other popular musical styles and artists.

66. Santelli, Robert. *The Big Book of Blues: The Fully Revised and Updated Biographical Encyclopedia*. New York: Penguin, 2001.

Explores the lives of 650 blues musicians, songwriters, producers, important British artists like Eric Clapton and John Mayall, and a few notable people connected to the genre like Alan and John Lomax. The biographical essays contain names of band members or individual artists, correct names if warranted, and birth and death dates. The entries, ranging in length from approximately 100 words for Eddie "Vann" Shaw to more than 600 words for Blind Lemon Jefferson, cover the performers' career, musicians who influenced or performed with them, hit records or singles, and style. Organized by individual or band name; contains cross-references to other artists covered in essays; includes a concise discography, a bibliography and an index.

67. Scott, Frank. *The Down Home Guide to Blues*. New York: A Cappella Books, 1991.

Assisted by the staff of *Down Home Blues*, this guide contains 3,500 reviews from twelve years of the newsletter's focus on blues recordings. The reviews are organized alphabetically by performer, with a section on pre- and post-war recordings and a list of essential recordings. Most entries give the song title, record label and issue number, a concise biographical overview of the musicians on the recording, and describe the style and quality of the recording. Of particular note, many of the recordings discussed are vintage and have either been reissued on foreign labels or, in the case of newer material, may be found on small independent labels.

68. Shadwick, Keith. *The Encyclopedia of Jazz and Blues*. London: Chartwell Books, 2003, 2005.

Biographical and other information on numerous artists and styles, including artists like Eric Clapton, B.B. King, Son House, Robert

Johnson, Louis Armstrong, Miles Davis, Duke Ellington and many more.

69. Shaw, Arnold. *Dictionary of American Pop/Rock: Slang and Shop Talk, Styles and Sounds, Fads and Fashions, People and Places, Dances and Diversions.* New York: Schirmer Books, 1982.

Covers blues, disco, jazz, rhythm and blues, gospel, rock, soul and more. The entries are arranged alphabetically and cover artists, terms, instruments, musical genres, people and more.

70. Shepherd, John, David Horn, Dave Laing and Paul Oliver, eds. *The Continuum Encyclopedia of Popular Music of the World.* New York and London: Continuum, 2003.

The volumes cover issues like media, industry and society; performance and production; and North America. Numerous references to persons and topics regarding blues, hip hop/rap, R&B, soul, rock and roll, and reggae.

71. Smith, Randall and John David, eds. *Dictionary of Afro-American Slavery.* Westport, CT: Praeger, 1997.

Contains information on African American folklore and slave songs, and their transformation into blues.

72. Sonnier, Jr, Austin. *A Guide to the Blues: History, Who's Who, Research Sources.* Westport, CT: Greenwood Press, 1994.

A biographical dictionary; begins with a discussion of African influences, and proceeds with an explanation of historical and musical insights (harmonic, melodic and scalar) and selected practitioners. Discusses major areas of blues activity and analyzes musical traits inherent in different blues styles. Another section of the book contains biographical portraits of nearly 400 artists; entries vary widely in length and importance. Numerous artists representing the Mississippi Delta, New Orleans, Texas and Chicago styles are profiled. Includes a selected filmography, bibliography and discography.

73. Southern, Eileen. *Biographical Dictionary of Afro-American and African Musicians.* Westport, CT: Greenwood Press, 1982.

Biographies of 1,500 musicians of African descent, living and deceased, from all musical genres. Includes famous and lesser known artists—Lavern Baker, Ruth Brown, Sam Cooke, B.B. King, Charley Patton, Joe Tex—who played a significant role in the history of blues, R&B and soul.

74. Steenson, Martin, compiler. *Blues Unlimited 1-50: An Index.* London: The Author, 1971.

The index covers the 1963–68 publications of this British blues journal, the first regular English-language blues journal. The index is important because the journal has been diligent in unearthing new and important biographical information on blues artists. The index focuses primarily on books and recording titles, but also includes articles, discographies, obituaries, record and book reviews organized by issue and page numbers. No generic subjects are indexed.

75. Stumble, Irwin and Lyndon Stambler. *Folk and Blues: The Premier Encyclopedia of American Roots Music.* Foreword by John Gorka. Third edn. New York: St Martin's Press, 2001.

The encyclopedia contains numerous interviews, lists of awards, information on Grammies, Folk Alliance and the Blues Foundation, photographs of numerous artists, and a comprehensive index of folk and blues music. Covers musical genres pioneered by African Americans and European immigrants, and their respective influence on global popular music. It also provides insight into why folk music and blues are distinct styles, but interact in ways to influence today's popular music.

76. Weissman, Dick and Craig Morrison. *Blues.* New York: Checkmark Books, 2006.

Part of the eight-volume *American Popular Music* set; includes numerous entries about artists, styles, events and terms. Each entry includes name, birth and death dates, musical role and biographical information. Organized alphabetically.

77. Williams, Michael W. *African American Encyclopedia.* Second edn. New York: Marshall Cavendish, 2001.

A set of eight volumes; the first contains a lengthy entry on blues, blues history and a review of blues styles. The series also includes concise biographies of blues and other popular musicians, and a selected discography for each artist.

78. Wilson, Charles, Charles Reagan and William Ferris, eds. *Encyclopedia of Southern Culture.* Chapel Hill: University of North Carolina Press, 1989.

Primarily focused on generic issues related to southern culture, including those directly associated with African Americans. Also includes information on the origins of blues and jazz. Examines the Mississippi Delta blues and its role and function within southern culture.

## AESTHETICS AND PHILOSOPHY

79. Garabedian, Steven Patrick. "Reds, Whites, and the Blues: Blues Music, White Scholarship, and American Cultural Politics." PhD dissertation, University of Minnesota, 2004.

An interdisciplinary study of white scholarship on African American blues music. Specifically, the author researches the changes in consensus about blues research and interpretation that have occurred, specifically from 1900 through World War II. Assesses the work of Lawrence Gellert, focusing on the rise and fall of the competitive discourse about blues politics and protest. The author concludes that although Sterling Brown and Langston Hughes were enamored with Gellert's work, after World War II his work was dismissed by conservative white cultural critics as fabrication, as an example of white left-wing propaganda rather than African American vernacular creativity. The author contextualizes the phenomena of white "discovery" and "denial" in the culture of the times.

80. Muyumba, Walton M. "Trouble No More: Blues Philosophy and Twentieth-Century African-American Experience." PhD dissertation, Indiana University Press, 2001.

Outlines the emergence of blues philosophy in contemporary American letters. Uses selected works by James Baldwin, Amiri Baraka, Ralph Ellison, Jamaica Kincaid and John Edgar Wideman to examine the impact of Ralph Ellison's *Invisible Man* regarding issues of identity, race and social hope. The essays delineate the pragmatist's qualities and aesthetics of the blues through various texts. Examines the shifting definitions of postmodern aesthetics to posit blues as a culturally appropriate starting point from which to discuss questions concerning contemporary human existence.

81. Oehler, Susan Elizabeth. "The Blues in Transcultural Contexts: Matters of Race, Culture, and Respect; An Introduction." In *African American Music: An Introduction*, eds Mellonee V. Burnim and Portia Maultsby, pp. 96–127. New York: Routledge, 2007.

Focuses on the many transcultural contexts in which the blues appear and its ability to mediate a variety of issues to survive. Topics include racial barriers and cultural interchange in the segregated era, the different cultural orientation of the music, blues transition in the past, shifting popularity of blues in the black community, black radio and white audiences, white blues scenes and more.

82. ———. "Aesthetics and Meaning in Professional Blues Performances: An Ethnographic Examination of an African-American Music in

Intercultural Context." PhD dissertation, Bloomington: Indiana University, 2001.

An ethnographic investigation of how blues performances reflect two cultural groups, African Americans and Euro-Americans, involved in professional blues scenes since the 1960s. Examines the intercultural interactions of blues performance, wherein bodies of people involved in a blues performance do not identify primarily with African American cultural values. Using the perspectives of professional African American blues performers, the author investigates how negotiations of ethnic orientations and racial dynamics affect the sounds and meanings of blues. She identifies qualities of blues performance that textual analysis has either omitted or failed to recognize, and notes that people negotiate aesthetics and meanings of blues through dynamics of cultural dominance, economic ownership, traditional re-creation and racial positions.

83. Powell, Richard J. *The Blues Aesthetic: Black Culture and Modernism.* Washington, DC: Washington Project for the Arts, 1989.

The catalogue of an exhibition presented by the Washington Projects for the Arts. It focuses on blues history, criticism, and the connection of blues to its social context. The catalogue contains contributions by Dwight Andrews and others.

## AUTOBIOGRAPHIES AND BIOGRAPHIES

### James Baldwin

84. Johnson, Gerald Byron. "Baldwin's Androgynous Blues: African American Music, Androgyny, and the Novels of James Baldwin." PhD dissertation, Cornell University, 1993.

The author believes that the injudicious application of socially and politically orientated criticism is one of the main reasons that Baldwin's novels have been consistently devalued, underestimated and misunderstood. Argues that a fuller and more accurate discussion of Baldwin's achievements is warranted; uses methods from mythology, psychology and music to analyze Baldwin's works. In addition to highlighting the continuity of Baldwin's works, the mytho-psychological-musical approach also maps the discontinuities and ruptures in his novels.

### Blind Blake

85. Blake, Blind and Stefan Grossman. *Blind Blake.* Van Nuys, CA: Alfred Publishing, 2007.

A book and CD in the Early Masters of Blues series. The book covers the story of Blake, considered the greatest ragtime blues guitarist of the 1920s. The accompanying CD contains several original recordings of his songs. The 18 transcriptions include "Georgia Bound," "Hey Daddy Blues," "West Coast Blues," "Policy Blues," "Wabash Rag" and several more.

## Michael Bloomfield

86. Bloomfield, Michael and S. Summerville. *Me and Big Joe*. London: Re-Search Publications, 1999.

    Bloomfield tells the story of his early days in Chicago, where he befriended Joe Lee Williams, aka "Big Joe." He recounts their visits to several blues clubs in the Midwest, where they encountered artists like KoKomo Arnold, Lightin' Hopkins, Tampa Red, Sonny Boy Williamson and many others.

87. Wolkin, Jan Mark, Bill Keenom and Carlos Santana. *Michael Bloomfield: If You Love These Blues*. New York: Backbeat Books, 2000.

    Covers blues guitarist Michael Bloomfield's life and music from his rise to fame in the 1960s with the Paul Butterfield Blues Band, his tenure with Bob Dylan and the Electric Blues Band, to Al Kooper's "Super Session." His story is chronicled through his own words and those of his brother, B.B. King, producer Paul Rothchild and many others. Includes a foreword by Carlos Santana and a CD of unreleased early studio tracks.

## Perry Bradford

88. Bradford, Perry. *Born with the Blues: The True Story of the Pioneering Blues Singers and Musicians in the Early Days of Jazz*. New York: Oak Publications, 1965.

    An autobiography of the blues composer and jazz musician (1895–1970) who wrote "That Thing Called Love," recorded by Mamie Smith in January 1920, and "Crazy Blues," recorded in August 1920. Permeated with insightful information on early jazz in New York and on early blues vocalists. Also includes a selection of Bradford's early songs, texts and tunes with piano accompaniment, numerous photographs and an index.

## William "Big Bill" Broonzy

89. Broonzy, William and Yannick Bruynoghe. *Big Bill Blues: William Broonzy's Story*. London: Cassell, 1955. Reprint, by New York: Oak Publications, 1964; New York: Da Capo Press, 1992.

Broonzy discusses his 30-year blues career, including his early life in Mississippi, Chicago experiences and details of his Arkansas farm. He provides the text and comments on the origins of eleven songs and discusses his method of conceptualizing song ideas. Also provides intimate insights into the careers and lives of Sleepy John Estes, Lonnie Johnson, Big Maceo Merriweather, Tommy McClennan, Memphis Minnie, Memphis Slim, Washboard Sam, Tampa Red and Sonny Boy Williamson. The book is conversational, anecdotal and humorous. Forewords by Charles Edward Smith and Stanley Dance; numerous drawings by Paul Oliver. The original discography by Albert McCarthy was revised by Ken Harrison and Ray Asbury for the 1964 reprint.

90. House III, Roger Randolph. "Keys to the Highway: William Big Bill Broonzy and the Chicago Blues in the Era of the Great Migration." PhD dissertation, Boston University, 1999.

Examines the life and analysis of the music of Big Bill Broonzy (1893–1958) and attempts to present a better understanding of this neglected composer of American music and his adjustment as a southern migrant to an urban culture. Uses methodologies from literary analysis, migrant studies and music to address issues like blues as a cultural vehicle of group preservation and resistance, and the influence of a musical genre created by a minority group upon international music making.

## William "Peetie Wheatstraw" Bunch

91. Garon, Paul. *The Devil's Son-in-Law: The Story of Peetie Wheatstraw and His Songs*. London: Studio Vista, 1971.

Draws upon the information and insights provided by colleagues and friends to piece together this portrait of William Bunch, the blues musician known as Peetie Wheatstraw. The author combines a discussion of his daily and musical life in St Louis and East St Louis with the text of 160 songs. The songs and his recording career are discussed chronologically with several textual quotations and some musical examples. No index.

92. Peel, David. *Oooh, Well, Well, It's the Peetie Wheatstraw Songs*. Bridgeport, PA: Belltower Books, 1972.

A 26-page companion monograph to the three reissued albums that were available in 1972. The text of 46 songs recorded between 1930 and 1937 are outlined in red on the left-hand page, and commentary for each song is printed in black on the opposite page. In addition, the author provides objective and valid commentary on authorship, imagery and performance practice.

## Chester "Howlin' Wolf" Burnett

93. Gash, Stephen Matthew. "Howlin' Wolf: Reconstructing the Social Forces Influencing His Approach to Music Making During the Chess Records Years, 1954–76." Masters thesis, Toronto: York University, 2002.

The author situates Howlin' Wolf's years with Chess Records within the social context of the time. His purpose is threefold: 1) to determine the elements that shaped his music making at Chess Records; 2) to probe the relationship between Howlin' Wolf and Chess Records producer, bass player and songwriter Willie Dixon; and 3) to examine Wolf in a live performance context. He also discusses Wolf's performance practices within the context of race, especially his decision to distance himself from white rock musicians and remain closely linked to his black audience in Chicago.

94. Segrest, James and Mark Huffman. *Moanin' at Midnight: The Life and Times of Howlin' Wolf.* New York: Da Capo, 2005.

A thoroughly researched biography of Chester Burnett (Howlin' Wolf) that captures his long and varied career. Traces his life from his Mississippi roots, where he was a victim of constant child abuse. His musical influences included Reggie Boyd, Charley Patton (who taught him to play the guitar), and Sonny Boy Williamson. His Chess recordings are also discussed.

## Leonard "Baby Doo" Caston

95. Titon, Jeff, ed. *From Blues to Pop: The Autobiography of Leonard "Baby Doo" Caston.* Special Series No. 4. Los Angeles: John Edwards Memorial Foundation (UCLA), 1974.

Although only twenty-nine pages long, this transcribed interview of the blues guitarist and pianist contains important information on his career with the Big Three Trio. The trio—Caston, Willie Dixon and Ollie Crawford—pioneered the singing of blues in harmony. Caston also discusses his life from his birth in Mississippi in 1917, his philosophy of blues, and what Titon calls his "commercial aesthetic." Several musical examples.

## Leonard Chess and Chess Records

96. Cohen, Rich. *Machers and Rockers: Chess Records and the Business of Rock and Roll.* New York: W.W. Norton and Co., 2004.

The author espouses the theory that Leonard Chess and some musicians he signed invented the idea of rock and roll. Discusses the importance of Chess's signing of artists like Chuck Berry, Bo Diddley, Muddy Waters, Little Walter and Howlin' Wolf, who all made significant contributions to rock. A story of the artists, ethical issues, and black musicians and Jewish businessmen who created R&B and inspired the development of rock and roll.

97. Cohodas, Nadine. *Spinning Blues into Gold: The Chess Brothers and the Legendary Chess Records.* New York: St Martin's Press Griffin, 2001.

Chronicles the life and musical success of Leonard and Phil Chess, who moved to Chicago in 1928 and founded an independent record label in 1950. Chess records produced numerous classics by rock and roll, gospel, jazz and soul artists. Traces the history of Chess and its many hit recordings, and the brothers' other recording labels, Argo/Cadet, Checkers and others. The hits discussed include Chuck Berry's "Rock and Roll Music," Etta James' "At Last," the Monotones' "Book of Love," Fontella Bass' "Rescue Me," and several more. In addition, the author discusses the popularity of Leonard Chess' Macomba Lounge, WVON (his radio station), and the delicate relationship that existed between the Jews who dominated the early indie record business and the African American artists whose music they produced.

98. Collis, John. *The Story of Chess Records.* New York: Bloomsbury USA, 1998.

Chronicles the Chess brothers and the founding of their company; illustrates that beginning with Muddy Waters in 1950, the company became immensely successful. Using blues, R&B and later rock and roll as the focal point, the author discusses artists and ethical issues like withholding royalties, investigates ten other successful small record companies, and examines the eventual decline of Chess Records after the death of Leonard Chess in 1969 and its subsequent sale to GRT.

**Eric Clapton**

99. Clapton, Eric. *Clapton: The Autobiography.* New York: Broadway, 2008.

Clapton tells his own story in a passionate and honest manner. Chronicles his musical evolution from the Yardbirds and Bluesbreakers to his relationship with Bob Dylan, Jimi Hendrix, The Rolling Stones and the Beatles. In addition, he discusses his failed marriage to George Harrison's ex-wife Pattie Boyd, details of his alcohol and drug addictions, the accidental death of his four-year old son, Conor in 1991, and the effect it had on him.

100. Ne'aumet, Jean-Emile and Patrick Eric Clapton. *Un Gentleman Guitariste*. Paris: Editions Durocher, 1994.

The author places Clapton on the same musical level as Jimi Hendrix, Bob Dylan and Bob Marley. Traces his career from the initial blues influences of Robert Johnson, Freddie King and Muddy Waters to his subsequent influence on Keith Richards of the Rolling Stones. Translated by Ne'aumet.

101. Sandford, Christopher. *Clapton: Edge of Darkness*. Revised edn. New York: Da Capo Press, 1999.

Paints a personal and musical profile of Clapton's career from the Yardbirds, John Mayall's Bluesbreakers, and Cream to his Grammy-winning solo career. In addition to covering issues like the use of alcohol and drugs, the author discusses Clapton's difficult adolescence and how tragedy shaped his life and music.

## Ida Cox

102. Davenport, Doris. "A Candle for Queen Ida." *Black Music Research Journal* 23(1–2) (Spring/Fall 2003): 91–203.

This article celebrates, acknowledges, honors and illuminates the life and musical attributes of Ida P. Cox. The essay analyzes and describes Cox as a vocalist, lyricist and poet. The author focuses on songs written by Cox, as well as her interpretations of other composers' songs, and her choice and presentation of songs.

## Rev. Gary Davis

103. Davis, Gary. *Rev. Gary Davis: The Holy Blues*, compiler and ed. Stefan Grossman. New York: Robbins, 1970.

A collection of 80 songs composed by Rev. Gary Davis with texts, tunes and guitar chords. The songs date from his early years in turn-of-the century South Carolina until his death in 1972. The "Holy Blues" designation was given to his style because he blended blues and ragtime music with gospel lyrics.

104. Davis, Rev. Gary and Stefan Grossman. *Rev. Gary Davis*. Van Nuys, CA: Alfred Publishing, 2007.

This book includes a short biography by Bruce Bastin and twelve transcriptions by Stefan Grossman, a student of Rev. Gary Davis. The transcriptions include lyrics and music, including chords.

Among the transcriptions are "Goin' to Sit Down on the Banks of the River," "Buk Rag," "You Better Mind," "Let Us Get Together," "Cocaine Blues," "The Angel's Message to Me," and several more. The book and accompanying CD are part of The Early Masters of Blues series.

## Willie Dixon

105. Dixon, Willie, Don Snowden and Elizabeth M. Snowden. *I Am the Blues: The Willie Dixon Story*. New York: Da Capo Press, 1989.

Captures Dixon's story from his birth into the racist culture of Vicksburg, Mississippi, his escape from a prison farm, and his draft refusal in 1942, to his work as a songwriter, bassist, arranger and record producer. Among the numerous artists he produced are Chuck Berry, Bo Diddley, Little Walter, Muddy Waters and Howlin' Wolf. In addition, his crossover appeal to artists like The Grateful Dead, Elvis Presley, The Rolling Stones, Stevie Ray Vaughan and Led Zeppelin is discussed.

106. Inaba, Mitsutoshi. "Willie Dixon's Work on the Blues: From the Early Recordings Through the Chess and Cobra Years, 1940–71." PhD dissertation, University of Oregon, 2005.

An exploration of Dixon's Chicago blues years from the 1940s through the early 1970s. Covers his life, his early performing groups—The Five Breezes, The Four Jumps of Jive, The Big Three Trio—and his work with both Chess and Cobra Records. The author examines Dixon's writing style and discusses how he helped artists like Muddy Waters, Howlin' Wolf and KoKo Taylor develop their public images. Includes a discussion of all recordings he made during the time period of the study.

## Thomas Dorsey

107. Harris, Michael Wesley. *The Rise of Gospel Blues: The Music of Thomas Andrew Dorsey in the Urban Church*. New York: Oxford University Press, 1994.

Investigates Dorsey's life from his birth in rural Georgia, his religious upbringing, his blues years, and his conversion and involvement in gospel music. The author contends that Dorsey represents the tension between the assimilationist and indigenous forms of African American music. His immense success as a composer of gospel music and his involvement with the Chicago African American community is also chronicled. Combines cultural and musical analysis to present a well researched and scholarly study.

108. ——. *The Advent of Gospel Blues in Black Old-Line Churches in Chicago, 1932–33, as Seen Through the Life and Mind of Thomas Andrew Dorsey.* PhD dissertation, Harvard University, 1982.

A study of Chicago's old-line churches' style of liturgy that reflected the assimilative attitudes found among some African Americans. Harris argues that until 1932, the music and worship service of the largest black Chicago churches varied little from their white counterparts. With the advent of Gospel Blues, the drift of old-line churches away from traditional black worship norms was halted. The history and evolution of this movement is traced from the choir at Ebenezer Baptist Church to a 1933 "convention" that was held at Pilgrim Baptist Church. Profiles Thomas Dorsey and his career, from his childhood exposure to "guitar pickin'," to his jobs as a "rent party" pianist and accompanist for Gertrude "Ma" Rainey, until 1928 when he began to compose sacred blues songs. Harris' primary conclusion is that blues transcends its acoustical properties and in some instances is the arbiter of the indigenous cultural values of black America.

## David "Honeyboy" Edwards

109. Edwards, David "Honeyboy," Janis Martinson and Michael Robert Frank. *The World Don't Owe Me Nothing: The Life and Times of Delta Bluesman "Honeyboy" Edwards.* Chicago: Chicago Review Press, 1997.

Dictated when he was 82 years old, this biography is a confluence of history, music and storytelling. Edwards describes community life, family events, the depression and the harsh realities of racial segregation, his arrests by white farmers and sheriffs, and the brutality he suffered because of his color and class. Reflects on his talent, and provides insights into the life and music of selected blues artists. The appendices include concise biographical portraits of blues performers and their recordings, and a discography of "Honeyboy's" recordings. Black-and-white photographs depict the artists and venues mentioned.

## Blind Boy Fuller

110. Fuller, Blind Boy and Stefan Grossman. *Blind Boy Fuller.* Van Nuys, CA: Alfred Publishing, 2007.

Grossman contributes nineteen transcriptions (including chords, music and lyrics) of Fuller's classic songs like "Black and Tan,"

"Meat Shakin Woman," "Low Down Ways," "Thousand Woman Blues," "Sweet Honey Hole," "Jitterbug Rag," "Lost Lover Blues" and "Worn Out Engine." Contains several photographs, a two-page biography by Bruce Bastin, and a CD of original recordings by this popular Piedmont blues guitarist. Part of The Early Masters of Blues series.

## Bob Geddins

111. Hildebrand, Lee. "A Conversation With Bob Geddins." In *California Soul: Music of African Americans in the West*, eds Jacqueline C. DjeDje and Eddie S. Meadows, pp. 112–24. Berkeley: University of California Press, 1998.

This conversation between Geddins and James Moore, Sr offers penetrating insight into the way that Geddins worked in the recording studio, artists he produced, how he coaxed vocalists into singing tunes his way, and his role and in creating Oakland blues.

## Buddy Guy

112. Wilcock, Donald E. with Buddy Guy. *Damn Right I've Got the Blues: Roots of Rock and Roll*. New York: Woodford Press, 1993.

An account of Buddy Guy's life and musical career. Permeated with interviews of blues, rock and musical industry notables. Guy is perceived as a link between Chicago blues pioneers like Howlin' Wolf and Muddy Waters and British artists like Eric Clapton and Jimmy Page. Discusses Guy's achievements, hardships and evolution from Louisiana poverty to fame as a Chicago blues musician. Contains numerous photographs and a thorough discography.

## W.C. Handy

113. Handy, W.C. *Father of the Blues: An Autobiography*, ed. Arna Wendell Bontemps with a foreword by Abbe Niles. New York: MacMillan, 1941; London: Sidgwick and Jackson, 1957; London: Jazz Book Club, 1961.

Chronicles Handy's life from his childhood in Alabama to his success in New York City. His first blues was an extension of the African American folk music he heard while growing up. Discusses the acquisition of knowledge that was forbidden by his parents (meaning any non-religious knowledge, especially regarding blues and worldly issues). Expounds on his years in Memphis, Chicago and New York, and the founding of his publishing business. Includes musical excerpts from several early and later blues; a chronological listing of his arrangements, books and compositions; and a name index.

114. Hurwitt, Elliot S. "W.C. Handy as Music Publisher: Career and Reputation." PhD dissertation, New York: City University of New York, 2000.

The focus is on the music publishing career of Handy and the intersection of the worlds of copyright and publishing of the blues, Tin Pan Alley, vaudeville and other popular genres between around 1900 and 1950. The author argues that Handy is the one person who brought these worlds together, and hails him as an essential figure in the transformation and transmission of black folklore materials.

115. Moore, Charles Eugene. "William Christopher Handy and *Uraeus Mi*: A Bantu-centered Philosophical and Intracultural Assessment." PhD dissertation, University of California, Los Angeles, 2000.

This dissertation advances a discursive strategy regarding the Bantu-centered philosophical and intracultural origins of *Uraeus Mi,* the blues music tradition. Describes Handy as a *Muntu* and covers his life and work as a pioneer who introduced blues to the world. He concludes that the theoretical and empirical data substantiates the origins of the *Uraeus Mi* tradition as an accretion of their epistemological, ontological and axiological logos.

116. Robertson, David. *W.C. Handy: The Life and Times of the Man Who Made the Blues.* New York: Knopf, 2006.

Covers Handy's life and accomplishments from his Alabama roots to his experiences on Beale Street in Memphis, Tennessee, and his subsequent success as a music publisher in New York City. The author argues that Handy was both the father and popularizer of blues, the first to bring African American culture to a mainstream audience through sheet music and the recording industry. Provides insight into some of Handy's most famous compositions, including the "Memphis Blues," "St Louis Blues," and "Blues for Mr Crump."

117. Thompson, Marilyn Angela. "W.C. Handy's Contribution to African American Solo Vocal Concert Music." EdD dissertation, Teachers College, Columbia University, 2007.

Examines Handy's involvement in academic music, with musical theater composers, classical composers and performers, and with the music publishing business. Asserts that Handy used his influence to provide opportunities for composers and performers, especially people of color, and promoted the publication of selected spiritual arrangements and art songs of six composers, Margaret Bonds, Lillian Evanti, W. C. Handy, Herbert Melts, Florence B. Price and William Grant Still. Profiles the composers, analyzes the songs and discusses each composition's compliance with ideals and sensibilities of either the Harlem or the Chicago Renaissance.

## Earl Hooker

118. Danchin, Sebastian. *Earl Hooker: Blues Master.* Jackson: University Press of Mississippi, 2001.

A biography woven together from interviews with Hooker's mother, relatives, friends and peers from 1975 to 1985. Elucidates Hooker's cultural milieu following Charles Keil's recommendation to document the culture of the ghetto through the prism of one central character. Hooker provides illuminating insights into the development of electric blues ensembles in the south and Chicago following World War II. Also discusses aesthetics, travel, Chicago blues and Hooker's recordings in Los Angeles.

## John Lee Hooker

119. Murray, Charles Shaar. *Boogie Man: The Adventures of John Lee Hooker in the American Twentieth Century.* New York: St Martin's Press, 2000.

In addition to a myriad of details about his life, the book contains a wealth of information on the blues revival, band personnel, associations with other musicians, and record labels. Also included is information on how Hooker survived the competition with other bluesmen and genres.

## Sam "Lightnin'" Hopkins

120. O'Brien, Timothy J. "Sam Lightnin' Hopkins: Houston Bluesman, 1912–60." Masters thesis, University of Houston, 2006.

The life and music of the artist are examined through manuscript collections, census data, court records and privately held correspondence. Songs, oral histories and videotapes chronicle his life and musical contributions to blues and guitar techniques.

**Linda Hopkins**

121. Barrow-Pryor, Erany. "Motherin' the Blues: Linda Hopkins; The Continuing Legacy of the Blues Woman." PhD dissertation, University of California, Los Angeles, 2005.

This dissertation records the life of Linda Hopkins, with its attendant tragedies, triumphs and challenges, and ability to embrace life. Situates her recording and performance achievements, talents and contributions within blues history, and demonstrates how her life and art have nurtured the blues and contributed to the ongoing legacy of blues women. Thorough coverage, with information on blues history as well as the particulars of Hopkins's contributions, influences and style. Released in paperback in 2008 by VDM.

**Langston Hughes**

122. Bonner, Patricia Elaine. "Sassy Jazz and Slo' Draggin' Blues as Sung by Langston Hughes." PhD dissertation, University of South Florida, 1990.

An exploration of the relationship between blues, jazz and the musico-poetry of Langston Hughes. Specifically focuses on the first two volumes of Hughes' poetry, *The Weary Blues* and *Fine Clothes to the Jew*, which exemplify the amalgamation of blues with jazz poetry. The author's analysis is concerned not only with Hughes' merging blues and jazz music, but also with union of the African American experience with written poetry, and the use of blues and jazz to chronicle African American life and experiences in North America.

123. Tracy, Steven C. *Langston Hughes and the Blues.* Urbana: University of Illinois Press, 2001.

Although not a biography or autobiography, this book is included here because of Hughes' affection and promotion of blues during the Harlem Renaissance. Originally published in 1988 this edition, with a significant new introduction, focuses on Hughes' use of blues forms and themes in his poetry throughout his stellar career. Specifically, he places poet and genre in historical, cultural and literary context, presents functional definitions of folklore and relates them to the marketing of blues in the 1920s, assesses the attitudes of Harlem intellectuals toward folk materials, and discusses the influence of James Weldon Johnson on Hughes' understanding and use of blues in his literary works. However, only scant attention is given to the numerous poems in which Hughes uses a blues sensibility without using a blues form. Extensive endnotes; online sources for blues CDs.

124. ——. "The Influence of the Blues Tradition on Langston Hughes's Blues Poems." PhD dissertation, University of Cincinnati, 1985.

The author explores both Hughes' attitudes toward the blues and his use of blues aspects in his works. Also examines the attitudes of Sterling Brown, W.E.B. DuBois, Zora Neale Hurston, James W. Johnson and Alain Locke. He places Hughes' discussions of blues within the context of other critics, and compares three of Hughes' poems to a variety of blues recordings. He concludes that Hughes was combining oral and literary traditions to create a poetry that contained little of the imagery that is contained in some of the best blues songs.

## Alberta Hunter

125. Taylor, Frank C. and Gerald Cook. *Alberta Hunter: A Celebration in Blues*. New York: McGraw-Hill, 1987.

Comprehensive and detailed account of Hunter's life and career beginning with her early years in Memphis, Tennessee, and culminating in her acceptance as an icon of blues. In addition to her experiences with sex and racial discrimination, the authors discuss her success prior to 1977, her comeback after 1977, and her noted tolerance of others. Also included are details of her vaudeville days, extensive travels in Europe and South America, entertaining American troops, work in films and more.

## Mississippi John Hurt

126. Hurt, Mississippi John and Aaron Stang, ed. *The Music of Mississippi John Hurt*. New York: Warner Brothers, 1993.

Contains a concise biography and the transcriptions in both notation and tablature of original Mississippi John Hurt's recordings of classics like "Shake That Thing," "Casey Jones," "Got That Blues," "Can't be Satisfied," "Nobody's Dirty Business," "Avalon Blues," "See See Rider," and "Stack O'Lee." The original recordings are included on the CDs that accompany the book.

127. Hurt, Mississippi John and Stefan Grossman. *Mississippi John Hurt*. Van Nuys, CA: Alfred Publishing, 2007.

A book and CD of 26 original recordings by Hurt. The book contains a short biography by Jas Obrecht that traces Hurt's life from the late 1920s to his musical renaissance after his rediscovery in 1963. The 26 transcriptions (chords, music and text) include "Shake That Thing," "Casey Jones," "Got The Blues," "Joe Turner Blues," "Make Me a Pallet on Your Floor," "Corinna Corinna," "Sliding Delta," "See See Rider," "Stack O' Lee," and several more. Part of The Early Masters of Blues series.

## John Jackson

128. Smarick, Nathan R. *John Jackson: Piedmont Blues and Folk Musician*. Masters thesis, University of Maryland, Baltimore County, 2008.

A biography of the Virginia musician John Jackson's life and career as a Piedmont blues and folk guitarist, banjoist and singer. Jackson supported the Civil Rights movement and emphasized African American history and culture by playing blues and supporting social causes related to African American Civil Rights, history and culture.

## Marion Walter "Little Walter" Jacobs

129. Glover, Tony, Scott Dirks and Ward Gaines. *Blues With a Feeling: The Little Walter Story*. New York: Routledge, 2002.

Chronicles the life and musical contributions of Marion Walter Jacobs ("Little Walter"). He learned from giants like Sonny Boy Williamson and, as a sideman with Muddy Waters, became known as the finest Chicago-style blues harmonica player of all time. The authors profile his musical life and describe Walters as a fiery, independent and fast-living artist who died tragically in a street fight at age thirty-seven.

## Elmore James

130. Franz, Steve. *Elmore James: The Ultimate Guide to the Master of the Slide Guitar*. St Louis: Bluesource Publications, 1994, 2003 (reprint).

This biography includes a detailed account of James' life from his Mississippi roots to his ascent to fame. The biography is supplemented with a detailed discography with full details of all known recordings by James; also includes information on sessions in which James performed as both a leader and sideman. Also included is a chronological listing of singles, albums, CDs, a guide to LP and CD issues, an index of musicians, images of nine vintage 45 rpm and 78 rpm labels, and an essay on the man and his music.

**Skip James**

131. Calt, Stephen. *I'd Rather Be the Devil: Skip James and the Blues.* Chicago: Chicago Review Press, 2008.

Discusses the lives of several musicians, but the primary focus is on Skip James, interviewed before his death in 1969. Covers his life, from his birth on a plantation in 1902, his abandonment by his father, and the impact and resulting popularity of his 1931 recording. He also discusses the popularity of songs like "22–20" and "Devil Got My Woman."

**Blind Lemon Jefferson**

132. Evans, David, ed. *Blind Lemon Jefferson.* Chicago: Black Music Research, 2001.

A special edition of the *Black Music Research* journal devoted to the life and music of Blind Lemon Jefferson. Essays authored by David Evans, Alan Govenar, Kip Lornell and Luigi Monge cover topics like myths and man, Blind Lemon and Leadbelly, the language of Jefferson, and musical innovations in his blues.

133. Groom, Bob. *Blind Lemon Jefferson.* Blues World Booklet No. 3. Knutsford, Cheshire, UK: Blues World, 1970.

Includes an introductory essay, "The Legacy of Blind Lemon," by Bob Groom and transcription of the lyrics of around 60 recordings. The recordings are cited in matrix number order with the take and Paramount release numbers and the approximate recording date.

134. Uzzel, Robert. *Blind Lemon Jefferson: His Life, His Death, and His Legacy.* Waco, TX: Eakin Press, 2002.

Covers Jefferson's life from his early years soliciting contributions with a tin can on the streets of small-town Texas to his move to Dallas in 1912. His performances in the Deep Ellum district, discovery by a Paramount Records talent scout, and arrival in Chicago in 1925 are discussed, along with an examination of the peak years of his recording, 1926–29, when he recorded more than a hundred titles. His travels and his influence on both African American and white musicians are also discussed.

**Lonnie Johnson**

135. Johnson, Lonnie and Stefan Grossman. *Lonnie Johnson.* Van Nuys, CA: Alfred Publishing, 2007.

Another book and CD in the Early Masters of Blues series. Contains a biographical sketch of the artist and 16 transcriptions of his music (chords, music and text) spanning Johnson's career from the early 1920s to the 1970s. The CD contains the original recordings by Johnson, including "Mr Johnson's Blues," "Love Story Blues," "To Do This," "You Got to Know," "Blues in G," "Sweet Woman You Can't Go Wrong," "I'm So Tired of Living All Alone," "Blue Ghost Blues," and several more.

## Pete Johnson

136. Mauerer, Hans J., compiler. *The Pete Johnson Story.* Bremen: Humburg, 1965.

An excellent tribute to the boogie-woogie and jazz pianist. Includes Johnson's own account of his career (reprinted from *Jazz Journal,* 1959), a biography by his wife (reprinted from *Jazz Report Magazine,* 1962), and a collection of comments and tributes from friends and reviewers. Includes analysis of individual compositions by James Wertheim, a selection of Johnson's letters written to Hans J. Mauerer between 1962 and 1965, a discography of 78-rpm and LP reissues, and a list of his compositions with publisher and recorded versions.

## Robert Johnson

137. Aisenpresser, Steven. "Come On In My Kitchen." Masters thesis, Edmonton, Alberta, Canada: Concordia University, 2004.

Transcends Johnson's music to present insights into the man and his passion for life. He straddles the boundary between past and present and alerts us to what we know and what we do not know. The overall focus is with Johnson's passion for life as a musician and lover.

138. Charters, Samuel. *Robert Johnson.* Photographs of Robert Johnson's Delta Country by the author. New York: Oak Publications; London: Music Sales, 1973.

Using information from interviews, Charters constructs a biographical profile and discusses Johnson's influence, style and themes. Contains transcriptions of the 29 blues recordings made by Johnson in Dallas and San Antonio between 1936 and 1937, grouped by recording session (there were five) and by matrix number. The melodic notation is supplemented with guitar chords. Charters also provides notes, comments and complete discographical information for each title.

139. Graves, Tom. *Crossroads: The Life of Blues Legend Robert Johnson.* Spokane, WA: Demers, 2008.

A well researched and lively narrative of the life and death of this Delta blues artist. Discusses the story behind the mythical talent that made Johnson a legend, but refutes that myth while still acknowledging the impact Johnson had on modern blues performers and fans.

140. Greenberg, Alan, Martin Scorsese and Stanley Crouch. *Love in Vain: A Vision of Robert Johnson.* New York: Da Capo Press, 1994.

Based on an unpublished and unproduced script by Greenberg, the book (originally written in the early 1980s) presents a factual account of Johnson's life from the cotton fields of Mississippi to his success as a blues performer in juke joints and other venues. His transformation from a raw blues performer into a successful singer and guitarist, and rumored pact with the devil are central plots in the story. Also discusses veteran Alabama guitarist Ike Zinnerman's influence on Johnson, his problems with alcohol and his romantic encounters. Blues poetry illustrates the harsh realities of life in the Mississippi Delta.

141. Groom, Bob. *Robert Johnson.* Fourth edn. Blues World Booklet No. 1. Knutsford, Cheshire, UK: Blues World, 1969.

Discusses Johnson's life in the social context of the Mississippi Delta, his musical influences, musical contributions, recordings, the details of his untimely death, and his debt to Charley Patton. Also discusses his pact with the devil, and provides specific insight into how Johnson's music was a reflection of African American life in the Mississippi Delta from the late 1880s until his death.

142. Guralnick, Peter. *Searching for Robert Johnson.* New York: Dutton, 1989.

This biography, first published in 1989 in anticipation of the first release of Johnson's complete recordings, conveys the power of Johnson's music, life, and myths about the place and time of his death. The author draws on the work of earlier scholars like Mike McCormick and clearly elucidates Johnson's origins, music and genius. He situates the artist within his sociocultural context in rural Mississippi between the two World Wars. In addition, he chronicles Johnson's debt to Charley Patton and Tommy Johnson.

143. Johnson, Robert. *Robert Johnson: King of the Delta Blues.* London: Immediate Music, 1966.

Transcriptions (text and melodies) of Johnson's twenty-nine recordings; transcribed from the first verse, and accompanied by guitar chords.

Of special note is the transcriber's use of 12/8 instead of 4/4 meter, important because it captures Johnson's unique style. Guitar introductions; alternative lyrics for three compositions; a concise biographical essay.

144. Komara, Edward. *The Road to Robert Johnson: The Genesis and Evolution of Blues in the Delta from the Late 1800s Through 1938.* Milwaukee: Hal Leonard, 2007.

Permeated with musical examples and biographical information on Johnson and his predecessors; follows the evolution of Johnson's music through the people and songs that influenced him, whether directly or indirectly. Portrays Johnson as a founder of blues and covers his life in the Delta from around the late 1800s until his controversial death in 1938. However, the book was written without interviewing Robert Lockwood, Jr, Johnson's stepson whom Johnson taught to play the guitar. Also includes historical photographs, maps, musical examples and more.

145. Mann, Woody. *Complete Robert Johnson.* New York: Music Sales Corporation, 1992.

Biographical information on the Delta blues legend. Also includes the tunings, tablature and voicings of 29 songs, including "22–20 Blues," "Come On In My Kitchen," "Crossroad Blues," "Dead Shrimp Blues," "Hell Hound on My Trail," Walkin' Blues," "Malted Milk," "Me and the Devil Blues," "Sweet Home Chicago," and several more.

146. McCulloch, Bill and Barry Lee Pearson. *Robert Johnson: Lost and Found.* Urbana: University of Illinois Press, 2003.

The authors deconstruct several publications on Johnson for the purpose of separating fact from fiction. Johnson's life, music, how he has been reinvented, and the views of artists, critics and fans are also discussed.

147. Schroeder, Patricia R. *Robert Johnson Mythmaking and Contemporary American Culture.* Chicago: University of Chicago Press, 2004.

Discusses Johnson's life and deconstructs the myths about Johnson making a pact with the devil, and the time and place of his death. Also covers his musical influences, contributions and legacy.

**Tommy Johnson**

148. Evans, David. *Tommy Johnson.* London: Studio Vista, 1971.

A biography drawn from interviews with Johnson's contemporaries in Louisiana and Mississippi. Traces his life, career, influences and significance as a blues artist. A summary of his repertoire is included along with examples of song texts, commentary and stylistic insights. Numerous photographs of his contemporaries; a discography of LP reissues; no index.

149. ——. "The Blues of Tommy Johnson: A Study of Tradition." Masters thesis, University of California, Los Angeles, 1967.

The author's premise is that blues compositions are highly individualistic and are reflective of the original artists or their imitators. To test this premise, he examines the life, music and musical tradition of Tommy Johnson from his early Mississippi roots to his recognition as one of the great Delta blues artists. All elements of Johnson's style are examined, including lyrics, melodies and instrumental accompaniment. Also discussed are the lives and styles of musicians who performed with Johnson as well as those who imitated his style.

### Pleasant "Cousin Joe" Joseph

150. Ottenheimer, Harriet Joseph. *Cousin Joe: Blues From New Orleans*. Chicago: University of Chicago Press, 1987.

A lively account of the life and musical career of New Orleans blues musician Cousin Joe. The book is based on 15 years of taped interviews with Pleasant "Cousin Joe" Joseph, in which he discusses his family, fellow musicians, friends and lovers. He also presents information on the changing relationships between blacks and whites during his long and productive musical career.

### B.B. King

151. Danchin, Sebastian. *"Blues Boy": The Life and Music of B.B. King*. Jackson: University Press of Mississippi, 1998.

Details his humble roots and early life in Mississippi, early years in Memphis, and emergence as a superstar. A scholarly account of King's evolution from the cotton fields of Indianola, Mississippi, to international stardom and performances in Los Angeles, London and Paris. Highlights some of King's most famous songs, discusses instances of poor professional management and parallels King's career with that of Elvis Presley. Mentions performers who influenced King (e.g. Charlie Christian, T-Bone Walker, "Peetie Wheatstraw," Wynonie Harris and Percy Mayfield), and King's subsequent impact upon artists like Eric Clapton, Jeff Beck, Little Joe Blue, Eddie C. Campbell and Robert Cray. Insightful analysis of song selections, touring strategies, management arrangements, and the role and impact of record companies on his eventual emergence as a superstar.

152. King, B.B. and David Ritz. *Blues All Around Me: The Autobiography of B.B. King.* New York: Avon Books, 1996.

An eloquent autobiography that traces King's life from the rural poverty of the Mississippi Delta to his assent to stardom as a blues guitarist/vocalist. Discusses the purchase of his first guitar at age twelve, his appearance on Sonny Boy Williamson's *King Biscuit Time* radio show, and his job as disc jockey at WDIA radio in Memphis. Also included is information on his encounters with Miles Davis and Stevie Ray Vaughan. Presents his views on the evolution of blues from country acoustic to urban electric, the birth and explosion of rock and roll, his success as a crossover artist, and his determination to remain true to the tradition while immersed in success.

153. Kostelanetz, Richard and B.B. King. *The B.B. King Reader: Six Decades of Commentary.* Milwaukee: Hal Leonard Publications, 2005.

A comprehensive collection of articles, interviews and reviews about King's life and musical career, from his Mississippi Delta roots to the late 1990s. Covers his career as a disc jockey at WDIA in Memphis, early tours and recordings, involvement in the blues revival and fame as a world renowned exponent of blues. An update of a 1997 edition.

154. McGee, David and B.B. King. *B.B. King: There's Always One More Time.* San Francisco: Backbeat Books, 2005.

The authors meld biography with discography to chart King's life from his childhood in the Mississippi Delta to his first recording session. McGee appraises King's career album by album, and also interviews his arrangers, engineers, musicians and producers.

155. Richardson, Jerry Scott. "The Blues Guitar Style of B.B. King." PhD dissertation, Memphis State University, 1987.

Focuses on the nature, sources and development of B.B. King's guitar style from his earliest recordings until 1987. Identifies a stylistic consistency in his blues improvisations that has influenced other blues guitarists. In addition to a personal interview with King, the author reviews the published research, presents an overview of the Mississippi Delta blues, and examines several tutors and guitar idols who influenced King. Transcriptions of twenty tunes are analyzed, along with several transcriptions of his predecessors, to discern either the uniqueness or similarity of motivic development in solos and vocal responses and any relationship to each other. Of particular note is the table that chronologically outlines the development of King's guitar style.

156. Shirley, David. *Everyday I Sing the Blues: Story of B.B. King.* New York: Franklin Watts, 1995.

Traces King's life and musical beginnings from the Mississippi Delta to his eventual success. Covers his tenure in Memphis as a disc jockey at WDIA radio, successful recordings, musical associations, musical influences upon him and his influence on others.

## Huddie "Leadbelly" Ledbetter

157. Jones, Max and Albert McCarthy, eds. *A Tribute to Huddie Ledbetter.* London: Jazz Music Books, 1946.

Although only twenty-six pages, this early tribute to Leadbelly contains a biographical portrait by Charles E. Smith from *Jazz Magazine*, an assessment of Leadbelly's performances by jazz scholar Frederic Ramsey, and a discography by Albert McCarthy and Frederic Ramsey. Several record reviews are also included.

158. Ledbetter, Huddie. *The Leadbelly Songbook: The Ballads, Blues, and Folk Songs of Huddie Ledbetter,* eds Moses Asch and Alan Lomax. New York: Oak Publications, 1962.

An expansion, with some overlapping, of Leadbelly's Folkways recordings. Included are 74 songs composed and adapted by Leadbelly, with melodies, text and chords; preceded by comments from Asch, Woody Guthrie, Frederic Ramsey, Pete Seeger and Charles E. Smith.

159. Lomax, Alan and John Lomax, eds. *Leadbelly: A Collection of World-Famous Songs.* Revised edn. Music ed. Holly Wood; special note on Leadbelly's 12-string guitar by Pete Seeger. New York: Folkways, 1965.

A collection of seventy songs (ten more than the original edition) transcribed from Leadbelly's (Huddie Ledbetter) Folkways recordings, with melodies, texts and guitar chords. Alan Lomax contributed a brief introduction.

160. Lornell, Kip and Charles Wolfe. *Introducing American Folk Music and the Life and Legend of Leadbelly.* New York: HarperCollins, 1992; New York: Da Capo Press, 1999.

Discusses folk musical traditions and artists, black and white approaches, and more. An in-depth examination of the life, music, contributions and legacy of Leadbelly, including details of his time in prison in Angola, his release from prison, his subsequent rise to fame, travels, Folkway recordings and more.

**Taj Mahal**

161. Mahal, Taj and Stephen Foehr. *Taj Mahal: Autobiography of a Bluesman*. London: Sanctuary Publishing, 2002.

    A frank portrayal of his life, musical contributions, associations, influences and musical philosophy. His penchant to mix Caribbean, blues, reggae and African musical elements in his musical compositions and performances is also discussed.

**Fred McDowell**

162. McDowell, Fred and Dan Bowden. *Fred McDowell: The Voice of Mississippi Delta Blues Guitar*. Pacifica, MO: Mel Bay, 2005.

    Traces his life from his roots in Rossville, Tennessee, to Como, Mississippi, and Memphis, Tennessee. This story of his rise to success includes a tutorial on his guitar technique with Raymond Payne; learning the bottleneck playing style is also briefly covered. In addition, his songs and influence on artists like Bonnie Raitt are covered.

**Brownie McGhee**

163. McGhee, Brownie. *Guitar Styles of Brownie McGhee*, ed. Happy Traum. New York: Oak Publications; London: Music Sales, 1971.

    The book contains an autobiographical profile of McGhee, and comments about each transcription. The transcriptions contain melodies, text, chords, breaks and accompaniment parts. This collection is out of print.

**J.D. Miller**

164. Leadbitter, Mike. *Crowley, Louisiana Blues: The Story of J.D. Miller and His Blues Artists, With a Guide to Their Music*. Bexhill-on-Sea, UK: Blues Unlimited, 1968.

    A 30-page monograph which focuses on musicians who recorded on Jay Miller's Excello label from the 1950s to 1966. In addition to discussing Miller's life and recording business, the author also discusses the recording careers and styles of Slim Harpo, Lazy Lester, Lightnin' Slim and Lonesome Sundown.

**Memphis Minnie**

165. Garon, Paul and Beth Garon. *Woman with Guitar: Memphis Minnie's Blues.* New York: DaCapo Press, 1992.

A carefully researched biography compiled from anecdotes from Memphis Minnie's friends, relatives and fellow performers. The book contextualizes the artist's life within her African American community, discusses her musical expertise, and examines some of her most famous songs (e.g. "Bumble Bee Blues," "I'm Talking About You," and "What's the Matter With the Mill"). Methodologies from psychoanalysis, critical theory, women studies and surrealism are employed to analyze her songs.

**Little Brother Montgomery**

166. Terkel, Studs. *Hard Times: An Oral History of the Great Depression.* New York: Pantheon Books; London: Allen Lane (The Penguin Press), 1970.

The primary focus of Terkel's book is to portray people's lives during the depression and to present their views and assessments. However, in the section entitled "The Fine and Lively Arts," Little Brother Montgomery is examined.

167. Zur Heide and Karl Gert. *Deep South Piano: The Story of Little Brother Montgomery.* London: Studio Vista, 1970.

Covers Montgomery's life from age eleven, when he left his Louisiana home, until 1940. Includes information on his time in New Orleans, Florida and Mississippi, until he finally settled in Chicago. Insider perspectives from blues pianists Pete Johnson, Otis Spann and Roosevelt Sykes provide important information on the development of blues piano to around 1940. Includes textual transcriptions of his songs, information on sessions in which he participated, and biographical data on other pre-1942 blues pianists. Many photographs and a name index.

**McKinley "Muddy Waters" Morganfield**

168. Gordon, Robert. *Can't Be Satisfied: The Life and Times of Muddy Waters.* Foreword by Keith Richards. New York: Little, Brown, 2002.

Covers the life of McKinley Morganfield ("Muddy Waters") from his birthplace in Issaquena, Mississippi, through his years working on a plantation to his success as a blues icon in Chicago. The book contains details of his associations with numerous artists, the Chess brothers, Alan Lomax, his Chicago years, travels, relationships with women, and overall contributions and significance to the history and evolution of blues.

169.  Rooney, James. *Bossmen: Bill Monroe and Muddy Waters.* London: Studio Vista; New York: Dial Press, 1971.

Discusses the lives of country legend Bill Monroe and blues icon Muddy Waters from their humble beginnings, associations, rise to fame, influences, music and the role of various persons in promoting their respective careers.

170.  Tooze, Sandra B. *Muddy Waters: The Mojo Man.* Foreword by Eric Clapton. Toronto: ECW Press, 1997.

In addition to chronicling Waters' life from his birth place in the Mississippi Delta to his immense success in Chicago, the book contains a wealth of information on the development of the post-war Chicago blues scene. Also includes thorough coverage of his musical career and associations with other musicians and with the Chess brothers, and excellent photographs and a detailed discography.

## Albert Murray

171.  Modeste, Jacquelynne Jones. "The Blues and Jazz in Albert Murray's Fiction: A Study in the Tradition of Stylization." PhD dissertation, College of William and Mary, 2004.

Uses blues as a critical theory, as a tool for crafting new possibilities for intellectual explorations. The author argues that studying blues as a cultural legacy is a significant means by which to identify the mechanisms that individuals and communities use to sustain themselves, and that blues are used to craft individual identities. Her primary focus is Albert Murray's *Scooter Series* wherein the blues is used as a heroic activity.

## Sam Myers

172.  Myers, Sam and Jeff Horton. *Sam Myers: The Blues is My Story.* Jackson: University Press of Mississippi, 2006.

Covers the musical roots and contributions of the Mississippi-born front man of Anson Funderburgh and the Rockets group. Discusses his life experiences, how he got started, his early career, and how he became associated with Anson Funderburgh.

**Charley Patton**

173. Calt, Stephen and Gayle Wardlow. *King of the Delta Blues: The Life and Music of Charlie Patton*. Newton, NJ: Rock Chapel Press, 1988.

Based on interviews with approximately fifty people over a period of seven years, the authors present a comprehensive and detailed account of Patton's life and music within his social context. They provide insights into the plantation system, barrelhouses and house frolics, and the "Race Records" which recorded African American musicians during Patton's time. The book also contains new information and insights which tend to demystify Patton's life and musical achievements. Also included are musical analyses of songs, maps of the region, a glossary of "Song Expressions," and more.

174. Evans, David. *Charlie Patton*. Blues World Booklet, No. 2. Knutsford, Cheshire, UK: Blues World, 1969.

In one of the earliest studies of this legendary artist, Evans discusses the man and his music within the sociocultural context of the Mississippi Delta. He provides insights into his beginnings, associations and venues where he performed, and a discussion of his musical style.

175. Fahey, John A. *Charlie Patton*. London: Studio Vista, 1970.

A musical and textual analysis of all but six of Patton's recorded songs. Following a short biography of Patton, Fahey analyzes Patton's compositions, classifies them by scales, and groups them according to guitar tunings and keys, notes played in each song according to scale, tune families and structured analysis. He also analyzes and provides the text and music of all but six of Patton's recorded compositions. He concludes that Patton's stanzas do not tend to be specific and organized thoughts; rather they seem to be sung at random without any reorganization.

176. ——. "A Textual and Musicological Analysis of the Repertoire of Charley Patton." Masters thesis, University of California, Los Angeles, 1969.

A detailed analysis of lyrics and music is presented with this concise biography of Delta blues guitarist Charley Patton. From the approximately thirty records issued by Patton between 1929 and 1934, forty different tune stanzas were transcribed and analyzed. The author concluded that Patton used a definitive mode, which included a tonic, major and minor third, perfect fourth and fifth, major sixth and minor seventh. He also concluded that while Patton's secular songs contain disjunctive traditional stanzas covering many different subjects, his religious songs deal with one subject only: religion.

## Yank Rachell

177. Congress, Richard. *Blues Mandolin Man: The Life and Music of Yank Rachell*. Jackson: University Press of Mississippi, 2001.

Contextualizes his life and musical career within an environment of art, entertainment, travels, family relationships, non music-related work, and local and national events. Rachell, a product of the West Tennessee blues scene, was one of only two major blues mandolinists and the only one to popularize that instrument in the blues revival scene of the early 1960s. This biography is important because many roots of modern blues can be traced to the groups with which Rachell played during the 1920s, 1930s and 1940s in West Tennessee. Foreword by David Evans. A selected discography, list of song lyrics and bibliography are also included.

## Ma Rainey

178. Lieb, Sandra R. *Mother of the Blues: A Study of Ma Rainey*. Boston: University of Massachusetts Press, 1983.

A thorough assessment of the vocalist's life and music, complete with anecdotes and factual information. Intimate details of her musical experiences, recordings, associations and travels are included. The book also contains a wealth of information on classic blues and Rainey's role in its dissemination.

179. ———. "The Message of Ma Rainey's Blues: A Biographical and Critical Study of America's First Woman Blues Singer." PhD dissertation, Stanford University, 1976.

A discussion of her musical life and contributions. The author postulates that Ma Rainey represents a merger between two important black traditions: country blues and minstrelsy. From 1923 to 1928, Rainey made ninety-two known recordings for the Paramount label and became immensely popular with black migrants to northern cities and southerners of both races as part of the national vogue of "race records." Rainey's songs are divided into several thematic categories; those with a love theme are the most numerous; other songs deal with humor, cynicism, slapstick, parody, vaudeville comedy, prison songs and more. The author concludes that even at their most skeptical level, the songs express a tough and realistic appraisal, an ability to see through pretense and a grudging acceptance of life.

180. Stewart-Baxter, Derrick. *Ma Rainey and the Classic Blues Singers*. London: Studio Vista, 1970.

Focuses on female blues singers of the 1920s whose styles were influenced by tent shows and vaudeville, and whose repertoires transcend the blues. Specifically, the careers of artists like Ida Cox, Rosa Henderson, Bessie Smith, Mamie Smith, Victoria Spivey and several others are examined, along with some lesser-known artists, the post-classic period, and individual styles and contributions. The book contains a discography of original releases and Microgroove reissue numbers for thirty-six artists.

## Jimmy Reed

181. Romano, Will. *Big Boss Man: The Life and Music of Bluesman Jimmy Reed*. San Francisco: Backbeat Books, 2006.

Details Reed's trials and tribulations on the road to becoming one of the most successful crossover artists of the 1950s with songs like "Big Boss Man" and "Blue Lights, Big City." Insights into his struggle with alcoholism and his musical career are provided by his family, fellow musicians and other associates.

## Nat Riddles and Sterling "Mister Satan" Magee

182. Gussow, Adam. *Mister Satan's Apprentice: A Blues Memoir*. New York: Vintage, 2000.

Written by a New Yorker who partnered with two New York street musicians, Nate Riddles and Mister Satan, in the mid-1980s. Riddles, a harmonica player, helped Gussow hone his technique, and guitarist Mister Satan (Sterling Magee) imparted life lessons. The duo of Satan and Adam recorded three albums, and toured Europe with Bo Diddley before eventually going their separate ways. The book chronicles the success of Adam and Satan at blues festivals and on albums, and discusses Riddles' battle with leukemia. The author also covers his work in the orchestra of a traveling production of *The Adventures of Huckleberry Finn*. Also included, a discussion of the life and music of Sterling Magee, whose career included stints with James Brown, Etta James and the Supremes.

## Bessie Smith

183. Albertson, Chris. *Bessie*. New York: Stein and Day; London: Barrie and Jenkins, 1972.

Albertson presents a thorough assessment of Smith's life and musical style, based on his belief that previous studies on Smith are either incomplete or inaccurate. In addition to a sketch of her formative years, the book covers her career from her first recording in 1923 to her death in a car accident near Clarksdale, Mississippi, in 1937. The book is based on numerous interviews, including the insights of Ruby Walker (Smith's aunt), many of which were previously published in various African American publications. Included are copious details of her touring, career as a recording artist, and private life. Limited coverage of her recordings.

184. Moore, Carman. *Somebody's Angel Child: The Story of Bessie Smith.* New York: Crowell, 1969.

Chronicles Smith's life and character from her birth in Chattanooga, Tennessee, in 1894 to her death in a car accident in 1937. The book is divided into four sections: early life, fame as a teenager, rise to stardom, and decline and death. The texts of some of her songs are included within the narrative. Contains a list of her compositions and an index.

185. Oliver, Paul. *Bessie Smith.* London: Cassell, 1959; New York: Barnes, 1961.

In this first monograph on her life, career and death, Oliver focuses on biographical information and an assessment of her recordings. The recordings, some of which are critiqued, are cited in chronological order. He also examines Smith's personality, influence, relationships, and the musical and social context of her life and music. Contains a concise bibliography and a selected discography of 78-rpm recordings in chronological order.

186. Scott, Michelle Renee. "The Realm of a Blues Empress: Blues Culture and Bessie Smith in Black Chattanooga, Tennessee, 1880–1923." PhD dissertation, Cornell University, 2002.

This study focuses on the environment and early life of the 1920s city and artist. The author is concerned with the various functions that Smith and blues culture served in African American working-class communities in the early twentieth-century south. The study is multifaceted and uses Smith's life as a central point from which to investigate numerous issues related to African American history, including migration, black women's culture, and black community development in the post-Reconstruction era. Chattanooga, Tennessee, is the research site wherein the author explores her hypothesis that the rise of blues culture and the success of a woman in the formerly male-dominated blues world is intrinsically connected to the rapid migrations and industrialization which occurred in the late nineteenth and early twentieth centuries. Additional sources used include slave narratives, Freedman Bureau's records, American Missionary Association archives, census records, city directories, black newspapers, police records and maps to trace the development of the Chattanooga black community from slavery to the onset of formal segregation.

187. West, James Steven. "Bessie Smith: A Study of Her Influence on Selected Works of Langston Hughes, Edward Albee, Sherley Anne Williams, and James Baldwin." PhD dissertation, University of Southern Mississippi, 1995.

Illuminates Smith's influence on the named writers. For Hughes, Smith's music bridged the gap between the "lowbrow" stereotypes of blues and its acceptance as a culturally valuable product of African American society. For Albee, she was an example of a wasted life and the perversion of possibility in a flawed society. For Williams, Smith served as a source for emulation and inspiration, while for Baldwin her music became the secular spiritual, a comfort in a lonely and confused world.

### Dick Heckstall-Smith

188. Heckstall-Smith, Dick and Peter Grant. *Blowing the Blues: A Personal History of the British Blues*. London: Clear Books, 2004.

This autobiography of British blues saxophonist Heckstall-Smith details his 1960s and 1970s stints with bands like Alexis Korner Blues Incorporated, The Graham Bond Organization, John Mayall's Bluesbreakers, and Coliseum. He discusses British R&B, racism and drug abuse, and provides anecdotes about Alexis Korner, Ginger Baker and Charlie Watts, among others.

### Otis Spann

189. DiFelice, Christy. "Searching for Otis Spann: The Life and Songs of Otis Spann." Masters thesis, Toronto: York University, 2008.

The primary goal of the thesis is to present Spann as an important figure in blues history. The work is divided into three sections that focus on his life, songs and voice. Also included are the lyrics of 182 of the 221 songs that Spann recorded between October 1954 and April 1970, with supporting discographical information.

### Hubert Sumlin

190. Romano, Will and Hubert Sumlin. *Incurable Blues: The Troubles and Triumph of Blues Legend Hubert Sumlin*. San Francisco: Backbeat Books, 2005.

Covers the life of Sumlin through his bouts with cancer, alcoholism, and personal and professional issues through his triumph as a Chicago blues artist. His contributions to the Chess recordings of Howlin' Wolf and his pick-less playing style, which influenced several blues and rock and roll artists like Jeff Beck, Eric Clapton, Keith Richards, John Mayer and Stevie Ray Vaughan, are also discussed.

## Henry Townsend

191. Townsend, Henry and Bill Greensmith. *Henry Townsend: A Blues Life*. Urbana: University of Illinois Press, 1999.

Townsend, born in Shelby, Mississippi, was a singer, songwriter, guitarist and pianist, whose discography comprises over 200 recordings. In addition to covering the life, music and associations of this little known but historically important musician, the book is permeated with details of the historic St Louis blues scene, distinctive St Louis sound and characteristic instrumentation. Presents insights into the performers and St Louis blues scene. Townsend dispels many of the myths associated with the music and musicians, especially Walter Davis, Lonnie Johnson and Roosevelt Sykes. Discography and bibliography.

## Stevie Ray Vaughan

192. Kitts, Jeff, Brad Polanski and Harold Steinblatt, eds. *Stevie Ray Vaughan*. Milwaukee: Hal Leonard Corporation, 1977.

A collection of essays and intimate interviews from the *Guitar World Magazine* that discuss the life and music of guitarist Vaughan. Included is information on his triumph over drug and alcohol abuse, and his return to his art. Andy Aledort's essay "Playing with Fire" provides an analysis of Vaughan's style from "Love Struck Baby" to "Scuttle Buttin."

193. Patoski, Joe Nick and Bill Crawford. *Stevie Ray Vaughan: Caught in the Crossfire*. London: Little, Brown, 1994.

The authors discuss Vaughan's beginnings in Texas, his introduction to blues, musical influences, style, encounters with abuse, and his triumphs and tragedies. His addiction to alcohol and drugs and his subsequent recovery to pursue a successful career as a guitarist and vocalist are also discussed.

## T-Bone Walker

194. Dance, Oakley Helen. *Stormy Monday: The T-Bone Walker Story*. Baton Rouge: Louisiana State University Press, 1987.

Dance organizes numerous interviews with Walker, members of his family and fellow musicians into a provocative narrative account of his life and music. She discusses his life on the road, family life, and immense influence on modern blues and bluesmen.

## Dinah Washington

195. Cohodas, Nadine. *Queen: The Life and Music of Dinah Washington*. New York: Pantheon, 2004.

An exhaustive biography of the vocalist once billed as the "Queen of the Blues." The author covers her musical career from her early success with Lionel Hampton to her death in 1963. Born Ruth Jones in Tuscaloosa, Alabama, in 1924, she left school at the age of thirteen; by eighteen her family had moved to Chicago. The book contains numerous interviews, and a discussion of her seven marriages, and other issues in her musical and personal life.

## Ethel Waters

196. Waters, Ethel. *To Me It's Wonderful*. Introduction by Eugenia Price and Joyce Blackburn. New York: Harper and Row, 1972.

Based on taped interviews, the book chronicles Waters' participation in Billy Graham's Crusades from 1957 until her death. The discography by George Finola of Waters' 259 recordings is accompanied by anecdotal comments on selected recordings.

197. Waters, Ethel and Charles Samuels. *His Eye is on the Sparrow: An Autobiography*. Garden City: Doubleday, 1951; London: Allen, 1951; London: Jazz Book Club, 1958; New York: Pyramid Books, 1967.

A candid discussion of both early life in Chester, Pennsylvania, and the role of singing in her life. Her career is covered, from talent contest winner to New York theater star, including her years touring, recording with Black Swan Records, and successes. After a dismal spell in the 1940s, her career experienced a revival in the 1950s. The account is permeated with insights into her life and career as a blues and jazz icon between 1921 and 1946.

## Josh White

198. Wald, Elijah. *Josh White: Society Blues*. Amherst, MA: University of Massachusetts Press, 2000.

Traces the life of White from his birth in South Carolina and duties as a "leadboy" for blind bluesmen to his success as a popular blues star in 1930s New York. He sang Civil Rights songs and was the first African American singer-guitarist to act in Hollywood films and to star on Broadway. The author also covers White's compromise with the blacklists, tenure in Europe, role in the folk revival of the 1960s, overall difficulty he experienced as an African American performer in a white society, and more.

## Mama Yancey

199. Bowers, Jane and William Westcott. "Mama Yancey and the Revival Blues Tradition." *Black Music Research Journal* 12(2) (Fall 1992): 171–213.

A study of the stylistic changes that occurred in post-war blues, as evidenced in Mama Yancey's repertoire of songs. The performances she recorded with her husband, blues and boogie woogie pianist Jimmy Yancey, in 1943 and 1951, serve as the basis for a discussion of changes in her vocal style. The authors also analyze recordings she made with Little Brother Montgomery, Art Hodes and Edwin Helfer to determine any possible influence of Jimmy's playing on the performances of artists who recorded with Mama Yancey.

## COLLECTIVE BIOGRAPHIES

200. Akamatsu, Rhetta. *Taint Nobody's Business If I Do: Women Blues Singers Old and New.* Scotts Valley, CA: Createspace, 2008.

The book asserts that strong women who took an unconventional path in their lives have changed music. The author explores the lives and legacies of 18 blues women, past and present, from Ma Rainey and Bessie Smith to Janis Joplin and Bonnie Raitt.

201. Awmiller, Craig. *This House on Fire: The Story of the Blues.* New York: Watts, 1996.

Presents a history of the blues from the 1930s to the mid 1990s. The author discusses African roots, blues influence on rock and jazz, and African American religious and work songs. Among the many blues and jazz artists profiled are Louis Armstrong, Eric Clapton, Robert Cray, Buddy Guy, B.B. King, Billie Holiday, Etta James, Blind Lemon Jefferson, Robert Johnson, W.C. Handy, Charley Patton and several others. He criticizes Billie Holiday's autobiography *Lady Sings the Blues* (1984) for embellishing the truth and creating myths. Overall, he combines synthesized information with some over-generalizations to produce a concise history of the blues.

202. Bohanon, Margaret Ann. "'Wild Women Don't Have the Blues': African-American Women Blues Singers and Working Class Resistance." PhD dissertation, Case Western Reserve University, 2001.

Focuses on the 1920s as a dominant period for women in blues. During that decade, African American women recorded and sold numerous recordings, traveled, and performed throughout the south and north. The author investigates how "classic blues" singers became symbols of female autonomy for African American working-class women and situates this phenomenon within the historical context of the south-to-north migrations. Contains a thorough discussion of classic blues singers' rejection of African American middle-class morality, and their choices to sing instead about sexuality, independence, resistance to societal and artistic roles, and subverted bourgeois ideals.

203. Booth, Stanley. *Rhythm Oil: A Journey Through the Music of the American South*. New York: Vintage Books, 1993.

The author reconstructs Robert Johnson's encounter with the devil, recounts the funeral of John Hurt, and his relationship with Furry Lewis. The importance of Memphis and the role of individuals/groups like the Bar-Kays, B.B. King, Otis Redding, Stax Records, Sam Phillips, Elvis Presley, ZZ Top and many more are discussed. The title is derived from a potion once sold on Beale Street in Memphis.

204. Bratcher, Melanie E. *Words and Songs of Bessie Smith, Billie Holiday, and Nina Simone: Sound Motion, Blues, Spirit, and African Memory*. New York: Routledge, 2007.

Explores the relationship between three African American female sensibilities within the context of a pan-African aesthetic. The author's purpose is threefold: 1) to show commonalties between Bessie Smith, Billie Holiday and Nina Simone's lives and original compositions; 2) to organize, examine and evaluate their selected song performances within the context of the "Nauru" pan-African theoretical model; and 3) to illuminate the vast sources of transformational values that an aesthetic analysis of African American song performance can foster.

205. Calt, Stephen, David Jansen, R. Crumb and Terry Zwigoff. *R. Crumb's Heroes of Blues, Jazz, and Country*. New York: Harry N. Abrams, 2006.

A combination of two works by R. Crumb, *Heroes of the Blues* and *Pioneers of Country Music*, which were originally released as trading card sets. The book is accompanied by a 21-track CD collection compiled by Crumb featuring original recordings by artists like Skip James, Dock Boggs, Jelly Roll Morton, Charley Patton and several additional artists.

206. Carruth, Hayden. *Sitting In: Selected Writings on Jazz, Blues, and Related Topics.* Iowa City: University of Iowa Press, 1993.

A collection of reprinted essays and poems which explore the forms and influences of blues and jazz. Specifically, the contributions, expressiveness, improvisations and spontaneity of artists like Joe Turner, Bessie Smith, Maxine Sullivan, Ben Webster and others are explored. Although much of the book focuses on literature alone, a strong interest in blues and jazz unifies the essays.

207. Charters, Samuel. *Walking a Blues Road: A Selection of Blues Writing 1956–2004.* New York: Marion Boyars, 2004.

Includes liner notes, essays and excerpts from Charters' books *The Legacy of the Blues* and *The Roots of the Blues.* In this compilation, he covers artists like Memphis Willie B., Blind Willie Johnson, Lightin' Hopkins, Robert Johnson, Memphis Slim, Bukka White, Big Joe Williams and Mighty Joe Young. He also analyzes styles, chords and repertoires in a comprehensive manner. A discography contains the content of twelve LPs recorded between 1962 and 1973.

208. ———. *The Blues Makers.* New York: Da Capo Press, 1991.

Contains the reprints of *The Bluesmen* and *Sweet as the Showers of Rain* (The Bluesmen, Vol. II). This edition adds a new chapter on Robert Johnson. Within each geographical area—Mississippi, Alabama, Texas to Memphis, the Atlantic Coast and the Carolinas— the author examines the lives and music of some of the most important artists: Skip James, James "Furry" Lewis, Sleepy John Estes, Robert Johnson, Blind Lemon Jefferson, Memphis Minnie, Willie McTell, Tommy Johnson, Ishman Bracey, Son House, The Memphis Jug Band, Charley Patton and many others. In addition to the excellent photographs, he uses music and textual analysis to illustrate his musical points.

209. ———. *The Country Blues.* 1959. Reprint, New York: Da Capo, 1975.

This is the first book-length study of early blues artists with a special focus on their backgrounds and musical styles. It provides insight into the social context which birthed the country blues, especially the post-Emancipation indignities suffered by the newly freed slaves. The author surveys the origins and early development of blues, the first published blues, and the critical role and function of record companies in the recording, dissemination and control of blues and its artists.

The careers of artists like Percy Bradford, Big Bill Broonzy, Rabbit Brown, Blind Lemon Jefferson, Leroy Carr, W.C. Handy, Lonnie Johnson, Furry Lewis, Robert Johnson, Blind Boy Fuller, Brownie McGhee, Lightin' Hopkins and Muddy Waters are discussed. He also examines Memphis Jug Bands and Medicine Show.

210.  ———. *The Legacy of the Blues: A Glimpse into the Art and the Lives of Twelve Guitar Great Bluesmen: An Informal Study.* London: Calder and Boyars, 1975.

The twelve portraits included here represent different styles of blues ranging from Mississippi Delta to urban styles. The author profiles Eddie Boyd, Juke Boy Bonner, Champion Jack Dupree, Snooks Eaglin, Lightin' Hopkins, Memphis Slim, Sunnyland Slim, J.D. Short, Bukka White, Big Joe Williams, Robert Pete Williams and Mighty Joe Young. He interviewed all but two, and focuses on their lives, styles and how their individuality reflects the "otherness" of African Americans in America.

211.  ———. *The Bluesmen: The Story and the Music of the Men Who Made the Blues.* New York: Oak Publications, 1967.

The first in a series of books devoted to the male blues singers of specific regions. This volume covers artists from Alabama, Mississippi and Texas. It begins with a discussion of the blues and Africa, followed by a discussion of the backgrounds, personalities and musical styles of artists from those states. Among the artists covered are Texas Alexander, Blind Lemon Jefferson, Son House, Robert Johnson, Charley Patton, Henry Thomas and Bukka White. The musical and text illustrations were transcribed from the original recordings. Also included is a list of the recordings cited and an index.

212.  Cohn, Lawrence. *Nothing But the Blues: The Music and the Musicians.* New York: Abbeville Press, 1993.

The essays trace the evolution of blues from its African roots, hollers, work songs and party music of the rural south to rock, urban blues and R&B. One chapter is devoted to female blues artists like Ma Rainey and Memphis Minnie. In addition, he covers white country blues artists, the impact of radio and recording technology on the popularity of blues, the link between gospel music and blues, and the blues revival of the 1960s.

213.  Davis, Angela Y. *Blues Legacies and Black Feminism: Gertrude "Ma" Rainey, Bessie Smith, and Billie Holiday.* New York: Vintage, 1999.

In this provocative book, the author examines how certain African American women became economically independent in a culture that had not previously allowed it. Through a detailed analysis of lyrics, which constitutes the second half of the book, Davis explores the meanings behind the performances of Rainey and Smith. She asserts that the songs do not portray a desolate and deserted woman, rather they portray independence, assertiveness and defiance. Davis also asserts that women's blues were personal, not political, and argues that their songs created awareness by naming the issues. Regarding Holiday, the author examines the social implications of her ability to transform inconsequential songs into complicated explorations of emotional issues.

214. Dicaire, David. *More Blues Singers: Biographies of 50 Artists From the Later 20th Century.* Jefferson, NC and London: McFarland and Co., Inc., 2001.

A follow-up to his earlier book on artists from the early twentieth century. Similarly, this book is divided into five sections, each with an introduction. The first section, "modern acoustic blues," covers artists who have been active on the contemporary blues scene, for example Taj Mahal, John Hammond, Jr, Keb' Mo', and Corey Harris. The second section, "contemporary Chicago blues," focuses on amplified blues artists like Lurrie Bell, Paul Butterfield, Melvin Taylor and Lil' Ed Williams. In section three, "modern American electric blues," artists like Jimi Hendrix, Kenny Neal, Robert Cray and Stevie Ray Vaughan are covered. Artists like Marcia Ball, Janis Joplin and Bonnie Raitt are discussed in "contemporary blues women." In the concluding chapter, "blues around the world," artists from several countries (including the UK, Ireland, Australia, France, the Netherlands, Sweden, Italy, Japan and Switzerland) are covered, including Javier Vargas (Spain) and Yuri Aaumov (Russia). Each entry includes biographical and critical information, and a complete discography. The appendix contains a discography of blues vocalists, a list of blues societies and foundations, and a bibliography.

215. ——. *Blues Singers: Biographies of 50 Legendary Artists of the Early 20th Century.* New York: McFarland and Co., 1999.

The reference includes biographies of fifty pioneers, innovators and stars of blues before 1940, like Blind Lemon Jefferson, Charley Patton, Son House, Robert Johnson, Ma Rainey and Bessie Smith. Each entry includes biographical and critical information, and musical information. The book is divided into five sections, beginning with the Mississippi Delta blues style and its transformation once it reached Chicago. Other sections cover the Texas blues, blues women, and the development of blues outside its main styles. He covers styles that range from the Virginia-Piedmont to Delta blues, from barrelhouse to boogie-woogie. The appendix includes a discography and bibliography.

216. Duffy, Tim. *Music Makers: Portraits and Songs from the Roots of America*. New York: Hill Street Press, 2002.

A collection of essays, photographs and lyrics by the author, co-founder of the Music Maker Relief Foundation, an organization founded in 1994 to assist artists working in blues, R&B, hillbilly and other roots music. The artists, all at least fifty-five years old, were either abused or ignored by mainstream record labels, and lived in poverty until the Foundation began to assist them. Among the seventy-five musicians whose lives and careers are featured, are Macavine Hayes, Mudcat, Coonie Stark, Drink Small and Beverly "Guitar" Watkins.

217. Federighi, Luciano. *Blues on My Mind*. Palermo, Italy: L'Eros Societa' Edittrie S.a.S. di Biagio C. Cortimiglia and Co., 2001.

In Italian. Well-researched and documented book, which offers connections between the blues of jazz artists like Eddie "Cleanhead" Vinson and Billie Holiday, and the blues of traditional artists like Lightin' Hopkins and others. The author also explores the blues ballad style, shouting styles, and offers a penetrating insight into blues culture. The discography includes entries on East Coast, California, Texas, Memphis, Chicago, Rhythm and Blues, and Zydeco. Translation by Federighi.

218. Fraher, James, ed. *The Blues is a Feeling: Voices and Visions of African-American Blues Musicians*. Chicago: Midwest Traditions, 1998.

A collection of one hundred duotone and black-and-white photographs of blues artists dating from the 1970s. The photographs are accompanied by quotations from selected interviews the author conducted with each artist he photographed. The quotations cover issues like the origins of blues, feelings about blues, what direction the music is headed, and the evolution of an artist. Among the numerous photographs and quotations are those of Buddy Guy, KoKo Taylor, Sunnyland Slim, Clarence "Gatemouth" Brown, Willie Kent, Junior Kimbrough, Bud Spires, Jimmy Lee Robinson, Mose Vinson, George Washington, Jr and many more.

219. Guralnick, Peter. *Lost Highway: Journey and Arrivals of American Musicians*. Boston: Godine, 1972.

A biographical history of blues, country and rock in essays covering artists like DeFord Bailey, Bobby Blue Bland, Howlin' Wolf, Otis Spann and Big Joe Turner. The essays focus on "the road" as a generic phenomenon that ties the experiences of the various artists together.

220. ——. *Feelin' Like Going Home: Portraits in Blues and Rock and Roll*. New York: Dutton, 1971.

The artists' profiles illustrate a progression from country blues to urban blues to rock and roll. The author begins with a reaction to rock and roll, and a concise history of blues which focuses on the contributions of artists like Blind Lemon Jefferson, Charley Patton, Son House, Robert Johnson and Tommy Johnson. This discussion is followed by several profiles, which are based on interviews, of blues artists like George "Mojo" Buford, Richard "Bigboy" Henry, George Higgs, Skip James, Johnny Shines, Muddy Waters, Robert Pete Williams and Howlin' Wolf, and rock and roll/country artists Jerry Lee Lewis and Charlie Rich. Each profile contains a biographical sketch, and an evaluation of the artist's style and influence. The role of Sam Phillips and Sun Records and the Chess family are also discussed. No index.

221. Harrison, Daphne Duval. *Black Pearls: Blues Queens of the 1920s*. New Brunswick, NJ: Rutgers University Press, 1988.

Considers the cultural and social impact of 1920s blues when the genre was dominated by African American females. The author focuses on Alberta Hunter, Victoria Spivey, Sippie Wallace and Edith Wilson as performers within their respective cultural contexts and includes the texts of some of their songs. She also addresses the social climate of the times, African American migration from the south to the north, performance opportunities and expectations of performers from the African American community. The book is permeated with new insights into the women and their musical legacy.

222. Hine, Darlene Clark, ed., Elsa Barkley and Rosalyn Terborg-Penn, assoc. eds. *Black Women in America: An Historical Encyclopedia*. Brooklyn: Carlson Publishing, 1993.

A comprehensive assessment of African American women in North America from the seventeenth century through the early 1990s. The entries focus on women who overcame adversity and worked to change their world. Among the musical artists profiled are Lavern Baker, Cleopatra Brown, Ruth Brown, Aretha Franklin, Ma Rainey, Bessie Smith, Dinah Washington and many more famous and lesser-known female musicians. The blues/jazz entries also include information on rhythm and blues.

223. Jackson, Buzzy. *A Bad Woman Feeling Good: Blues and the Women Who Sing Them*. New York: W.W. Norton and Co., 2005.

This book is an out-growth of a doctoral dissertation idea at the University of California, Berkeley. The author argues that female blues singers have inspired American women in general to express their creativity, to strive for success and to live unconventional lifestyles. She discusses artists like Ma Rainey, Bessie Smith, Billie Holiday, Etta James, Aretha Franklin, Janis Joplin and Tina Turner.

224. Leadbitter, Mike. *Delta Country Blues.* Bexhill-on-Sea, UK: Blues Unlimited, 1968.

Discusses some of the post-war Mississippi Delta artists by tracing their northern migration and examining their recording sessions. He discusses Upper Delta artists like Howlin' Wolf, Sonny Boy Williamson, Elmore James, Willie Love and Charlie Booker, and from the Lower Delta, he includes Dr Ross, Ike Turner and B.B. King. In addition, he covers the importance of Memphis radio station WDIA and the beginnings of the Sun Record label.

225. Lester, Julius. *Blues Singers: Ten Who Rocked the World.* Boston: Jump Sun, 2001.

Profiles of ten blues or blues-inspired artists, including Ray Charles, B.B. King, Billie Holiday, Bessie Smith, Muddy Waters, Aretha Franklin, Mahalia Jackson and Little Richard. Each concise profile discusses the performers' singing or playing style as well as the author's personal connection to the artist. Permeated with quotes and comments from the artists themselves. Contains a bibliography and a "Recommended Listening" list.

226. McClary, Susan. *Conventional Wisdom: The Content of Musical Form.* Ernest Bloch Lectures. Berkeley: University of California Press, 2001.

The essays were adapted from a series of Ernest Bloch Lectures given at the University of California, Berkeley. McClary focuses on the ideas and context of conventions agreed to by society and musicians, and uses instrumental and vocal examples from the seventeeth to the twentieth centuries to make her case. In addition to Scarlatti, Mozart and Beethoven, she uses blues examples of Robert Johnson, Bessie Smith and others, as well as references to rap, to discuss how cultural context has defined or challenged the concept of musical convention.

227. Oliver, Paul. *Conversations With the Blues.* London: Cassell; New York: Horizon Press, 1965; London: Jazz Book Club, 1967.

A compendium of seventy recorded conversations with Oliver that were made in 1960. The artists reflected on the nature of blues, and their lives and careers. The author also covers blues in Chicago and Detroit, the relationship of blues to the church and the character of the blues. There are eighty photographs, biographical notes and an index.

228. O'Neal, Jim and Amy Van Singel, eds. *The Voice of the Blues: Classic Interviews from* Living Blues Magazine. New York and London: Routledge, 2002.

A collection of interviews that were first published in *Living Blues Magazine*. Whereas some of the interviews were conducted while the editors lived in Chicago, others were conducted elsewhere by volunteer contributors. With the exception of the earlier Muddy Waters interview, all were conducted in the 1970s. Some interviews, like the Thomas Dorsey, Freddie King, Jimmie Nixon, Sleepy John Estes, Houston Stackhouse, T-Bone Walker, Little Walter, Esther Phillips and Freddie Kings, are expanded versions of the interviews first published in *Living Blues Magazine*. Informative and insightful.

229. Pearson, Barry Lee. *Sounds so Good to Me: The Bluesman's Story.* Philadelphia: University of Pennsylvania Press, 1984.

A scholarly collection of interviews with blues artists. Pearson concentrates on bluesmen's lives rather than an analysis of music or discussion of social issues. He covers Georgia Tom Dorsey, Honeyboy Edwards, W.C. Handy, Sunnyland Slim, James Thomas and many more. In addition to their lives, he discusses the musicians' ties to their instruments, abuse of alcohol, violence, rip-offs, parental recognition of their talent, opposition from some members of society, and more.

230. Robertson, Brian and R. Crumb. *Little Blues Book.* New York: Algonquin Books, 1996.

A guidebook to blues that features lyrics from songs, mini-biographies of blues men and women, and illustrations by R. Crumb. The author recounts stories of many blues legends, using the lyrics of artists like Son House, Blind Lemon Jefferson, Muddy Waters and others. The book is a primer for those who desire information on the first wave of blues musicians.

231. Rubin, Dave. *Inside the Blues, 1942–1982: Four Decades of the Greatest Blues Guitarists.* Milwaukee: Hal Leonard, 2007.

The author covers forty years of blues history, with special emphasis on the guitar stylings of Buddy Guy, Jimi Hendrix, Elmore James, Albert King, B. B. King, Otis Rush, Stevie Ray Vaughan, T-Bone Walker, Muddy Waters, Johnny Winters and others. Includes many musical examples, a discussion of regional styles, information on guitar tunings, and over twenty rare photographs.

232. Russell, Tony. *The Blues: From Robert Johnson to Robert Cray.* New York: Gale Group, 1997; New York: Schirmer Books, 1998.

Begins with blues influence and dissemination, and covers legends from the Mississippi Delta to geographical areas like Los Angeles and London. The book includes European artists, record labels and festivals as well as artists and record labels from the United States. The five sections focus on chronology, historical issues, an alphabetical listing of biographical entries, a bibliography and an annotated discography. Music festivals from Ascona, Switzerland, to Snowbird, Utah are also listed. Although the biographical portraits are concise, they cover numerous blues artists, black and white, famous and not-so-famous, including Charley Patton, Sun House, Robert Johnson, Big Bill Broonzy, B.B. King, Robert Cray, Eric Clapton, Stevie Ray Vaughan and many more. Includes a blues timeline of significant people and events in blues history from 1912 to 1992, a selected filmography, bibliography and discography.

233. Shadwick, Keith. *Blues: Keeping the Faith*. New York: Book Sales, 1998.

Contains concise portraits of a wide variety of artists, past and present. Included are profiles of artists like Big Bill Broonzy, Son House, Robert Johnson, Furry Lewis, Willie McTell, Charley Patton, Black Ace, Eric Clapton, Albert King, B.B. King and many others. The portraits also include many less famous artists, and it is a good introduction to the life and music of blues artists.

234. Silvester, Peter J. *A Left Hand Like God: A History of Boogie-Woogie Piano*. With a special contribution from Denis Harbinson. New York: Da Capo Press, 1989.

Provides insight into the southern turpentine and logging camps of north-east Texas, northern Louisiana and southern Arkansas (known as Arklatex), where boogie-woogie was born. The book contains biographical material on the giants of boogie-woogie piano, ranging from Albert Ammons, Pete Johnson and Meade Lux Lewis to Axel Zwingenberger. Coverage includes information on the music and the unique approaches employed by its practitioners.

235. Surge, Frank. *Singers of the Blues: Brief Biographies of 17 Singers and Musicians Who Helped Develop The Blues Style and Became Legendary Performers During Their Lifetime*. Minneapolis: Lerner Publications, 1969.

For younger readers. The concise biographies include background information, including birth, death and concise details of their musical careers.

236. Tanner, Lee and Lee Hildebrand. *Images of the Blues*. San Francisco: Metro Books, 1998.

A companion to Tanner's *Images of Jazz*, this narrative contains candid quotes from numerous blues musicians. The numerous and concise profiles contain information on the life and musical careers of the artists.

237. Taylor, Dennis. *Blues Saxophone: An In-depth Look at the Styles of the Masters.* Milwaukee: Hal Leonard, 2001.

This book and companion CD provide an overview of the styles and techniques popularized by some of the greatest blues saxophonists. Among the artists covered are A.C. Reed and Eddie Shaw of Chicago, and the organ/soul stylings of Willis "Gator" Jackson and jazz saxophonist Stanley Turrentine. The book includes historical analysis, blues exercises based on blues chord changes, and musical transcriptions. Also includes a short history of each stylist and an analysis of the solo being performed; the CD contains the author playing the solos.

238. Tipaldi, Art. *Children of the Blues: 40 Musicians Shaping a New Generation of Blues Tradition.* New York: Backbeat Books, 2002.

First-person recollections from a new generation of artists who adapted the life lessons and musical techniques of the fathers of the blues. The book covers forty-nine artists who have infused traditional blues forms with new voices and material: Marcia Ball, Rory Block, Robert Cray, Taj Mahal, Keb' Mo,' Charlie Musslewhite, Bob Margolin, Duke Robillard, Tommy Shannon, Junior Watson, Stevie Ray Vaughan and many more.

239. Trynka, Paul and Val Wilmer. *Portrait of the Blues: America's Blues Musicians in Their Own Words.* New York: Da Capo Press, 1997.

A guide to the evolution and development of blues as gleaned from over fifty blues and blues-influenced performers. Trynka fashioned excerpts from interviews into a narrative account of the development of the blues. Among the numerous performers interviewed are Buddy Guy, John Lee Hooker and B.B. King. The book also includes about 120 photographs, taken by Val Wilmer over thirty years, of the rural south and urban blues centers like Chicago, Memphis and New Orleans.

240. Wardlow, Gayle Dean. *Chasin' That Devil Music: Searching for The Blues.* Introduction by Edward Komara, ed. San Francisco: Backbeat Books, 1998.

Stories of blues musicians are pieced together from personal interviews, public records and door-to-door canvassing. The book begins with Wardlow's 1967 Solomon Hill article, and ends with his return visit twenty years later. He covers the seeds of his research, numerous biographical entries, a lengthy interview of Ishman Bracey and portions of interviews with numerous others. Of special interest is his essay on "Tips, Leads and Documents," which contains case studies from his research, including death certificates, oral interviews and telephone directories. He covers famous and not-so-famous bluesmen like Tommy Johnson, Willie Brown, Skip James, Charley Patton, Bukka White and many more. Interestingly, he does not include information on blues icons Son House, Memphis Minnie, Muddy Waters, or Howlin' Wolf. Includes a CD with nineteen recordings and a list of the 78-rpm recordings cited in the text.

241. Waterman, Dick, Peter Guralnick and Bonnie Raitt. *Between Midnight and Day: The Last Unpublished Blues Archive.* New York: Da Capo, 2003.

A collection of rare images, supplemented with the author's commentary, of 120 blues artists. The authors offer their perspectives on artists like Chuck Berry, Ray Charles, Bob Dylan, Buddy Guy, John Lee Hooker, Lightnin' Hopkins, "Mississippi" John Hurt, Skip James, Janis Joplin, B.B. King, Fred MacDowell, Bonnie Raitt, Otis Rush, Roosevelt Sykes, Big Mama Thornton, Sippie Wallace, Muddy Waters, Junior Wells, Bukka White, Howlin' Wolf and many more. The book also includes contributions by Peter Guralnick, Chris Murray and Bonnie Raitt.

242. Wyman, Bill and Richard Havers. *Bill Wyman's Blues Odyssey: A Journey to Music's Heart and Soul.* London: DK Adult, 2001.

Wyman, author and former bassist with the Rolling Stones, chronicles the African American musical experience from 1619 to the contemporary sounds of Eric Clapton and Bonnie Raitt. The book, permeated with quotes from musicians, covers the contributions of artists like Papa Charlie Jackson, John Lee Hooker, Ma Rainey, Bessie Smith, Fats Waller and many others. Among the tidbits included in the book is a list of battles won by the Confederacy.

## COLLECTIONS OF MUSIC

243. Ball, Tom, compiler. *The Nasty Blues: Bawdy Blues Songs with Biographies, Lyrics, & Guitar Chords.* Anaheim Hills, CA: Centerstream Publishing, 1990.

Transcriptions of thirty blues songs with not-so-subtle sexual innuendos from the classic era (like "Sam, the Hot Dog Man," "Banana in Your Fruit Basket," and of course the classic Bessie Smith tune

"Empty Bed Blues"). Each song is accompanied by information on the recording: artists (including well known artists like Smith, Alberta Hunter, Lonnie Johnson and Ethel Waters, and lesser known artists like Lil Johnson and Lillie Mae Kirkland), sidemen, date and location of recording, label of issue and reissue, and label number. The compiler also includes anecdotes about the performers and recordings, and some interesting insights and instructions about how to play these songs. Includes photos of the performers (both candid and posed) and significant locations, advertisements for recordings, jacket art, photos of disc labels and cartoons by R. Crumb. Good introduction by the compiler. Limited bibliography.

244. Berendt, Joachim Ernst. *Blues.* Munich: Nymphenburger Verlagshandlung, 1957.

In German. This anthology is designed to introduce Germans to blues and contains the text of forty-eight songs in English, with German translations, and twenty-seven melodies. The transcriptions are preceded by a 26-page essay, in German, on the nature and significance of blues, including musical and rhythmic concepts, themes, a discussion of racial discrimination, sociocultural elements, double meanings, the relationship between blues and jazz, and more. Translation and coverage by the author.

245. Ellington, Duke. *Piano Method for Blues.* New York: Robbins, 1943.

Designed to introduce the musical features of blues. The focus is on form, harmonic structure (with a chart that demonstrates variations in blues), melodic structure and rhythmic characteristics. The author explains stylistic features, bass styles and boogie woogie. The book includes numerous examples including seven piano adaptations of recordings by the Duke Ellington orchestra.

246. Garwood, Donald. *Masters of Instrumental Blues Guitar.* New York: Oak Publications, 1968.

The author explains the techniques used by several country blues guitarists, such as the finger-picking technique of Gary Davis, John Hurt, Mance Lipscomb and Frank Stokes. The discussion of the stylistic features of Hurt and Lipscomb are especially informative. Also included are the solos to numerous songs, musical notation and chords to two songs by Bo Carter.

247. Grossman, Stefan. *Stefan Grossman's Early Masters of American Blues Guitar.* Van Nuys, CA: Alfred Publishing, 2007.

This collection contains fourteen songs from seven pivotal early Mississippi Delta blues guitarists/vocalists: Willie Brown's "Future

Blues," "M&O Blues," and "Ragged and Dirty"; Son House's "Dry Spell Blues," and "My Black Mama"; Skip James' "Devil Got My Woman," "Hard Time Killin' Floor," and "Special Rider"; Hambone Willie Newbern's "Roll and Tumble Blues"; Charley Patton's "Screamin' and Hollerin' The Blues," "Stone Pony Blues," and "34 Blues"; Arthur Pettis' "Good Boy Blues"; and Robert Wilkins' "That's No Way to Get Along." The transcriptions include melodies, chords and text. Accompanied by a CD of the original recordings of the respective artists.

248.  ———. *Country Blues Guitar*. Van Nuys, CA: Alfred Publishing, 2007.

This collection comprises twenty-two transcriptions of recordings by eight early country blues guitarists: Scrapper Blackwell's "Bad Day Blues" and "Kokomo"; Blind Blake's "Georgia Bound"; Big Bill Broonzy's "Big Bill Blues," "Mississippi River Blues," "Mr Conductor Man," "Saturday Night Rub," "Stove Pipe Stomp," and "Worryin' You Off My Mind"; Rev. Gary Davis' "Cincinnati Flow Rag," "Italian Rag," "Sally Where'd You Get Your Liquor From," and "Two Step Candyman"; Blind Lemon Jefferson's "Easy Rider Blues," "Hot Dogs," and "One Kind Favor"; Lonnie Johnson's "Go Back to Your No Good Man," and "Life Saver Blues"; Charley Jordan's "Hunkle Tunkie Blues," and "Keep it Clean"; Josh White's "Jesus Gonna Make Up My Dying Bed" and "Little Brother Blues." Transcriptions of chords, melodies and text. Includes a CD of the original recordings. Part of the The Early Masters of the Blues series.

249.  ———. *Country Blues Songbook*. New York: Oak Publications, 1973.

An anthology of 142 transcriptions of chords, melodies and texts of country blues. Approximately seventy were transcribed from the 1960s and 1970s recordings made by Son House, Mississippi John Hurt, Skip James, Mance Lipscomb, Bukka White and Robert Wilkins. The remainder were transcribed from the original 1920s and 1930s recordings of artists like Blind Boy Fuller, Robert Johnson and Charley Patton. The collection includes an essay by Stephen Calt entitled "The Country Blues as Meaning," wherein he reassesses the blues based on its expedient, functional and eclectic qualities.

250.  ———. *Ragtime Blues Guitar*. New York: Oak Publications, 1970.

A collection of twenty-one transcriptions by the author—eighteen songs and three instrumentals—of artists from different geographical regions of the south who share a ragtime-influenced guitar style. Texts are provided for all songs, and the guitar accompaniments are provided in both tablature and conventional notation. Most of the transcriptions are from recordings by Blind Blake, Big Bill Broonzy,

Blind Boy Fuller and Blind Lemon Jefferson. Also includes transcriptions of Rev. Gary Davis, Blind Willie McTell, Willie Moore and Anglo-American blues guitarist Sam McGee.

251. ———. *Delta Country Blues*. New York: Oak Publications, 1969.

Contains twenty-six transcriptions of songs of Mississippi Delta bluesmen, including transcriptions of two songs by Skip James and one transcription each of Robert Johnson, Willie Brown, Son House, Tommy Johnson, Fred McDowell, Charley Patton and Bukka White. Each transcription is preceded by a discussion of its stylistic features; the transcriptions contain the text and musical accompaniment in tablature and conventional notation.

252. Handy, W.C. *Blues: An Anthology; Complete With Words and Music of 53 Great Songs*. Revised by Jerry Silverman. New York: Macmillan; London: Collier-Macmillan, 1972.

The 1972 edition replaces more than a dozen titles cited in the first edition (1926) with new songs and five additional reproductions from sheet music. The essays from the first edition are divided into three categories in this edition: "background" (folksongs arranged primarily by Handy), "blues" (popular, commercial blues by Handy and others), and "blues-songs" (blues-influenced popular songs by Handy and others). The discussion of Handy, other blues pioneers, and influence of blues remains intact from the first edition. Notes on each song, with titles, and a name index is also included in this edition. See also items 253, 254 and 255.

253. ———. *A Treasury of the Blues: Complete With Words and Music of 67 Great Songs From "Memphis Blues" to the Present*. Second edn. Historical and critical text by Abbe Niles. New York: Boni, 1949.

This second, expanded edition includes 48 transcriptions of Handy's songs, plus two excerpts by George Gershwin, and folk songs that either preceded or influenced blues. Also includes African American and Euro-American songs that were influenced by blues from the first edition. See also items 252, 254 and 255.

254. ———. *Blues: An Anthology*. Introduction by Abbe Niles; illustrations by Miguel Covarrubias. New York: Boni, 1926.

Published fourteen years after Handy composed "Memphis Blues," this original edition contains transcriptions of forty-eight songs by Handy, plus two excerpts by George Gershwin, all arranged for piano and voice. The collection includes folksongs that either preceded or influenced blues, and some African American and Euro-American compositions influenced by blues. The introduction contains a discussion of textual and musical features by Abbe Niles. Notes on each song appear in the index, with titles and a name index. See also items 252, 253 and 255.

255.  Handy, W.C. and Miguel Covarrubias. *Blues: An Anthology; Complete Words and Music of 53 Great Songs.* 1926. Reprint, New York: Da Capo Press, 1990.

Originally published in 1926, this most recent edition compiles songs by W.C. Handy and Gershwin, arranged for piano and voice. Introduction by William Ferris. The collection is significant because it was compiled by the person most responsible for making blues popular and known worldwide. The collection also contains historical notes, text, tunes and arrangements, notes for each song, a bibliography, and guitar chords illustrated by Miguel Covarrubias. See also items 252, 253 and 254.

256.  Jahn, Janheinz, ed. *Blues und Work Songs: Tiberttragen und Herausgegeban Von Janheinz Jahn, mit Melodi Enotiernungen und Einem Essay bon Alfons Dauer.* Frankfurt: Fisher, 1964.

In German. Essays on the characteristics of blues poetry by author Jahn and the musical characteristics of blues by Alfons Dauer. The essays are followed by over sixty blues texts in English and German and the melodies of forty tunes. No information is provided on the printed sources of either the blues texts or melodies. Translation and coverage by Jahn and Dauer.

257.  Keepnews, Orin and John Hammond. *The Blues Book.* 1963. Reprint, New York: Alfred Publishing, 2001.

A collection of 100 blues songs; includes biographical and discographical information on each song. Preface by John Hammond; introduction by Orin Keepnews. The titles include "Barefoot Blues," "Cherry Red," "The Dirty Dozen," "Gulf Coast Blues," "Jailhouse Blues," "See See Rider," and many more. This book is permanently out of print.

258.  Kriss, Eric. *Barrelhouse and Boogie Piano.* New York: Oak Publications, 1974.

The second set of a series of transcriptions by the author, this collection contains twenty-two transcriptions of different artists. The transcriptions are categorized, but contain errors in both the musical and textual elements. Among the transcriptions are "Honky Tonk Train," "Sugarland Blues," "Jelly Roll Blues," "Cow Cow Blues," and "Atlanta Boogie."

259.  ——. *Six Blues-Roots Pianists.* New York: Oak Publications, 1973.

A collection of seventeen transcriptions of six blues pianists: Champion Jack Dupree, Little Brother Montgomery, Speckled Red, Otis Spann, Roosevelt Sykes and Jimmy Young. In addition to the introductory essay on the beginning of blues piano, the collection contains a biographical sketch of each pianist and a discussion of the character and structure of each transcription. The collection also includes an annotated bibliography, a discography, a list of solo performances by the six artists, and a list of other available recordings for each artist, arranged by label.

260. Lomax, John A. and Alan Lomax, eds. *Negro Folk Songs as Sung by Leadbelly, "King of the Twelve-String Guitar Players of the World," Long-Time Convict in the Penitentiaries of Texas and Louisiana.* Transcribed, selected and edited by John A. Lomax and Alan Lomax. New York: Macmillan, 1936.

A collection of the life and songs of Leadbelly, with linking narrative by the editors and an account of his experiences with the editors since his release from prison in 1934. Transcriptions of forty-eight songs were done, primarily from discs made for the Library of Congress by George Herzog who attempts to reproduce the nuances of Leadbelly's singing. The transcriptions are divided into reels, work songs, hollers, blues, talkin' blues, ballads and miscellaneous. Each song is preceded by an editorial introduction. The song texts are supplemented with Leadbelly's chanted interpolations and explanations.

261. Mann, Woody. *Six Black Blues Guitarists.* New York: Oak Publications, 1973.

A compilation of twenty-eight transcriptions of the blues of Blind Blake, Big Bill Broonzy, Rev. Gary Davis, Blind Willie McTell, Memphis Minnie and Rev. Robert Wilkins. Includes texts, musical notation and tablature for instruction. A concise introduction to the history of the blues, and the lives and musical styles of the artists.

262. Richards, Tim. *Improvising Blues Piano.* New York: Schott, 2001.

Focuses on teaching how to improvise the twelve-bar blues, complete with chords, riffs, turn-arounds and tags. The styles include barrelhouse blues, bags groove, sad blues, smooth blues and others. Illustrated with diagrams, side bars and dialogue boxes.

263. Sackheim, Eric. *The Blues Line: A Collection of Blues Lyrics.* Illustrations by Jonathan Shahn. New York: Grossman, 1964.

A comprehensive collection of the texts of 270 blues from the mid-1920s to the mid-1950s. Organized geographically by states and cities, and further divided into sections like "female blues artists," "piano blues artists," and "the 1940s and 1950s." Textual passages are italicized whenever their accuracy is in doubt. Also includes quotes from blues artists combined with similar themes from other world literature. Illustrations by Jonathan Shahn of seventy-seven artists, a contents list, but no index.

264. Shirley, Kay, ed. *The Book of the Blues*. Annotated by Frank Griggs; record research by Joy Graeme; music research by Bob Hartsell. New York: Leeds Music, 1963.

This collection of 100 blues includes melodies, guitar chords and texts representing country, classic and urban blues styles from the 1930s and 1940s. Also includes compositions by Clarence Williams, several piano blues and some jazz instrumentals. Each song contains notes on recorded versions (but without dates) and tablature for guitar and tenor banjo. Includes an index of song titles.

265. Silverman, Jerry, ed. and arr. *Folk Blues: 110 American Folk Blues*. For voice, piano and guitar. New York: Macmillan, 1958; New York: Oak Publications, 1968.

An anthology of music and text. Although the songs are primarily of African American origin, white blues and country artists like Woody Guthrie and Jimmie Rodgers are also represented. Each song has accompaniment for both guitar and piano, a brief discussion on its theme, and acknowledgment of the composer, if known. In the intro-duction, Silverman describes the musical heredity of Blind Lemon Jefferson, Leadbelly, Jimmie Rodgers, Woody Guthrie and Josh White, as well as technical aspects of the blues. Includes a bibliography, discography and index of song titles.

266. Titon, Jeff Todd. *Downhome Blues Lyrics: An Anthology From the Post-World War II Era*. Boston: Twayne Publishers, 1981.

A collection of folk blues lyrics composed and sung by African Americans and sold on commercial records during the years follow-ing World War II. The author listened to 3,000 blues records by black singers that were originally geared to the black community; he transcribed those he thought were the best, based on his assessment of the merit of the lyrics.

## DISCOGRAPHIES AND LISTENING GUIDES

267. N.A. *African American Song*. Alexander Street Press, 2006, www. alexanderstreet.com.

The first online service to document blues, gospel, jazz and other genres and to offer them as part of an online listening service. The collection, which includes recordings from the late nineteenth century up to contemporary times, is not available anywhere else online. Listeners must subscribe to the free online newsletter, but then they can access recordings by the top names in each style, including Alberta Hunter, Skip James, Leadbelly, Ma Rainey, Memphis Jug Band, Blind Willie McTell, Memphis Minnie, Bessie Smith, Charley Patton, Irma Thomas, Son House, Muddy Waters and many more. Of the 50,000 recordings by more than 2,300 performers, around 5,000 are considered rare or have never before been published. In addition to licensed recordings from Document Records, the Library of Congress, Rounder Records and others, previously unpublished field recordings from the Alan Lomax collection, the Jelly Roll Morton series and the Leadbelly series are included.

268. Bogdanov, Vladimir, Stephen Thomas Erlewine and Chris Woodstra, eds. *All Music Guide to the Blues: The Definitive Guide to the Blues.* New York: Backbeat Books, 2003.

A concise and comprehensive guide to the best blues, past and present. The editors reviewed and rated 8,000 recordings of all major styles from Delta blues to Louisiana, Memphis, Chicago, Texas and beyond; from classic female singers to jump blues, slide guitar, blues in jazz, soul blues, blues-rock, modern acoustic and electric blues, and more. The profiles of 1,200 artists and thirty essays are supplemented with "music maps" that chart the evolution of blues, its various styles, instruments used, key artists and more. See also item 273.

269. Cowley, John and Paul Oliver, eds. *The New Blackwell Guide to Recorded Blues.* Oxford: Blackwell Publishers, 1996.

This guide has been rewritten to account for the nearly 6,000 blues CDs by African American musicians that were issued or reissued just prior to 1996. Essays by American and British scholars are organized into thirteen chapters, arranged primarily in chronological order. Each author includes his choice of ten "essential" recordings that, in turn, are coupled with thirty additional appraised recordings, for a recommended list of around 550 CDs. The guide also contains introductory essays by the editors, a bibliography, suggestions for additional reading arranged by subject, a list of recordings arranged by label, and an index of recordings by performer.

270. Dixon, Robert M.W. and John Godrich. *Recording the Blues.* London: Studio Vista, 1970.

A thorough account of the race record industry from 1920 to 1942. This book is a companion to the authors' discography *Blues and Gospel Records 1902–1942.* They discuss the urban studio sessions of classic blues vocalists (1923–26), the peak period for recordings (1926–30), the decline of recordings (1931–34), the success of urban blues recordings (1934–40), and the last years for race recordings (1941–45). The authors discuss the trends and consumer markets inherent in the record data they collected; methods of discovering, recording and marketing the blues; and the impact of the Great Depression on the recording of blues artists. A graph links the number of issues per year (1919–42) with significant social and historical events that occurred during that time period. This book was combined with *Savannah Syncopators* by Paul Oliver and *Blacks, Whites, and Blues* by Tony Russell and published as *Yonder Come the Blues: The Evolution of a Genre* (1970). See also items 271, 277, 336, 341 and 343.

271.  Dixon, Robert M.W. and John Godrich, eds. *Blues and Gospel Records 1902–1942*. Fenton, Middex: Steve Lane, 1964. Revised edn, London: Storyville Publications, 1969.

This original edition attempts to list all African American folk music recorded up to the end of 1942, excluding genres derived from other styles. The introduction includes lists of field recording trips made by companies that recorded "race records" as well as selected information on the companies. The discography contains an alphabetical listing of artists and groups, details on personnel, instrumentation, dates, venues, and matrix take and issue numbers. In addition, Microgroove reissues are cited and the book contains a Microgroove index. Additions and corrections have appeared regularly in the journal *Storyville* since 1969. See also item 270.

272.  Dixon, Robert M.W., John Godrich and Howard Rye. *Blues and Gospel Records*. Fourth edn. New York: Oxford University Press, 1997.

Since their first edition in 1964, the authors have compiled recordings made for the commercial market (whether released or not) and for the Library of Congress Archive of Folk Songs. This edition includes approximately 20,000 recordings representing about 3,000 artists. In addition to standard discographical information, information on race records and a list of field trips to the south by persons interested in the preservation of the music is included. Howard Rye helped to enlarge and revise this fourth edition, including adding numerous new artists and new information, and listing records by educational or institutional groups like the Fisk, Pace, and Tuskegee Institute Singers. Rye, continuing the work of Dixon and Godrich, expands the work to cover the 1890–1943 period. See also item 271.

273.  Erlewine, Michael, Vladimir Bogdanov, Chris Woodstra and Cub Koda, eds. *All Music Guide to the Blues: The Experts' Guide to the*

*Best Blues Recordings.* All Music Guide Series. San Francisco: Miller Freeman Books, 1999.

This book, devoted to blues, is another premiere reference in Backbeat's *All Music Guides.* The guide contains reviews of 8,900 recordings and profiles of 1,200 artists. It differs from guides like Robert Santelli's in that it contains very concise biographies and only lists what the editors consider essential recordings. This edition continues the album ratings, first-buy recommendations, musical roots descriptions and maps that are found in previous editions. See also item 268.

274.　Guralnick, Peter. *The Listener's Guide to the Blues.* New York: Quarto Marketing Ltd, 1982.

A beginner's guide to listening to the blues. The author discusses the transformation of the blues and pays homage to artists who defy stated connections and styles. The fifteen chapters range in topic from "discovering the blues" to geographical styles and "post-modernism: Chicago." Also included are numerous references to recordings.

275.　Hadley, Frank-John. *The Grove Press Guide to the Blues on CD.* New York: Grove Press, 1993.

Arranged alphabetically by performer, the guide includes 700 entries for recent or reissued compact discs. Each entry includes the title of the album, recording company, a star rating by the author and three contributors, a description and critical annotation, and the year of the issue or reissue. In addition, the guide contains a thirty-page section of compact disc-anthology entries arranged alphabetically by CD title.

276.　Kenney, William Howland. *Recorded Music in American Life: The Phonograph and Popular Memory, 1890–1945.* New York: Oxford University Press, 1999.

The author discusses three interrelated processes in recorded music history: 1) The effect of the financing and cultural production on products that become available to the public; 2) patterns of audience reception; and 3) the manner in which produced music generates meaning. He discusses the adoption of jazz and popular musical styles by record companies, and the various societal forces that advocated for and against "race music," swing bands and other musical genres.

277.　Leadbitter, Mike and Neil Slaven, eds. *Blues Records: January 1943 to December 1966.* London: Hanover Books, 1968; New York: Oak Publications, 1969.

A continuation of the Godrich and Dixon compilation, but limited to blues recordings made after 1942 and any subsequent reissues of those recordings. The series covers blues from a wide variety of artists. The artists are listed alphabetically and each entry contains some biographical information. Recordings are listed chronologically, supplemented with data on personnel, instrumentation, matrix numbers, location and dates of recordings, and release numbers. Alternative names and joint performances are cross-referenced. See also items 270, 271, 336, 341 and 343.

278. Mahony, Daniel. *The Columbia 13/1400-D Series: A Numerical Listing*. Second edn. Stanhope, NJ: Walter C. Allen, 1966.

A listing of 689 recordings that were recorded on "race" labels between September 1923 and April 1933. Includes blues and vaudeville songs, male and female performers, instrumental groups, and popular and religious music. The entries are arranged by catalog number and include release dates, artists' credits by instrument and accompaniment, matrix and take numbers, recording session location and date, song title, composer credit, publisher and copyright dates, and more. The book also contains indices of song titles and artists.

279. Minton, John. *78 Blues: Folksongs and Phonographs in the American South*. Jackson: University Press of Mississippi, 2008.

A study of the first "hillbilly" and "race" records and their impact on diverse artists and audiences. The recordings were released between the 1920s and World War II, and Minton argues exploded into urban blues, R&B, honky-tonk, and western swing, gospel, soul, and rock and roll. The recordings preserve the work of artists like Blind Lemon Jefferson, Robert Johnson, Charlie Poole and Jimmie Rodgers, and simultaneously map the evolution of modern American popular music and the growth of the recording industry.

280. Moore, Allan, ed. *The Cambridge Companion to Blues and Gospel Music*. Cambridge, UK: Cambridge University Press, 2002.

This reference is focused on two distinct but related genres of African American music: blues and gospel. Unlike the two other Cambridge companions that are devoted to pop/rock and jazz, there is no section devoted to personalities herein. A chronology and two-page editorial preface precede the essays by contributing scholars (among the strong points about the book) including Graeme M. Boone, Barb Jungr, Allan Moore, Guido Van Rijn, Steve Tracy and Jeff Todd Titon. The work concludes with a comprehensive and thorough essay by Dave Headlam on "appropriations of blues and gospel in popular music," which includes the only two examples of musical notation found in the book. Although there are some errors and inconsistencies in the referencing system and bibliography, this is a valuable resource for studying blues and gospel music.

281. Rucker, Leland, Al Cooper and Tim Schuller, eds. *Music Hound Blues: The Essential Album Guide.* Detroit: Visible Ink Press, 1998.

Examines more than 600 performers and their original or reissued recordings. Includes contributions by forty-two contributing editors, including Jeff Hannusch, Craig Morrison, Robert Sacra and Joel Salvin. The biographical entries include birth and death dates, a concise profile of each artist, critical advice about recordings, and information on the artists' influences and who they influenced in turn. The editors reviewed more than 700 blues groups and individuals representing historical blues styles from Mississippi Delta country blues to the electric blues of Chicago, big-band jump blues of the 1940s to the blues-rock of the 1990s. The author also includes lists of books, magazines, newspapers, radio stations, record labels, websites, compilation albums, exceptional blues albums and more. The four indices include information on band members, producers, roots and categories of blues. A CD featuring artists like Lonnie Brooks, Otis Clay and Taj Mahal accompanies the guide.

282. Russell, Tony and Chris Smith. *The Penguin Guide to Blues Recordings.* With Neil Slaven, Ricky Russell and Joe Faulkner. New York: Penguin, 2006.

An A–Z guide that surveys the recorded work of more than 1,000 blues artists, from Charley Patton and Robert Johnson to B.B. King, Buddy Guy and Stevie Ray Vaughan. They reviewed almost 6,000 recordings.

283. Vreede, Max E. *Paramount 1200/1300 Series.* London: Storyville Publications, 1971.

A discography of blues and jazz recordings on the Paramount label from the 1920s and 1930s. Each entry contains information on the ztitle, composer, principal and secondary artists, whether it is an instrumental or vocal performance, label, wax and take numbers. The book also includes information on the various labels, month of release, wax colors, and date of first advertisement. The nine labels are illustrated in color and are accompanied by their original advertisements from the *Chicago Defender* newspaper.

284. Williamson, Nigel. *The Rough Guide to Blues I.* New York: Rough Guide, 2007.

Profiles the best blues singers, bottleneck guitarists, divas, harmonica players and more. Includes detailed information about artists, critical reviews of their best albums, and essays on the history and evolution of blues from the Delta to cities like Chicago to its current international status. Also includes information on boogie-woogie and gospel music.

## FICTION

285. Jimoh, A. Yemisi. *Spiritual, Blues, and Jazz People in African American Fiction: Living a Paradox.* Knoxville: University of Tennessee Press, 2002.

The author investigates how blues and jazz have influenced literature from Jean-Paul Sartre's *Nausea* to Philip Roth's *The Human Stain.* This thorough historical examination begins with blackface minstrels of the 1840s, and proceeds to the urban migration of African Americans in the early twentieth century and the Civil Rights movement of the 1960s. Highlights the music of each era and the black literature that emerged from it. Also demonstrates how spirituals reflect the pain and suffering of the nineteenth century slave experience, how W.C. Handy's "Memphis Blues" and Mamie Smith's "Crazy Blues" reflected urban life of the time, and how 1960s jazz parallels the individualistic, free and self-contained experience within the context of broader themes. Examines the literature of writers like James Baldwin, Ralph Ellison, Paul Lawrence Dunbar, Zora Neal Hurston, Nell Larsen and John Edgar Wideman. One slight drawback to the book is the lack of a theoretical foundation.

286. Murray, Albert. *The Hero and the Blues.* The Paul Anthony Buck I.E. Brick Lectures, Ninth Series. Columbia: University of Missouri Press, 1973.

A witty and insightful collection of essays that examine aesthetics, blues, tragedy and improvisation. The author looks at the relationship between fiction and blues, and weaves a narrative between life and art that leaps from Hemingway and Duke Ellington.

## GENDER

287. Bynoe, L.T. "African-American Blues Women's Contribution to Womanist Theory: An Ethnographic Educational Study." EdD dissertation, University of San Francisco, 1996.

An African-centered epistemology and womanist theory study that surveys the identity of seven African-American blues women: Ruth Brown, Shirli Dixon-Nelson, Pam Hawkins, Sista Monica, Laura Petaway, E.C. Scott and KoKo Taylor. Specifically, the author's

objectives are to ascertain what contributions they made to womanist theory; what young women can learn about love, identity, community reciprocity and survival from these women; and the depth of
the transformative power of their messages to change the condition
of people. Also presents an interesting look at the healing elements
identified through generational reciprocity, historical knowledge,
family spirituality, community transformation and self identity.

288. Harrison, Daphne Duval. "Blues." In *African American Music: An
Introduction*, eds Mellonee V. Burnim and Portia Maultsby, pp. 508–28.
New York: Routledge, 2007.

Discusses several topics that are germane to the historical role of
women in blues, including the first blues recording, aesthetics of blues
performance, impact on radio, film and recording studios, and the
contributions of contemporary blues artists like Denise LaSalle, Big
Maybell, Big Mama Thornton, KoKo Taylor and Dinah Washington.

289. Johnson, Theodore Wallace. "Black Images in American Popular
Music, 1840–1910." PhD dissertation, Northwestern University, 1975.

A thorough study of the images and portrayals of African Americans
in popular sheet music between 1840 and 1910. Discusses the black
male character as portrayed in minstrels, an image that portrayed
African Americans as happily enslaved on the plantation of a kind
"massa," a childlike person who worked all day and danced all
night. The images also portray the consequences of losing that "kind
massa"; the result is to be mourned as a freedman. The author concludes that, from the beginning, popular songs functioned as a medium
wherein white Americans revealed their preoccupation with race
through images they wished to project upon African Americans.

290. Wright, Delane Elizabeth. "Poppin' Their Thang: African American
Blueswomen and Multiple Jeopardy." Masters thesis, University of
North Texas, 1997.

The author uses Frances Beal's concept of "double jeopardy" (1969)
to investigate what, if any, relationship existed between female African
American blues artists and the music they came to perform. Also she
researched whether "multiple jeopardy" emerged when African
American blues singers discuss their lives and careers as performers
in an unidentified Texas city.

## HISTORIES AND SURVEYS

291. Adelt, Ulrich. "Black, White and Blue: Racial Politics of Blues
Music in the 1960s." PhD dissertation, University of Iowa, 2007.

The dissertation explores the racial taxonomies of blues, specifically the changes that transpired in the 1960s when blues was reconfigured from a black to a white performance context in its production and consumption while retaining a notion of authenticity connected to constructions of "blackness." The author argues that within the context of the Civil Rights and counterculture movements, blues audiences became increasingly white and European. Furthermore, he argues that in their romantic embrace of poverty of choice, white audiences and performers engage in discourses of authenticity; in the commodification, racialization and gendering of sounds and images; and in the confluence of blues music's class origins.

292. Armentrout, David and Patricia Armentrout. *Jazz and Blues*. New York: Rourke Book Co., 1999.

    For younger readers. A concise overview of blues and jazz history geared to adolescents. Hence, the coverage of blues and jazz styles, including boogie woogie, is very limited. In addition, there is virtually no coverage of blues or jazz styles after the 1930s and 1940s big band era in jazz. Includes a one-page glossary, table of contents and recommendations for further reading.

293. Asirvatham, Sandy and Jennifer Peltak. *The History of Blues: African-American Contributions*. New York: Chelsea House, 2003.

    A comprehensive assessment of the history and evolution of blues. In addition to tracing the blues from its rural origins and success in urban areas, the authors discuss musicians like Blind Lemon Jefferson, Robert Johnson, Charley Patton, B.B. King and many others who were involved in creating blues history.

294. Awmiller, Craig. *This House on Fire: The Story of the Blues*. New York: Franklin Watts, 1996.

    An introduction to the blues from its origins to the urban centers and the success of artists like Robert Johnson, Blind Lemon Jefferson, B.B. King, Ma Rainey, Bessie Smith and Muddy Waters. Traces the blues from the Mississippi Delta to Chicago, and provides insights into the blues influence on popular music of the 1960s.

295. Bane, Michael. *White Boy Singin' the Blues*. New York: Penguin Books, 1982.

    The author is a music critic, former editor of *Country Music*, and author of *Who's Who in Rock*. The primary focus of the book is on the impact of African American popular music on white songs and singers in 1940–70. Memphis serves as the location from which the author discusses the interplay between black and white music and musicians. While he accepts the fact that rock and roll has its origins in black music, he also believes that the music is not exclusively African American. He describes how white artists like the Allmans, Janis Joplin and Elvis Presley struggled to capture the roots of the black sound.

296. Barlow, William. *Looking Up at Down: The Emergence of Blues Culture.* Philadelphia: Temple University Press, 1989.

A comprehensive history of the blues permeated with lyrics that illustrate the impact that the music has on musicians and their listeners. Covers the social and musical evolution, changes and social evolution that blues has undergone from its origins to World War II. Of special note is the discussion of the way in which blues is interwoven with social conditions, concerns, conflicts and shifts in the consciousness of African Americans. Rare recordings, oral histories and interviews are used to trace the evolution of blues from the rural south to the urban cultures of areas like Memphis, St Louis and Chicago. In short, he brings to life the blues culture that served as African American cultural resistance to white domination.

297. Bekker, Peter O.E. *The Story of the Blues.* Life, Times and Music Series. New York: Friedman/Fairfax Publishing, 1997.

Attempts to cover the origins, history and evolution of blues from its southern roots to cities like Chicago, Memphis and Kansas City. Discusses persons associated with Delta, classic and other blues styles.

298. Brooks, Lonnie, Cub Koda and Wayne Baker Brooks. *Blues for Dummies.* New York: For Dummies, 1998.

For younger readers. An elementary tour guide through the history and evolution of blues from artists like Son House and Robert Johnson to Gatemouth Moore, B.B. King, Robert Cray, John Lee Hooker, Etta James, KoKo Taylor, Stevie Ray Vaughan, Muddy Waters, Buddy Guy and several others.

299. Charters, Samuel. *The Roots of the Blues: An African Search.* Reprint, New York: Da Capo Press, 1991.

The author traces the roots of blues from West Africa to African American culture. He discusses selected West African traditional musical idioms and their perceived relationship with blues by quoting lyrics, and drawing upon his fieldwork in West Africa.

300. ——. *The Poetry of the Blues.* Photographs by Ann Charters. New York: Oak Publications, 1963.

A study of the context, technique and significance of the texts of blues. The author begins by describing features of African American society that produced the blues, then moves to an analysis of blues texts. His discussion focuses on feeling, form, poetic technique, themes, and their affects on the musicians and their music. Issues of social protest and sexual innuendo are also examined.

301. Cohn, Lawrence. *Nothing but the Blues: The Music and Musicians.* Introduction by B.B. King. New York: Abbeville Press, 1993.

A compilation of eleven essays about the beginnings and history of the blues. The focus is on informing, educating, entertaining and engendering interest among the readership of this volume. The topics range from roots and influences, to women blues singers, urban blues and the blues of today. Among the authors of essays are Samuel Charters, who wrote on the roots of blues, David Evans on Texas and deep south blues, Mark A. Humphrey on the gospel and urban traditions of blues, and Richard K. Spottswood on women and blues. Other essayists include Mary Katherine Aldine, Bruce Bastin, John H. Cowley, Jim O'Neal, Barry Pearson and Charles Wolfe. There are 320 illustrations and photographs of record contracts and performers making music.

302. Collis, John. *The Blues: Roots and Inspiration.* New York: Smithmark Publishers, 1997.

Explores pre-blues forms of blues and other African American music and the ways in which blues have been used to inspire people.

303. Collis, John and Buddy Guy. *The Story of Chess Records.* New York: Bloombury Publishers, 1998.

A history of the blues record label founded in 1950 by Leonard and Phil Chess. Originally named Aristocrat, they later changed the name of the label to Chess. Their first big hit was "I Can't be Satisfied" by Muddy Waters in 1948. The book is permeated with information on their associations with and marketing of artists like Bo Diddley, Chuck Berry, Willie Dixon, Howlin' Wolf, Muddy Waters and Sonny Boy Williamson. The expansion of the Chess catalogue to include more genres, beginning in the 1950s, is also discussed. Well-written and thoroughly detailed.

304. Cook, Bruce. *Listen to the Blues.* Reprint, New York: Da Capo Press, 2000.

The fifteen chapters in this book deal with issues ranging from a definition of blues to the importance of the Delta, Chicago, Texas and Tennessee in the history and evolution of blues. Addresses the appropriation of blues and his premise of the mutual influence between blacks and whites in blues and other musical genres. Also included are interviews with musicians and references to non-blues musicians like Clifford Brown, Dizzy Gillespie, Charlie Parker, Hank Ballard and Lavern Baker. A limited discussion of blues as poetry or social conscience is also included. Permeated with emotional, personal and anecdotal observations and conclusions.

305. Davis, Francis. *The History of the Blues: The Roots, the Music, the People.* Reprint, New York: Da Capo Press, 2003.

This is a companion volume to the three-part PBS series of the same name, an interpretative study that explores the history and evolution of the blues throughout the rural south and on its way northward. Discusses artists like Bessie Smith, Robert Johnson, Muddy Waters, Johnny "Stovepipe" Watson, Charley Patton and many others. Whereas a whole chapter is devoted to Robert Johnson, nothing is included on the urban blues artists of the 1930s like Bumblebee Slim, Johnny Temple, or Jimmy Gordon. Includes an extensive bibliography, discography and a timeline that links blues milestones to corresponding events in art and history.

306. Dickerson, James. *Mojo Triangle: Birthplace of Country, Blues, Jazz and Rock and Roll.* New York and London: Schirmer Tradebooks, 2005.

Focuses on the development of popular music and the major figures who shaped it within a geographical triangle encompassing Natchez, New Orleans, Memphis, Nashville and the Delta. Discusses the importance of Muscle Shoals, Alabama, as home of one of the most significant soul music rhythm sections of the 1960s–70s. Dickerson also includes a lengthy discussion of the role that climate and weather played in the area's musical development and history.

307. Eastman, Ralph. "Country Blues Performance and Oral Tradition." *Black Music Research Journal* 8(2) (Fall 1988): 161–77.

The author argues that in discussions of early blues, many writers have separated lyrics and music from the act of performance. Furthermore, his thesis is that by focusing almost exclusively on lyrics and musical transcriptions, and not on the *process* of the blues phenomenon, scholars "have unintentionally misstated and obscured the nature and function of blues" (p. 161). Therefore, the author attempts to demonstrate that country blues are rooted in oral tradition and that confusion ensued when scholars misapplied literary criteria when discussing this folk tradition.

308. Ellison, Mary. *Extensions of the Blues.* London: John Calder; New York: Riverrun Press, 1989.

Argues that blues are representative of all facets of life, ranging from joy and happiness to hate, despair, laughter and suffering. The author traces blues evolution as it reflects African American trials and tribulations in American society. Of particular note are her views on "Blues in American poetry" (pp. 107–71), and "Blues in American Fiction" (pp. 171–219).

309. Elmer, Howard. *Blues: Its Birth and Growth*. New York: Rosen Publishing Group, 1999.

A basic introduction to the topic that traces the evolution of blues from its African roots to its success in urban areas. After his introduction on African influence and oral tradition, the author discusses the structure of blues. Photographs of several early blues artists and later white artists like Janis Joplin in a section entitled "American Noise."

310. Evans, David. "Blues: A Chronological Overview." In *African American Music: An Introduction*, eds Mellonee V. Burnim and Portia Maultsby, pp. 77–96. New York: Routledge, 2006.

This overview includes a discussion of the background and context of blues, African and European musical elements, contexts for blues performance, role of instruments, the electric guitar, and blues texts, forms, recordings and much more. Well researched and well written.

311. Finn, Julio. *The Bluesman: The Musical Heritage of Black Men and Black Women in the Americas*. New York: Interlink Publishing Group, 1992.

The author traces the roots of blues from before American slavery, and theorizes that blues are inseparable from black religion in Africa and the diaspora. He discusses rituals and religious traditions in Africa and their transformation to syncretic expressions in Haiti, Jamaica, Cuba, Brazil and the United States. He focuses on sects and religious practices in the New World which have contributed to the development of blues, rather than on specific performers, compositions, or genres.

312. Flaherty, Ed. *The Blues Alive: A Timeless Tradition*. New York: SCH Distributors, 2005.

The author synthesizes anthropology and history with personal experiences to discuss how playing blues has influenced his life. He also discusses how African music, the music of Bengali, flamenco and gypsy musics have all been used to express a broken heart, to achieve spirituality and to denote sexuality.

313. Floyd, Jr, Samuel A. *The Power of Black Music: Interpreting Its History From Africa to the United States*. New York: Oxford University Press, 1996.

Floyd traces the development of African American music genres from early spirituals through blues, jazz, rhythm and blues, gospel, Motown, pop and concert-hall art music. The discourse mentions the contributions of many artists in all genres. He uses Henry Louis Gates, Jr's concept of "signifyin[g]" and the significance of call and response to the aesthetics, performance and understanding of African American musical traditions. Floyd argues that the performance is more important than the piece performed.

314. Goldman, Albert. *Sound Bites.* New York: Turtle Bay Books (Random House), 1992.

Although the author is primarily concerned with the sound and scenes of rock and roll, he covers the blues but offers no new insights. He also discusses artists like Aretha Franklin and Albert King, and topics like the importance of Memphis, Tennessee, why whites sing "black," and whether or not soul music has sold out.

315. Groom, Bob. *The Blues Revival.* London: Studio Vista, 1971.

Discusses the evolution of white interest in blues and the affect of that interest on the genre. Provides insight into the European visits of Big Bill Broonzy and Leadbelly, examines the influence of blues on 1950s popular music, and the subsequent rise in interest once the previously mentioned influence was discovered. He also discusses field recording trips, reissues, the growth of blues research and literature, and the popularity of blues festivals.

316. Guralnick, Peter, Robert Santelli, Holly George-Warren and Christopher John Farley, eds. *Martin Scorsese Presents the Blues: A Musical Journey.* New York: Amistad Press, 2003.

Companion volume to the documentary series *Martin Scorsese Presents the Blues.* The chapters in the book correspond to a segment of the documentary; each is introduced by an essay from the film's director: "A Century of the Blues" (directed by Robert Santelli), "Feel Like Going Home" (dir. Martin Scorsese), "Warmin' by the Devil's Fire" (dir. Charles Burnett), "The Road to Memphis" (dir. Richard Pearce), "The Soul of a Man" (dir. Wim Wenders), "Godfathers and Sons" (dir. Marc Levin), "Red, White, and Blues" (dir. Mike Figgis), and "Piano Blues and Beyond" (dir. Clint Eastwood). Also included are archival essays from Stanley Booth, Mack McCormick and Paul Oliver; newly-commissioned essays from David Halberstam, Elmore Leonard, Suzan-Lori Parks and John Edgar Wideman; in-depth conversations with artists like Eric Clapton, John Lee Hooker, Robert Johnson and Bessie Smith; and related literary excerpts from writers James Baldwin, Ralph Ellison, William Faulkner, Langston

Hughes, Zora Neal Hurston and Eudora Welty. Preface by Martin Scorsese, foreword by Alex Gibney, and an introductory note by editor Peter Guralnick. Illustrated with rare, vintage photographs.

317. Gussow, Adam. *Seems Like Murder Here: Southern Violence and the Blues Tradition*. Chicago: University of Chicago Press, 2002.

Based on a blues lyric by Charley Patton, the author believes that blues evolved as a response to the lynching and violence against African Americans in the southern United States. He includes interpretations from songs and literary works, ranging from the autobiographies of Honeyboy Edwards, B.B. King and W.C. Handy, to the poetry of Langston Hughes and the novels of Zora Neal Hurston to make his case. His chapter on Mamie Smith's "Crazy Blues" is particularly provocative.

318. Hamilton, Marybeth. *In Search of the Blues*. New York: Basic Books, 2008.

The author questions why historians who write about blues do not apply methodological rigor. The focus is on white folklorists and record collectors whose purpose was to interpret and promote African American folk blues from 1900 to the early 1960s. She deconstructs selected works by Alan and John Lomax, Howard Odum, Frederic Ramsey, James McKune and Dorothy Scarborough, addressing meaning in the music and their racial attitudes and political agendas. She also argues that the "Delta blues" label was invented by whites who toured the south searching for black voices of frustration and rage.

319. Handyside, Chris. *Blues: History of American Music*. New York: Heinemann, 2006.

For younger readers. Geared to high school readers, this concise history covers the Mississippi Delta, Chicago and other cities, and briefly discuss giants like Charley Patton, Robert Johnson, B.B. King and others. This is an overview rather than an in-depth discussion of the topic.

320. Haydon, Geoffrey Jennings. "A Study of the Exchange of Influences Between the Music of Early Twentieth-century Parisian Composers and Ragtime, Blues, and Early Jazz." DMA dissertation, University of Texas at Austin, 1992.

The author discusses the musical exchange of ideas among classical European composers like Claude Debussy, Darius Milhaud, Maurice Ravel, Eric Satie and Igor Stravinsky, all of whom infused their compositions with elements of American popular music. He points out that American jazz artists like Bix Beiderbecke and George

Gershwin were simultaneously utilizing French Impressionistic devices into their compositions and improvisations. He cites and analyzes compositions from French and jazz composers and improvisers to illustrate the aforementioned relationship.

321. Jackson, Bruce. *Wake Up Dead Man: Hard Labor and Southern Blues.* Athens, GA: University of Georgia Press, 1999.

     Based on fieldwork in Texas prisons in 1964–66, this study contains authentic commentary on folklore, music and other topics. A new heading indicates another speaker, time and place. The author collected numerous songs from a brutal era in Texas prison life, as well as songs that accompany a variety of work situations.

322. Keil, Charles. *Urban Blues.* Chicago: University of Chicago Press, 1966.

     An excellent study of the mid-1960s blues scene in Chicago. Beginning with a discussion of acculturation and kinship, Keil elaborates on the exclusion of contemporary blues (with the exception of Baraka's *Blues People*, [1963] 1999) from blues criticism. He provides reasons for stylistic and thematic changes, and suggests that rationalization has taken place. In addition, he discusses how economic, legal and technical factors affect communication, artists' roles, audience response, group solidarity and more. Contains an interview of B.B. King and an examination of Bobby "Blue" Bland's stage performance. The appendices include a discussion of identity theories, a framework for musical discussion and an annotated outline of blues styles.

323. Koopmans, Andy. *The History of the Blues.* New York: Lucent Books, 2005.

     For younger readers. Written for grades 9–12, this concise chronological overview of blues history traces the music's development from its African roots, the influence of spirituals, field hollers and work songs, to its acknowledgment as a significant contribution to world culture. He alludes to the influence of blues in all contemporary American popular music.

324. Kubik, Gerhard. *Africa and the Blues.* Jackson: University Press of Mississippi, 1999.

     The author uses his vast field experience and research on African musical traditions to discover a link between blues and west-central Sudanic music, and uses performance practices and musical characteristics to illustrate the connections. Traces blues out of and back to Africa where he argues that Mexican innovations now enrich contemporary African sound.

325. Lehmann, Theo. *Blues and Trouble*. Berlin: Henscheluerlag, 1966.

     In German. The monograph is concerned with expressive issues that
     have permeated blues since its origins rather than a historical evolution
     of blues. The author discusses ambiguity, integrity, frankness, realism
     and superstition in the blues. In addition, he describes the musical
     styles of several blues vocalists, and includes forty-one blues texts in
     English and German. Translation and coverage by the author.

326. Leiser, Willie. *I'm a Road Runner Baby*. Bexhill-on-Sea, UK: Blues
     Unlimited, 1969.

     A thirty-eight-page diary of a Swiss blues enthusiast's visit to the
     United States from December 1968 to January 1969. During his visit
     he met and heard several blues and gospel artists perform in Chicago,
     Philadelphia, Washington, DC and San Francisco. The diary contains
     interesting insights and observations on the music and musicians.

327. Marcus, Greil. *Mystery Train: Images of Rock and Roll Music*. New
     York: Dutton, 1975.

     A classic devoted primarily to rock and roll artists, but does include
     a scholarly discussion of blues artists like Harmonica Frank, Robert
     Johnson and Sly Stone, and their musical styles. Surveys their effect
     on musical trends and the difficulty rock stars experience in sustaining
     creativity after initial success.

328. Middleton, Richard. *Pop Music and the Blues: A Study of the
     Relationship and its Significance*. London: Gollancz, 1972.

     The book is divided into two sections. The first focuses on blues'
     relationship to the black cultural experience in America. A discus-
     sion of the black/white cultural clash leads to a description and
     analysis of the basic musical elements of blues in which the author
     demonstrates that these musical elements are the result of that cul-
     tural clash. Also discusses how blues is a reflection of the changing
     situation of blacks in America. In the second section, the author
     explores the relationships between white popular music and blues,
     and between white Western and non-Western cultures, and the influ-
     ence of blues on the music of the Beatles, Bob Dylan, Jimi Hendrix,
     Frank Zappa and others.

329. Mitchell, George. *Blow My Blues Away*. Baton Rouge: Louisiana
     State University Press, 1971.

     Although primarily concerned with the roots of jazz, the author
     connects it to early forms of African American music, including the
     blues. He also discusses meaning and the impact of blues on jazz.

330. Muir, Peter C. "Before Crazy Blues: Commercial Blues in America, 1850–1920." PhD dissertation, City University of New York, 2004.

The study begins with an exploration of the reasons why pre-1912 blues has been neglected in blues scholarship. Examines the identity of early commercial blues and commercial proto-blues, compositions displaying blues characteristics that were published before the beginning of the commercial blues industry in 1912. Then the focus moves to blues that flourished in the second decade of the twentieth century, when more than 700 blues compositions were copyrighted and over 1,000 recordings (disc, cylinder and piano roll) were made.

331. Murray, Albert. *Stomping the Blues.* 1976. Reprint, New York: Da Capo Press, 1989.

An examination of the mythologies, sources and styles of the blues. Discusses aesthetic values, their origin in African American culture, their individual stylizing within the society and the ways in which they evoke ritual responses to life. Provides meanings and interpretations of the blues within its cultural context by discussing topics like "Blues Face to Face," "Singing, Playing and Swinging the Blues," "Kansas City Four," "Folk Art and Fine Art," and much more. The coverage is provocative and stimulating.

332. Oakley, Giles. *The Devil's Music: A History of the Blues.* Second edn. New York: Da Capo Press, 1997.

Combines sociological and musical insights to demonstrate that historical blues were more than mere entertainment. Traces the rise and development of blues in relationship to other African American musical genres, examines its social context, and relates the interesting experiences of some musicians. Covers blues icons like W.C. Handy, Leadbelly, Charley Patton, Ma Rainey and Bessie Smith, and the music scene in cities like Atlanta, Chicago, Memphis and St Louis. A discussion of meaning and musical change is also included.

333. Obrecht, Jas, ed. *Rollin' and Tumblin': The Postwar Blues Guitarists.* San Francisco: Backbeat Books, 2000.

Comprehensive coverage of the pioneers of electric blues guitar from Chicago, the Mississippi Delta, Louisiana, Texas and the west coast. Extensive interviews of some contemporary artists and concise portraits of historical blues figures like John Lee Hooker, Lightnin' Hopkins, T-Bone Walker and Muddy Waters. Includes an essay on the history of the blues guitar.

334. Oliver, Paul. *Broadcasting the Blues: Black Blues in the Segregation Era.* New York: Routledge, 2005.

Summarizes the influence and impact of blues on a myriad of musical movements. Covers the influence of blues on artists in a wide variety of musical movements, including gospel, jazz, soul, rhythm and blues, and more.

335.  ———. *Blues off the Record: Thirty Years of Blues Commentary.* New York: Da Capo Press, 1988.

A compilation of essays and critiques first published in other sources. An exhaustive examination of themes like the origin of the blues, the effects of recording on blues development, the extent that recorded blues are representative of blues as they were sung, and the limitation of content. Focuses on six themes: the treatment of Christmas, attitudes of blues singers toward religion, the relationship between early blues and gospel music, patterns of continuity in the development and treatment of blues, black heroes and escapism.

336.  ———. *Savannah Syncopators: African Retentions in the Blues.* London: Studio Vista, 1970.

An outline and discussion of issues and questions involved in the transmission of African musical traditions to America. The author discusses the notions and misconceptions of jazz historians, examines the characteristics of West African music and musical instruments of the Savannah regions, and relates the aforementioned to the development of the blues in North America. He espouses that musical practices from the Savannah regions of West Africa, rather than rainforest, were reinterpreted into the blues. This volume was combined with two other books, *Blacks, Whites and Blues* by Tony Russell (1970) and *Recording the Blues*, in *Yonder Come the Blues* (2001). See also items 270, 271, 277, 336, 341 and 343.

337.  ———. *Screening the Blues: Aspects of the Blues Tradition.* New York: Da Capo, 1968, 1989.

Examines the many variants of the blues and relates them to African American musical and religious traditions. Also traces the origins of blues, discusses "the dozens," Christian rituals and sexual imagery aspects of blues. Extensive source notes, many photographs, a discography and an index of song titles and singers.

338.  ———. *Blues Fell This Morning: The Meaning of the Blues.* Foreword by Richard Wright. New York: Collier, 1963. Reprinted and retitled *Blues Fell This Morning: Meaning in the Blues.* New York: Cambridge University Press, 1990.

Explores the historical context of blues lyrics, rooting the text in the varied sociocultural experiences of African Americans in the south.

The 350 textual transcriptions from the early decades of the twentieth century highlight issues like love, devotion, marriage, gambling, religion, natural disasters, racism, religion, poverty, prostitution, punishment, sickness, sex, slum housing and work. The author meticulously transcribed the text of hundreds of 78-rpm blues recordings and categorized them according to how they reflect social and historical events in African American history.

339. Oliver, Paul, Max Harrison and William Bolcom. "Blues." In *The New Grove: Gospel, Blues and Jazz, With Spirituals and Ragtime*, pp. 36–178. New York: W.W. Norton and Co., 1986.

Derived in part from *The New Grove Dictionary of Music and Musicians* (1980), Paul Oliver covers some interesting and provocative issues regarding blues, especially questions regarding shifting perceptions and identities within blues. Addresses blues origins before delving into a discussion of the history of the blues from its origins to the late 1970s. Discusses blues singers; string, jug and washboard bands; Zydeco groups, piano blues, southern blues, post-war blues on the West Coast, white blues, blues structure, and blues styles like folk, classic and urban blues. Includes a bibliography and discography.

340. ——. *The Story of the Blues*. London: Barrie and Rockliff; Philadelphia: Chilton, 1969; Harmondsworth, UK: Penguin Books, 1973.

Discusses the evolution and distinctive features of blues styles, relationship of blues to African American society, and how individual artists influenced the history and evolution of the genre. Organized chronologically, beginning with the slave trade, followed by chapters on strings bands, boogie woogie, tent shows, rural and urban idioms, and more. Includes an index of nearly 700 artists.

341. Oliver, Paul, Tony Russell, Robert M.W. Dixon, John Godrich and Howard Rye. *Yonder Come the Blues: The Evolution of a Genre*. Cambridge, UK: Cambridge University Press, 2001.

This volume combines *Savannah Syncopators* by Paul Oliver; *Blacks, Whites and Blues* by Tony Russell; and *Recording the Blues* by Dixon and Godrich, three books that were published separately in 1970. The compilation includes new essays and a discussion of the most significant sociocultural factors that shaped the blues as identity among African Americans. The authors emphasize the significance of the African heritage, generic aspects of black and white music, and the role of recordings in consolidating blues. See also items 270, 271, 277, 336 and 343.

342. Robertson, Brian. *Little Blues Book*. New York: Algonquin Books, 1996.

Permeated with stories about the men and women of early blues, and includes a discussion of black women expressing themselves via the blues in the 1920s. He profiles numerous artists who made up the first wave of creative artists in the genre.

343. Russell, Tony. *Blacks, Whites and Blues.* London: Studio Vista, 1970.

Examines the interaction between the folk music of African Americans and whites to the late 1930s. He discusses minstrelsy and the folk repertoire common to blacks and whites, with a focus on different approaches and styles. Discusses the blues influence on Jimmy Rodgers, interplay between Western and Eastern styles, urbanization of blues and changes in country music. Contains a bibliography, a discography that is divided into artists and anthologies, and an artist index. This book was combined with *Savannah Syncopators* by Paul Oliver and *Recording the Blues* by Dixon and Godrich and published as *Yonder Come the Blues: The Evolution of a Genre* (2001). See also items 270, 271, 277, 336 and 341.

344. Schneider, Thomas A. "Blues Cover Songs: The Intersection of Blues and Rock on Popular Music Charts (1955–95)." PhD dissertation, University of Memphis, 2001.

An investigation of songs on the Billboard Pop Charts originally recorded by blues or R&B artists that were later reintroduced to the mainstream audience through "covers" by (mostly) white pop and rock artists. Analyzes the bestselling records between the years 1955 and 1995; over 275 pop titles, 297 blues and R&B recordings, and 421 pop/rock recordings are discussed. Includes background information on each song title, a musical comparison between the cover and original, and selected information about the writer, producer, or recording process. Also included is information on each original blues artist, an essay on the evolution of blues as a musical style, emergence of early rock and roll, and a discussion of the general practice of recording cover versions in pop music.

345. Shockett, Bernard Irwin. "Stylistic Study of the Blues, 1917–31, as Practiced by Jazz Instrumentalists." PhD dissertation, New York University, 1964.

Traces stylistic trends in the historical evolution of the blues as demonstrated by jazz artists. The format follows *Brian Rust's Guide to Discography* (1980). The compositions, recorded between 1917 and 1931, were categorized and analyzed according to form, introductions, key signatures, modulations and tempi. The author also lists some characteristics of pre-1932 blues structure.

346. Springer, Robert, ed. *Nobody Knows Where the Blues Come From: Lyrics and History.* Jackson: University Press of Mississippi, 2007.

A collection of essays that focus on blues as a neglected form of oral history that African Americans use to identify and record significant events. The essays offer an interesting and provocative intersection between oral history and a vibrant and varied assessment of the history of the songs.

347. Springer, Robert and Andre J.M. Prevos. *Authentic Blues: Its History and Its Themes.* Studies in the History and Interpretation of Music, Vol. 47. New York: Edwin Mellen Press, 1996.

The authors advocate that blues is a genuine form of cultural and literary education, and that its transmission via recordings was as significant as its oral transmission. They also argue that blues is more than a collection of imitative formulae because tradition and evolution are always present in the lyrics.

348. Taft, Michael Ernest. "The Lyrics of Race Records Blues, 1920–42: A Semantic Approach to the Structural Analysis of a Formulaic System." PhD dissertation, St Johns, Newfoundland, Canada: Memorial University, 1977.

Focuses on the lyrics of African American blues recordings produced between 1920 and 1942, especially the short, aphoristic pronouncements and the concise poetic imagery. Studies the nature of the formulaic structure and highly creative lyrics of "race records." The text, structure and context of the blues is covered in part one of the dissertation; the structure of the blues is examined in part two. The author concludes that the formula is both a theoretical construct and a concrete reality of blues composition. The structure of the blues formula becomes more concrete and acquires definable boundaries when one moves from compositional competence to blues performance, and at the level of blues performance, rather than blues competence, the formula becomes useful in the study of blues structure.

349. Titon, Jeff Todd. *Early Downhome Blues: A Musical and Cultural Analysis.* Urbana: University of Illinois Press, 1977.

The book is divided into three parts. In part I Titon considers the place of downhome blues in African American culture in the first part of the twentieth century and attitudes of musicians toward their music over a longer period of time. In part II he uses a representative sample of early downhome recordings and analyzes the music and text. Part III is concerned with the response of the record industry to downhome blues and black culture during the jazz age. Very thorough and scholarly.

350. Tracy, Steven, ed. *Write Me a Few of Your Blues: A Blues Reader.* Amherst, MA: University of Massachusetts Press, 1999.

A compilation by several authors, primarily nonperformers. The book documents the aesthetics and history of the blues, and its importance in the authors' lives. The forty-nine previously published essays were chosen because of their aesthetic, artistic, political and social significance. Published between 1911 and 1998, the essays are organized around themes like Africa, folklore, other folk music, religion, style, performance, racism and social protest, recordings, literature and criticism, and blues influence. Includes essays by Houston Baker, Angela Davis, Francis Davis, David Evans, Bill Ferris, LeRoi Jones, Charles Keil, Albert Murray, Larry Neal, Robert Palmer, Rosetta Reitz, Richard Wright and others. The essays are documented and some, like Jerry Richardson's essay on B.B. King, include musical analysis. Good discographies.

351. Van Rijn, Guido. *Kennedy's Blues: African-American Blues and Gospel Songs on JFK.* Jackson: University Press of Mississippi, 2007.

A comprehensive compilation of the blues and gospel texts written about President John F. Kennedy. The songs are organized by topic, ranging from the Cold War and the economy, to the space race and the Civil Rights movement. The accompanying CD by Agram Records contains twenty-eight tracks. The author helps us understand the multiple ways that African Americans responded to the personality and politics of the president. Foreword by Brian Ward.

352. ———. *Roosevelt's Blues: African-American Blues and Gospel Songs on FDR.* Jackson: University Press of Mississippi, 1996.

This is the first book of the author's research into the connection between blues texts and a specific American president. This comprehensive assessment of 1930s and 1940s blues lyrics that describe Roosevelt's influence on black Americans is accompanied by thirty-five illustrations, a bibliography, discography, and a foreword by Paul Oliver.

353. Weissman, Dick. *The Basics: Blues.* New York and London: Routledge, 2006.

A historical overview of the evolution of blues from its roots to contemporary times. The book is organized chronologically and focuses on the major styles and issues in blues development and blues' relationship to rhythm and blues. A selected bibliography, discography and filmography is included, along with a timeline of significant social and historical events.

**Regional studies**

354. Barlow, William Brook. "Voices From The Heartland: A Cultural History of the Blues." PhD dissertation, University of California, Santa Cruz, 1983.

Song texts, interviews, oral histories and recordings, and other secondary sources are used to document the cultural history of blues from the perspective of the creators. The work is divided into three sections: the first deals with the origins and infancy of blues in the Mississippi Delta, East Texas and the Piedmont from the 1890s to the 1930s. The second section covers the formation of a vaudeville blues tradition. The final section traces the birth and maturation of the urban blues tradition in major metropolitan areas from 1900 to World War II. The author also reassesses the role of the blues tradition in American culture and within the context of the historical data presented in this work.

355. ———. *Beale Street, U.S.A.: Where the Blues Began.* Bexhill-on-Sea, UK: Blues Unlimited, 1981.

This reissue of a twelve-page booklet produced by the Memphis Housing Authority presents a picture of Beale Street in Memphis from around 1900 with a primary focus on the buildings and their occupants. Contains important historical and social information for blues scholars.

356. Bastin, Bruce. *Red River Blues: The Blues in the Southwest.* Urbana: University of Illinois Press, 1995.

Extensive interviews and primary sources are used to chronicle a history of the performers of south-eastern blues. In addition to the social context of a specific tradition, the author provides a wealth of biographical details of the artists, and mentions performers whom he associates with a specific style of south-eastern blues.

357. ———. *Crying for the Carolinas.* London: Studio Vista, 1971.

A study of Piedmont blues and blues vocalists from North and South Carolina, northern Georgia and part of Virginia. The author conducted field work in North Carolina (Atlanta, Charlotte and Durham) and South Carolina (Greenville and Spartanburg), and describes blues activities and distinctive features of the blues in this region. He dedicates chapters to Blind Boy Fuller and other vocalists who moved north, including Brownie McGhee and Sonny Terry. Several photographs, a selected bibliography and discography, and an index.

358. Bearden, William. *Memphis Blues: Birthplace of a Music Tradition.* Mt Pleasant, SC: Arcadia Publishing, 2006.

The author argues that Memphis is the heart of the blues world, and that the rebirth of Beale Street acts as the spiritual center of the blues revival in Memphis. He covers blues history from the Delta to cities like Chicago, and thereafter to international destinations like the UK.

359. Cheseborough, Steve. *Blues Traveling: The Holy Sites of Delta Blues.* Jackson: University Press of Mississippi, 2001.

Much more than a guidebook, the book is a well researched history of blues traveling in the Mississippi Delta. It contains lines from blues lyrics that refer to specific sites, names and locations of blues music stores, blues museums, blues clubs and juke joints, and anecdotes about artists like "Mississippi Fred" McDowell. "Guidelines for Good Times," a resource for first-time travelers to the Mississippi Delta, includes information on food and drink, accommodations, church music, casinos, photography, etiquette in blues clubs, and sites like the Clarksdale Station where Muddy Waters boarded the train for Chicago.

360. Dickerson, James L. *Goin' Back to Memphis: A Century of Blues, Rock and Roll, and Glorious Soul.* Reprint, New York: Cooper Square Press, 2000.

A history of the evolution of popular musical genres in Memphis, with special emphasis on the recording studios. Uses interviews and personal experiences to discuss Stax and the Stax records house band, Sun owners and producers Sam Phillips and Chips Moman, and musicians Elvis Presley and Jerry Lee Lewis. In addition to discussing turn-of-the-century Beale Street, he profiles the role and function of artists like Walter "Furry" Lewis, "Fiddling Abe" Fortas (who later became a Supreme Court Justice), "Memphis Minnie" (Lizzie Douglas), the Box Tops, Booker T. and the MGs, Isaac Hayes, Otis Redding and Roy Orbison. The book is informative but more anecdotal than scholarly.

361. Dolan, Mark K. "Cathartic Uplift: A Cultural History of Blues and Jazz in the Chicago *Defender*, 1920–29." PhD dissertation, University of South Carolina, 2003.

Focuses on the *Defender's* handling of advertisements for blues and jazz during the period as a reflection of its readers' interests and needs. Immersed in the theories of James Carey, Sidney Kobre, Robert Park and others, the author concludes that the *Defender's* content was determined by outside factors, including a rich and growing audience and appetite for African American music on the south side of Chicago. Analyzes the editorial content of the entertainment pages and the other themes covered in the paper, including issues dealing with "uplift" and the "emotion-charged" advertising dealing with the appearances of artists like Louis Armstrong, Blind Lemon Jefferson, Lonnie Johnson, Mamie Smith and Bessie Smith.

362. Dube, Caleb. "Between Starvation and Stardom: Chicago Blues Musicians as Cultural Workers." PhD dissertation, Northwestern University, 2001.

Investigates blues musicians' struggle to make a living in Chicago's tourist blues scene, one of the few centers of blues activities to survive. Uses Bourdieu and de Certeau's theories of "cultural workers" to study the tactics that musicians use to address the problem and how they utilize the various opportunities that arise at different work sites. The two-year study focused on a core of ten Chicago blues musicians, and used participant observation of the artists at their homes, nightclubs, the Chicago Blues Festival and miscellaneous work sites. Each artist was interviewed about his life history and the daily struggle to find music jobs. The author notes that the musicians tap into opportunities made available by the blues economy such as commodification of blues.

363. Dunas, Jeff. *State of the Blues: The Living Legacy of the Delta.* New York: Aperture, 2003.

Concerned with the influence and power of blues. In this collection of intimate portraits and interviews, the author focuses on many of the greatest blues performers of our time, including John Lee Hooker, B.B. King, Clarence "Gatemouth" Brown, Charley Musslewhite, Bonnie Raitt, KoKo Taylor and many more. The interviews are supplemented with evocative photographs of the landmarks and byways of the "Blues Highway" that leads from New Orleans to Chicago. William Ferris provides the cultural and historical context for the author's photographs. Introduction by John Lee Hooker.

364. Evans, David Huhn. *Big Road Blues: Tradition and Creativity in the Folk Blues.* Berkeley: University of California Press, 1982.

Discusses the processes of folk blues tradition and composition by focusing on the blues tradition of Drew, Mississippi. Interviews with 1960s and 1970s blues icons like Son House, Robert Johnson, Tommy Johnson, Charley Patton and Muddy Waters, and lesser known artists like Mager Johnson, Fiddlin' Joe Martin, Matt Willis and Willis Taylor provide deep insight into their lives, how blues are composed, elements of blues, origins, and how singers and songs relate to form a tradition. The author contends that songs are not composed by individuals but arise out of local tradition. He analyzes Tommy Johnson's "Big Road Blues" to demonstrate how musicians improvise on a core set of musical elements to create a "new" song each time they perform. Also examines the styles of Matt Willis, Mager Johnson, Charley Patton, Howlin' Wolf, A. Youngblood and others.

365.  ———. "Tradition and Creativity in the Folk Blues." PhD dissertation, University of California, Los Angeles, 1976.

Focuses on the processes of composition, learning, re-composition, transmission and handling of repertoire in the folk blues tradition, based on extensive fieldwork conducted in Mississippi and other states between 1964 and 1973. The author recorded about 700 blues performances by more than 80 artists. In addition to distinguishing between folk blues and popular blues, the author argues that folk blues can be divided into two broad categories: regional and local, and includes a detailed breakdown of both styles, but with a special emphasis on the musical elements of the local tradition of Drew, Mississippi. Combines elements of various methodologies—comparative, oral formulaic, artist-centered, and functional, psychological, sociological, structural and performance-centered approaches—to analyze the music and to draw conclusions.

366.  Ferris, William R. *Blues from the Delta*. London: Studio Vista, 1970; Garden City, NY: Anchor Press/Doubleday, 1978; New York: Da Capo Press, 1988.

This study expands on the author's folklore dissertation ("Black Folklore from the Mississippi Delta," University of Pennsylvania, 1969) through conversations and correspondence with scholars like John Blassingame, B.B. King, David Evans, Alan Lomax, Paul Oliver, Robert Ferris Thompson and Jeff Titon, and performers like Shelly "Popa Jazz" Brown, Wallace "Pine Top" Johnson, Lee Kizart, Jasper Love, Maudie Shirley and James "Son" Thomas. The book is divided into three parts: "blues roots," "blues composition" and "blues house party." Of special note is the focus on verse structure and its relationship to the composition and performance of blues. An excellent bibliography and discography.

367.  ———. "Blues Roots and Development." *Black Perspective in Music* 1(2) (Fall 1974): 122–27.

Traces the origin of blues to the nineteenth century, and links the origin to African musical practices. He discusses gifted singers, bottleneck guitar playing, Mississippi Delta blues and urban blues.

368. Gioia, Ted. *Delta Blues: The Life and Times of the Mississippi Masters Who Revolutionized American Music*. New York: W.W. Norton and Co., 2008.

Depicts the history and evolution of Mississippi Delta blues from its roots to its rise to global influence, field hollers and plantation music to contemporary artists performing in the Delta tradition. The author discusses Charley Patton, Son House, Robert Johnson, Tommy Johnson, Muddy Waters, John Lee Hooker, Howlin' Wolf, B.B. King and several others. Includes thirty-eight illustrations.

369. Gordon, Robert. *It Came from Memphis*. New York: Atria (Simon and Schuster), 2001.

The author, a native of Memphis, focuses on the unheralded artists like Insect Trust, Mudboy, and the Autrons. He also discusses John McIntire, wrestling legend Sputnick Monroe and more.

370. Govenar, Alan. *Living Texas Blues: The Rise of Contemporary Sound*. College Station, TX: Texas A&M University Press, 2008.

Documents Texas blues from its beginnings in the cotton fields to its acceptance across age, racial, economic and geographical boundaries. The book includes 495 black-and-white illustrations, including photographs of Blind Lemon Jefferson, Aaron "T-Bone" Walker, Delbert McClinton, Sam Lightnin' Hopkins, Baldemar "Freddie Fender" Huerta, Stevie Ray Vaughan and many more.

371. ———. *Meeting the Blues: The Rise of the Texas Sound*. Dallas: Taylor, 1989.

Chronicles the history and personalities associated with historical Texas blues, including Blind Lemon Jefferson, Texas Alexander and other contemporary exponents of the genre.

372. Grazian, A.S. (David). *Blue Chicago: The Search for Authenticity in Urban Blues Clubs*. Chicago: University of Chicago Press, 2003.

Researched by a sociologist trained at the University of Chicago, this ethnographic study focuses on a myriad of sociomusical issues. Discusses blues from the perspective of the commodification of popular culture in America, the contemporary relevance of urban subcultures, race relations in the post-Civil Rights era, and the shift from factory production to entertainment consumption. Primary research (interviews and participant observations) was conducted in two north side Chicago blues clubs, B.L.U.E.S. and its satellite B.L.U.E.S. Etcetera. Although these clubs are located in different cultural settings, their primary clientele was white. However, to deepen his understanding of the two venues, he conducted additional observations in thirty-six blues-oriented bars, clubs and restaurants in Chicago's African American neighborhoods. Based on fieldwork for his dissertation.

373. ———. "Blue Chicago: Cultural Commerce and the Search for Authenticity in the Nocturnal Metropolis." PhD dissertation, University of Chicago, 2000.

Covers race relations after the Civil Rights era, issues involved in converting a factory culture to modern consumption, and the relationship of blues to the consumption of modern cultural artifacts.

374. Gussow, Adam Stefan. "Seems Like Murder Here: Southern Violence and Blues Texts, 1890–1996." PhD dissertation, Princeton University, 2000.

Presents a new reading of blues culture and the blues tradition. The author proposes that the "blues subject" emerged as an African American response to student lynchings in the turn-of-the-century south. He argues that if such texts were a way of "making whiteness" and "exorcising blackness," then they presented black audiences with an image of hopelessness whose essence blues texts attempt to describe. Examines the autobiographies of artists like W.C. Handy, B.B. King and Sammy Price, and ruminates on the legacy of lynching as portrayed in the novels of Clarence Major, Arthur Flowers, Chester Himes and Zora Neale Hurston, and in Mamie Smith's "Crazy Blues" and Robert Johnson's "Terraplane Blues." Also examines the conflicted role of interracial violence in blues culture.

375. Hay, Fred J., ed. *Goin' Back to Sweet Memphis: Conversations with the Blues.* Transcriber, ed. and annotator Fred Hay; illustrator George D. Davidson. Athens and London: University of Georgia Press, 2001.

Interviews and recollections of numerous blues artists who were born, raised, or performed extensively in Memphis. Essays on Bukka White, Big Memphis, Ma Rainey, Tommy Gary, Furry Lewis, Ernest "Boose" Taylor, Little Laura Dukes, Amos Patton, Joe Willie Wilkins and Houston Stackhouse, conducted by two college freshman during Memphis' "second blues renaissance." The interviews focus on their lives, music and contacts with other artists. Selected bibliography and discography.

376. Hildebrand, Lee. " Oakland Blues, Part I." In *California Soul: Music of African Americans in the West*, eds Jacqueline C. DjeDje and Eddie S. Meadows, pp. 104–12. Berkeley: University of California Press, 1998.

Traces the history, influences, and transformations that led to the development of Oakland blues, and describes that style. The primary focus is on producer Bob Geddins, who worked with artists like Lowell Fulson, K.C. Douglas, Roy Hawkins, Sugar Pie DeSanto, Jimmy McCracklin and Mercy Dee Walton.

377. Jackson, Bruce, ed. *Wake Up Dead Man: Hard Labor and Southern Blues.* Athens, GA: University of Georgia Press, 1999.

Deals with southern convict culture, its music of perseverance and resistance, and songs used to ease the rigors of work and convict life. The sixty-five work songs included recall a brutal period in the deep south. Profiles singers and identifies the Africanisms embedded in songs like "Hammer Ring," "Ration Blues," "Yellow Gal," and "Jody's Got My Wife and Gone."

378. Johnson, Pableaux. *Legends of New Orleans.* New Orleans: Blue Marble Music, 2001.

Although not devoted solely to blues, this book combines a CD of performances by several musical icons. Includes a concise guide to hotel and musical hot-spots beyond Bourbon street. The author is a native of Louisiana's Bayou Country, and an expert on New Orleans food culture.

379. Joyner, David Lee. "Southern Ragtime and its Transition to Published Blues." PhD dissertation, University of Memphis, 1986.

Traces the development of published ragtime in the south and its publishers and composers through historical investigation and musicological analysis of the sheet music. Uses a survey of published research on blues to define blues and ragtime. Discusses the importance of the Jesse French Piano Company of Nashville, Tennessee, in the development of ragtime. The study is limited to a geographical area covering Tennessee to Georgia to Texas; includes a discussion of previously unknown local artists like Geraldine Dobyns, H.A. French and Elma Ney McClure. A noteworthy discussion and comparison of selected blues of W.C. Handy with other Memphis blues composers who were active during Handy's time in Memphis.

380. Lawson, Rob Alan. "Jim Crow's Counterculture: The Blues and African-Americans in the Lower Mississippi Valley, 1890–1945." PhD dissertation, Vanderbilt University, 2003.

The dissertation begins with a question about human behavior: How do people respond to sustained discrimination and exploitation? The author asserts that black southerners from the lower Mississippi Valley region created blues as a larger cultural response to white supremacy during the Jim Crow era (1890–1945). The author illustrates the myriad ways that blues was used as accommodation and resistance to Jim Crowism, and provides specific details regarding cultural forms used to achieve the desired results.

381. Leadbitter, Mike. *Delta Country Blues*. London: Blues Unlimited, 1968.

Covers the context and music as it evolved in the Mississippi Delta. Includes information on blues icons like Son House, Robert Johnson and Charley Patton. An early effort to illuminate both the persons who produced the music and the cultural context in which it was produced.

382. Lee, George W. *Beale Street: Where the Blues Began*. Foreword by W.C. Handy. New York: Ballot, 1934. Reprint, College Park, TX: McGrath Publishing, 1969.

George W. Lee, an African American Army lieutenant, chronicles incidents, activities and personalities of respectable business people and the night life associated with the street from the 1860s to the 1930s. Discusses dope, gambling and saloons on Beale Street. Chapter eight describes the bands and their leaders from the end of the Civil War. Chapter nine focuses on W.C. Handy and the sources of some of his songs.

383. Lomax, Alan. *The Land Where the Blues Began*. New York: Pantheon Books, 1993.

An account of the author's travels in the Mississippi Delta in the 1940s; documents his interviews with several blues musicians. He discusses Big Bill Broonzy, Son House, Robert Johnson, Muddy Waters and others. Examines the music and complex melodies that often defy conventional Western notation. In an attempt to document "true facts" regarding Coahoma County, Mississippi laborers, he teamed with novelist Zora Neale Hurston in 1935, and later with John Work for musical analysis, and Charles Johnson, Chair of Sociology at Fisk University, who aided in documenting social context.

384. Lornell, Kip and Tracey E.W. Laird, eds. *Shreveport Sounds in Black and White*. Jackson: University Press of Mississippi, 2008.

The musical distinctiveness of Shreveport, Louisiana, identified as one of the nation's most important "regional-sound" cities, shaped country, blues, R&B, rockabilly and rock, and contributions from artists like Leadbelly, the Melody Makers, Jimmie Davis, Hank Williams, Taylor-Griggs Melody Makers, and Eddie Giles. In addition to glimpses into the lives and contributions of respective artists representing different genres, the editors also discuss the musical mixture that has emerged from the cultural interactions of the city's black and white musicians.

385. McGinley, Paige A. "Sound Travels: Performing Diaspora and the Imagined American South." PhD dissertation, Brown University, 2008.

An investigation of four "Sound Travels" performances that draw upon the song-collecting travels of John and Alan Lomax, "blues tourism" in the Mississippi Delta and commemorations of the black diaspora that followed Hurricane Katrina. Examines how the black diaspora has been used as a performance trope and is represented and reinvented to replace other modes of travel. Investigates specific questions regarding migration, travel and representation, including how and why various artists employ performance tropes of migration and diaspora, and how performances of black migration create and contest mythologies of the American open road.

386. McKee, Margaret and Fred Chisenhall. *Beale Black and Blue: Life and Music on Black America's Main Street.* Baton Rouge: Louisiana State University Press, 1993.

Discusses the political relationship between the black community and the Memphis political and social scene. The book contains interviews with Bobby "Blue" Bland, Sam Chatmon, John Estes, B.B. King, "Furry" Lewis and Big Joe Williams. They discuss how they came to the blues, their survival in the music business and their career from success to obscurity to rediscovery in the 1960s and 1970s.

387. Merrill, Hugh. *The Blues Route.* New York: William Morrow, 1990.

Traces the migration of the blues, beginning with the juke joints and plantations of the Mississippi Delta, through its development from Atlanta, Memphis and New Orleans, to the "promised lands" of Chicago and Los Angeles. Essentially an oral history of blues migration and the people involved in it, the book includes quotes from blues fans as well as Rufus Thomas of Sun and Stax Records, Bruce Iglauer, KoKo Taylor, Eddie "Cleanhead" Vinson, trumpeter Gregory Davis of the Dirty Dozen, singer Valerie Wellington, and German-born Chris Strachwitz, the first person to record Louisiana Zydeco.

388. Minton, John Stephen. "Phonograph Blues: Folksong and Media in the Southern United States before the Second World War." PhD dissertation, University of Texas, 1990.

Focuses on the relationship between folk song and the commercial phonograph industry in the southern United States before World War II. Limited to the 78-rpm discs known as "race" (African American) and "hillbilly" (white) music; theorizes an intimate connection between the two, and researches how performers and audiences instantaneously experience these recordings as cultural events. Concludes that electronic media are culturally specific and cross-culturally variable; the encoding and decoding of messages through these media is conditioned by their interrelation with and the prominence and influence of that culture's other means of expressive communication.

389. Mitchell, George. *Blow My Blues Away*. Baton Rouge: Louisiana State University, 1971.

Based on field work conducted in Mississippi in the summer of 1967. Interviews with Ada Mae Anderson, Jessie Mae Brooks, William Diamond, Rosa Lee Hill, Robert Diggs, Other Turner and Robert Johnson, conducted after each had sung. Includes some lyrics and several photographs. Important because it provides insight into some lesser known Delta blues musicians.

390. Newman, Mark. *Entrepreneurs of Profit and Pride: From Black-Appeal to Radio Soul*. Media and Society Series. Westport, CT: Praeger Press, 1988.

Outlines the development of black radio and early black appeal, to its triumph as a symbol of cultural pride. Describes "narrowcasting" to a specific audience (as opposed to network broadcasting for mass appeal), developed by Jack L. Cooper in Chicago. Also discussed, the importance of WDIA of Memphis, Tennessee, in the 1950s, and the longest continuous blues program in Helena, Arkansas, the schism between black appeal and white programming, and the two distinct and different radio experiences that resulted.

391. Nicholson, Robert. *Mississippi: The Blues Today*. Photographs by Logan Young. New York: Da Capo Press, 1998.

The Scottish-born London resident conducted extensive research in the southern US, and presents a vivid account of today's music among an economically impoverished people. Paints lively portraits of the lives and music of current exponents of Mississippi Delta blues and examines the social context of 1990s blues, including issues like racial tensions and violence. Profiles contemporary artists like Booba Barnes, Scott Dunbar, Lonnie Pitchford and Son Thomas.

392. Oliver, Sylvester Walker, Jr. "African-American Music Traditions in Northeast Mississippi." PhD dissertation, University of Memphis, 1995.

Examines the role of religious and secular oral musical traditions in six African American communities of north-eastern Mississippi. The focus is fourfold: 1) an ethnography of the African American community; 2) the religious musical traditions; 3) the secular musical traditions (e.g. blues, string bands, fife and drum bands, and the fiddle and banjo traditions); and 4) a concise history of the Rust College Singers and their impact. Transcriptions and analyses of fourteen examples of religious and secular music.

393. Olsson, Bengt. *Memphis Blues and Jug Bands*. London: Studio Vista, 1970.

An investigation of blues, jug bands and medicine show musicians, including Robert Burse, Gus Cannon, "Furry" Lewis, Jim Jackson, the Memphis Jug Band and Frank Stokes. Not a detailed study, but provides some insights into the artists and their music. Appendices list Brunswick Recordings made in Memphis.

394. Oster, Henry. *Living Country Blues*. Detroit: Folklore Associates, 1969.

An important annotated collection of 230 blues recorded in Louisiana between 1955 and 1961, many of which were recorded in Angola State Penitentiary; arranged into nineteen categories, including farming, drinking, gambling, wandering, love, sex, imprisonment and more. Includes chapters on the definition, history and cultural context of the country blues. Primary focus is on literary and sociological aspects of country blues. Sixteen photographs, bibliography, title index, and the discography of performances by artists discussed in the book.

395. Ottenheimer, Harriet Joseph. "The Blues Tradition in St. Louis." *Black Music Research Journal* 9(2) (Fall 1989): 135–53.

Discusses the early blues scene in St Louis, and the city's role in the development of blues. Covers the influence of W.C. Handy, publication of the first scored twelve-bar blues, the transformation from ragtime to blues, the popularity of boogie-woogie style piano, and the comments and impact of Henry Townsend.

396. Palmer, Robert. *Deep Blues: A Musical and Cultural History of the Mississippi Delta*. New York: Penguin, 1982.

Covers the history of Mississippi Delta blues. The highlight of the book is the insider perspectives provided by Roosevelt "Booka" Barnes, Jessie Mae Hemphill, Jack Owens, Lonnie Pitchford, Bud Spres, Napoleon Strickland and others. They discuss their music, influences and ascent to popularity on a national and international level. The project is important because it focuses on guitars, mouth harps and full bands. Companion volume to a film directed by Robert Mugge.

397. Pearson, Barry Lee. "Appalachian Blues." *Black Music Research Journal* 23(1–2) (Spring/Fall 2003): 23–53.

Possibly the first essay on Appalachian blues. Discusses the history and evolution of blues in selected counties in Alabama, Georgia, Kentucky, North Carolina, South Carolina, Tennessee, Virginia and West Virginia. Includes comments from artists like Nap Turner, John Jackson, Etta Baker, Ida Cox, Lucille Bogan and Pink Anderson. Also discusses the race record industry and other topics.

398. ——. "The Life Story of the Blues Musician: An Analysis of the Traditions of Oral Self-Portrayal." PhD dissertation, Indiana University Press, 1977.

Investigates the ways in which tradition influences the oral self-portraits of black American musicians, primarily from Mississippi. Argues that these musicians have emulated a specific stereotyped role and lifestyle. The author examines life story as folklore and compares it to anthropological studies of personal documents and personal histories. Within this context, the stereotypical characteristics of the blues musician are described and the artist is shown to be aware that he is following a stereotype.

399. Pinkney, Cheryl Williams. "Cultural Implications of Indigenous Blues Music in the Mississippi Delta." EdD dissertation, Cleveland, MS: Delta State University, 2006.

Focuses on the blues phenomenon in the Mississippi Delta as it relates to culture, the benefits of culture, and educational curricula. Among the primary issues examined are the search for alternative, supplemental materials and methods of adding academic rigor to the curriculum, and the need for educators to use blues as a vehicle to spark interest and to enhance the educational experience. The study focused on four artist informants (*emic* participants) and four policy makers (*etic* participants).

400. Prevos, Andre J.M. "Four Decades of French Blues Research in Chicago: From the Fifties into the Nineties." *Black Music Research Journal* 12(1) (Spring 1992): 97–112.

Discusses the growing interest in blues history and research in French journalism since the 1950s. Characterizes the efforts and conclusions of French blues researchers and in Chicago. Jacques Demetre and Marcel Chauvard documented Chicago blues of the 1950s. Kurt

Mohr researched Chicago blues of the 1970s. Emmanuel Choisnel took photographs of many blues artists. Sebastian Danchin musician and scholar researched Chicago blues of the late 1970s. Jacques Lacava, cinematographer, musician and researcher was interested in Chicago blues of the 1980s. To this group of scholars, Prevos adds French blues musicians Marc Loison, Alain Françoise, Bernard Marie and Thierry Anquetil who went to Chicago to meet and interact with as many blues musicians as possible, and used what they learned in both their recordings and performances. In addition to their respective research and musical interests, Prevos also cites some of their most important fieldwork studies.

401. Rotella, Carlo. *Good With Their Hands: Bluesmen and Other Characters From the Rust Belt.* Berkeley: University of California Press, 2002.

An assessment of postindustrial society, the decline of "Rust Belt" cities, and the passing of a working class culture whose members were respected because they were "good with their hands." Presents connections and disconnections between post-industrial urban ethnic, historical and geographical sectors, regardless of present culture and condition. The chapter of interest here is about Buddy Guy and the Chicago blues scene. Other loosely connected chapters focus on the film *The French Connection* (1971) as an example of post-industrial crime, a female boxer from Erie, Pennsylvania, and efforts to restore the former home of boxing great Rocky Marciano.

402. Rowe, Mike. *Chicago Breakdown.* London: Edison Press, 1973.

A history of the 1940s and 1950s Chicago blues scene, specifically focused on the rise and fall of blues recording companies and the careers and styles of post-war artists. Discusses the urbanization of blues, Chicago blues of the 1930s, African American migration patterns, the Chicago club scene, and the influence of record companies like Chess on the careers of blues artists. Musicians discussed: Floyd Jones, Elmore James, Johnny Shines, Sunnyland Slim, Little Walter, Howlin' Wolf, Muddy Waters and Sonny Boy Williamson. Includes a list of Chicago R&B hits, 1945–59.

403. Rowe, Mike and Ronald Radano. *Chicago Blues: The City and the Music.* New York: Da Capo Press, 1981.

Covers the demographic changes and social issues that led to the development of Chicago blues. The migration of Mississippi Delta musicians to Chicago and the role of Chess and Jax record labels is chronicled. Numerous blues artists who worked in Chicago, on the south side and near-west side, are discussed: Big Bill Broonzy, Elmore James, John Lee Hooker, Tampa Red, Jimmy Reed, Otis Rush, Little

Walter, Junior Wells, Muddy Waters, Sonny Boy Williamson, Otis Spann, Eddie Taylor, Mighty Joe Young and more. Thorough coverage until around the mid-1970s; includes Billboard rating charts and a discography by artist.

404. Simas, Art. *Boston's Blues: Musicians' Profiles, History, Festivals and Radio Listings of Blues Music in Boston.* Bloomington, IN: 1stBooks Library (Author House), 2005.

In-depth coverage of the contemporary blues scene of greater Boston. Includes numerous interviews with musicians, blues disc jockeys and photographers, regional festival listings, radio stations and a concise history of the blues in Boston.

405. Spaulding, Norman W. "History of Black Oriented Radio in Chicago 1929–63." PhD dissertation, University of Illinois, 1981.

A cultural and historical analysis of black-oriented radio programming in Chicago between 1929 and 1963. Demonstrates how black radio became a major element in the changing culture of the black community. Argues that black-oriented radio influenced not only mainstream American radio broadcasting, but also America's musical traditions and styles, especially the changing blues traditions and the emergence of R&B and soul music.

406. Spencer, Jon Michael. "The Diminishing Rural Residue of Folklore in City and Urban Blues, Chicago 1915–50." *Black Music Research Journal* 12(1) (Spring 1992): 25–43.

Follows the dissemination of blues from rural south to urban north, and the subsequent decline of rural residue of folklore in city blues as it transformed into contemporary urban blues. Author argues that rural folkways that were integral to country blues were diminished in urban blues but never completely forgotten, because city and urban blues were the offspring of country blues, and reflected the conditioning of rural immigrants from the south to their new urban experience.

407. Tracy, Steven. *Going to Cincinnati: A History of the Blues in the Queen City.* Urbana: University of Illinois Press, 1993.

A chronology of the evolution of the African American community and blues in Cincinnati from the post-Civil War era to the present. Begins with a sixteen-page history of the city's African American community up to World War I; includes the author's definition of "what is the blues." Recordings, record company documents and interviews are used to construct insightful portraits of local artists like Sam "Stovepipe" Jones, Bob Coleman, Sweet Papa Tadpole, Kid

Coley, Big Ed Thompson and Robert Singleton, and blues pianists Pigmeat Jarrett, James Mays and Big Joe Duskin. Notes the importance of King Records and the careers and music of H-BOMB Ferguson and Albert Washington. Thoroughly researched; well written.

408. Wood, Roger. *Down in Houston: Bayou City Blues.* Austin: University of Texas Press, 2003.

Traces the history and influence of blues in Houston. The author interviewed "Gatemouth" Brown, Albert Collins, Johnny Copeland, Lightnin' Hopkins and many lesser known artists associated with Houston blues. Includes many descriptive photographs taken by James Fraher.

409. Worley, William S. *Beale Street: Crossroads of America's Music.* Lenexa, KS: Addax, 1998.

Covers the history and importance of Memphis's famed Beale Street in the development of blues, as an entertainment mecca that histori-cally attracted a myriad of African American musicians, from jug bands to blues musicians. In contemporary times, it is a place that attracts tourists to B.B. King's night club and to view the statue of W.C. Handy. Includes never-before-published photographs of artists like B.B. King, Martin Luther King and Elvis Presley.

## Global studies

410. Brunning, Bob. *Blues: The British Connection.* London: Helter Skelter Publishing, 2003.

The author, a former sideman with Savoy Brown and Fleetwood Mac, gives his perspective on the history and evolution of blues in the UK. Discusses the changes that took place after Muddy Waters and other American blues artists visited the UK in the 1950s, and the influence of the 1960s blues explosion on artists like The Animals, The Spencer Davis Group, Eric Clapton, Mick Jagger, Manfred Mann, John Mayall, and The Pretty Things. Discusses the pros and cons of white British bands working with visiting American blues musicians.

411. Coolen, Michael. "The Fodet: A Senegambian Origin for the Blues." *Black Perspective in Music* 10(1) (Spring 1982): 69–85.

Citing the few attempts to examine all possible connections between specific African traditions and the blues, the author suggests possible links between Africa and African American musical traditions. Discusses the Senegambia slave trade, the Wolof Xalam tradition, Senegambian retentions in the United States, and blues and the Fodet.

412. Makuluni, Dean Edison. "Narrating the Blues: Music and Discursive Strategies in Selected African-American, Afro-Caribbean and Black South African Fiction." PhD dissertation, University of Iowa, 1999.

A response to novelist Toni Morrison's call for criticism of her fiction and that of other black women to be judged on its own rather than in terms of the Anglo-American canon. Focuses on ways in which music provides myths of identity for literary texts, how music can authorize a novel historically, and how music can orient a work toward specific political ends. Studies texts that engage blues and jazz as expressive codes shared by black writers from the United States, the Caribbean and South Africa, arguing that the writers critiqued engage in acts of identity through the use of blues and their creative work.

413. Narvaez, Peter. "The Influences of Hispanic Music Cultures on African-American Blues Musicians." *Black Music Research Journal* 14(2) (Fall 1994): 203–25.

Portia Maultsby's theory of interruptions between African Americans and mainstream cultures is used to illustrate how such interactions affect musical creativity and musical identity, and then to draw conclusions about Hispanic influences on blues. Discusses these influences in Texas and Mexico, and in New Orleans, especially in the music of Professor Longhair and Jelly Roll Morton. Social history, blues lyrics, musical evidence and selected life histories reveal the musical interaction.

414. Schwartz, Roberta Freund. *How Britain Got the Blues: The Transmission and Reception of American Blues Style in the United Kingdom.* New York: Ashgate Publishing Co., 2007.

An in-depth study of how British youth first encountered the blues in the early 1960s. Significant insight on how critics influenced the artists and styles. The impact of blues on the music of Eric Clapton, John Mayall, The Rolling Stones and others is chronicled.

415. Wynn, Neil A., ed. *Cross the Water Blues: African American Music in Europe.* American Made Music Series. Jackson: University Press of Mississippi, 2007.

A unique collection of essays on jazz, spirituals, shuffle and orchestral music that examine the flow of African American music and musicians to Europe from slavery to the twentieth century. The essays use historical, musicological and philosophical perspectives and focus on the reception and influence of blues on British, French,

German and Dutch audiences. Includes documentation of previously unknown recordings and performances of African American musicians in Europe. The authors include Christopher G. Bakriges, Jeffrey Green, Bob Groom, Ranier Lotz, Paul Oliver and Neil Wynn.

## LITERATURE, CRITICISM AND LYRICS

416. Baker, Barbara Anne. "The Blues Aesthetic and the Making of American Identity in the Literature of the South." PhD dissertation, Auburn University, 1999.

Investigates the manner in which blues aesthetics are manifested in southern literature. Uses the theories of Ralph Ellison and Albert Murray, which espouse that blues is at the heart of African American vernacular tradition, and that blues has had an indelible impact on American culture and art. Concludes that the African American experience is diffused throughout southern literature regardless of the racial heritage of the author. Uses selected works by Charles W. Chestnutt and Zora Neale Hurston to discuss how African American and non-African American cultural attributes can be fused to create an identity.

417. Baker, Houston. *Blues, Ideology and Afro-American Literature: A Vernacular Theory.* Chicago: University of Chicago Press, 1985.

Baker calls for a decanonization and decentering of African American literature and its critical discourse. Engaging and scholarly, this work situates blues as a vernacular paradigm of American culture and relates blues themes and attitudes to both American literary and critical history and to African American expressive culture. Uses anthropology, Marxist criticism, and semiotics to deconstruct selected writings by Paul Laurence Dunbar, Ralph Ellison, Frederick Douglass, Harriet Jacobs (Linda Brent) and Richard Wright.

418. Burns, Loretta Susie. "A Stylistic Analysis of Blues Lyrics." PhD dissertation, University of Michigan, 1977.

Posits that the patterns of imagery, theme and other structural elements of blues are controlled by situation and response. The major structural elements include flexibility, fatalism or optimism, objectification of personal experience, irony and expression. The author concludes that the two major themes in blues, love and wandering, are conceived according to the thematic dictates of the underlying framework, and organized around concepts of ambiguity and opposition. In addition, she asserts that the blues perspective demonstrates detachment, restraint and a controlled acceptance of absurdity.

419. Dougan, John M. "Two Steps From The Blues: Creating Discourse and Constructing Canons in Blues Criticism." PhD dissertation, College of William and Mary, 2001.

Examines three phenomena: the development of blues criticism in its various forms from the 1920s to the 1990s, the role of blues criticism in the emergence of a blues discourse and history, and the codification of a blues canon. He analyzes blues discourse—a cadre of complex relationships that exist between writers, musicians, fans, record collectors and independent entrepreneurs—primarily as the creation of critics, historians, musicologists. Of special note is his analysis of women blues writers, their rhetorical approach, and the impact they have had on decentering the male-authored blues canon and recreating contemporary blues discourse.

420. Duncan, Christopher M. "The Blues Voice of Houston Baker, Jr. as Political Theory: An (Other) American Paradigm." *New Political Science* 22(2) (June 2000): 231–48.

Duncan decodes Baker's theoretical perspective about the distinctive language that African Americans share, and the special circumstances that have developed that perspective. He discusses both the assumptions and political theory behind Baker's transfiguration of American cultural discourse.

421. Evans, Howell. "The Literature of the Blues and Black Cultural Studies." PhD dissertation, Gainesville: University of Florida, 2004.

This research is heavily invested in cultural studies, and focuses on the use of blues in advertising, corporate sponsorship, festivals and tourism. Investigates how blues serve as a signifier of authenticity and anti-commercialism (even when it is being used to create a marketing image for companies like Volkswagen), and how the discourse surrounding the blues create colonial subjects and stereotypes. The author concludes that blues is best thought of as a form of colonial discourse in which matters of literacy, race and sexuality are negotiated.

422. Hall, Chekita Trennel. "The Blues as a Paradigm of Cultural Resistance in the Works of Gloria Naylor." PhD dissertation, Bowling Green State University, 1995.

Explores the various ways that African American author Gloria Naylor depicts the liberating potential of the complex position occupied by black women in America. Focuses on various strategies of resistance that Naylor developed to circumvent the negative images imposed upon black women by a racist society. The author argues that Naylor's strategies of resistance are grounded in an indisputably black aesthetic: the blues. Furthermore, she defines the blues as a paradigm of cultural resistance which, in turn, enables her to explore black female cultural resistance within a black aesthetic.

423. Heldrich, Philip Joseph. "Big City Blues: A Novel With a Critical Preface Exploring Blues Form and Theme in Contemporary Literature." PhD dissertation, Oklahoma University Press, 1997.

Studies the relationship between the African American tradition of the blues and contemporary writing. Discusses specific stylistic and thematic qualities of blues novels that serve as a self-conscious, self-critical voice to emphasize themes of improvisation and survival. Also explores the story of Chicagoan Mark Callahan who uses vamping and riffing to survive the streets of his Wrigleyville neighborhood.

424. Kitts, Lenore Lee. "Lay it Down: The Specter of Slave Music in Toni Morrison's *Beloved.*" PhD dissertation, University of California, Berkeley, 2006.

Discusses the blues, spirituals, lullabies and work songs that fill the 1987 novel *Beloved* by Toni Morrison. Provides information on how Morrison uses music to provide insight into historical consciousness, how she tropes and models her prose style, how she recreates the genre's participatory style, and more.

425. McGeachy, Margaret Gillian. "Lonesome Words: The Vocal Poetics of the Old English Lament and the African American Blues Song." PhD dissertation, University of Toronto, 1999.

Investigates the similarity between the tenth-century Old English lament and the twentieth-century African American blues song, and their use of emotive expression of personal and social struggle. Argues that both voices are immediate yet elusive and truthful but mysterious. Juxtaposes the texts of selected Old English songs and blues songs and their respective critical receptions to determine the features that characterize the vocal poetics of each. Assumes that the poet of laments and the blues singer both optimize specific musical features such as the first-person speaker and certain formulae to simulate live performance within the text, and concludes that both are recontextualized by the anthology and, as a result, are reinterpreted in a new setting.

426. Page, Yolanda Williams. "'I Won't be Blue Always: Music as Past in August Wilson's *Joe Turner's Come and Gone, Ma Rainey's Black Bottom, The Piano Lesson,* and *Fences.*" PhD dissertation, Louisiana State University and Agricultural and Mechanical College, 2001.

Illustrates how August Wilson's earliest plays, specifically *Joe Turner's Come and Gone, Ma Rainey's Black Bottom, The Piano Lesson*, and *Fences*, reference and reflect the disabling impact of the slave past and offer strategies to overcome the effects of slavery. Using music as a vehicle, the author demonstrates that the past can become an enabling mechanism for acceptance and reconciliation. Also included, an overview of Wilson's life, a history of African American theater, a lengthy discussion of each play, transcription of a personal interview, a list of recommendations for further research, and more.

427. Prince, Valerie Renee Sweeney. "Finding a Place of My Own: Home and the Paradox of Blues Expressiveness." PhD dissertation, University of Michigan, 1998.

This research was predicated on the belief that, in post Great Migration literature, the creation of a home represented the creation of a safe place in which to nurture a threatened people. The author postulates that when home fails to be that protective space, blues is evoked as a metaphorical shelter offering safety and rest.

428. Raussert, Wilfried. "Blues-memory and Jazz-vision: The Historical Imagination in Selected Twentieth-century African American Novels." PhD dissertation, University of Mississippi, 1994.

Researches the influences of blues and jazz upon the imagination of African American writers from the early twentieth century to the present. The influence is characterized by continuity and change, and can be divided into five basic forms: the impact of music on literary form and theme; use of music as a paradigm for understanding historical time; blues and jazz cultural roots as related to novels; the presence of musical content and character; and the importance of blues and jazz in African American culture in general. Analyzes selected novels of Ralph Ellison, Langston Hughes, Toni Morrison and Ishmael Reed, and concludes that blues and jazz not only informs the historical and social visions of the novelists, they also shape the diction, syntax and literary structure, especially in the works of more recent authors.

429. Taft, Michael. *Blues Lyric Formula*. New York: Routledge, 2006.

A structural analysis of the formulae used in the composition of blues lyrics commercially recorded by African Americans prior to World War II. Includes a detailed account of how blues artists created a commercially acceptable form of blues, and the rules inherent in formulaic structures of blues.

430. ——. *Talking to Myself: Blues Lyrics, 1921–1942*. New York: Routledge, 2005.

A compendium of blues lyrics by artists representing the classic era of blues. The collection includes over 2,000 lyrics transcribed from the original recordings and covering a myriad of topics. Among the topics covered are gender issues, love, illness, employment and work, politics and other issues that characterize the African American experience. The author includes the text from both famous and obscure artists, including KoKomo Arnold, Blind Blake, Leadbelly, Son House, Skip James, Robert Johnson, Blind Lemon Jefferson, Charley Patton and dozens more.

431. Tribbett, Marcus Charles. "Lyrical Struggles: Hegemony and Resistance in English Broadside Ballads and African-American Blues." PhD dissertation, Washington State University, 1996.

The study is concerned with the meanings of verbal and visual signs used to reflect and represent the position of various groups and individuals. Focuses on the intersection of popular cultural voices with the dominant ideologies of class, race and gender formation, using case studies from English broadside ballads and African American blues to show how this has operated historically in Western cultures. Outlines the historical and cultural contexts of the ballads and argues that balladeers had leeway to resist structures of authority in the sixteenth and seventieth centuries. Discusses the cultural contexts of African American blues to 1940, and devotes chapter five to "Memphis Minnie" Douglas, who challenged white-supremacist ideology.

## PHOTOGRAPHY

432. Charters, Ann and Samuel Barclay Charters. *Blues Faces: A Portrait of the Blues.* New York: Godine, 2000.

A collection of blues portraits, including some taken from Samuel Charters' work, depicting numerous artists; many of the images have been used on book jackets and record labels. Samuel Charters adds commentary to the photographs.

433. Connor, Anthony and Robert Neff, photographer. *Blues (Music/ Photography).* Boston: Godine, 1975.

A collection of photographs of many major artists, taken during performances and recording sessions.

434. Coughlin, Jack and Steven Tracy. *The Blues: 26 Portraits.* New York: Rep House LLC, 1997.

The twenty-six photographs by Coughlin depict a myriad of individuals, situations and social context issues, including Blind Lemon

Jefferson, Son House, B.B. King, Bessie Smith and Sonny Boy Williamson. Tracy provides the commentary.

435. Cowdery, Charles K. and Raeburn Flerlage. *Blues Legends*. New York: Gibbs Smith, 1995.

Contains twenty photo-biographies that trace blues history from the Delta and Arkansas, through the independent strains that developed in the south-east and south-west, to its influence on rock and roll in the 1960s and 1970s. Featured artists are B.B. King, John Lee Hooker, Memphis Minnie, Muddy Waters, T-Bone Walker and fifteen others.

436. Day, Lisa, ed., and Raeburn Flerlage, photographer. *Chicago Blues as Seen from the Inside – The Photographs of Raeburn Flerlage*. London: ECW Press, 2000.

A collection by one of the most respected photographers of Chicago blues. His photographs have graced the covers of magazines and recordings from the most important blues labels, like Chess, Delmark, Prestige and Testament. The photographs were shot in concert performances, club shows, interviews and studio sessions, and include artists like Bobby "Blue" Bland, B.B. King, James Cotton, John Lee Hooker, Son House, Otis Spann, Little Walter, Howlin' Wolf, Martha Reeves and Jackie Wilson.

437. PoKempner, Marc and Wolfgang Schorlau. *Down at Theresa's – Chicago Blues: The Photographs of Marc PoKempner*. Illustrated. New York: Prestel, 2000.

Black and white photographs capture the atmosphere at Theresa's Lounge in Chicago in the late 1960s. The images depict the working-class people who frequented the lounge.

438. Raccuglia, David. *Darker Blues*. Oxford, MS: Fat Possum Records, 1993.

Features the work of photographer Raccuglia and classic Fat Possum photographs. The photographs reflect the spirit of the label and depict authentic images of real blues culture. The book is accompanied by two CDs featuring Solomon Burke, Junior Kimbrough and other artists.

439. Watermann, Dick, Bonnie Raitt and Peter Guralnick. *Between Midnight and Day: The Last Unpublished Blues Archive*. New York: Da Capo, 2003.

A collection of rare images, supplemented with the author's commentary, of 120 blues artists. The authors offer their perspectives on artists like Chuck Berry, Ray Charles, Bob Dylan, Buddy Guy, John Lee Hooker, Lightnin' Hopkins, "Mississippi" John Hurt, Skip James, Janis Joplin, B.B. King, Fred MacDowell, Bonnie Raitt, Otis Rush, Roosevelt Sykes, Big Mama Thornton, Sippie Wallace, Muddy Waters, Junior Wells, Bukka White, Howlin' Wolf and many more. The book also includes contributions by Peter Guralnick, Chris Murray and Bonnie Raitt.

440. Withers, Ernest C. and Daniel Wolf. *The Memphis Blues Again: Six Decades of Memphis Music Photographs.* New York: Viking Press, 2001.

A continuation of Withers' fifty-year photographic documentation of the Memphis music scene in and around Beale Street. Many historically important photographs—taken in auditoriums, churches, dancehalls, recording sessions and the streets of Memphis—of artists from the 1940s, 1950s and 1960s who either lived or recorded in Memphis, including James Brown, Ray Charles, Sam Cooke, Aretha Franklin, Al Green, W.C. Handy, Isaac Hayes, Helen Humes, Ike and Tina Turner, Elvis Presley, Otis Redding and Muddy Waters. Wolf selected the photographs and wrote the introduction and informative captions.

## RELIGION

441. Cone, James H. *The Spirituals and the Blues.* New York: Seabury, 1972.

A provocative sociocultural assessment of the meaning and depth of African American music as expressed in blues and spirituals. Proceeding from the notion that blues and spirituals are a powerful tool in the black struggle for survival, the author asserts that a deeper level of experience that transcends objective historical research is available only to those who share the spirit and participate in the faith of those who created the songs. He believes the world of thought that underlines the meaning, role and function of slave songs has not yet been analyzed thoroughly; blues and spirituals flow from the same bedrock of experience, and so share the same mood and ethos.

442. McCarthy, S. Margaret. "The Afro-American Sermon and the Blues." *Black Perspective in Music* 4(2) (Fall 1976): 269–78.

Discusses the influence of the church on the lives and the music of African Americans. Argues that the influence of the church can also be seen in the secular music of African Americans, especially in blues. A comparison of biblical quotes and blues texts demonstrates connections in language and meaning.

443. Nichols, Stephen J. *Getting the Blues: What Blues Music Teaches Us About Suffering and Salvation.* Grand Rapids, MI: Brazos, 2008.

Illustrates how blues provides insight into biblical narrative. He weaves biblical stories together with the lives of blues musicians, and demonstrates how blues teaches about sin, suffering, alienation and worship. Also discusses the Psalms, some of the prophets and the writings of Paul to support his position.

444. Spencer, Jon Michael. *Blues and Evil.* Knoxville: University of Tennessee Press, 1993.

Revises the traditional perspectives on the mythology and theology found in the poetry of the blues. Uses the work of Amiri Baraka, James Cone and Julio Finn to underscore the contention that academia has consistently misinterpreted the hidden cultural messages inherent in blues because it insists on forcing the interpretation of blues into existing categories used by European and Christian scholarly traditions. In doing so, Spencer demonstrates that blues are not wholly European or Christian, but a blend of European and West African elements. Emphasizes how important it is to properly contextualize blues before it can be viewed as an integrated statement of religion and social philosophy.

445. Spencer, Jon Michael, ed. *Sacred Music of the Secular City.* Durham, NC: Duke University Press, 1992.

A special edition of *Black Sacred Music: A Journal of Theomusicology.* Includes essays by scholars like Dwight D. Andrews, James Cone, Michael Eric Dyson, Rod Gruver, William T. Turner and Cornell West. Essay topics include blues, jazz, soul and rap (with a strong religious and philosophical perspective), and artists like Duke Ellington, Marvin Gaye, Madonna, Bruce Springsteen, the Impressions and the Temptations.

# II

# Funk, rhythm and blues, and soul resources

## GENERAL

446. Bennett, Bobby and Sarah Smith. *The Ultimate Soul Trivia Book: 501 Questions and Answers About Motown, Rhythm and Blues, and More.* New York: Citadel Press, 2000.

The book is designed to challenge and inform music fans about persons involved in teaching and researching the genres. The hundreds of questions focus on top R&B and soul singers from 1950 to around 2000.

447. Billi, Michael. *Rock 'N' Roll Jews: Judaic Traditions in Literature, Music, and Art.* Syracuse: Syracuse University Press, 2001.

Billi argues that Jews were not only involved with the business side of American popular music, but the creative and promotion sides as well. Inherent in his discourse is the help that Jews provided to African American musicians. Specifically, Chess Records recorded African American musicians like Chuck Berry, Bo Diddley and Muddy Waters when no one else would. Discusses Alan Freed's role in promoting R&B, and extols the importance of Jewish composers Jerry Leiber and Mike Stoller's compositions to rhythm and blues music and musicians. Also discusses the creative contributions of Bob Dylan, Leonard Cohen, Lou Reed and Paul Simon to American popular music.

448. Clark, Jim Logan. *Temples of Sound.* New York: Chronicle Books, 2003.

Profiles of the legendary studios where some of the most popular funk, jazz, pop and soul music was made. They discuss Sun Records, Stax and Rudy Van Gelder's studio where some John Coltrane and Miles Davis sessions were recorded. Includes interviews of the musicians and producers. Foreword by Quincy Jones.

449. Davis, Robert. "Who Got da Funk? An Etymophony of Funk Music From the 1950s to 1979." PhD dissertation, University of Montreal, 2006.

This study deals with the etymophony (origins) of funk's development through an investigation of its sonic text by creating a conceptual framework for understanding the process of genre formation. Looks at how the network of intertextual musical relationships, situated within their sociocultural context, act as points of departure for stylistic and genre formation. The author asserts that a musicological investigation is necessary to avoid the myth of personalities and sociocultural constructs that are not directly related to the complexity of the intertextual process, and that this type of investigation will enable us to reexamine the contributions of individual artists and the social context that sustains music making, and more.

450. George, Nelson. *Post-Soul Nation: The Explosive, Contradictory, Triumphant, and Tragic 1980s as Experienced by African Americans.* New York: Viking, 2004.

The author posits that the 1980s represent a transitional departure from the gains of the Civil Rights era and music of James Brown when compared with tangible gains of the post-soul years. Presents the African American community as amorphous; focuses on cultural and political figures like Michael Jordan, Spike Lee, Eddie Murphy, Clarence Thomas, Mike Tyson and Oprah Winfrey. Explores the political potency of Louis Farrakhan and Jessie Jackson, and the generational change in the arts as espoused by Toni Morrison, Jean-Michael Basquiat, Vernon Reid and Run-DMC.

451. ———. *The Death of Rhythm and Blues.* Reprint, New York: Penguin, 2003.

Chronicles the rise and fall of "race music," its eventual transformation to rhythm and blues, and its subsequent dilution into crossover music. He summarizes the contributions of artists like Chuck Berry, James Brown, Aretha Franklin and Michael Jackson. A provocative discussion of the links between black social and economic affairs, changes in contemporary black culture, and how white culture has changed black music.

452. Kamin, Jonathan Liff. "Rhythm and Blues in White America: Rock and Roll as Acculturation and Perceptual Learning." PhD dissertation, Princeton University, 1976.

Views rock and roll as the result of the acculturation of white musical standards with African American rhythm and blues, a phenomenon facilitated by perceptual learning of black music by white audiences. Changes in rock and roll are seen as the contrasts between African American musical traditions and Euro-American musical traditions, and addresses white versions of "cover songs" as a style intermediate between the two cultures. Uses theoretical perspectives by Neil Leonard and Richard Peterson, and in the latter case views black musical elements as acceptable but subordinate to European musical elements.

453. Moorefield, Virgil Edwin. "From the Illusion of Reality to the Reality of Illusion: The Changing Role of the Producer in the Pop Recording Studio." PhD dissertation, Princeton University, 2001.

Examines the transformation of the recording studio over the last fifty years, and argues that the role and function of the producer has expanded from that of merely a technician to encompass conceptual and artistic issues, as evidenced by the careers of producers like Phil Spector and George Martin. Also discussed, musical forms and production on recordings from the 1960s, such as the Beach Boys' "Good Vibrations" and the contributions of Brian Eno. This work is included here because of George Martin and Phil Spector producing R&B, and the importance of the producer/engineer/artist in disco, hip hop and electronic music.

454. Neal, Mark Anthony. *Songs in the Key of Black Life: A Rhythm and Blues Nation.* New York: Routledge, 2003.

The author's premise is that contemporary African American musicians use a cultural memory to build on the musical traditions of the past and suggests connections between modern black musical genres and the griot tradition of West Africa. Posits that black music must be considered within the lived realities of black communities, and that black songsters narrate the real and perceived experiences of the black race. The section titled "rhythm" discusses African Americans' use of music to shape racial identity. The second section, "and blues," focuses on publicly relevant spaces—black community cultural spaces and theaters—in which debates can take place and racial identity can be negotiated.

455. ———. *Soul Babies: Black Popular Culture and the Post-Soul Aesthetic.* New York: Routledge, 2002.

Focuses on the last three decades of black images and representations with an emphasis on African American popular culture since the Black Power and Civil Rights movements. Introduces the concept of the "post-soul aesthetic" to black cultural criticism. In addition, explores a myriad of issues and values by discussing a wide range of influential individuals, from Sanford and Son to Snoop Dogg.

456. ———.*What the Music Said: Black Popular Music and Black Public Culture.* New York: Routledge, 1999.

An interpretation of the cultural and political divide that has evolved from African Americans' two separate but overlapping lives: the first life involving the organic connection to the formal and informal black institutions like juke joints, the second involving the connection between black cultural production and mass consumerism in which black agency is dominated by commercial interests. A special discussion of consumer economics, hip hop and black rhetoric as the heartbeat of inner-city life and ideology. Presents a convincing argument regarding the history of African American music's interaction with American culture at large and a tale of both diminished and distorted returns.

457. Phinney, Kevin. *Souled America: How Black Music Transformed White Culture.* New York: Billboard Books, 2007.

For the general reader; traces the history of race relations in America as evidenced through music, including blues, country, gospel, jazz, rhythm and blues, rap and other genres. Includes perspectives of gospel music scholar Horace Boyer and Ziggy Marley of reggae fame. Discusses Eminem as a white performer in black face and "sepia Sinatras" like Johnny Mathias. Focuses on Mariah Carey, analyzes the singing style of Nat "King" Cole, and includes interviews of Ray Charles, B.B. King, Sly Stone, Bonnie Raitt, Donna Summer and more.

458. Redd, Lawrence N. *Rock is Rhythm and Blues: The Impact of Mass Media.* East Lansing: Michigan State University Press, 1972.

Attempts to illustrate the author's contention that R&B and rock are the same. Covers the history of mass media's impact upon the musical culture of black America. Traces the evolution of blues, its marriage to jazz and the birth of R&B. In addition, the book contains several interviews with "soul poets" Jerry Butler, Dave Clark, Arthur "Big Boy" Crudup, B.B. King, Brownie McGhee and Jessie Whitaker.

459. Shapiro, Peter. *Turn the Beat Around: The Secret of Disco.* New York: Faber and Faber, 2006.

Although the primary focus here is disco, the author discusses the impact and influences of artists like James Brown, Donna Summer and Barry White. Discusses the clubs, DJs and producers that shaped the disco sound and traces the evolution of the music from its inception in the New York City boroughs and gay clubs in Manhattan, to its mainstream acceptance throughout America. Ties the music to an emerging and empowered African American community and the gay freedom movement.

460. Straw, William G. "Popular Music as Cultural Commodity: The American Recorded Music Industries, 1976–85." PhD dissertation, McGill University, 1990.

An analysis of the historical change within those cultural industries involved in the dissemination and production of popular music. Researches the relationship between US recording and radio industries between 1976 and 1985; investigates the manner in which crises arise and are resolved, and the emergence and integration of disco and New Wave in music-related industries. The role of aesthetics in creating audiences for different genres is also examined.

461. Sykes, Charles E. "A Conceptual Model for Analyzing Rhythmic Structure in African-American Popular Music." DME dissertation, Indiana University, 1992.

Identifies, describes and categorizes rhythmic components of African American popular music and proposes a theoretical framework for defining general principles of rhythmic organization; also determines the implications of this analytical study for music education. The original thesis was that musical structure is related to its relevant sociocultural context. Analyzes twenty-four commercial recordings of R&B and soul music from 1949 to 1979.

462. Werner, Craig Hansen. *A Change is Gonna Come: Music, Race and the Soul of America*, revised edn. Ann Arbor: University of Michigan Press, 2006.

A comprehensive assessment of the connection between music and race in America. In sixty-five concise chapters, traces gospel, blues and jazz "impulses" through American, British and Jamaican music, and demonstrates how music produced under oppressive conditions has become an integral part of contemporary urban music. Of special note is his discussion of how hip hop filled the musical vacuum left when disco faded out. Explores the connection between music and race by deconstructing the relationship between Martin Luther King, Jr's dream and the music of Motown, Public Enemy's disagreements with a "Reaganized" America, and Aretha Franklin's place in the 1960s Black Power movement.

## REFERENCES

463. Danchin, Sebastian. *Encyclopedia du Rhythm and Blues et da la Soul.* Paris: Fayard, 2002.

In French. Numerous biographies of artists and executives, and discussions of other topics germane to the history, evolution and dissemination of R&B and soul music. Coverage by the author.

464. Everett, Walter. *Expression in Pop-Rock Music: Critical and Analytical Essays.* Second edn. New York: Routledge, 2007.

A collection of critical essays on a variety of popular and rock musical topics. The numerous scholars use a wide variety of cultural, social and stylistic approaches and methods to analyze the text of songs by artists like Tori Amos, James Brown, Genesis and Frank Zappa, to name a few. Of particular importance is the variety of ways in which he demonstrates how phrases and sections of songs, including R&B, can be combined melodically, harmonically and by rhythmic invention. He references numerous songs, including those by Motown artists like The Supremes and the Temptations. This edition includes three new essays that cover musical changes that have occurred since the first edition, including the rise of hip hop.

465. Given, Dave. *The Dave Given Rock 'n' Roll Stars Handbook: Rhythm and Blues Artists and Groups.* Miami: Exposition Press of Florida, 1980.

Contains numerous profiles of individuals and groups who achieved stardom in rock and roll and rhythm and blues. Profiles accompanied by extensive discographies.

466. Gulla, Bob. *Icons of R&B and Soul: An Encyclopedia of the Artists Who Revolutionized Rhythm.* 2 vols. Westport, CT: Greenwood Press, 2007.

The two-volume survey examines the contributions and innovations of twenty-four R&B and soul artists. Special emphasis on their contributions to the history and evolution of their genres, the impact of the styles on American culture, and how that impact is manifested in contemporary politics, trends and social issues. Entries contain biographical information history on hit recordings, the social context of the time and a discography. Artists covered include James Brown, Ruth Brown, Ray Charles, Sam Cooke, Fats Domino, Aretha Franklin, Etta James, Curtis Mayfield, Smokey Robinson, the Supremes, the Temptations, Ike and Tina Turner, Otis Redding, Stevie Wonder, and British recording artist Dusty Springfield. Also includes information on Berry Gordy and Motown records, and Kenneth Gamble and Leon Huff of Philadelphia International records.

467. Larkin, Colin. *The Virgin Encyclopedia of R&B and Soul.* New York: Virgin Publishing, 1998.

Covers numerous individuals and topics that focus on productivity and accomplishments. Useful information on individuals, groups and styles; however, there are occasional errors in the discographical information (e.g. when referring to a person/group like Archie Bell and the Drells [sic]).

468. Rosalsky, Mitch. *Encyclopedia of Rhythm and Blues and Doo-Wop Vocal Groups.* Metuchen, NJ: Scarecrow Press, 2002.

Gathers historical data that addresses the different R&B and doo-wop groups from multiple perspectives. Covers individuals and groups, and topics like individual members' stints with groups, the geographical roots of members, background information, and provides discographical information. Entries are organized alphabetically and include obscure groups like the Altairs, Goldentones, the Crests and Five Satins.

469. Talevski, Nick. *The Unofficial Encyclopedia of the Rock and Roll Hall of Fame.* Westport, CT: Greenwood Press, 1998.

Examination of the Rock and Roll Hall of Fame selection process. Includes a review of the annual induction ceremony and provides career biographies of 150 inductees, who include artists, producers, record company founders and DJs: Alan Freed, Hank Ballard, Booker T and the MGs, James Brown, Ruth Brown, Leonard Chess, the Coasters, Drifters, Bo Diddley, Marvin Gaye, Little Willie John, Aretha Franklin, Frankie Lymon, Leiber and Stoller, Clyde McPhatter, Smokey Robinson, Alan Toussaint, the Soul Stirrers, Stevie Wonder and many more.

470. Tee, Ralph. *Who's Who in Soul Music.* New York: Weidenfeld and Nicholson, 1991.

Comprehensive and thorough listing of numerous soul artists, writers, producers, arrangers, instrumentalists and significant industry figures, with birth and death dates, musical style and influence, and more. Entries cover the "Bird groups" (e.g. the Orioles, the Cardinals, the Flamingos, the Penguins, the Crows), as well as artists associated with Atlantic, Motown, Stax and Philadelphia Soul music.

471. Vernon, Paul. *African-American Blues, Rhythm and Blues, Gospel and Zydeco on Film and Video.* New York: Ashgate Publishing, 1999.

An important reference book; contains details of numerous films and videos that deal with blues, rhythm and blues, gospel and Zydeco.

472. Whitburn, Joel. *The Billboard Book of Top 40 R&B and Hip-Hop Hits*. North Hollywood, CA: Billboard, 2006.

Offers comprehensive information on the most popular R&B and hip hop songs and artists to be listed on Billboard's Top 40 charts from 1942 to 2004. Entries include artists like The Ink Spots, Roy Brown, Ray Charles, Fats Domino to Kurtis Blow, Grandmaster Flash and the Furious Five.

## AUTOBIOGRAPHIES AND BIOGRAPHIES

### Arthur Alexander

473. Younger, Richard. *Get a Shot of Rhythm and Blues: The Arthur Alexander Story*. Tuscaloosa: University of Alabama Press, 2000.

A biography of the singer and songwriter whose songs influenced many 1960s rock musicians, including the tune "Get a Shot of Rhythm and Soul." Covers Alexander's successes and influences, his failures, and the sadder time of this obscure artist.

### Ashanti

474. Torres, Jennifer. *Ashanti*. Hockessin, DE: Mitchell Lane, 2006.

For younger readers. Geared toward grades 9–12; a concise biography covers her life from the early years in New York, her meeting and collaboration with P. Diddy, her name change and rise to musical success.

475. Walters, Rosa. *Ashanti*. Broomall: Mason Crest, 2007.

Traces the life and success of Ashanti Shequolya Douglass from her Glen Cove, New York roots to her Grammy-award debut album *Ashanti*, other albums and hits. Mentions her discovery and signing by P. Diddy to Bad Boy Records at the age of 14, her athletic accomplishments, her ability to compose songs, her contract with other labels, and more.

### Jack Ashford

476. Ashford, Jack. *Motown: The View From the Bottom*. West Sussex, UK: Bank House Books, 2005.

Discusses his life, musical success, relationships and his participation as a sideman on many Motown recordings. Of special note is the information on his relationship with the legendary Funk Brothers, the Motown in-house rhythm section that was so integral in the creation of the Motown sound. Includes anecdotes about Motown stars, recording situations and being scouted to join Motown by Marvin Gaye.

### Nicholas Ashford and Valerie Simpson

477. Norment, Lynn. "Ashford and Simpson." *Ebony,* February 1979, 136.

Focuses on both their musical career and life as husband and wife. Includes details of their early years in the church and their subsequent rise to musical success. Offers in-depth coverage of their songwriting career, including composing for Warner Brothers and Glover records, and for artists like Ray Charles, Chaka Kahn, Marvin Gaye, Quincy Jones, Tammi Terrell and many others.

### Erykah Badu

478. Badu, Erykah. *Erykah Badu-Baduizm.* Milwaukee: Hal Leonard, 1999.

A concise biography with lyrics and music of 14 songs from her 1997 solo album *Baduizm.* The songs include "On and On," "Appletree," "Certainly," "4 Leaf Clover," "No Love," "Sometimes," and more.

479. McIver, Joel. *Erykah Badu: The First Lady of Neo Soul.* London: Sanctuary Publishing, 2002.

Covers her life from her Dallas, Texas roots, home life, early exposure to the theatrical productions of her mother, Kollen Maria Gipson, studies at Grambling University, and her eventual success and status as an icon of the neo-soul movement.

### Lavern Baker

480. N.A. "Tweedle Dee Girl." *Ebony,* April 1956, 106.

Follows Baker's life from obscurity as a blues singer to immense success as a pop singer. Mentions her economic success (making $75,000 per year) and covers her recording of several of her own compositions, including "That's All I Need," "So Long," "Fire," and "Can't Hold Out Any Longer."

## Florence Ballard

481. N.A. "Ex-Supreme Talks." *Ebony*, February 1969, 83.

An interview with former Supreme Florence Ballard. She discusses Motown records, Diana Ross and Mary Wilson, her departure from the group, her replacement Cindy Birdsong, her recordings since leaving the Supremes, and her new family life with husband Thomas Chapman.

482. Benjaminson, Peter. *The Lost Supreme: The Life of Dreamgirl Florence Ballard*. Chicago: Lawrence Hill Books, 2008.

Attempts to resurrect the reputation of Ballard who left the Supremes and descended into legal difficulties with Motown and a battle with alcohol. This interview, just a year before her death in 1976, traces her life from her drop-out years, the impact of rape, joining the Supremes, and loss of money through questionable contracts. He also discusses her unscrupulous managers, costly clothes, feud with Diana Ross and more.

## Al Bell

483. Person-Lynn, Kwaku. "Insider Perspectives on the American Afrikan Popular Music Industry and Black Radio." In *California Soul: Music of African Americans in the West*, eds Jacqueline C. DjeDje and Eddie S. Meadows, pp. 179–213. Berkeley: University of California Press, 1998.

Covers the careers of Al Bell and Pam Robinson. Bell was national director of promotions, national sales manager, executive vice-president, and eventual owner and board chairman of Stax records; the article covers his career before, during and after his Stax years, contributions to the music, Stax and Motown musical philosophies, Stax concerts in Los Angeles and more. The interview with Pam Robinson, program manager of KGFJ radio, focuses on black radio in Los Angeles, 1980–87, and offers information on KGFJ, KACE, playlists, formatting, rotation, sales, ratings and more.

## Chuck Berry

484. Berry, Chuck. *Chuck Berry: The Autobiography*. New York: Random House, 1989.

In this candid and honest portrayal, Berry discusses everything from his invention of the "duck walk," his early years in segregated St

Louis, his recording career at Chess Records, sexual adventures, legal issues and time in prison, and details of his recording sessions. Includes a discography and filmography.

485. Chapman, Deborah. *Chuck Berry*. London: Music Sales, 1997.

A discussion of his life and musical contributions, influence upon other artists, life in St Louis, legal issues including prison sentences and a tax evasion problem, his career with Chess Records and more.

486. Collis, John. *Chuck Berry: The Biography*. London: Aurum Press, 2002.

Interviews with family members and people who worked with him delve into the truth about Berry's life in St Louis. Important events in his life and career are covered, from stints in prison, recordings, the integration of his 1950s audiences, his recordings with Chess records, crossover appeal, tax evasion, compositions, and his impact on European audiences and on groups like the Rolling Stones.

487. Pegg, Bruce. *Brown Eyed Handsome Man: The Life and Hard Times of Chuck Berry*. New York: Routledge, 2006.

Chronicles Berry's life from his early years growing up in segregated St Louis to his successes and failures throughout his career. His achievements and failures at Chess Records, legal problems and rise to international fame are discussed. The author also examines Berry's recordings, business acuity, and levels scathing criticism at some of Berry's activities.

488. Reese, Krista. *Chuck Berry: Mr. Rock 'n' Roll*. Saline, MI: Proteus, 1982.

Traces Berry's roots and the beginning of his career in St Louis, and touches upon issues like his introduction to music, early encounters with the law, career with Chess Records, success in both black and white communities, and influence upon other musicians.

489. Rothwell, Fred. *Long Distance Information: Chuck Berry's Recording Legacy*. Upper Poppleton, York, UK: Music Mentor Books, 2001.

A detailed analysis of every recording that Berry made, stories about his famous compositions, full session details, and a listing of his key American and British vinyl and CD releases, and TV and film appearances. Includes a concise overview of his life, career and influences.

## Black Rock Coalition

490. Mahon, Maureen. *Right to Rock: The Black Rock Coalition and the Cultural Politics of Race*. Durham: Duke University Press, 2004.

Important questions about the power and limits of racially influenced aesthetics in social, artistic and political contexts are discussed, focusing on the struggles of black rock and roll bands such as Screaming Headless Toros, Bad Brains, Living Colour and Fishbone. The author argues that by the 1980s rock music produced by African Americans was no longer considered to be authentic black music. Discusses the 1985 founding of the Black Rock Coalition in New York, a group of musicians and writers, to challenge that myth and to create outlets for black rock music. A second coalition was organized in Los Angeles.

491.   ——. "The Black Rock Coalition and the Cultural Politics of Race in the United States." PhD dissertation, New York University, 1997.

Analyzes the social relations and cultural productions of the Black Rock Coalition (BRC), an organization of African American musicians based in New York and Los Angeles. During her fieldwork between May 1993 and May 1995, the author examined the organization and its membership, participated in and observed events, attended meetings and rehearsals, and collected stories from twenty-eight members of BRC. She argues that BRC members live out experiences shaped by a new configuration of race-, class- and generation-specific factors that are part of a post-Civil Rights era wherein African American music and musical activities provided discourse about race and culture in the United States.

## Toni Braxton

492. King, Jason Gregory. "Blue Magic, Stardom, Soul Music and Illumination." PhD dissertation, New York University, 2002.

The author begins his study with some questions: How do we detect feeling in music? How do we hear "soul" in music? How do we feel "love" in a singer's rendition of a song? These questions highlight the contemporary black soul music star in performance. The author considers issues in black representation, stardom and soul, and how they inform the concept of illumination. He uses the theoretical perspectives of James Baldwin, Randy Martin, Michael Taussig and others to ascertain how to perform an intuitive reading and/or surplus elements of a given commoditized performance of Toni Braxton in objective representation. The study demonstrates that dualism, individualism and hierarchy are important components in the performances of Toni Braxton.

493. Kinnon, Joy Bennett and Kim Garcia, photographs. "Toni Braxton and Kerri Lewis' Newest Production: Baby Denim." *Ebony*, April 2002, 44–50.

Discusses the birth of their first child, how they met, and provides some insight into Lewis' background before they met. Also, contains information on her life and tribulations before their marriage, and her recent musical success.

## James Brown

494. N.A. "The Explosive Mr. Brown." *Ebony*, March 1965, 57.

Explores the on- and off-stage personalities of Brown, and his attention to detail. Contains information on his appeal to audiences, business holdings and his wardrobe. Brown offers insight into the enjoyment of blacks and whites at a James Brown concert in Memphis. Includes information on his drummer Nat Kendrick and manager Ben Bart.

495. Brown, Geoff. *Life of James Brown*. New York: Omnibus Press, 2008.

A revision of the author's book previously released under various titles (including *James Brown: Doin' it to Death*). Covers Brown's early years in Macon, Georgia, his marriages, relationships with his sidemen, legal issues, and success as a bandleader and business man. Also discusses his music and his role in making soul music an international economic and musical success. A limited discography is included.

496. Brown, James. *I Feel Good: A Memoir of a Life of Soul*. New York: Nal Publishers (Penguin), 2005.

A garrulous, vernacular memoir written with the help of Marc Eliot. Traces Brown's transformation from a grade-school drop out to gospel singer, showman and musical innovator, who broke the color barrier in the 1950s and 1960s. He discusses soul as a statement of race, of force, of stature and of pride. In addition, his life in the music industry and his legal, financial and political views are discussed.

497. Brown, James, Danilo Ecker and Ed Brown. *James Brown*. Rome: Galleria Civica, 1995.

Covers his life from the early poverty years through his acclaim as the Godfather of Soul. Includes discussions of his music, music and business associates, social concerns, private life, trouble with drugs, issues with the law, and marriages.

498. Brown, James, Al Sharpton, and Bruce Tucker. *James Brown: The Godfather of Soul*. New York: Da Capo Press, 2003.

This autobiography was originally published in the late 1980s, before his brushes with the law. Much is said about his penchant for social involvement and his feelings about his music and place in the world. He includes some interesting historical facts: he could only find Asian and white students to shout "Say it loud, I'm black and proud" on his historic recording; mentions that Elvis Presley wanted to record with him.

499. Costa, Jordi. *James Brown*. Madrid: Salvat, 1993.

In Spanish. Covers his early years in Macon, Georgia, forming of bands, musical style, success in running King records, issues with women and more. Written before some of Brown's legal and other problems he experienced in the late 1980s and the mid-1990s. Coverage by the author.

500. Danielsen, Anne. *Presence and Pleasure: The Funk Grooves of James Brown and Parliament*. Middletown, CT: Wesleyan University Press, 2006.

An exploration of funk grooves with a special emphasis on the late 1960s and 1970s music of James Brown and George Clinton and Parliament. Investigates the creation of funk grooves, and the role of race in the construction and consumption of funk. Also discusses the cross-over appeal of the music and white listeners' response to 1980s funk.

501. Fandel, Jennifer. *James Brown*. Chicago: Raintree, 2004.

A concise account of Brown's life, musical contributions and popularity, supplemented with several photographs. She discusses his perseverance and unique ability to overcome hardships and adversity to achieve his goals. Geared primarily to young readers.

502. George, Nelson and Allan Leeds, eds. *The James Brown Reader: Fifty Years of Writing About the Godfather of Soul*. New York: Blume (Barnes and Noble), 2008.

The first comprehensive collection of writings about the man and his music. The writings chronicle his professional and personal struggles and triumphs, the essence and significance of the man himself, and his role in promoting soul music to international acclaim. The coverage runs from the 1960s to 2007. It is extensive, scholarly and the best collection of writings on Brown to date.

503. Rhodes, Don. *Say it Loud: My Memories of James Brown, Soul Brother No.1*. New York: The Lyons Press, 2008.

Written by a long-time friend and colleague of Brown who recounts the story of Brown's life and music. He discusses his musical style, social activism, world travels and habit of challenging anyone who had wronged him. His troubles with the law and marriages are also discussed.

504. Slutsky, Allan and Chuck Silverman. *The Funk Masters: The Great James Brown Rhythm Sections.* New York: Warner Brothers, 1997.

This book deconstructs the function of Brown's bass, drummers and guitarists, and profiles the performers, including Bootsy Collins. Transcriptions isolate each part.

505. Sullivan, James. *The Hardest Working Man: How James Brown Saved the Soul of America.* New York: Gotham Publishers, 2008.

Tells the story of Brown's historic Boston Garden concert in the racially charged atmosphere following the assignation of Martin Luther King, Jr. Chronicles Brown's efforts to present the concert over the objections of the mayor, the performance itself, and the significant role that Brown played in keeping Boston quiet and free of a racial rebellion. Also discusses Brown's transformation from childhood poverty to a self-made millionaire musician and business man.

506. Wolk, Douglas. *James Brown's Live at the Apollo.* New York: Continuum International Publishing Group, 2004.

Discusses a concert that was given in October 1962 at the Apollo Theater in Harlem. The discussion is important because the concert took place before Brown had become famous. The author describes the context of the concert, music and what took place.

507. Zisman, Marc. *Le Funk: De James Brown à Prince.* Paris: J'ai Lu, 2003.

In French. Covers the history and evolution of Brown's life, and his acclaim as an international star and promoter of soul music. Discusses his music, popularity of soul outside the United States, and troubles with drugs, legal issues, marriages and more. Coverage by the author.

## Ruth Brown

508. N.A. " Ruth Brown." *Ebony,* May 1952, 53.

Hailed as one of the greatest singers of her generation, Ruth Brown quickly rose to the top of the rhythm and blues charts. Her excellence is compared with that of Ella Fitzgerald, Billie Holiday and Sarah Vaughan. The article asserts that she was at her best when singing songs that deal with frustration and passion.

509. Brown, Ruth and Andrew Yule. *Miss Rhythm: The Autobiography of Ruth Brown, Rhythm and Blues Legend.* New York: Dutton Publishers, 2006.

Begins with a discussion of her life from her humble beginnings to her marriage at the age of eighteen, and an accident while on her way to an Apollo Theater audition in 1948. Chronicles her signing with Atlantic Records and subsequent hit records and success. The book also covers her declining popularity, her work as a cleaning lady, her comeback with a role in *Hairspray* in 1988, her legal victory over Atlantic records in 1988, and her Tony Award for her role in *Black and Blue on Broadway* in 1989.

### Jerry Butler

510. N.A. "Jerry Butler: History's Hottest Iceman." *Ebony*, December 1969, 64.

Discusses his personal and musical background and his long-awaited success. Includes an examination of the messages in his lyrics, popular recordings and on-stage style. Also contains information on Curtis Hayfield and the Impressions, songwriters Leon Huff and Kenny Gamble, Vee Jay and Mercury record companies, and other individuals and record companies.

### Mariah Carey

511. Nickson, Chris. *Mariah Carey*. New York: St Martin's Press, 1998.

Discusses her humble roots on Long Island, her opera-singing mother, her discovery, singing, career management and marriage to Tommy Mottola (then head of CBS Columbia records). Her meeting and collaborating with Sean "Puffy" Combs, her search for perfection on her recordings, and encounters with racial discrimination are discussed.

512. Tracy, Kathleen. *Mariah Carey*. Hockessin, DE: Mitchell Lane Publishers, 2006.

For younger readers. Geared to grades 9–12, this is a concise account of her life from her New York roots, meeting Tommy Mottola and signing with Columbia records, and her rise to success.

### Ray Charles

513. N.A. "The Soul of Ray Charles." *Ebony*, September 1960, 99.

The article covers several facets of Charles' life and success, including his personal background and musical beginnings, information about his wife, Della and sons, Ray, Jr and David James, and his evolution to musical greatness. The article also alludes to his past experience with drugs and schism with religious issues.

514. Charles, Ray and David Ritz. *Brother Ray: Ray Charles' Own Story.* New York: Da Capo Press, 1992.

Chronicles his success in overcoming poverty, blindness, loss of his parents, and the endemic racism of his early life until his acclaim as a musical genius. The biography is the result of many conversations with Ritz, whom Charles trusted to interpret his musical and personal life experiences. Ritz covers his travels, bouts with drugs, and encounters with musicians, club owners, fans and women. Includes information on his relationship with his mother, his stay in Seattle, Washington, his relationship with Quincy Jones, and the art of combining jazz, soul and country musical elements into cross-over appeal. First published in 1978, this 1992 edition contains new material, a discography and notes.

515. Lydon, Michael. *Ray Charles: Man and Music.* New York: Routledge, 2004.

Traces Charles' life from his early years in Florida, stays in Seattle, Washington, and New York City, to his eventual settling in Los Angeles. Examines how Charles merged country music with R&B and gospel into his own unique musical expressions. The author discusses Charles' drug addition and his relationships with agents, club owners, fans and women. Of specific note is the discussion of Charles' business acuity, especially his insistence on retaining ownership of record masters.

516. Robinson, Louie. "The Enduring Genius of Ray Charles." *Ebony,* October 1974, 12.

Discusses his childhood, educational and musical background, and musical influences. Also covers his stay in Seattle, friendship with Quincy Jones, and his undeniable influence on R&B and country music. Also discussed, his business acumen, expertise as a recording engineer, and association with The Beatles, Lowell Fulson, Georgia Gibbs, Elvis Presley and Stevie Wonder.

## Chubby Checker

517. N.A. " Chubby Checker." *Ebony,* January 1961, 40.

Profiles the artist, his family and social background and his role in making "The Twist" a dance craze in the 1960s. Also provides details of his artist-in-residence position at South Philadelphia High School, and the influence of Dr Josephine Gaporade, Dr Maurice Wasserman and Clarice Young on his musical success.

## Sam Cooke

518. Guralnick, Peter. *Dream Boogie: The Triumph of Sam Cooke.* San Francisco: Backbeat Books, 2006.

Presents an extensive account of Cooke's childhood and grounding in Gospel music, and the deep racism he suffered while touring throughout the south with the Soul Stirrers. The author conducted several interviews with various acquaintances, and includes their comments about Cooke's personality. He also covers his interactions with record companies, marriage issues and black show business concerns before and after the Civil Rights movement.

519. Robinson, Louie. "The Tragic Death of Sam Cooke." *Ebony*, February 1965, 92.

The article covers the events and people associated with the untimely death of Sam Cooke in a Los Angeles motel. He discusses Lisa Boyer, the woman he was accused of attacking, and the woman who shot him. Robinson also covers his family's strong musical background, his two marriages, and the influence of artists like Bobby Blue Bland, Ray Charles and Lou Rawls.

## Bo Diddley

520. Kiersh, Edward. *Where Are You Now, Bo Diddley? The Artists Who Made U Rock and Where They are Now.* New York: Dolphin/ Doubleday, 1986.

In addition to Bo Diddley, the book covers the stories of forty-seven artists (mostly pop) including Chuck Berry, James Brown, Chubby Checker, Dave Clark, Chuck Berry, Jimi Hendrix, Little Richard, Martha Reeves and Phoebe Snow. Relates their stories of survival, including efforts to combine spiritual rebirth, self-discipline and psychotherapy to combat drug abuse, money issues, mental issues and more.

521. Lee, Chris. "Bo Diddley, 79: Singer-Songwriter's Beat Made Rock 'n' Roll." *Los Angeles Times* Obituaries. June 3, 2008.

A concise but thorough assessment of his life and career from his Mississippi and Florida roots to his achievement of fame. Details his rise to fame, his associations and influence on other artists, and contribution to the history and evolution of rock and roll. Also covers Diddley's unique rhythm, guitar sound, stage act and more.

522. White, George. *Bo Diddley: Living Legend, The Man With the Most Famous Beat in the World.* London: Sanctuary Publishing, 1998.

Discusses Ellas Otha ("Bo Diddley") Bates' life from his birth in McComb, Mississippi, and early Florida roots until he achieved international success. His role in the transition from blues to rock and roll, the "Bo Diddley beat," his success in the 1950s and 1960s, and technical innovations. He was inducted into the Rock and Roll Hall of Fame and was awarded the Rhythm and Blues Foundation Pioneer Lifetime Achievement Award.

## Antoine "Fats" Domino

523. N.A. "King of Rock 'n' Roll." *Ebony*, February 1957, 26.

Focuses on Domino's popularity as a recording star. It mentions that his recording of "Blueberry Hill" made him more popular than Elvis Presley and Pat Boone, and that between 1952 and 1957 he sold over 10 million records. Also chronicles the importance of composer and singer Dave Bartholomew, who wrote several of Domino's classics, including "Ain't That A Shame," "Poor Me," and "Don't Blame It on Me."

524. Coleman, Rick. *Blue Monday: Fats Domino and the Lost Dawn of Rock 'n' Roll.* New York: Da Capo Press, 2006.

He argues that Domino's 1949 recordings of "Thunderous Rocker" and "The Fat Man" were the first rock and roll songs, not Elvis Presley's "That's All Right." He believes Domino's role and contributions in rock and roll are under-appreciated and under-researched. He also discusses Domino's drinking and gambling problems, life on the road and recording sessions. Argues that Domino is a bridge between New Orleans R&B giants like Professor Longhair and artists like Ernie K-Doe.

525. Massaquoi, Hans. "Fats Domino." *Ebony*, May 1974, 155.

The article details Domino's nonmusical issues. Specifically, Domino discusses how he lost $2 million during his visits to Las Vegas, and how and why he eventually quit gambling. He also discusses his wife Rosemary, their eight children and Elvis Presley.

## Earth, Wind and Fire

526. N.A. "Earth, Wind and Fire Members Build Their 'Dream' Homes." *Ebony*, December 1977, 154.

The article includes the comments of three members of the group discussing how they built their dream homes. Also included are Philip Bailey, Al McKay, and Freddie, Maurice and Verdine White discussing their abstinence from alcohol and drugs, and their respective real estate holdings.

527. Robinson, Louie. "Earth, Wind, and Fire." *Ebony*, February 1975, 66.

Profiles its founder Maurice White and attributes the group's popularity to their theatrics and hard-driving music. Also discusses White's compositional style as a fusion of blues, pop, rock, jazz and African beat.

## Joe Evans

528. Evans, Joe and Christopher Brooks. *Follow Your Heart: Moving With the Giants of Jazz, Swing, and Rhythm and Blues.* Urbana: University of Illinois Press, 2008.

Discusses Evans' thirty-two-year career in the music business, as a music executive, entrepreneur, musician and promoter for artists like Ray Charles, the Manhattans, the Pretenders, and for Ray Charles' Tangerine record label. Also discusses life on the road with Lionel Hampton, the significance of musical venues like the Apollo theater, the Savoy ballroom, Minton's playhouse and the Rhythm Club.

## Roberta Flack

529. Garland, Phyl. "Roberta Flack: New Musical Messenger." *Ebony*, January 1971, 54.

This interview with Flack profiles her personal and musical background, and her choice to leave her job as a school teacher to pursue a career as a professional singer and pianist. Covers her background in classical music (singing arias and Italian songs on recitals). Flack mentions the influence of artists like Jerry Butler, Aretha Franklin and Les McCann on her soulful musical style.

## Aretha Franklin

530. Garland, Phyl. "Aretha Franklin—Soul Sister." *Ebony*, October 1967, 47.

Profiles Franklin's unsuccessful beginning and subsequent success as a soul singer. In the interview, she discusses her gospel background, singing in the church choir, musical influences, and the personal and musical problems she experienced in her early career. She comments on her father, Rev. C.L. Franklin, and also mentions James Cleveland, John Hammond, Clara Ward and Jerry Wexler.

531. Sanders, Charles L. "Aretha and Glynn." *Ebony*, July 1979, 104.

Chronicles the marriage of Aretha to actor Glynn Thurman. She responds to doubts expressed about the wedding, and he gives his opinions about male-female relationships and his courtship of Aretha. Includes several photographs of the wedding.

532. ———. "Aretha." *Ebony*, December 1971, 124.

Primarily an exposé on her success and popularity, with comments on her family, associates and personality. Discusses her personality on and off stage, how audiences response to her performances, and her musical protégé Billy Always.

## Kenneth Gamble and Leon Huff

533. Bennett, Joy T. "For the Love of Philly." *Ebony*, June 2008, 104–6, 108.

Profiles the legendary songwriters and their success in revitalizing Philadelphia's sound. Bennett acknowledges the duo's immense success as songwriters of hits like "Cowboys to Girls," "Wake Up Somebody," "You'll Never Find Another Love Like Mine," "Turn Off The Lights," and "Me and Mrs. Jones," to name a few, recorded by artists like The Intruders, Harold Melvin and the Blue Notes, The O'Jays, Billy Paul, Teddy Pendergrass and many more. Discusses how the two are using profits from their hit songs to revitalize their own neighborhood and to create low-income housing.

## Veta Gardner and the Coasters

534. Gardner, Veta. *Yakety Yak I Fought Back: My Life With the Coasters.* Bloomington, IN: Author House, 2007.

The story of a Tyler, Texas native who moved to Los Angeles and aspired to become another Nat "King" Cole or Billy Eckstine. Instead, Gardner founded the Coasters along with Billy Guy, Will Jones and Cornell Gunter, and became the group's lead singer. He discusses the group's successes and failures, their relationships with songwriters, and their ability to create and maintain their unique musical identity.

**Marvin Gaye**

535. Calman, Stephanie. "The *Ebony* Interview With Marvin Gaye." *Ebony*, March 1981, 58.

An in-depth, provocative interview with the artist that covers the gamut of his personal and musical careers. Gaye discusses his father, growing up in Washington, DC, and joining the army at age seventeen. His rise to musical prominence is covered, from establishing a group called The Moonglows to his move to Motown Records. Details how he survived twenty-four years in the music business; mentions Berry Gordy, Jr, Princess Margaret, Quincy Jones, The Moonglows, and Frankie, Janis and Anna Gordy Gaye.

536. Douglas, Carlyle C. "Marvin Gaye." *Ebony*, November 1974, 5.

This interview took place after Gaye ended his five-year hiatus and resumed his touring. He discusses issues like marriage, religion, sex, his father, mother, wife, and former singing partner Tammi Terrell.

537. Dyson, Michael Eric. *Mercy Mercy Me: The Art, Loves, and Demons of Marvin Gaye*. New York: Basic Civitas Books, 2004.

A bio-criticism of Gaye's music and personal life. Analyzes the cultural significance of "What's Going On." Mixes psychoanalytic theory and other insights to draw conclusions on issues like the abuse by his father, why his father shot him, his relationships with Tammi Terrell and Berry Gordy, and things that motivated him to achieve musical greatness.

538. Edmonds, Ben. *Marvin Gaye: What's Going' On and the Last Days of the Motown Sound*. Edinburgh, Scotland: Conongate Books, 2001.

Examines the making and impact of Gaye's album *What's Going On*. The author argues that the recording made America examine its social and political dogma during the Civil Rights movement and the Vietnam War. He interviewed several musicians and record company executives before drawing conclusions about the meaning and impact of the recording.

539. Gaye, Frankie. *Marvin Gaye, My Brother*. San Francisco Backbeat Books, 2003.

He reconstructs his brother's life, their tough childhood and abusive father. Also discusses his rise to fame, contributions, fears and successes, drug problems, paranoia, Marvin composing "What's Happening, Brother" for Frankie upon his return from Vietnam, his relationships with women and more.

540. Ritz, David. *Divided Soul: The Life of Marvin Gaye.* New York: Da Capo Press, 2003.

Interviews conducted before Gaye's death provide details of his life and musical success, from his tortured childhood and abusive father to the achievement of international success. Also discussed, his associations with Berry Gordy, Smokey Robinson, Stevie Wonder and other executives; fears and paranoia; his relationships with Tammi Terrell and other women; drug abuse; and other topics.

541. ——. "Marvin Gaye: The Shocking, Tragic Story of His Last Days." *Ebony,* June 1985, 160.

An excerpt from the author's book *Divided Soul* focuses on the months preceding Gaye's untimely death. Provides details of the troubled relationship between Marvin and his father, relationship with his mother Alberta, and insight into his relationship with former wives, Anna Gordy and Janis Hunter, his sons Frankie and Marvin III, and daughter Nona.

## Gloria Gaynor

542. Gaynor, Gloria. *I Will Survive: The Book.* New York: St Martin's Press, 1997.

Her story begins with the early years in Newark, New Jersey, proceeds to the 1960s years with the Soul Satisfiers, and covers the rise to success after she recorded "Never Can Say Goodbye." Also covers her immense success after recording "I Will Survive" in 1978, her career's decline after the death of her mother, use of drugs, conversion to Christianity, and the revival of her career in the early 1990s.

543. ——. *Soul Survivor: My Story.* Peabody, MA: Zondervan Publishing, 1995.

A discussion of her rise to success after recording "Never Can Say Goodbye," which helped launch the disco movement in the 1970s. She addresses the importance of her hit "I Will Survive," her depression after the death of her mother, squandering her newfound wealth on alcohol, drugs and parties, her turn to religion in the 1980s, and the revival of her career in the early 1990s.

## Berry Gordy, Jr.

544. N.A. "Triumph of a Stay-at-Home." *Ebony,* February 1966, 32.

Covers his rise to success and developing the Motown sound as the founder of Motown Records. Gordy comments on his plan to expand into television, and offers his comments and insights into some of Motown's artists, including Marvin Gaye, The Four Tops and Stevie Wonder.

545. Gordy, Berry. *To Be Loved: The Music, The Magic, The Memory of Motown; An Autobiography.* New York: Warner Books, 1995.

Discusses his life from the time he worked in the automobile industry to the founding and success of Motown. Also discussed, his relationships with artists like Smokey Robinson, Stevie Wonder and Diana Ross, his musical philosophy, expansion to do films, and business acuity.

546. Robinson, Lisa, contrib. ed. "The Music, The Magic, The Memories of Motown: A Tribute to Berry Gordy." *Vanity Fair* (December 2008): 1–33.

Gordy labels this article the fairest portrayal of him and Motown, apart from his own autobiography (1995) [see item 545]. This thirty-three-page account is filled with quotes and insider perspectives by Gordy and many Motown artists. The oral history and other insights are provided by Berry Gordy, Duke Fakir of the Four Tops, Smokey Robinson, Martha Reeves, Otis Williams of the Temptations, Lionel Ritchie, Stevie Wonder, executive Suzanne De Passé and etiquette teacher Maxine Powell. Many interesting and provocative topics: Gordy's frustration with attempts to categorize Motown's music, being labeled a gangster, his relationships with the artists, the abrupt departure of Holland-Dozier-Holland from Motown over money issues, lawsuits, his initial reluctance to sign the Jackson Five, and the assessments of Gordy, Reeves and Robinson about misrepresentations in the film, *Dreamgirls.* Beautiful photographs, some rare, including shots of Gordy and Smokey Robinson, Holland-Dozier-Holland, Martha Reeves and Maxine Powell, The Supremes, The Temptations, the Four Tops, Stevie Wonder and others.

## Al Green

547. Bailey, Peter. "Al Green: Apostle of Love." *Ebony*, November 1973, 104.

In this interview, Green discusses his musical career, gives an overview of his background in Grand Rapids, Michigan, and his reaction to his successful career. He identifies James Brown, Sam Cooke, Claude Jeter and Jackie Wilson as musical influences, and presents his views on drugs and marriage. Includes a list of his most popular recordings.

548. Norment, Lynn. "Al Green." *Ebony*, March 1978, 84.

Discusses the impact of religion on his life. Describes how his life changed after the break-up of his marriage, and how religion helped to relieve the pressure that he was experiencing. This is a very important article because many people questioned Green about his musical identity, whether sacred or secular; this article offers important insights into this paradox.

549. ——. "How Tragedy Has Affected the Life of Al Green." *Ebony*, October 1976, 176.

Covers Green's reaction to the death of a rejected admirer, information on his private life, his switch to sacred music and subsequent success in that genre, and a summary of his musical accomplishments to date. Elton John, the Rolling Stones and Stevie Wonder are mentioned in the article.

**Donny Hathaway**

550. Cheers, D. Michael. "The Mysterious Death of Donny Hathaway." *Ebony*, April 1979, 61.

Describes the way the New York police handled Hathaway's death, especially their explanation of his fall from a hotel window. Also covers his career from high school to Howard University, and his association with Roberta Flack, Aretha Franklin, Rev. Jessie Jackson and Curtis Mayfield.

**Isaac Hayes**

551. Garland, Phyl. "Isaac Hayes: Hot Buttered Soul." *Ebony*, March 1970, 82.

Detailed coverage of his birth into poverty and eventual climb to musical and acting success. Special attention is given to his personal background and impoverished childhood. Also discusses his songwriting partner David Porter and the soul duet of Sam and Dave.

552. Higgins, Chester. "Ex-Con Dancer Finds Savior in Black Moses." *Ebony*, May 1972, 133.

Profiles Helen Washington's family background, stint in prison and street life prior to working with Hayes. Also covers her relationship and work with Hayes.

553. Mason, J. "Isaac Hayes' New Wife, New Image, New Career." *Ebony*, October 1973, 173.

In this interview, Hayes discusses his new lifestyle, career direction and wife, Mignon. He also offers information on his impoverished background, material possessions, rise to success and popular recordings, and pays tribute to James Brown, Marvin Gaye, Donny Hathaway, Joe Simon and Bobby Womack.

554. Powers, Ann and Valerie J. Nelson. "'Black Moses' Led Pop to New Ground." *Los Angeles Times.* August 11, 2008.

A profile of his career as a musician, composer, producer and film star, written after his untimely death in 2008, at his home near Memphis, Tennessee. Covers his association with David Porter, with Stax records, his 1972 Academy Award for Best Song ("Shaft"), and his appearances in more than 60 movies and television shows, including his final film appearance in *Soul Men* with Samuel Jackson and Bernie Mac. A selective discography is also included.

## Jimi Hendrix

555. Black, Johnny. *Jimi Hendrix: The Ultimate Experience.* New York: Da Capo Press, 1995.

Uses quotes, interviews and thirty-two pages of photographs to present a chronological account of Hendrix's life from his childhood in Seattle to his immense international musical success, including his final appearance at Ronnie Scott's in London. Quotes from books, magazines, newspapers, television and radio documentaries, and internet sites are used to weave this account of Hendrix's life. The interviews feature comments from Eric Clapton, David Crosby, Paul McCartney and Pete Townsend.

556. Boot, Adrian and Chris Salewicz. *Jimi Hendrix: The Ultimate Experience.* New York: Boxtree Ltd, 1995.

A biography as well as essays on specific areas of Hendrix's life and musical influences. The contributors include Bob Dylan, Marianne Faithful, Sting, Germaine Greer, Charles Shaar Murray and Oliver Stone.

557. Brown, Tony. *Jimi Hendrix: Concert File.* Malvern, Australia: Omnibus Press, 2000.

A detailed catalogue of Hendrix's many concerts between 1969 and 1970 in Europe and America. Also documents Hendrix's accomplishments as a sideman to many vocalists prior to going to London in 1967. Additionally, the catalogue contains a list of locations, songs played, and specific details of each set.

558. Cross, Charles R. *Room Full of Mirrors: A Biography of Jimi Hendrix.* New York: Hyperion, 2006.

He covers Hendrix's early years in Seattle, living in poverty with alcoholic and largely absent parents, his stint as an army paratrooper, playing clubs in the 1960s, his stays in New York and London, his break-out performance at the Monterey Pop Festival in 1967, and more. Also includes family squabbles, issues regarding his untimely death, and Hendrix's caring and thoughtful personality. The author conducted 300 interviews with family members, musicians and others.

559. Doggett, Peter. *Complete Guide to the Music of Jimi Hendrix.* Malvern, Australia: Omnibus Press, 2004.

An in-depth and informative examination of each song in Hendrix's extensive recorded repertoire. The discussions include the date, time and place of specific recordings, information on his sidemen, and an assessment of the song.

560. Egan, Sean. *Jimi Hendrix and the Making of Are You Experienced.* The Vinyl Frontier Series. Chicago: Chicago Review Press, 2002.

Traces a myriad of events that led up to Hendrix's debut, provides amusing stories about the origin of songs, reveals Hendrix's love of science, and his ability to master a song in one or two takes. Includes information on London Rock Scene artists like The Who, the Rolling Stones and the Beatles who came out to watch him perform while he was in London.

561. Hanford, III, John C. "With the Power of the Soul: Jimi Hendrix in *Band of Gypsys.*" PhD dissertation, University of Washington, 2003.

Investigates Hendrix's historic and live recording of *Band of Gypsys* as a showcase for Hendrix's skills as an improviser and live performing artist. An analysis of four compositions—"Who Knows," "Machine Gun," "Power to Love," and "Message to Love"—is used to demonstrate Hendrix's use of continuity and change, maintaining traditional stylistic concepts while exploring new musical concepts. The formation of the band is discussed.

562. Henderson, David. *'Scuse Me While I Kiss the Sky: Jimi Hendrix; Voodoo Child.* New York: Atria, 2008.

This biography was first published in 1978 as *Jimi Hendrix: Voodoo Child of the Aquarian Age.* It has been revised and updated, and melds the original text of Hendrix's interviews with new material, including details of lawsuits and his death. This edition includes more of Hendrix's personal writings, covers his romantic life and provides insights into the creation of his music.

563. Hendrix, James Al. *My Son Jimi*. Seattle: Aljas Enterprises, 1999.

Jimi's father presents an accurate account of his role as father, and a detailed assessment of his life, from his perspective. He portrays himself as a hardworking person whose wife, Lucille, was sleeping around, leaving Jimi to be raised primarily by his aunts, uncles and grandmothers, all important details of Jimi's life and factors that shaped his music. He also discusses Jimi's premature death and his legal battle for control of Jimi's estate.

564. Hendrix, Janie and John McDermott. *Jimi Hendrix: An Illustrated Experience*. New York: Atria, 2007.

Presented through text, rare color photographs, and reproductions of memorabilia and documents. Includes reproductions of drawings from his childhood, handwritten song lyrics and rare photographs. The seventy-minute audio CD contains interviews and unreleased material from a live concert and a jam session at a record plant.

565. Kramer, Edward E. and John McDermott. *Hendrix: Setting the Record Straight*. New York: Grand Central Publishing, 1992.

A detailed definitive account of Hendrix's life based upon first-person recollections, musicians' observations, and the views and recollections of key people in his life. Kramer, his long time producer, provides important insights into Hendrix's creative processes.

566. Lawrence, Sharon. *Jimi Hendrix: The Intimate Story of a Betrayed Musical Legend*. New York: Harper, 2006.

Written by a former UPI reporter and confidante of Hendrix. Presents an overview of his early years: being abandoned by his mother, performing in high school rock bands and briefly becoming a paratrooper. The author also discusses his time in New York and London, his drug abuse, lawsuits, paranoia, the ground-breaking performance at the Monterey Pop Festival in 1967, and his untimely death.

567. McDermott, John, with Eddie Kramer and Billy Cox. *The Ultimate Hendrix: An Illustrated Encyclopedia of Live Concerts and Sessions*. San Francisco: Backbeat Books, 2005.

Chronicles all of Hendrix's recording sessions, with vivid new descriptions of each concert from 1963 to 1970. Richly illustrated with many photographs.

568. ——. *Jimi Hendrix: Sessions; The Complete Studio Recording Sessions*. London: Little, Brown and Co., 1996.

A detailed examination of Hendrix as a musician and of his studio sessions that begins with his 1963 collaboration with Curtis Knight and the Isley Brothers. Provides an in-depth account of each recording, explains how Hendrix manipulated the out-dated recording technology, and discusses the new musical directions that he was pursuing around the time of his death. Handwritten lyrics, studio memorabilia, more than 100 photographs.

569. Murray, Charles Shaar. *Crosstown Traffic: Jimi Hendrix and The Post-War Rock 'n' Roll Revolution.* New York: St Martin's Griffin, 1991.

This British author presents a broad-based study of African American music, including blues, jazz, rhythm and blues, and soul, and discusses how they influenced Hendrix and how he influenced them. Of special note is the author's assessment of the cultural contradiction of a black performer with a white audience, excelling in a musical genre that was popularized by whites but rooted in black musical culture.

570. Rody, Steven. *Black Gold: The Lost Archives of Jimi Hendrix.* North Hollywood: Billboard Books, 2002.

A comprehensive biography of Hendrix's lost sessions, previously unknown collaborations, and rare film and video documents. Uses unreleased and commercially-unavailable recordings (in studio, live and personal) to document each stage of Hendrix's life. Research also included interviewing Hendrix's father, Carlos Santana, John McLaughlin, Kathy Etchingham and many others. Of special note is the author's exploration of Hendrix's experiments with jazz artists like Miles Davis, Rashaan Roland Kirk and John McLaughlin, blues icons like Buddy Guy, B.B. King and Johnny Winter, and his early backing of rap pioneers like the Last Poets.

571. Shadwick, Keith and Jimi Hendrix. *Jimi Hendrix, Musician.* San Francisco: Backbeat Books, 2003.

Presents a fresh look at Hendrix by deconstructing his style as guitarist, composer and singer. Traces his musical career and situates him historically in the 1960s, but also discusses his life before and after the 1960s. Contains new information about Hendrix's musical creativity, and Douglas J. Noble, a Hendrix expert, discusses the instrument and equipment that Hendrix used to create more expressive and exciting sounds. The book contains over 300 photographs.

572. Shapiro, Harry and Caesar Glebbeek. *Jimi Hendrix: Electric Gypsy.* New York: St Martin's Griffin, 1995.

Shapiro and Glebbeek, founders and curators of the Hendrix Information Center in Ireland, cover his childhood in Seattle, his time in

New York and London, drug addiction, lawsuits and more. Quotes, anecdotes, mini-biographies of his sidemen and song analyses present a thorough picture of Hendrix as a brilliant composer and a musical perfectionist. Includes a discography over 100 pages long, and over 200 pieces of correspondence, mementos and photographs.

573.  Stubbs, David. *Jimi Hendrix: Voodoo Child; The Stories Behind Every Song.* New York: Da Capo Press, 2003.

Follows Hendrix through his early gigs on the "Chitlin Circuit" in the mid-1960s, his discovery by Chas Chandler, musical journeys to New York and London, and the formation of his band. Discusses Hendrix's albums, musical associations, insight into his creative processes. Complete discography, 90 photographs.

574.  Tate, Grady. *Midnight Lighting: Jimi Hendrix and the Black Experience.* Chicago: Lawrence Hill Books, 2005.

Focuses on the social meaning, sexual mystery and scientific inquiry of Hendrix from an African American perspective. Looks at the phenomenon of a black musician being an icon in the white rock and roll world, the tools of his trade, romances, and his ability to affect American culture.

575.  Willett, Edward. *Jimi Hendrix: Kiss The Sky.* Berkeley Heights, NJ: Enslow Publishers, 2006.

Explores Hendrix's family back to the 1800s, Hendrix's childhood in Seattle, his performances in high school and other bands, time in New York and London, breakout performance at the Monterey Pop Festival in 1967, drug issues, lawsuits, the Woodstock performance and his death from an overdose of pills.

## Lauryn Hill

576.  Furman, Leah and Elina Furman. *Heart of Soul: The Lauryn Hill Story.* New York: Ballantine, 1999.

Covers her family and her life from childhood; discusses her role in establishing and touring with the Fugees, and the role her two children played in her rise to success. A highlight of the book is the discussion of Hill singing "Killing Me Softly."

577.  Hill, Lauryn, *The Miseducation of Lauryn Hill.* Milwaukee: Hal Leonard, 1999.

In addition to a concise biographical sketch of the artist, the folio contains several songs. Among the songs are "Doo Wop," "Everything is Everything," "Ex-Factor," "Forgive Them Father," "Lost Ones," "Superstar," and many more.

578. Laslo, Cynthia. *Lauryn Hill.* Hartford: Children Press, 2000.

For younger readers. Geared to teenagers, this concise account traces her life from humble beginnings through the role that her children and family played in her attainment of success. Also contains a discussion of her career with the Fugees, and eventual success as a solo entertainer.

579. Nickson, Chris. *Lauryn Hill: She's Got That Thing.* New York: St Martin's Press, 1999.

This biography was written without interviewing Hill, but is engaging and contains depth. Discusses her rise from obscurity to fame and success with the Fugees, and transformation to eventual stardom as a solo act. Her love of her children and family support are also discussed.

## Brenda Holloway

580. Browne, Kimasi. "Brenda Holloway: Los Angeles's Contribution to Motown." In *California Soul: Music of African Americans in the West*, eds Jacqueline C. DjeDje and Eddie S. Meadows, pp. 321–53. Berkeley: University of California Press, 1998.

Browne discusses her tenure with Motown during its formative years (1964–68), and her role as a singer, songwriter, instrumentalist and fashion innovator. Furthermore, he argues that she was an individual who resisted the caste mold of Motown, and provides reasons why she left Motown after a short four-year stint.

581. ——. "Variation in the Vocal Style of Brenda Holloway: Soul Singer and 1960s Motown Recording Artist." Masters thesis, University of California, Los Angeles, 1995.

Transcriptions and analyses of two of Holloway's vocal performances, "Every Little Bit Hurts" (1964) and "You've Made Me So Very Happy" (1967), focus on four methods of variation in melody, rhythm and text. He concludes that melismas, slurs, leaps, additive rhythms and textual interpolations are characteristics of her vocal style.

## Whitney Houston

582. N.A. "Whitney Houston." *Ebony,* December 1985, 155.

Discusses her success at the age of twenty-two, before her marriage to Bobby Brown. Covers her background and childhood in East Orange, New Jersey, her early musical experiences in the choir of a Baptist Church where her mother was Minister of Music, and travels with her cousin, Dionne Warwick. Her recordings and television appearances are discussed along with her influences and associations with artists and business people like Chaka Khan, Aretha Franklin, Jermaine Jackson, Luther Vandross and Clive Davis.

## Ink Spots

583. Watson, Deek. *The Story of the Ink Spots.* New York: Vantage Press, 1967.

   Recounts how the group came together, their individual backgrounds, their rise to success, and their ability to navigate through deep-seated racism. Their choice of music, ability to please black and white audiences, and rise to fame are also discussed.

## Michael Jackson and the Jackson Five

584. N.A. "New Heights for the Jackson Five." *Ebony*, September 1971, 126.

   Focuses on the continuing success of the group, their forthcoming ABC television cartoon series, and details of their two-year contract for the series.

585. Boucher, Geoff and Elaine Woo. "A Major Talent, A Bizarre Persona." *Los Angeles Times* Obituaries. June 26, 2009, 12–13.

   Provide a comprehensive assessment of Jackson's life and musical achievements from his beginnings in Gary, Indiana, to his untimely death on June 25, 2009. In addition, they discuss his fantasies, tragedies, relationship with Motown Records, Quincy Jones, Diana Ross, and the stern discipline of his father, Joseph Jackson. His fame, impact on popular music and love for his three children are also discussed. The obituary contains several excellent photographs.

586. Johnson, Robert. "The Michael Jackson Nobody Knows." *Ebony*, December 1984, 155.

   A discussion of the business acuity of the artist-songwriter. Discusses his many music companies, his childhood singing career with the Jackson Five, his decision to go solo and the success he has enjoyed since launching his solo career.

587. ——. "Michael Jackson Sets A World Record." *Ebony*, May 1984, 163.

Deals with the immense success of the *Thriller* album, which sold 25 million copies. Covers the success of the album internationally, including in Australia, Holland, Japan and Spain. The article mentions CBS records, producer Quincy Jones and the fact that the album was cited in the *Guinness Book of World Records* as the best-selling record ever.

588. Overby, Theresa. *Michael Jackson.* Hockessin, DE: Mitchell Lane Publishers, 2005.

An overview of his life and musical accomplishments for young readers. Traces his life from his Gary, Indiana, the beginning of the Jackson Five, Michael's early solo career, his relationship with Diana Ross and his contributions to popular music.

589. Robinson, Louie. "Family Life of the Jackson Five." *Ebony*, December 1974, 3.

An insightful portrait of the off-stage life of the family; includes concise information on Jackie, Janet, Jermaine, Joseph, Katherine, Latoya, Marlon, Michael, Randy, Rebbie and Tito.

590. ———. "The Jackson Five." *Ebony*, September 1970, 150.

An account of the group's "discovery" by Diana Ross, their signing with Motown records and their rise to fame. Also profiles brothers Jackie, Jermaine, Marlon, Michael and Tito.

591. Ryan, Harriet, Chris Lee, Andrew Blankstein and Scott Gold. "Singer Was About to Start Series of Comeback Shows." *Los Angeles Times.* June 26, 2009: A11.

Covers the events surrounding Jackson's untimely death, and the anticipation that had preceded his comeback tour. Quotes from Dick Clark, Quincy Jones, Madonna, Tommy Mottola and Lisa Marie Presley about Jackson's musical achievements, significance and preparation for the comeback tour. In addition to these articles, the *Los Angeles Times* also includes related articles on Jackson's death, including "His Style Was as Iconic as His Sound" by Booth Moore (p. 14) and "An Appreciation: A Star Who Transcended Boundaries" by Ann Powers (p. 15). Similar obituaries and tributes can be found in the *New York Times, Washington Post* and most major newspapers and news outlets worldwide during the week of June 25, 2009.

592. Sanders, Charles. "Michael." *Ebony*, December 1982, 126.

In this interview, Sanders covers the potential success of Michael's upcoming albums, including his upcoming *Thriller* album, and his role in the film *E.T.* Also discusses his relationship with Tatum O'Neal, Diana Ross and Brook Shields.

593. ———. "Jermaine and Hazel Jackson: Love-Family Style." *Ebony*, August 1981, 74.

Profiles their marriage and their two children. Discusses their life-style, Jermaine's decision to leave the Jackson Five in 1976 to start a solo career, surviving a major family crisis, and the treatment that the Jacksons received from Motown Records.

594. ———. "The Jacksons." *Ebony*, September 1979, 33.

Discusses the origins and success of the group, from Gary, Indiana, to Motown. Examines the success of *Destiny*, which sold over 1 million copies, and their hit single "Shake Your Body," which sold 2 million copies. Discusses the brothers, father Joe Jackson, and the group's involvement with Ryan O'Neal's family.

## James Jamerson

595. Slutsky, Alan and James Jamerson. *Standing in the Shadow of Motown: The Life and Music of Legendary Bassist James Jamerson*. Milwaukee: Hal Leonard, 1989.

Slutsky interviewed hundreds of people to paint a picture of Jamerson's life and musical brilliance, his role and function in Motown recording sessions, his problems with drugs and alcohol, and his demise after Motown moved to Los Angeles. Includes forty-nine transcriptions of musical scores, fifty rare photographs and a 120-minute CD. Slutsky's 2002 documentary of the same name won the New York Film Critics' Award for "Best Documentary of the Year."

## Etta James

596. James, Etta and David Ritz. *Rage to Survive: The Etta James Story*. New York: Da Capo Press, 2003.

Covers her life from her birth to a fourteen-year-old mother from south central Los Angeles, singing in the St Paul Baptist church choir, drug addiction, prison sentences, involvement with men and issues with her mother. Her musical success, life after drugs and her relationship with Johnny Otis are also discussed.

## Ted Jarrett

597. Jarrett, Ted and Ruth White. *You Can Make It If You Try: The Ted Jarrett Story of Rhythm and Blues in Nashville*. Hillsboro, NH: Hillsboro Press, 2005.

Covers Jarrett's career as a musician, label chief, talent scout, artist's manager, songwriter, producer and disc jockey in the Nashville R&B scene since the 1950s. Discusses his tenure with record labels and radio stations, and how he discovered, managed and nurtured talent. His compositions were first recorded by Nashville R&B stars like Gene Allison, Earl Gaines and Christine Kittrell, and later by artists like Hank Ballard, Ruth Brown and the Rolling Stones.

## Rodney Jerkins

598. Norment, Lynn. "Rodney Jerkins: Master Maestro on a Mission." *Ebony*, June 2002, 106–12.

Covers the life and career of Jerkins—considered at the time to be pop music's youngest hit-making genius—from his childhood in Pleasantville, New Jersey, to winning a Grammy Award for producing and songwriting. Mentions his classical piano and embryonic musical experiences in his father's church. Only twenty-four years old at the time of this interview, he owned his own recording studio, Darkchild Productions and Recording Studio, and was the youngest person to have secured a distribution deal with a major record label (Sony). He helped create hits for Mary J. Blige, Toni Braxton, Brandy, Destiny's Child, Kirk Franklin, Whitney Houston, Michael Jackson, Jennifer Lopez, Brian McKnight, Monica, Britney Spears, N'Sync and many more.

## Louis Jordan

599. N.A. "Louis Jordan." *Ebony*, January 1949, 24.

Profiles the Arkansas-born and former minstrel show performer known as "King of the Juke Boxes." His advice-laden topical songs deal with the economy, military and romance. He reveals that he often auditioned and incorporated songs written by others. Also included is a discussion of persons he recorded with, including The Andrew Sisters, Bing Crosby and Ella Fitzgerald.

600. N.A. "Whatever Happened to Louis Jordan?" *Ebony*, April 1973, 182.

The article recounts Jordan's past greatness and chronicles his current activities. Also discusses the popularity of his band, The Tympani Five, during the 1940s. Also mentions the influence of his wife Martha and artists like Cab Calloway, Damita Jo, Jimmy Rushing and Fats Waller.

601. Chilton, John. *Let the Good Times Roll: The Story of Louis Jordan and His Music*. Ann Arbor: University of Michigan Press, 1994.

A well researched and thorough account of the life and music of this exceptional vocalist and saxophonist. Chilton details his band's personnel, evolution of his style and influences on his playing, and analyzes and critiques his recordings. Includes numerous interviews, stories about Jordan's encounters with racism, and battles of big bands. Insightful but somewhat tepid coverage of some events in Jordan's life, for example when he was stabbed by one of his wives.

## Alicia Keys

602. Bankston, John. *Alicia Keys*. Hockessin, DE: Mitchell Lane Publishing, 2004.

   For younger readers. Geared toward grades 9–12 and only thirty-two pages long. Chronicles her life and interest in music from her early childhood in New York City, exposure to a myriad of free concerts, her audition and acceptance to the Professional Performing Arts School, and the signing of her first record contract. Her move from Columbia Records and her association with Clive Davis and J Records is also discussed.

603. Brown, Terrell. *Alicia Keys*. Broomall, PA: Mason Crest, 2007.

   Covers her early life, her debut recording of *Songs in A Minor* and her immense success. Includes some discussion of her musical influences, and acknowledgment of her mercurial rise to become the first female rhythm and blues performer to have eight consecutive releases debut at No.1 on the Billboard 200 album charts.

604. Graham, Ben. *Maximum Alicia Keys: The Unauthorised Biography of Alicia Keys*. CD Audio Series. New Maiden, UK: Chrome Dreams, 2004.

   An audio biography that includes comments and interviews by Keys and an eight-page illustrated booklet and fold-out poster. Background music by Amanda Thompson; read by Nancy McLean.

## Gladys Knight and the Pips

605. N.A. "Gladys Knight and the Pips." *Ebony*, November 1980, 45.

   This article deals with the revival of the group after its success in the 1960s and 1970s. Discusses the successes and failures since the peak of their success, and why the group revived their career. Covers Gladys' marriage, members of the group and more.

606. Mason, B.J. "Gladys Knight and the Pips: It's A Family Affair." *Ebony,* June 1973, 172.

Profiles the group as a family and discusses their success. The interview focuses on both the Knight family and the families of the Pips (William Quest, Merald Knight and Edward Patten). Covers the group's beginnings and difficulties they encountered on their road to success. The group also pays tribute to Sam Cooke and Jackie Wilson.

**Beyoncé Knowles**

607. Celebrities Art Center. *Beyoncé Knowles, The Marvelous Queen.* New York: Mi-Productions, 2007.

For younger readers. Written for ages 9–12 to praise her as a queen of R&B and hip hop. The plot presents a beauty queen artist and her many fans walking on Hollywood boulevard; the crowd praises her and she responds in kind. The book is presented as a musical.

608. Hodgson, Nicola. *Beyoncé Knowles.* New York: Raintree Publications, 2005.

Only forty-eight pages, this concise biography covers her childhood in Houston, her early introduction to music, her parents' role in developing her career, the success of Destiny's Child, and her rise to success in music and films.

609. Tracy, Kathleen. *Beyoncé.* Blue Banner Biographies. Hockessin, DE: Mitchell Lane Publishers, 2006.

For younger readers. Geared to ages 9–12, the book covers her early years in Houston, her beginning interest in music, role of her parents, and the founding and eventual success of Destiny's Child. Discusses her expansion into movies, and her meeting and marriage to Jay-Z.

610. Walters, Rosa. *Beyoncé.* Broomail, PA: Mason Crest, 2007.

Part of a series of books on rhythm and blues and rap artists, this concise biography traces her life from her Houston roots, discusses the role of her parents in molding her career, the origin of Destiny's Child, her sister, meeting Jay-Z and her rise to superstardom.

611. Webster, Christine. *Beyoncé Knowles.* New York: Weigi Publishers, 2005.

Only twenty-four pages, this concise account covers her life and family in Houston, interest and success of Destiny's Child, role of her father as her manager, and rise to stardom.

## Patti LaBelle

612. Sanders, Charles. "Patti LaBelle's on Her Own and Doing Great."
     *Ebony*, September 1978, 162.

     Discusses the changes in her career after the breakup of her group
     Labelle. Also discusses the role and functions of her husband, Armstead
     Edwards, manager Vicki Wickham, son Zuri, and Labelle members
     Nona Hendriz and Sarah Dash.

613. Weston, Martin. "Labelle." *Ebony*, May 1976, 100.

     Describes the transformation of the Labelles from 1960s R&B icons
     to rock stars in the 1970s. Also provides information on their sexy
     shows, their on-stage characters, off-stage personalities, and members
     Patti LaBelle, Nona Hendrix and Sarah Dash. Other important figures
     in their careers—producers, managers, musical associates, celebrities—
     are also mentioned, including Carol Burnett, Michael Callahan, James
     Ellison, Eddie Martinez, Carmine Rojas and Vickie Wickham.

## Leiber, Jerry and Mike Stoller

614. Leiber, Jerry and Mike Stoller, with David Ritz. *Hound Dog: The Leiber
     and Stoller Autobiography*. New York: Simon and Schuster, 2009.

     A joint oral autobiography of one of the most successful R&B song-
     writing teams, told in alternating blocks between Lieber and Stoller.
     Copious details of their musical careers, supplemented with com-
     ments on songs composed for artists like The Coasters, Little Willie
     John, Ben E. King, Big Maybell, Elvis Presley and many others. Among
     their numerous hits are "Charlie Brown," "Jailhouse Rock," "Hound
     Dog," "On Broadway," "Stand By Me," "Spanish Harlem" (Leiber with
     Phil Spector), and "Poison Ivy," to name a few. Discusses their col-
     laborations with artists like Peggy Lee and their mentoring relationship
     with Burt Bacharach and Phil Spector.

## Preston Love

615. Love, Preston. *A Thousand Honey Creeks Later: My Life in Music
     From Basie to Motown and Beyond*. Introduction by George Lipsitz.
     Hanover and London: Wesleyan University Press/ University Press
     of New England, 1997.

     Love's autobiography details his long, productive and eclectic career
     in the music business, encounters with racism, musical associations

and achievements. Begins with Love's days with Count Basie in the 1940s, his studio days in Los Angeles, and endless travels to perform in cities like St Cloud, Minnesota; Guthrie, Oklahoma; and Honey Creek, Iowa. Of special note is his discussion of his relationships with jazz icons Ray Charles, Dizzy Gillespie, Jo Jones and Lester Young, and his role as a sideman with soul icons Aretha Franklin, Marvin Gaye, Gladys Knight and the Pips, Smokey Robinson, The Temptations and Stevie Wonder. Many significant insights into the evolution of jazz and the emergence of the Motown sound.

### Frankie Lymon

616. Peters, Art. "Comeback of an Ex-Star." *Ebony*, January 1967, 42.

In this interview, Lymon discusses his heroin addiction and the breakup of his group The Teenagers. He covers his childhood, origins of the Teenagers, beginning in the music industry and his attempt to revive his career.

### Curtis Mayfield and the Impressions

617. Anderson, Monroe. "Curtis Mayfield: From Super Fly to Super Star." *Ebony*, July 1973, 66.

In this interview, Mayfield discusses his recent success, his extensive musical background and his achievements with the Impressions. He also discusses some of the hit songs he composed, and his business relationship with Jerry Butler and Gene Chandler, his mother, Mrs Marion Jackson, and wife, Toni.

618. Turner, Jr, William C. "Keep on Pushing: The Impressions." *Black Sacred Music: A Journal of Theomusicology* 6(1) (Spring 1992): 206–18.

An introspective assessment of the role and function of some of the Impressions' most famous songs. Included is a thematic and textual analysis of "Keep on Pushing," "I'm So Proud," "Why Do We Keep On Doing What We Are Not Suppose To Do," "Get Up and Move," "Gypsy Woman," and "We're Moving On Up."

### James McGowan / Four Fellows

619. McGowan, James. *Hear Today, Here to Stay.* Salthill, Galway, Ireland: Sixth House Press, 1983.

Discusses McGowan's life and musical career from its beginnings in the 1950s, when he teamed up with Larry Banks, David Jones and

Teddy Williams to form the R&B quartet The Four Fellows. He discusses the group's decline, and his personal accomplishments and contributions after the decline of the group's popularity.

## Booker T and the MGs

620.  Garland, Phyl. "Booker T. and the MGs." *Ebony*, April 1969, 92.

Discusses how Booker T. Jones, studio musician for Stax records, helped popularize the "Memphis Sound." The interview covers the group's individual and collective talents, including engineering, producing and songwriting. Also covered are the individual backgrounds of the members (Steve Cropper, Donald Dunn, Al Jackson and Booker T. Jones), and a list of artists with whom they worked, including Eddie Floyd, The Staple Singers, Johnny Taylor and Carla Thomas.

## Bruce "Cousin Brucie" Morrow

621.  Morrow, Cousin Bruce. *Cousin Brucie: My Life in Rock 'n' Roll Radio.* Sag Harbor, NY: Beech Tree Books, 1987.

The autobiography of the 1960s WABC-AM New York radio personality "Cousin Brucie." Traces his life from Brooklyn, through radio stints in Bermuda and Miami until he landed in New York. His musical association with Bando, his associate, marriages, fears, and success in programming rock and roll, rhythm and blues, and soul music are also discussed.

## "Prince" Rogers Nelson

622.  Norment, Lynn. "Prince: What is the Secret of His Amazing Success." *Ebony*, June 1985, 160.

By the mid-1980s, Prince had won three American Music Awards, three Grammy Awards and an Academy Award for his *Purple Rain* soundtrack. Included are details of his personality, musical creativity and business skills. Also mentioned are many personalities he admires or has been associated with, including David Bowie, Boy George, Rod Stewart and Vanity.

623.  ——. "Prince: The Story Behind Passion For Purple." *Ebony*, November 1984, 66.

"Prince" Rogers Nelson discusses the secrets of his successful movie *Purple Rain* (1984). He outlines the roles of the people involved with the project, reveals his future recording plans, and discusses his religious beliefs and stage attire.

## The O'Jays

624. Rhoden, Bill. "The O'Jays: There's a Message in Their Music." *Ebony*, September 1977, 90.

Written to commemorate the twentieth anniversary of their show-business career, this article provides insight into their beginnings as a group, careers, musical philosophy and family lives. The musicians pay tribute to and acknowledge the influence of artists like the Dominoes, the Drifters, Frankie Lymon, Clyde McPhatter, Jackie Wilson and several others.

## Johnny Otis

625. Otis, Johnny. *Upside Your Head: Rhythm and Blues on Central Avenue.* Hanover and London: Wesleyan University Press/ University Press of New England, 1993.

Although this author/musician is most often identified with rhythm and blues, this work also encompasses his blues and jazz achievements and associations. Includes information on his associations with artists like Count Basie, Count Otis Matthews, Wynonie Harris, Little Esther Phillips, T-Bone Walker, Big Mama Thornton, Roy Milton, Lester Young and Eddie "Cleanhead" Vinson. Otis provides personal insight into the musical scene and historical significance of Central Avenue in Los Angeles from 1940 to 1970. Also discussed, his involvement in the Civil Rights movement and the 1991 beating of Rodney King.

## Richard "Little Richard" Penniman

626. White, Charles. *The Life and Times of Little Richard, Quasar of Rock.* Third edn. Malvern, Australia: Omnibus Press, 2003.

An authorized biography that includes information on Little Richard's early 1990s comeback, a complete discography and accounts of his recording sessions. Insights from his family, friends, fellow musicians and Richard himself were woven into this account of his life. He discusses his stage antics, flaunting of racial taboos, sexual experiences, personality, public image, career in show business and in the church, and revival of his career.

## Wilson Pickett

627. Llorens, David. "Soulin' With 'Wicked' Pickett." *Ebony*, October 1969, 130.

     Covers a variety of issues regarding his personal background, his transition from gospel music to soul, and his eventual success as a soul singer. Alludes to his time in Memphis, his eventual signing with Atlantic Records, and the influence of George Patterson and Jack Philpot.

## Otis Redding

628. Freeman, Scott. *Otis!: The Otis Redding Story*. New York: St Martin's Press, 2002.

     Traces Redding's musical life from his roots in Macon, Georgia, which, the author notes, was also home to James Brown and Little Richard. Also delves into Redding's cross-over appeal after he recorded "Dock of the Bay" in 1967, Redding's relationship with Phil Walden, his success at Stax Records, and how Motown and Stax crafted their respective styles.

629. Schiesel, Jane *The Otis Redding Story*. New York: Doubleday and Co., 1973.

     A concise look at Redding's life and musical achievements from his early years in Macon, Georgia, to his musical experiences at Stax Records and acclaim as a soul superstar. Discusses the influence of Dee Clark, Sam Cooke, James Brown, the Charms and Little Richard, his success in Europe and eventual crossover appeal.

## Martha Reeves and the Vandellas

See also item 662, Martha and the Vandellas.

630. Reeves, Martha and Mark Bego. *Dancing in the Street: Confessions of a Motown Diva*. New York: Hyperion Books, 1995.

     Reeves recounts the excitement and energy of Motown in its heyday, and the frustrations she experienced in making a musical comeback. She downplays her feuds with Berry Gordy and Diana Ross, discusses exploitation by her managers, her drug addiction and her unsuccessful romantic relationships.

## Lionel Richie and The Commodores

631. Harris, Ron. "The Commodores." *Ebony*, May 1979, 62.

The article covers the origins, roots, road to success and recordings of this popular soul group. Of special note is the insight provided about the individuals who formed and made the group successful, including Ronald LaPread, Thomas McClary, Walter Orange, Lionel Richie and Milan Williams.

632. Johnson, Robert. "Will Superstardom Spoil Lionel Richie." *Ebony,* January 1985, 27.

Details Richie's background and success as a composer and pianist. Johnson discusses his education at Tuskegee Institute, his organization of a group called the Jays while at Tuskegee, and the transformation of the Jays into The Commodores. Richie tells how he deals with success, and mentions some people who helped to develop his career.

**Smokey Robinson and the Miracles**

633. Banks, Lacy. "The Miracle of the Miracles." *Ebony,* October 1971, 164.

Covers the fourteen-year history and eleven years of hit songs of Smokey Robinson and the Miracles (including Pete Moore, Bobby Rogers, Claudette Robinson and Ronnie White). Smokey Robinson's position as vice-president of Motown Records is also discussed.

634. Moore, Trudy S. "Smokey and Claudette Robinson." *Ebony,* October 1982, 120.

This article profiles the couple who married in 1959. Discusses their singing together in high school and the recording of their first song, "Get a Job" in 1958. Smokey talks about his children, his job as vice-president of Motown records, the music business and the Miracles.

**The Ronettes**

635. N.A. "The Ronettes." *Ebony,* November 1966, 184.

Profiles the formation of the group known as the Ronettes (Estelle Bennett, Ronnie Bennett and Nedra Talley). Covers their musical backgrounds, touring with the Beatles, the impact of meeting Phil and his oversight of their career.

**Diana Ross and The Supremes**

636. N. A. "Diana Ross: A Quartet of Superstars." *Ebony,* March 1977, 156.

This article covers Ross' portrayals of four different blues singers during a television special. Includes a discussion of costumes, make-up and props. She is shown to be a versatile and talented star who possesses both acting and musical skills, hence her success in impersonating other singers.

637. N.A. "There's No Place Like Home for Diana Ross." *Ebony*, July 1973, 100.

This article focuses on her life as a wife and mother. It includes insights into her new-found happiness, her adjustment to married life and motherhood, juggling her new life with a musical career, and her reaction to the Oscar nomination for her role in *Lady Sings the Blues*.

638. N.A. "The Supremes Make it Big." *Ebony*, June 1965, 80.

Deals with the group's success and discusses their three consecutive hits, "Where Did Our Love Go," "Baby Love," and "Come See About Me." Mentions Berry Gordy, Jr, Hitsville U.S.A. and Motown records in their assent to musical success.

639. Ifkovic, Ed. *Diana's Dogs: Diana Ross and the Definition of Diva.* New York: Universe, Inc., 2007.

Discusses Diana Ross' international celebrity from an idiosyncratic perspective, from her Detroit roots to her Connecticut mansion. There is information on her temper tantrums, eating habits, homes, cars and other issues that have appeared in tabloid headlines. However, it contributes insight into her personality, which, in turn, was reflected in her music. Of special interest is the section on her Detroit roots.

640. Ribowsky, Mark. *The Supremes: A Saga of Motown Dreams, Success, and Betrayal.* New York: Da Capo, 2007.

Provides details of Florence Ballard, Diana Ross and Mary Wilson evolving from their beginning as The Primettes to stardom as The Supremes. He covers their first meeting with Berry Gordy, signing with Motown Records and their rise to popularity under the guidance of the Holland-Dozier-Holland writing team. Of special note are details about the interrelationships of the group and why they broke up.

641. Robinson, Louie. "Why Diana Ross Left The Supremes." *Ebony*, February 1970, 120.

Details why Ross left the Supremes, her achievements as a Supreme, her relationship with Barry Gordy, Jr, and why Florence Ballard left the group. Also mentions her role in the discovery of the Jackson

Five, views on marriage, future plans, and comments on both the original Supremes (Florence Ballard and Mary Wilson) and the singers who replaced them (Cindy Birdsong and Jean Terrell).

## David Ruffin

642. Sapin-Ruffin, Genna. *A Memoir: David Ruffin—My Temptations.* Bloomington, IN: Author House, 2002.

The author discusses her pursuit of Ruffin while he was still married, her eventual marriage to him and his mistreatment of her (e.g. cheating, beatings). She asserts that Ruffin's true love was Tammi Terrell, vents her anger at Ruffin and Otis Williams, and portrays herself as a victim.

## Raynoma Gordy Singleton

643. Singleton, Raynoma Gordy. *Berry, Me and Motown.* New York: McGraw-Hill, 1995.

Berry Gordy's second wife portrays him as a former pimp and a manipulator with a split personality, and reveals family secrets. More importantly, she relates her creative and administrative contributions to Motown's success, her role as co-founder of Motown, and the creation of the Motown sound.

## Phil Spector

644. Brown, Mick. *Tearing Down the Wall of Sound: The Rise and Fall of Phil Spector.* New York: Vintage Books, 2008.

He provides background information on the Beatles, Rolling Stones, Sonny and Cher, the Ronettes and how Spector became a significant record producer. He also recounts more lurid events in Spector's life, such as waving a gun in either jest, anger, or in a jealous or bullying manner.

## The Spinners

645. Douglas, Carlyle. "The Spinners." *Ebony,* July 1976, 40.

An overview of the group's beginnings and people who helped to develop their career. Discusses members of the group (B. Cameron, Henry Fambrough, Billy Henderson, Pervis Jackson and Phillippe Wynne) and the difficulty of starting a musical career. Mentions some of their hit records.

**Donna Summer**

646. Howard, Josiah. *Donna Summer: Her Life and Music.* Cranberry Township, PA: Tiny Ripple Books, 2003.

For younger readers. The book provides insight into her years in Europe, living in Greenwich Village, betrayal by loved ones, hit records and her influence as a star of disco music.

647. Smith, Kenny, Bryan P. Rooney and Vince Falzone. *Backstage With Bryan Rooney: From Liverpool to Donna Summer.* Northwich, Cheshire, UK: Arley Productions, 2008.

British roadie Rooney discusses the highs and lows of the music business, and life on the road and as a sideman for Donna Summer. He also discusses concert riots in the Frisian Islands and Milan, and a negative encounter with a policeman in Malibu, California. Also mentions other artists he toured with, including The Beatles, Keith Moon and Harry Nilsson.

648. Summer, Donna and Marc Eliot. *Ordinary Girl: The Journey.* New York: Villard Books, 2004.

Describes her years living in Europe and Greenwich Village. Discusses her Christian faith, represents her as loving, kind, talented and giving person, and mentions how some loved ones took advantage of her. Also discusses the homophobia controversy of the 1980s and provides insight into the creative process behind some of her hit recordings.

**The Temptations**

649. Cox, Ted. *The Temptations (African-American Achievers).* New York: Chelsea House, 1997.

For younger readers. Geared toward grades 9–12. Discusses the impact of Motown on the careers of many African American musicians in the 1960s. Explains how the Temptations got together, their struggles and frustrations (e.g. egos and drug issues), and the discipline they needed to achieve stardom, their decline in popularity, personnel changes, and their ability to survive and be successful in spite of the changes transpiring in African American popular music.

650. Higgins, Chester. "The Temptations." *Ebony,* April 1971, 64.

Deals with the Temps' Detroit origins, success, longevity and ability to relate their music to current trends. Information on members

Dennis Edwards, Melvin Franklin, Eddie Kendricks, Otis Williams and Paul Williams is included.

651. Robinson, Louie. "The Temptations." *Ebony*, July 1975, 114.

Discusses the group's return to the road after a four-month hiatus to rework their act. The changes included expanded use of the stage, new choreography, use of cordless microphones and the addition of new personnel. Each member of the group is introduced: original members Dennis Edwards, Melvin Franklin and Otis Williams, and new members Glenn Leonard and Richard Street.

652. Williams, Otis. *Temptations Update*. New York: Cooper Square Press, 2002.

Original Temps member Williams discusses a myriad of issues with the group, including the good and bad times, quarrels, alcohol and drug abuse, suicide and his efforts to keep the group together. Also includes how Motown instructed its group in charm, musical skills, choreography, how to dress and other skills.

## Tammi Terrell

653. Peters, Art. "The Ordeal of Tammi Terrell." *Ebony*, November 1969, 94.

Deals with her health issues, her six operations, her discovery by Berry Gordy, Jr, and her popular recordings with Marvin Gaye. Also discusses her musical background and plans for the future.

## Ike and Tina Turner

654. N.A. "Ike and Tina Turner." *Ebony*, May 1971, 88.

The article covers background of each performer, how they met and became a duo, and their eventual success. It also covers their appeal to a multiracial audience, their appearances on television shows and their tour with the Rolling Stones.

655. Christian, Margena A. "The Last Days of Ike Turner: The Story of a Rock and Roll Legend Who Lived Hard, Loved Life But Couldn't Quite Let Go of His Past." *Ebony*, October 2008, 94–100.

An in-depth provocative discussion of Ike Turner's contributions, relationships with his family and others, and the effect of drugs on his life. Written after his death on December 12, 2007 of cocaine toxicity; details the impact of his 1976 divorce from Tina Turner, and discusses his several divorces, his early years in Clarksdale, Mississippi and his contributions to music. Extensive input from associates and family members, including Falina Rasool (a background singer and his personal assistant and caregiver), his sister Ruby Aillene Selico, and Ronnie Turner, Ike and Tina's only child together.

656.  Collis, John. *Ike Turner: King of Rhythm.* New York: Do-Not Press, 2004.

Profiles his career beginning at Sun Records where his song "Rocket 88" was first recorded, and his success and meeting Anna Mae Bullock (Tina Turner). In addition to their numerous hits, including "Proud Mary," Collis discusses Ike's drug abuse, abuse of Tina, prison time and the rehabilitation of his career.

657.  Norment, Lynn. "Tina Turner: Sizzling at 45." *Ebony,* May 1985, 76.

This article covers her career in the ten years after leaving Ike Turner, her husband and musical partner, in 1975. The article details the hit songs she has recorded as a solo artist (e.g. *Private Dancer*), and the diversification of her career (e.g. a role in the film *Mad Max: Beyond Thunderdome*). Also mentioned are Turner's associations with Mick Jagger, Al Green, Lionel Richie, Martin Short, The Rolling Stones, and Craig, Ron and Ike Turner.

658.  ——. "Tina Turner: Single, Sassy and Going Strong." *Ebony,* June 1982, 66.

Tina discusses her twenty-year musical career, as both a member of the Ike and Tina Turner Revue and later as a solo performer. She traces the beginning of her act with Ike back to Tennessee and later to St Louis. She also discusses her children, touring with the Rolling Stones, early concerts and recordings, and her Buddhist beliefs.

659.  Turner, Ike. *Taking Back My Name: The Confessions of Ike Turner.* New York: Virgin Books, 1999.

This autobiography covers his life from his birth in Clarksdale, Mississippi. Discusses his work with Sun Records and his contributions to R&B and rock and roll. Little Richard credits Ike with being the "architect of rock and roll." Ike blames Tina Turner for most of their marital problems and presents his version of their relationship.

660.  Turner, Tina and Kurt Loder. *Tina.* New York: William Morrow and Co., 1986.

Tina presents an honest and forthright account of her life and career. She covers life issues ranging from her abandonment at age ten to her teaming with Ike Turner at the age of eighteen. She also discusses her marriage, divorce, recordings, her return to success with the *Private Dancer* album, and her staying power since then.

## Usher

661. Torres, John-Albert. *Usher*. Blue Banner Biographies. Hockessin, DE: Mitchell Lane Publishers, 2005.

For younger readers. In this thirty-two-page biography for ages 9–12, Torres discusses his experiences in New York, the influence of Michael Jackson, role of Jermaine Dupri and his rise to success.

## Martha and the Vandellas

See also item 630.

662. N.A. "Martha and the Vandellas." *Ebony*, February 1968, 83.

Describes the group's efforts to emerge from the shadow of the Supremes and establish their own musical identity. In addition to their individual and musical backgrounds, the article illuminates their beginning in show business and discusses their club dates.

## Luther Vandross

663. Normet, Lynn. "Luther Vandross." *Ebony*, December 1985, 83.

Discusses his career to the age of forty-four, when this article was written. His career is detailed from stints as a background singer with The Average White Band, Carly Simon, Sister Sledge, Ringo Starr and other performers. Includes information on his early years in New York, his one year at Western Michigan University and his success as a crooner. His song "Everybody Rejoice," which was included in *The Wiz*, is discussed.

## War

664. Robinson, Louie. "The Funky Sound of War." *Ebony*, March 1975, 84.

This group formed in the late 1960s as Eric Burden and War. Robinson discusses War's major hits and albums, two noteworthy concerts in the north-west, and the importance of audience reaction in creating their reputation. Jimi Hendrix and Sly and the Family Stone are mentioned as musical influences.

## Billy Ward and the Dominoes

665. N.A. "The Dominoes." *Ebony*, February 1954, 23.

Discusses the popularity of the group in its heyday and its enormous record sales. Contains important information on Billy Ward, the group's arranger and coach. The article profiles Ward's beginnings and success as a composer of more than 600 songs, several of which sold over 1 million copies. Other members of the quintet and their hits are mentioned.

## Fred Wesley, Jr.

666. Wesley, Fred. *Hit Me, Fred: Recollections of a Sideman*. Durham: Duke University Press, 2005.

A thoroughly engaging memoir of his life in music written in graphic language, and permeated with information on his work with James Brown. In addition, he discusses his career struggles in Los Angeles, playing jazz in Denver, overcoming a cocaine habit, and his role and function as James Brown's bandleader for many years.

## Jerry Wexler

667. Lewis, Randy. "Record Producer was Godfather of R&B." *Los Angeles Times*. August 16, 2008: B6.

A detailed obituary of Jerry Wexler. He joined Ahmet Ertegun in the business and production side of R&B from the 1950s to the 1970s they ran Atlantic Records, one of the most successful and influential record labels in music history. He signed and produced many influential artists, including Ray Charles, The Coasters, The Drifters, Aretha Franklin, Wilson Pickett, Led Zeppelin and many more. In addition to exposing mainstream white Americans to African American music, while a reporter at Billboard magazine, Wexler is credited with changing the chart category from "race records" to rhythm and blues. Photograph of Ertegun, Big Joe Turner and Jerry Wexler.

668. Wexler, Jerry and David Ritz. *Rhythm and the Blues: A Life in American Music*. New York: St Martin's Press, 1994.

This memoir discusses Wexler's career highs and lows. He produced artists like Ray Charles, Bob Dylan, Solomon Burke, Etta James, Aretha Franklin and Wilson Pickett. Discusses his relationship with Ahmed Ertegun, bad business decisions, his troubled family, personal feuds and his role as co-owner of Atlantic Records.

## Barry White

669. N.A. "Barry White." *Ebony*, March 1979, 41.

Addresses the lavish lifestyle of the composer-singer, and discusses his $1.5 million home, his family, and his penchant for acquiring eels, fish, horses and sharks. A special feature of the article is the coverage of his wife Glodean White, and his numerous awards and accomplishments in the recording industry.

670. White, Barry and Marc Eliot. *Love Unlimited: Insights on Life and Love*. New York: Virgin Books, 2001.

The singer unveils both his life and philosophy from his early years in south central Los Angeles. The eleven chapters are permeated with advice on how to find, cherish, keep and make love last forever. He also covers his gang membership, prison sentence and his life before he became a famous musician. This is important information because it explores contexts and issues that shaped his music.

## Norman Whitfield

671. Lewin, Randy. "Motown Producer, Songwriter Won 2 Grammies." *Los Angeles Times*. September 18, 2008: B6.

The obituary of the famous and productive producer and songwriter Norman Whitfield covers his contributions to rhythm and blues and soul music at Motown in the 1960s and 1970s. Includes a discussion of songs he wrote for artists like Marvin Gaye, Barrett Strong, the Temptations, Edwin Starr and several others. His many hits include "Beauty is Only Skin Deep," "Ain't Too Proud to Beg," "Papa Was a Rolling Stone," "I Heard it Through the Grapevine," and "Just My Imagination."

## Jackie Wilson

672. Douglas, Tony. *Jackie Wilson: Lonely Teardrops*. New York: Routledge, 2005.

Covers Wilson's life from his early childhood, through his drug addiction, to stardom an as international proponent of R&B. Discusses his hits, crossover appeal, appearances on white TV shows hosted by icons like Dick Clark, and his death.

## Mary Wilson

673. Wilson, Mary. *Dreamgirl and Supreme Faith, Updated Edition: My Life as a Supreme*. New York: Cooper Square Press, 2000.

Discusses the singer's life, musical growth, and issues surrounding her career and her split from the Supremes. Offers her insights on relationships with Berry Gordy, Diana Ross and Florence Ballard. She is portrayed as someone who always defended the Supremes and Diana Ross throughout her musical and public life.

### Bob "Wolfman Jack" Smith

674. Jack, Wolfman and Byron Laursen. *Have Mercy!: Confessions of the Original Rock and Roll Animal.* New York: Warner Brothers, 1995.

Discusses the life and achievements of Bob Smith ("Wolfman Jack"). He recounts his childhood passion for black music that dates to the 1950s, his humble beginnings in Norfolk, Virginia, and his experiences as a radio disc jockey near the Mexican border. He pays tribute to Chuck Berry, Ray Charles, Elvis Presley and many others.

### The Womenfolk

675. N.A. "The Womenfolk." *Ebony*, June 1964, 182.

A concise description of a racially-mixed, all-female R&B group that was active on the west coast in the early 1960s. Their lifestyles before and after the establishment of the group and how they came together is discussed. The group's members are discussed, consisting of Jean Amos, Leni Ashmore, Barbara Cooper, Judy Fine and Joyce James.

### Stevie Wonder

676. Altman, Linda Jacobs. *Stevie Wonder: Sunshine in the Shadow (Men Behind the Bright Lights)*. New York: EMC, 1976.

A concise thirty-eight pages; covers his life from his humble beginnings in an abusive home, meeting Berry Gordy, Jr and signing with Motown records. His rise to success, hit records, influences and deep concern for social issues are also discussed.

677. Davis, Sharon. *Stevie Wonder: Rhythms of Wonder*. London: Anova Books, 2006.

Provides insights and assessments of his life from poverty to superstardom. His early years, sight impairment, discovery by Motown, signing a contract with Berry Gordy, Jr, involvement in Civil Rights and other social issues, and an assessment of his many musical hits and musical contributions are also included.

678. Haskins, James. *The Story of Stevie Wonder.* New York: Dell, 1979.

Focuses on Wonder's early years, attracting the attention of Berry Gordy, Jr, strong interest in Civil Rights and relationship with Martin Luther King, Jr, his immense success with hit recordings, his overall contributions to R&B and soul, and more.

679. Hughes, Timothy S. "Groove and Flow: Six Analytical Essays on the Music of Stevie Wonder." PhD dissertation, University of Washington, 2003.

This dissertation is a collection of six analytical essays on soul and funk songs recorded by Stevie Wonder between 1972 and 1974. Concerned specifically with Wonder's use of repeated musical figures, how grooves function, and his use of "flow" to give songs shape and life. Explains the musical concepts of groove and flow and how they are connected to funk and soul. Also discusses Wonder's Clavinet-based funk music, and analyzes songs like "Superstition," "Higher Ground," "You Haven't Done Nothing," and "Golden Lady." The overall focus is on the grooves that are so essential to funk, and their function in providing power and life to the genre.

680. Lodder, Steve and Stevie Wonder. *Stevie Wonder: A Musical Guide to the Classic Albums.* San Francisco: Backbeat Books, 2008.

Tells the story of Wonder from a new perspective by concentrating on his most productive years, 1971–81. Covers his background, meeting Berry Gordy, Jr and the early years with Motown. Assesses the musical characteristics and influences found on Wonder's classic 1970 albums, including *Music of My Mind, Innervisions, Songs in the Key of Life,* and *Talking Book.* Lodder also discusses the lyrical influence of Marvin Gaye and Sly Stone. Eighty color and black-and-white photographs.

681. Love, Dennis and Stacy Brown. *Blind Faith: The Miraculous Journey of Lula Hardaway, Stevie Wonder's Mother.* New York: Simon and Schuster, 2007.

The authors conducted extensive interviews with both Hardaway and Wonder, and profiles them in this book. Regarding Wonder, they discuss his musical abilities, good nature, commitment to social issues and musical success. Hardaway's life is covered from her birth into poverty, through marriage to Calvin Judkins, an abusive, alcoholic husband who forced her into prostitution, and more. The authors make it a major point in the book to show that once Wonder became successful he improved her life.

682. Marvis, B. and Nathan I. Huggins. *Stevie Wonder.* New York: Chelsea House, 1995.

For younger readers. This account of his life for young adults concentrates on his journey from the early years in poverty to the cultivation of his talent, and eventual success with Motown Records. Wonder's ability to overcome adversity to achieve success is an important message.

683. Slater, Jack. "Stevie Wonder." *Ebony*, January 1977, 29.

A detailed description of his background, early life, and eventual success as a composer and performer. The article covers his early life in Detroit, his career with Motown and how it began, and his rise to musical greatness. Of special note is his discussion of how his music reflects his personal experiences and thoughts on many topics, from romance to social justice to spiritual motivation. He also mentions Berry Gordy, Jr, Ronnie White and the Miracles.

684. Swenson, John. *Stevie Wonder.* Medford, MA: Plexus Publishing Ltd, 1989.

Begins with his early years in poverty and the cultivation of his talent on the harmonica; discusses his sight impairment, meeting Berry Gordy, Jr and signing with Motown records. Includes insights into his rise to musical success, hit records, influences and deep concern for social issues, especially the Civil Rights movement and the cause of Martin Luther King, Jr.

685. Taylor, Rick. *Stevie Wonder: The Illustrated Disco/Biography.* New York: Cherry Lane Music, 1985.

The biographical details of his life and musical success are supplemented with numerous illustrations. There are no new details on his life; the coverage focuses on his early years to his rise to international success. The illustrations cover a myriad of situations dealing with his life and musical success.

686. Troupe, Quincy and Lisa Cohen. *Little Stevie Wonder.* Boston: Houghton Mifflin, 2005.

For younger readers. Written for grades 2–4, this concise account of Wonder's life focuses on his rise to prominence from poverty, musical contributions, affinity with others and musical success. Wonder frames his discussion within the context of his recording of "Isn't She Lovely."

687. Williams, Tenley and James Scott Brady. *Stevie Wonder (Overcoming Adversity).* New York: Chelsea House, 2001.

For younger readers. This concise account of his life is geared to young readers, specifically grades 7–10, and follows Wonder's life from poverty to world renown. The central theme is that although he was born into poverty, his talent and hard work enabled him to achieve and to become an icon in the music world.

688. Wonder, Stevie. *The Stevie Wonder Anthology.* Milwaukee: Hal Leonard, 2002.

This is one of several collections of Wonder's music. Includes seventy-five songs from 1963–98, like "Reggae Woman," "Ebony and Ivory," "Fingertips (Part 2)," "Higher Ground," "Part Time Lover," and "You are the Sunshine of My Life."

## COLLECTIVE BIOGRAPHIES

689. Baptista, Todd R. *Group Harmony: Echoes of the Rhythm and Blues Era.* Paducah, KY: Collectables, 2007.

A study of the men and women of rhythm and blues, featuring numerous biographies of individuals and vocal harmony groups from the 1950s. Many interviews, several rare photographs, and good discographies.

690. Berry, Bill. "The Hottest of the Hot Groups." *Ebony,* July 1978, 32.

Discusses the history and musical style of five popular musical groups of the time: The Commodores; Bootsy's Rubber Band; Earth, Wind and Fire; Rufus Featuring Chaka Khan; and Parliament/Funkadelic.

691. Bogle, Donald. *Brown Sugar: Over 100 Years of America's Black Female Superstars.* London: Continuum, 2007.

Originally published in 1980, this version covers the "dark divas" to around 2006. He examines the lives, careers, contradictory images and private anxieties of artists like Ma Rainey, Josephine Baker, Ethel Waters, Billie Holiday, Lena Horn, Marian Anderson, Dorothy Dandridge, Pearl Bailey, Diana Ross and the Supremes, Aretha Franklin, Donna Summer, Lauren Hill, Queen Latifah, Beyoncé and many more. Bogle was the first author to apply the operatic term "diva" to pop goddesses. Many illustrations.

692. Brooks, TaKeshia. *Dream Factory Deferred: Black Womanhood, History and Music Video.* New York: I. Universe, Inc., 2007.

Discusses the stage on which black females have performed since the days of Sarah Bartmann, "The Hottentot Venus," wowed Europe. Within this context, the author discusses the gender-related issues that have confronted neo-soul artists like Erykah Badu, Lauryn Hill,

India.Arie, Macie Gray, Meshell Ndegeocello, Jill Scott and Angie Stone.

693. Broven, John. *Record Makers and Breakers: Voices of the Independent Rock and Roll Pioneers.* Urbana: University of Illinois Press, 2008.

Traces the history of the independent rock and roll industry from its regional beginnings in the 1940s with R&B and hillbilly music to its decline in the 1960s. Covers the nurturing of artists like Chuck Berry, Fats Domino, B.B. King, Elvis Presley and others. Interviews with majors players in the independent record business like Joe Bihari of Modern Records, Marshall Chess of Chess Records, Jerry Wexler, Ahmet Ertegun and Miriam Penstock of Atlantic records, Sam Philips of Sun Records, Art Rupe of Specialty Records, as well as Mimi Trepel of London records, music publishers Gene Goodman and Freddy Bienstock, and disc jockey Bill "Hoss" Allen of WLAC radio in Nashville, Tennessee.

694. Deffa, Chip. *Blue Rhythms: Six Lines in Rhythm and Blues.* Music in American Life Series. Urbana: University of Illinois Press, 1996.

Although the title indicates rhythm and blues, three of the six profiled artists are also known and respected as blues artists. The inclusion of Charles Brown, Floyd Dixon and Jimmy Witherspoon lends a blues flavor to his profiles of Lavern Baker, Ruth Brown and Little Jimmy Scott. Covers the trials and tribulations of their careers and the musical, racial, social and cultural complexities of performing and presenting their music. Extensive notes and a selected discography.

695. Fitzgerald, Jon. "Black Pop Songwriting, 1963–66: An Analysis of the U.S. Top Forty Hits by Cooke, Mayfield, Stevenson, Robinson, and Holland-Dozier-Holland." *Black Music Research Journal* 27(2) (Fall 2007): 97–141.

Traces the evolution of black songwriters from the early successes of Sam Cooke and Curtis Mayfield to the crossover success of Motown composers and others. Concise biographies of Cooke, Mayfield, Smokey Robinson, William Stevenson and Holland-Dozier-Holland. Identifies the hits of these composers from 1963–66. Informative analyses of lyrics, melodies and rhythms.

696. Freeland, David. *Ladies of Soul.* Jackson: University Press of Mississippi, 2001.

Penetrating insights into the lives and rise to fame of seven female soul singers in the 1960s: Maxine Brown, Ruby Johnson, Denise LaSalle, Bettye LeVette, Barbara Mason and Timi Yuro. The author situates the artists within the social context of the 1960s, and chronicles their encounters with racism, sexism in the music industry, conflict with male managers, hardships on the road, competition within the music business, and the hopes, desires and dreams of each singer. Nine photographs, a bibliography, discography and introduction.

697. Garland, Phyl. "The 'In' Groups of the Big Beat." *Ebony*, June 1967, 38.

Covers groups include Little Anthony and the Imperials, Mills Brothers, The Marvelettes, The Miracles, The Supremes, The Temptations, Martha and the Vandellas, and Sam and Dave. Discusses the success of the major vocal groups of 1967, white acceptance of African American music in the media, and biographies of selected individuals within the groups.

698. Hildenbrand, Lee. *Stars of Soul and Rhythm and Blues: Top Recording Artists and Showstopping Performances, From Memphis and Motown to Now.* New York Watson-Guptill Publishes (Crown), 1994.

Profiles numerous soul and R&B artists with a emphasis on the hit makers. Covers vocalists, bandleaders and composers; many photographs.

699. Hirshey, Gerri. *Nowhere to Run: The Story of Soul Music.* City: Southbank Publishing, 2006.

An oral history of artists like James Brown, Ray Charles, Marvin Gaye, Screamin' Jay Hawkins, Aretha Franklin, Smokey Robinson, Diana Ross, Mary Wilson and Wilson Pickett. Interviews provide facts about their music, associations, successes, failures, and contributions to soul music.

700. Kohl, Paul Robert. "Who Stole the Soul? Rock and Roll, Race, and Rebellion." PhD dissertation, University of Utah, 1994.

This dissertation investigates the reactive music from African American artists who followed the Civil Rights movement and integration, with a focus on James Brown and Berry Gordy, Jr. The author argues that while Brown's recordings reflected the separatist philosophies of political activists like Malcolm X, Gordy's work with Motown Records paralleled the integrationist stance of Martin Luther King, Jr. In addition, he discusses the music of Marvin Gaye, Sly and the Family Stone, and some rap musicians regarding the commercial success of African American traditions.

701. Landau, Jon. *It's Too Late to Stop Now: A Rock and Roll Journal.* San Francisco: Straight Arrow Books, 1970.

A compilation of journalistic and critical essays, many of which were published in *Rolling Stone* between 1966 and 1971. The book is divided into two sections, "white rock" and "black rock." The latter section contains essays on Ray Charles, King Curtis, Aretha Franklin, B.B. King, Sly and the Family Stone, Valerie Simpson, Otis Redding, Wilson Pickett, and Motown.

702. Nathan, David. *The Soulful Divas: Personal Portraits of Over a Dozen Divas, from Nina Simone, Aretha Franklin and Diana Ross to Patti LaBelle, Whitney Houston and Janet Jackson.* New York: Billboard Books, 1999.

In addition to the artists cited in the title, also profiles Esther Phillips, Doris Troy, Gladys Knight, Chaka Khan, Millie Jackson, Natalie Cole, Phyllis Hyman, Roberta Flack and Anita Baker. The author interviewed each artist and includes quotes and background information. General purpose is to pay respect to female artists who have impacted his life and the lives of others. The book is arranged in the order in which he met the artists.

703. Robertson, Regina R. "Ladies First." *Essence*, June 2008, 122–31.

Provocative and insightful interviews with Mary J. Blige, Alicia Keys and Jill Scott, discussing how they rely on the elements (voice and artistry) that drew them to the music. They also reveal how they pen hits, embrace success, and the steps they take to stay ahead of the musical curve and their competition.

704. Warwick, Jacqueline. *Girl Groups, Girl Culture: Popular Music and Identity in the 1960s.* New York: Routledge, 2007.

The author addresses 1960s girl group music from the perspective of teenage girls, using methodologies from psychology and sociology to gauge the role and function of the repertoire in the emotional development of young girls of the baby boom generation. Also addresses class, gender, race and sexuality.

705. Werner, Craig. *Higher Ground: Stevie Wonder, Aretha Franklin, Curtis Mayfield, and The Rise and Fall of American Soul.* New York: Crown, 2004.

A biography of three artists who became major soul creators and stars. Demonstrates how historical events impacted their lives and discusses each singer's individual impact on the culture and music. He attributes their success to their creativity, ability to write and perform songs that appeal to the public, and their ability to combine gospel and soul musical elements. He also argues that the migrations of African Americans from the south into mid-western and north-eastern cities created an audience for the music in those areas.

## DISCOGRAPHIES AND LISTENING GUIDES

706. Bogdanov, Vladimir, John Bush, Stephen Thomas Erlewine and Chris Woodstra, eds. *All Music Guide to Soul: The Definitive Guide to R&B and Soul.* San Francisco: Backbeat Books, 2003.

The latest in a series of books on related topics, this comprehensive guide to soul and rhythm and blues includes around 8,500 reviews of 1,500 artists. Filled with reviews that lead users to the best recordings by their favorite artists and introduces them to new music and artists in similar genres. Includes biographies, essays and "music maps" that trace the history and evolution of soul music from its roots in blues and gospel music to its flowering in Memphis and Motown and its many musical branches of today. Complete discographies, with important out-of-print albums and import-only releases.

707. Graff, Gary, Josh Freeman Du Lac, Jim McFarlin and Kurtis Blow, eds. *Musichound R&B: The Essentials Album Guide.* New York: Schirmer Books, 1998.

Reviews of 1,000 individuals artists and groups, including a significant number of hip hop and rap artists. Thorough and replete with biographical and other information. The book is interesting because it gives equal treatment to diverse artists like Bobby Brown, Toni Braxton, Sheena Easton, Sam Cooke, and the Stax and Motown recording artists. Few pre-rock artists are included, and several classic 1960 soul artists like Garnett Mimms, a regional star with several hit recordings, are omitted. Useful appendices include fan sites; a companion CD contains several gems from the Mercury Records catalog.

708. Hansen, Barret Eugene. "Negro Popular Music, 1945–53." Masters thesis, University of California, Los Angeles, 1967.

The author analyzes numerous recordings of R&B, blues and other tunes that enjoyed mass acceptance by African Americans during the period of his research, and isolates the vocal characteristics of each. The compositions were taken from the lists of top tunes from Billboard and the Harlem Hit Parade. Among the many recordings discussed are those of Roy Brown, Ruth Brown, the Clovers, the Dominoes, Louis Jordan, Joe Liggins, Amos Milburn, Willie Mae "Big Mama" Thornton, the Five Royales, Jimmy Witherspoon and many others.

709. Pavlow, Al. *Big Al Pavlow's the R and B Book: A Disc-History of Rhythm and Blues.* Second edn. New York: Music House Publishers, 1983.

     First released in 1983, the book focuses on doo-wop and R&B in the 1950s, but also includes information on black music of the 1940s. Documents thousands of 45-rpm and 78-rpm recordings that are important to the history and evolution of R&B and the roots of rock and roll. Written by a record store owner in Providence, Rhode Island, the book fills a void in American popular music to 1983.

710. Pruter, Robert, ed. *The Blackwell Guide to Soul Recordings.* Blackwell Reference. London: Blackwell Publishers, 1993.

     This guide to soul recordings is permeated with information about artists and recordings ranging from some of the earliest performances to the early 1990s. In addition to covering pioneering artists like James Brown, Marvin Gaye, Aretha Franklin, Stevie Wonder and the Temptations, he covers numerous other artists like Gladys Knight, Al Green, The Shirelles and many more.

711. Shapiro, Peter. *The Rough Guide to Soul and R&B.* New York: Rough Guides, 2006.

     A comprehensive guide to musicians, singers, songwriters and record labels that encapsulates the history from gospel and doo-wop to disco, hip hop and R&B. Includes interviews of more than 300 artists, reviews of numerous albums, recommended playlists and many photographs.

712. ———. *The Rough Guide to Soul: 100 Essential CDs.* New York: Rough Guides, 2000.

     A concise collection of 100 essential soul recordings, formatted in a pocket size. Because of its small size, not all albums are reviewed in detail; the reviews range from decent to informative.

713. Tee, Ralph. *The Best of Soul: The Essential CD Guide:* San Francisco: Collins Publishers, 1993.

     Contains CD suggestions from Atlantic, Motown, Stax and Philadelphia International recording artists. The CDs are supplemented with background information, including the date of the recording and side personnel.

714. Thompson, Dave. *Funk: Third Ear—The Essential Listening Companion.* San Francisco: Backbeat Books, 2001.

     A listening companion of approximately 1,500 recordings, divided into categories like prefunk, classic funk, disco funk and new school funk. Also contains succinct annotations of many recordings, and discussions of topics like the psych-funka-delic experience, Motown's treatment of funk, blaxploitation films and funk music, the British funk connection, the decline of funk, and more.

715. Whitburn, Joel. *Joel Whitburn's Top Rhythm and Blues Records 1972 Through 1977*. 5 vols. New York: Record Research, 1978.

Comprehensive and thorough annotations of numerous recordings dating back to some of the Bird groups. Also lists the recordings of Motown, selected Stax, and some of Philadelphia International Records stars.

716. White, Adam and Fred Branson. *The Billboard Book of Number One Rhythm and Blues Hits*. New York: Billboard Books, 1993.

Tells the stories behind twenty-five years of hits for recording labels like Atlantic, Motown, Stax, Philadelphia International and others. More than a list of hits, the book contains historical background on many hits, including Smokey Robinson's "Being With You," originally written for Kim Carnes after her success with a cover of Smokey Robinson and the Miracles' song "More Love."

717. White, George. *The Complete Bo Diddley Sessions: Bo Diddley Discography*. Upper Poppleton, York, UK: Music Mentor Books, 1993.

A complete discography of Diddley's American and British recordings until 1993. Includes details of his bands' histories, session details, recordings from 1955 to 1992 (including his BBC recordings), film and video performances, label shots, guest appearances on other artists' sessions, and vintage ads.

## HISTORIES AND SURVEYS

718. Busnar, Gene. *The Rhythm and Blues Story*. New York: Julian Messner, 1985.

For younger readers. Traces the history of rhythm and blues from its African roots through its influence on artists like Michael Jackson, Prince and Bruce Springsteen. The book is geared to grades 6–9, and is permeated with personal but undocumented statements.

719. Garland, Phyl. *The Sound of Soul*. Chicago: Henry Regency, 1969.

An analysis and history of soul music from its roots to the late 1960s. Focuses on recording in Memphis (Stax records, musicians, context) and artists like B.B. King, Nina Simone and Aretha Franklin. Includes a provocative discussion of soul in jazz with a focus on then-modernists like John Coltrane.

720. Goosman, Stuart. *Group Harmony: The Black Urban Roots of Rhythm and Blues*. Philadelphia: University of Pennsylvania Press, 2005.

The book is based on the author's fieldwork for his doctoral degree in Ethnomusicology at the University of Washington. Presents a deep awareness of the convictions, energies, talent and traditions that gave rise to the harmony used by rhythm and blues groups. He covers the contributions of the Cardinals, Clovers, Orioles and Swallows, and includes the recollections of groups like the Dunbar Four, Four Bars of Rhythm, Five Blue Notes, the Hi Fives and individuals like Deborah Chessler, Maurice Hulbert, Al "Big Boy" Jefferson, Jimmy McPhail, Jessie Stone and others.

721. ——. "The Black Authentic: Structure, Style, and Values in Group Harmony." *Black Music Research Journal* 17(1) (1997): 81–101.

A concise discussion of issues regarding mixing and re-mixing African and European vocal concepts in post-war black popular music, especially the harmonizing styles of groups like the Cardinals, Clovers, Orioles and the Swallows. The author is concerned with the concept of doubleness—deriving more than one meaning from a word or phrase—in black cultural forms, and whether music derives any special power from doubleness. He draws on fieldwork conducted in Washington, DC, and Baltimore, Maryland.

722. Grendysa, Peter A. *Atlantic Rhythm and Blues, 1947–1974*. New York: Atlantic Recording Corporation, 1991.

Covers the lives and music of several Atlantic R&B stars, including Aretha Franklin and Wilson Pickett. He discusses the roles of Jerry Wexler and Ahmet Ertegun in founding the label, signing talent and producing numerous hit recordings.

723. Gribin, Anthony J. and Matthew M. Schiff. *Doo-Wop: The Forgotten Third of Rock 'n' Roll*. New York: Krause Publishers, 1992.

A good history of the music from the 1950s through the early 1970s. Defines and provide illustrations of the music that lies, stylistically, somewhere between R&B and rock and roll. Sixty-four musical examples, over 100 photographs, and a list of the prices of 1,000 doo-wop recordings.

724. Haralambos, Michael. *Soul Music: The Birth of a Sound in Black America*. New York: Da Capo Press, 1985.

Discusses the blues roots of soul music and its transformation of soul from its earliest styles to the mid-1980s. Covers the history from 1950s when black pride, self-awareness and black consciousness were at their peaks. Contains lots of information on musicians who were active as both artists and promoters of the music, like Ray Charles, Bobby Blue Bland, James Brown, King Curtis, Little Milton, The Impressions, Johnnie Taylor, Sonny Boy Williamson, Stevie Wonder and others.

725. ——. *Right On: From Blues to Soul in Black America.* New York: Drake Publishers, 1975.

Covers the evolution of soul music from its blues roots, and includes a discussion of musicians, issues and context. Focuses on soul music from the 1950s to the mid-1970s.

726. Herbert, Sharmine S. "Rhythm and Blues, 1968–72: An African-Centered Rhetorical Analysis." PhD dissertation, Howard University, 2000.

The author advocates that R&B has served as a tool for expression and entertainment continuously from its advent in the 1940s until it was used as an outlet for social protest (ca. 1968–72). Analyzes selected R&B songs of James Brown, Marvin Gaye, Curtis Mayfield, Gil Scott-Heron, The Last Poets and Nina Simone that were released during the time period of the study. Using a multifaceted methodology (including an African-centered rhetorical analysis of selected, notions of Africology, revolutionary rhetorical analysis and black cultural analysis), the author illustrates that themes from the songs align with the dominant themes of the Black Power movement during that same time period.

727. Jones, Alan, Jussi Kantonen and Joel Brodsky. *Saturday Night Forever: The Story of Disco.* Chicago: Chicago Review Press, 2000.

Covers the history of disco from its underground venues of New York City through its rise to international acclaim. Provides instruction on how to dance the Hustle and the Bus Stop; also covers fashions, gay subculture, drugs, clubs, the influence of James Brown, Gloria Gaynor, and more.

728. Jones, Ferdinand and Arthur C. Jones, eds. *The Triumph of the Soul Cultural and Psychological Aspects of African American Music.* Westport, CT: Praeger, 2001.

A collection of essays by writers like Peter R. Aschoff, Leonard Brown, Michael White, Angela M.S. Nelson, Cheryl Keyes, William Lowe and the editors focus on the deep aesthetical and cultural meanings of genres like blues, jazz, rap, spirituals and gospel music.

729. Mahon, Maureen. "Rock: Race, Gender, and Genre; The Power Dynamics of Rock." In *African American Music: An Introduction,*

eds Mellonee Burnim and Portia Maultsby, pp. 558–85. New York: Routledge, 2006.

Although gender, race and genre are the primary areas of discussion, the essay is also relevant to history because the author discusses the significant contributions of black women and their influence on whites and blacks, male and female, throughout the history of rock and roll. Specifically, the author illustrates that black women are an extricable part of rock and roll, and demonstrates that the form as we know it today would not have developed without their influence. Also discusses foundational figures like Ruth Brown and Etta James, girl groups like the Ronettes, black backups, Patti LaBelle, and the influence of artists like Willie Mae "Big Mama" Thornton on Elvis Presley, Tina Turner on Mick Jagger, and more.

730. Maultsby, Portia. "Funk." In *African American Music: An Introduction*, eds Mellonee V. Burnim and Portia Maultsby, pp. 293–315. New York: Routledge, 2006.

Describes funk as a form of urban dance music, also known as party music, which emerged in the late 1960s and owes its origins to the musical creations of R&B and jazz musicians. Covers early architects like James Brown and Sly and the Family Stone, funk lyrics, party themes, social and political commentary, male and female relationships, performance aesthetics, disco and electro-funk, the role of artists like George Clinton, and much more. The most comprehensive discussion of the genre to date.

731. ——. "Rhythm and Blues." In *African American Music: An Introduction*, eds Mellonee V. Burnim and Portia Maultsby, pp. 245–71. New York: Routledge, 2006.

A historical overview of the style from 1939 to contemporary times. Discusses the social context and migration of southern blacks during World War II, the musical roots of R&B, first-generation performers, combos like those of Louis Jordan and Nat "King" Cole, vocal harmony groups, second-generation performers, crossover formulas, and much more. Thorough and well written.

732. ——. "Soul." In *African American Music: An Introduction*, eds Mellonee V. Burnim and Portia Maultsby, pp. 271–93. New York: Routledge, 2006.

Describes soul music as a form of urban black popular music, derived from rhythm and blues of the 1950s, which crystallized in the late 1960s and peaked in the mid-1970s. The author presents the architects of soul (especially the contributions of Ray Charles, James Brown and Sam Cooke) and discusses the social and historical roots of the music, soul lyrics, Civil Rights and Black Power, the soul musical aesthetic, the decline of the soul era, neo soul and more. The essay is more definitive than most on the topic.

733. McCutcheon, Lynn Ellis. *Rhythm and Blues: An Experience and Adventure in its Origin and Development.* Arlington, VA: Beatty, 1971.

Divides the development of rhythm and blues into three eras: the pioneer era from 1946 to 1956, the rock and roll era from 1955 to 1963, and the soul era from 1964 to 1971. The origins of rhythm and blues are covered in the first section. The second presents a chronological account of record labels, artists, records and events. Major artists and R&B in the early 1970s is covered in the last section.

734. Meadows, Eddie S. "A Preliminary Analysis of Early Rhythm and Blues Musical Practices." *Western Journal of Black Studies* 7(3) (Fall 1983): 172–83.

Focuses on the origin and naming of groups, role of instruments in R&B orchestras, soloists/groups vocal practices, and the role that independent record companies played in the success or failure of soloists and groups. Limited historical information (1946 to the early 1960s) supplements the primary focus on soloists and groups.

735. Merlis, Bob and Davin Seay, eds. *Heart and Soul: A Celebration of Black Music Style in America 1930–1975.* New York: Stewart-Tabori and Chang (Abrams), 1997.

The author, an executive at Warner Brothers Records, a Board Member of the Blues Foundation, and a member of the Rock and Roll Hall of Fame Nominating Committee, tells the story of the evolution of black music by recalling stories about Lavern Baker, Solomon Burke, Jay Hawkins, Frankie Lymon and O.V. Wright. Some 400 photographs of advertisements, magazine covers, publicity shots, posters and programs.

736. Morrow, Bruce with Rich Maloof. *Doo-Wop: The Music, The Times, The Era.* Foreword by Neil Sedaka; introduction by T.J. Lubinsky. New York: Sterling Publishers, 2007.

Disc jockey Cousin Brucie traces the roots of doo-wop from early African American slave songs to its heyday in the 1950s and decline in the late 1960s. Covers popular prolific groups like the Platters and lesser-known "one-hit wonders" like the Chords. Also discusses art, architecture, politics and popular culture of the era.

737. Ortizano, Giacomo Luigi. "On Your Radio: A Descriptive History of Rhythm-and-Blues Radio During the 1950s." PhD dissertation, Ohio University, 1993.

Focuses on the era when network radio was losing its audience to television and examines related issues: the 1950s, R&B, the radio format, radio stations, advertising, sexually suggestive song lyrics, and payola. Data was collected from books, periodicals, reports, sound recordings and personal interviews. The author argues that the payola scandal of 1959 contributed to the decline of 1950s R&B radio, that British rock and soul took away the market for music with an earlier 1950s sound, and new developments—broader radio formats, Latin rhythm and blues and the pioneers of the oldies radio—helped to keep the music on the air, albeit at a lesser level than in the 1950s.

738. Ripani, Richard J. *The New Blue Music: Changes in Rhythm and Blues, 1950–1999*. Jackson: University Press of Mississippi, 2006.

An outgrowth of the author's doctoral dissertation at the University of Memphis. Analyzes the music of artists like Louis Jordan, John Lee Hooker, Ray Charles, James Brown, Earth, Wind and Fire, Michael Jackson, Public Enemy, Mariah Carey and Usher. Focuses on African influences in melody, harmony, rhythm and form as illustrated in the top twenty-five R&B songs from each decade. Demonstrates the connection between R&B and genres like blues, country, gospel, jazz, religious music, and rock and roll. Sixty-five musical examples, fifteen tables and graphs, and a bibliography. [See also item 739.]

739. ——. "The New Blue Music: Changes in Melody, Harmony, Rhythm, and Form in Rhythm and Blues, 1950–99." PhD dissertation, University of Memphis, 2004.

The study of a super genre called the *blues system* that comprises a number of American popular and sacred genres (including blues, jazz, gospel, country, rock and roll, and rhythm and blues) with common musical features—styles, forms, content—from both the African and European musical traditions. Tracks the changes that occurred in the top twenty-five R&B songs of each decade, specifically the use of I, IV and V chords, number of chord types used, blue notes, the triplet swing concept, twelve-bar blues form and more. Concludes that the minor mode became more prominent in the 1970s, while the use of traits like the triplet swing concept declined. The dissertation was published as a book in 2006. [See also item 738.]

740. Schaefer, George W. "Drumset Performance Practices on Pop and Rhythm and Blues Hit Recordings, 1960–69." PhD dissertation, Arizona State University, 1994.

The author investigates the premise that the only difference between rhythm and blues and rock and roll was the race of the performer, and whatever performance practices are implied by the race of the performer. The author transcribed drumset performances from 145 R&B and rock recordings and quantified six characteristics: drumset audibility, tempo stability, rhythmic improvisation, proportion of drum fills and meter. Findings indicate that no significant differences exist between the two styles. However, his findings also indicate that the rhythms used in R&B were significantly more syncopated than those of rock and roll, and duple meters predominated in the second half of the decade.

741. Selman-Earnest, Cora. "Black Owned Radio and Television Stations in the United States From 1950–82: A Descriptive Study." PhD dissertation, Wayne State University, 1985.

Examines African American ownership of broadcast facilities in the United States. A questionnaire of ninety-one black-owned commercial radio stations identified the major owners of the station, the roles of the general public and community in the formulation of procedures, the types and numbers of programs produced (including music programming) to meet specific needs, and more. Among the author's findings were that more than 60% of the black-owned stations are located in the mid-west and south, and that more than half feature a rhythm and blues format.

742. Shaw, Arnold. *Black Popular Music in America: From the Spirituals, Minstrels, and Ragtime to Soul, Disco, and Hip-Hop.* New York: Schirmer Books; London: Collier Macmillan, 1986.

The author argues that American popular music is a confluence of black and white musical influences, best understood from a black perspective. Discusses five African American styles—minstrels, spirituals, ragtime, jazz and blues—by focusing on origins, developments, and important artists and songs. Demonstrates that African American songwriters, vocalists and musicians were the source of musical styles during the Jazz Age, Ragtime Years, Swing Era and Age of Rock. Discusses what he terms the "white synthesis," showing that white musicians have profited greatly from African American musical creations. His final chapter covers the contemporary scene (1980s).

743. ———. *Honkers and Shouters: The Golden Years of Rhythm and Blues.* New York: Macmillan Publishing Co., 1978.

Recreates the era of the electric guitar, honking tenor saxophonist, Big Joe Turner's Kansas City shouts and the harmonies of Harlem's Sugar Hill Street-corner groups. Includes over twenty conversations with musicians and businessmen, including the last interviews given by Louis Jordan and T-Bone Walker. Discusses the rural and urban roots of R&B, boogie woogie, blues bands, pioneering independent record labels, disc jockeys and songwriters, and the sociocultural context that produced the music. Also covers the musical contributions of Bo Diddley, B.B. King, The Drifters, The Coasters, Fats Domino, Little Richard, Big Mama Thornton, Muddy Waters and Dinah Washington.

744. ———. *The World of Soul: Black America's Contribution to the Pop Music Scene.* New York: Cowles Book Co., 1970.

Discusses blues, the pop realm of Billy Eckstein and Nat "King" Cole, rhythm and blues, soul and gospel music. Covers the contributions of numerous artists, including Son House, Robert Johnson, Blind Lemon Jefferson, Dinah Washington, Fats Domino, the Platters, Willie Mae Thornton, Percy Mayfield, James Brown, Ray Charles, Aretha Franklin, The Coasters, Holland-Dozier-Holland, Johnny Taylor and many more. Also includes information on record labels and jazz singers.

745. Stephens, Robert W. "Soul: A Historical Reconstruction of Continuity and Change in Black Popular Music." *Black Perspective in Music* 12(1) (Spring 1984): 21–44.

Focuses on the underlying messages, philosophies and the musical influences of soul. Covers the history and evolution from its sacred and secular roots in Africa, the relationship of its cultural context to historical and sociopolitical events, and its musical character and dissemination through emergent contemporary styles. Discusses specific blues styles, geographical styles (northern and southern), and the role of Motown and Stax records in the history and evolution of soul music.

746. Thompson, Dave. *Funk.* San Francisco: Backbeat Books, 2001.

A compendium of recordings organized by categories like pre-funk, classic funk, disco funk and new school. Contains anecdotal biographies, reviews, ratings, photographs; several concise essays cover funk from its roots to around 2001.

747. Vincent, Ricky. *Funk: The Music, The People, and the Rhythm of the One.* New York: St Martin's Press, 1996.

Examines the black blues and jazz roots of funk and how African American music has often been appropriated by other cultural groups. Funk has remained considerably free of industry greed and gentrification because of its illicit power. Discusses James Brown, George Clinton, Miles Davis, Dr Dre, Earth, Wind and Fire, Jimi Hendrix, The Ohio Players, Sly Stone and several others.

748. Ward, Brian. *Just My Soul Responding: Rhythm and Blues, Black Consciousness, and Race Relations.* Berkeley: University of California Press, 1998.

Argues that R&B reinforces white stereotypes of blacks and promotes the continuation of segregation, and that many whites who attended the concerts of artists like Chuck Berry, James Brown, Ray Charles and Aretha Franklin never supported equal rights or the dismantling of segregation. Covers the history of R&B from the Chords release of "Sh-Boom" in 1954 through the mid-1970s. Also discusses the role of Berry Gordy and Motown. Well researched and well written.

749. Young, Malanie Catherine. "Soul Shakedown: The Politics of Soul Music." Masters thesis, University of Nevada, Las Vegas, 2005.

Uses the hegemonic theory of politics to discuss the importance of commercially popular music in the political socialization process. Reviews the literature on soul music, and analyzes the lyrics of soul songs recorded between 1965 and 1975. Illustrates that soul lyrics of the 1960s and 1970s celebrated African American culture through themes of freedom, pride and power.

## Regional studies

750. Bernard, Shane K. *Swamp Pop: Cajun and Creole Rhythm and Blues.* Jackson: University Press of Mississippi, 1996.

Focuses on the sources and sounds of "Swamp Pop," the Cajun and Creole equivalent to R&B. Thirty black-and-white photographs; discography; CD.

751. Berry, Jason, Jonathan Fosse and Tad Jones. *Up From the Cradle of Jazz: New Orleans Music Since World War II.* New York: Da Capo Press, 1992.

Provides insight into the many cultures, customs, beliefs and social groups in New Orleans. Discusses the social context that fostered the birth and development of jazz, and traces the evolution of rhythm and blues, soul and other genres.

752. Booth, Stanley. *Rhythm Oil: A Journey Through the Music of the American South.* New York: Pantheon Books, 1991.

A collection of previously-published magazine articles that explore the contributions of Memphis and its musicians to the history and development of popular music. Includes interviews, stories, tales and folktales about Robert Johnson, Beale Street, Mississippi John Hurt, Charlie Freeman, Stax Records, James Brown, Sam and Dewey Phillips, Otis Redding, B.B. King, Phineas Newborn, Jr and Elvis Presley. Draws heavily on the perspectives of Furry Lewis and highlights the songwriting/ recording session that produced Otis Redding's "Dock of the Bay."

753. Bowman, Rob. "Stax." In *African American Music: An Introduction*, eds Mellonee V. Burnim and Portia Maultsby, pp. 452–70. New York: Routledge, 2006.

Covers the history of Stax records from its origins in Memphis, Tennessee, where it was founded by white country fiddler Jim Stewart. Divides Stax's development into two periods: 1959–70/71 and 1971/ 72–76. Discusses the role of Al Bell, and performers like Isaac Hayes, Sam and Dave, Booker T. and the MGs, Otis Redding, The Staple Singers and others in Stax's success. Details the Columbia-Stax distribution deal and lists the musical characteristics of the Stax sound.

754. ——. *Soulville U.S.A.: The Story of Stax Records*: New York: Schirmer Books, 2003.

An in-depth story of the people, origins, history and evolution of Stax, situated in the social context of Memphis, Tennessee. Covers the contributions of artists, composers and producers like Al Bell, Isaac Hayes, Booker T and the MGs, David Porter, Otis Redding and others. Also discusses important concerts held in Ghana and Los Angeles. The book jacket contains endorsements from Al Bell, Isaac Hayes, Booker T. Jones, Mavis Staples, and several more artists and executives associated with Stax records. Based on the author's dissertation from the University of Memphis. [See item 755.]

755. ——. "Stax Records: A Historical and Musicological Study." PhD dissertation, University of Memphis, 1993.

He divides the history of Stax into two periods: 1959–70/71 and 1971/72–76 (time periods possibly related to Al Bell's tenure as CEO with Stax, although not specifically stated). Interviews, records, Stax's in-house literature, journal and magazine articles, and books were used to compile this study. Focuses on material recorded, written, performed, or produced by Memphis-based artists. Gives a detailed assessment of the recordings issued until around 1971. Analyzes ninety-five representative recordings for musical characteristics and lyrical content.

756. Broven, John. *Rhythm and Blues in New Orleans*. Gretna, LA: Pelican Publishing, 1974.

First published in the UK as *Walking to New Orleans: The Story of New Orleans Rhythm and Blues* (1974) by Blues Unlimited. Covers R&B (1946–55), rock and roll (1955–59), and the local record scene (1955–63). Information on black and white artists (Dave Bartholomew, Fats Domino, Dr John, Willie Tee, Polka Dot Slim, Lee Dorsey, The Neville Brothers, The Meters, Professor Longhair, Allan Toussaint, Earl Palmer) and their record labels.

757. Collins, Willie. "California Rhythm and Blues Recordings, 1942–72: A Diversity of Styles." In *California Soul: Music of African Americans in the West*, eds Jacqueline C. DjeDje and Eddie S. Meadows, pp. 213–44. Berkeley: University of California Press, 1998.

He discusses some of the most significant R&B recordings made in California between 1942 and 1972, several contributors, musical styles, gospel-based rhythm and blues, Oakland-based R&B, and the unique contributions of Charles Brown, Lowell Fulson and T-Bone Walker.

758. Country Music Hall of Fame. *Night Train to Nashville: Music City Rhythm and Blues, 1945–1970*. Nashville: CMF Press, 2004.

Focuses on Nashville's title as Music City USA and the time period when cultural icons like Little Richard and Jimi Hendrix were residents of the city, Etta James recorded her *Live* album at the New Era Club, and Arthur Gunter recorded *Baby Let's Play House* for Excello Records. Covers the importance of radio stations like WLAC and WSOK in developing all-black formats, the collaborations between R&B singers and songwriters and Music Row musicians such as Hank Garland, Boudreaux Bryant and Floyd Cramer.

759. Dickerson, James. *Goin' Back to Memphis: A Century of Blues, Rock 'n' Roll and Glorious Soul*. New York: Macmillan Publishers, 1996.

Recounts the many artists who made Memphis their home (e.g. B.B. King, Jerry Lee Lewis, Elvis Presley, the Bar-Kays, Booker T and the MGs), and the importance of Sun and Stax records. Focuses on the importance of Memphis to the evolution and history of blues, rock and soul music.

760. Early, Gerald. *One Nation Under a Groove: Motown and American Culture*. New York: Ecco Publishers (HarperCollins), 1995.

Begins by covering Frank Sinatra, but thereafter focuses on the Motown sound because of its pervasive influence in American culture. Analyzes Motown records.

761. Eastman, Ralph. "Pitchin' Up A Boogie: African-American Musicians, Nightlife, and Music Venues in Los Angeles, 1930–45." In *California*

*Soul: Music of African Americans in the West*, eds Jacqueline C. DjeDje and Eddie S. Meadows, pp. 79–104. Berkeley: University of California Press, 1998.

A scholarly in-depth discussion of the breadth and depth of contributions made in Los Angeles to blues, jazz, and rhythm and blues, an area often overlooked. Discusses the contributions of Curtis Mosby, Nat "King" Cole, Lionel Hampton, Cee Pee Johnson, performance venues and the social context of the music.

762. ———. "Central Avenue Blues: The Making of Los Angeles Rhythm and Blues, 1942–47." *Black Music Research Journal* 9(1) (Spring 1989): 19–35.

In this historically significant essay, Eastman examines specific reasons why west coast R&B musicians in general, and Los Angeles artists in particular, developed distinctive sounds. He discusses venues; musicians like Aaron "T-Bone" Walker, Charles Brown, Johnny Otis and Gene Phillips; independent record companies and radio stations; and more.

763. Elmore, Charles J. *All That Savannah Jazz: From Brass Bands, Vaudeville, to Rhythm and Blues.* Savannah, GA: Savannah University Press, 1999.

A historical overview of jazz in Savannah, Georgia. Presents the stories of performers who passed through the city, and discusses performance venues like the Flamingo Lounge, the Star Theater and the Old City auditorium, and bands like Bobby Dilworth's. Filled with names, dates and performances of jazz and rhythm and blues in historical Savannah.

764. Fikentscher, Kai. "'You Better Work': Music, Dance, and Marginality in Underground Dance Clubs of New York City." PhD dissertation, Columbia University, 1996.

Focuses on subject matter, methodology and theory in Underground Music (UDM). UDM represents a confluence of topics: the relationship between music and dance, the role of the disc jockey as the central figure within a specific context, and music as primary identifier of an urban subculture that has been shaped primarily by gay, African American and Latino New Yorkers. The connection between music and marginality, and the role of New York City as musical center is also investigated.

765. Flory, Jonathan Andrew. "I Hear a Symphony: Making Music at Motown, 1959–79." PhD dissertation, University of North Carolina, Chapel Hill, 2006.

Researches the intersections between social status and musical production at Motown between 1959 and 1979. Focuses on Motown's strong relationship with the African American middle class by linking the music and creative processes to pressing issues facing the community, and by situating the founding of the company within Detroit's middle class of the late 1950s. Motown's huge success (1963–67) highlights the musical and troping concepts of Holland-Dozier-Holland, the success of the Four Tops and the Supremes, the company's move into more racialized song topics in the late 1960s, and more.

766. Govenar, Alan. *The Early Years of Rhythm and Blues: Focus on Houston.* Houston: Rice University Press, 1990.

The focus is on the numerous photographs of 1950s R&B stars by Benny Joseph. The text, although limited to only fifteen pages, chronicles the endemic racism in the music business during the 1950s and 1960s.

767. Groia, Philip. *They All Sing on the Corner: A Second Look at New York City's Rhythm and Blues Vocal Groups.* New York: P. Dee Enterprises, 1983.

Discusses several African American R&B and doo-wop groups of the 1950s. Numerous interviews with singers, musicians and choreographers; discographies; forty rare photographs of early pioneers like the Cadillacs, Dominos, Five Keys, Flamingos, Harptones, Frankie Lymon, Moonglows, Orioles, Solitaries, Teenagers and Ravens. More than 700 references to R&B artists.

768. Guralnick, Peter. *Sweet Soul Music: Rhythm and Blues and the Southern Dream of Freedom.* New York: Harper and Row, 1986.

A narrative historical account based on interviews with over 100 people. The author traveled to all parts of the United States to collect information. Covers the role of Stax records in the history and evolution of the music, the importance of Memphis, and artists like Solomon Burk, James Brown, Ray Charles, Sam Cooke, Aretha Franklin and Otis Redding.

769. Hamusch, Jeffery. *I Hear You Knockin': The Sound of New Orleans Rhythm and Blues.* Fourth edn. Ville Platte, LA: Swallow Publications, 1985.

Recounts the stories of more than two dozen figures in the New Orleans rhythm and blues scene, including DJs, instrumentalists, producers, singers and record label entrepreneurs.

770. Helper, Laura. "Whole Lot of Shakin' Going On: An Ethnography of Race Relations and Crossover Audiences for Rhythm and Blues

and Rock and Roll in 1950s Memphis." PhD dissertation, Rice University, 1997.

An ethnographic history of urban segregation and popular culture in 1950s Memphis, specifically focusing on the role of race and music in a rich musical scene with new mass media. Although the music and its distribution crossed class and racial boundaries, the research revealed that residential and musical juxtapositions almost never led to friendships or equal relationships across racial lines. Explores the interrelationships of theory and experience in music and geography, issues of production and reception, local meanings, and the ways in which whites encouraged segregation by describing African Americans and other poor persons as "dirty, infectious, and polluting." This dissertation is based on sixteen months of fieldwork in Memphis, and a year of archival work at the Smithsonian National Museum of American History.

771. Jackson, John A. "Philadelphia International." In *African American Music: An Introduction*, eds Mellonee V. Burnim and Portia Maultsby, pp. 470–91. New York: Routledge, 2006.

Founded in 1971 by the esteemed writing duet of Kenneth Gamble and Leon Huff, Philadelphia International rose to international fame. Discusses several of the label's artists (Patti LaBelle, McFadden and Whitehead, the O'Jays, Billy Paul, Teddy Pendergrass and Lou Rawls) and their production of nine platinum and fifteen gold albums. Also examines the Gamble and Huff sound, the revival of the label and its eventual decline.

772. ——. *A House on Fire: The Rise and Fall of Philadelphia Soul.* New York: Oxford University Press, 2004.

Focuses on the creation, expansion and dissolution of Philadelphia International Records, whose artists and songs were popular in the 1970s. Specifically, he covers the careers of Kenneth Gamble, Leon Huff and Thom Bell whose talents catapulted artists like Teddy Pendergrass, The O'Jays, Harold Melvin and the Blue Notes, The Spinners and the Stylistics to international stardom.

773. Koster, Rick. *Louisiana Music: A Journey From R&B to Zydeco, Jazz to Country, Blues to Gospel, Cajun to Swamp, Pop to Carnival Music and Beyond.* New York: Da Capo Press, 2002.

A general overview of a broad topic; because of its breath and depth some artists (especially Louis Armstrong and Jelly Roll Morton) receive limited coverage. Discusses musical genres, the connection between the Neville Brothers and the 1976 album by the Wild Tchoupitoulas, Ernie K-Doe, Leadbelly, Trent Reznor and more.

774. Lee, Gary and Patti Meyer Lee. *Don't Bother Knockin' ... This Town's A Rockin': A History of Traditional Rhythm and Blues and Early Rock 'n' Roll in Buffalo, New York.* Buffalo, NY: Buffalo Sounds Press, 2000.

Covers selected local and national events that led to a Buffalo style of rhythm and blues. Discusses local artists like Dyke and the Blazers, Darrell Banks, Stan Szelast and Gary Mallaber, and the contributions of Buffalo DJ George "Hounddog" Lorenz.

775. Lisle, Andria and Mike Evans. *Waking Up in Memphis.* New York: Sanctuary Publishing, 2003.

A personal tribute to the history and evolution of the Memphis music scene, from W.C. Handy to 2003. Covers Sun Records, Beale Street, taxes, and the importance of Memphis artists in formulating creativity in blues, R&B, and rock and roll. Discusses artists including Isaac Hayes, Al Green, Jerry Lee Lewis, Willie Mitchell, Phineas Newborn, Carla Thomas, Rufus Thomas, Elvis Presley and Ike Turner. One glaring error is the labeling of the Rock and Roll Hall of Fame and Museum in Cleveland, Ohio as the Pyramid in Memphis, Tennessee.

776. McKnight, Mark. "Researching New Orleans Rhythm and Blues." *Black Music Research Journal* 8(1) (1988): 113–34.

Discusses the history and evolution of New Orleans rhythm and blues; describes its sound, and identifies important piano players and vocalists. Includes research sources, bibliographic sources, historical sources, indexes and periodicals, sound recordings, interviews, research centers, and a chart of international blues and R&B serials.

777. Morse, David. *Motown and The Arrival of Black Music.* New York: Collier, 1972.

A searching commentary on the nature of the Motown sound compared with other musical genres and companies at that time. Discusses the performers, the Motown formula for success, social and political issues that arose because of their success, the business of Motown, and the work ethic and style of its performers.

778. Newman, Mark Allan. "Entrepreneurs of Profits and Pride: From Black-Appeal to Radio Soul (Illinois, Arkansas, Tennessee)." PhD dissertation, University of California, Los Angeles, 1986.

Investigates racial issues that precluded African Americans from full participation in the radio craze of the 1920s. Black roles, whether comedic or dramatic, still mirrored images of blackface minstrelsy stereotypes; racial issues and black demographics (pre-World War II) blinded white executives to the viability of the black audience and the black consumer market. Investigates problems faced by blacks in broadcasting and solutions found in locally-oriented narrowcasting, and analyzes radio's influence on black consciousness and culture. Research was conducted in Chicago, Illinois; Helena, Arkansas; and Memphis, Tennessee between 1929 and 1960.

779. O'Meara, Caroline Polk. *New York Noise: Music in the Post-Industrial City, 1978–1985*. PhD dissertation, University of California, Los Angeles, 2006.

Focuses on how noise and ideas of noise organize the composition and reception of much late twentieth-century music. The author argues that understanding how these ideas operate in a specific time and place deepens our understanding of contemporary musical culture as a whole. The focus is on New York City in the late 1970s and early 1980s, and on music ranging from that of avant-garde classical composer Glenn Branch to the early hip hop disc jockeys, disco and punk. Each chapter examines a small group of works within its cultural, historical and geographical context, and although a formal musical analysis is presented, theoretical space is left for the music to generate disorder, to sound as noise.

780. Orchard, Jonathan Booth. "The Aesthetic of Sound and Performance in Rock 'n' Roll: Its Roots in the Rural South." Masters thesis, University of Texas, Dallas, 1984.

Illuminates the cultural synthesis that occurred between Anglo-Americans and African Americans living in close proximity in an agrarian society. Traces the aesthetic of sound and performance in rock and roll to its roots in the American south, specifically the influence of blues, country music and gospel music. Discusses the styles of Chuck Berry, Jerry Lee Lewis, Carl Perkins, Elvis Presley and Little Richard.

781. Posner, Gerald. *Motown: Music, Money, Sex, and Power.* New York: Random House, 2007.

The author researched public court documents in Detroit to ascertain how Berry Gordy dealt legally with artists like Marvin Gaye, Smokey Robinson, Diana Ross, the Temptations and Stevie Wonder. He demonstrated that Motown was not a mob-run company, discussed the Holland-Dozier-Holland lawsuit, Florence Ballard's dismissal from the Supremes, and more.

782. Pruter, Robert. *Doowop: The Chicago Scene.* Music in American Life Series. Urbana: University of Illinois Press, 1991.

A history of Chicago as one of the major centers for the distribution and production of the music. Covers the soul music industry from its rise in the early 1960s to its decline and virtual disappearance in the early 1980s. Permeated with new insights on Vee Jay, Okeh, Chess, the ABC-Paramount Chicago connection, Brunswick, Mercury and Curton record labels. Discusses artists like Jerry Butler, the Chi-Lites and Curtis Mayfield, and topics like the Chi-Sound and demise of the Chicago soul industry.

783. Rosin, James. *Rock, Rhythm and Blues: A Look at the National Recording Artists From the City of Brotherly Love.* Philadelphia: Autumn Road Co., 2004.

Discusses the history of 1950s Philadelphia music, the artists associated with Philadelphia International Records, Kenneth Gamble and Leon Huff, the role of Dick Clark and *American Bandstand*, and other talented stars who emerged from the city.

784. Ryan, Jennifer. "'Can I Get a Witness?': Soul and Salvation in Memphis Music." PhD dissertation, University of Pennsylvania, 2008.

The author contends that soul music's creation in the early 1960s was a result of musicians blending the sounds of African American church music with the secular themes of R&B, and that some religious musicians who participated were torn between their faith and career. Discusses the processes by which past and present soul musicians negotiate their faith in a secular context. Findings reveal that a persistent religious world view existed among musicians, even those who performed in nightclubs or juke joints.

785. Ryan, Marc W. *Trumpet Records: Diamonds on Farish Street.* Jackson: University Press of Mississippi, 2004.

The history of a regional record company and the blues, gospel, and rhythm and blues artists that it catapulted to national success. Information was gathered from interviews (including with Henry McMurry, the founder of the label), company documents, archival recordings and reviews. Sixty black-and-white photographs and a discography.

786. Scott, Colin and Martin Hawkins. *Good Rockin' Tonight: Sun Records and the Birth of Rock 'n' Roll.* New York: St Martin's Griffin Press, 2002.

Contends that Sun Records was the birthplace of rock and roll because Sam Phillips was the first to blend country music with R&B. He recorded artists like Johnny Cash, Jerry Lee Lewis, Elvis Presley, Howlin' Wolf, Ike Turner and many others. Also documents some of Phillips' mistakes, flaws and failures.

787.  Smith, Suzanne. *Dancing in the Streets: Motown and the Cultural Politics of Detroit.* Cambridge: Harvard University Press, 2001.

Motown is the focal point for an examination of the shift in African American protest ideologies from integration to separatism. Motown sprang from Detroit's most important black institutions but, according to the author, failed to change with the times. Argues that Motown's move to Los Angeles in 1972 was evidence of the bankruptcy of its version of African American capitalism.

788.  Sykes, Charles. "Motown." In *African American Music: An Introduction,* eds Mellonee V. Burnim and Portia Maultsby, pp. 431–52. New York: Routledge, 2006.

A history of Motown from its origins as Hitsville USA to its subsequent world renown. Covers influences, performers, assembling the sound, different stages of its development, the role of writers like Holland-Dozier-Holland, Motown's move to Los Angeles and more.

## Global studies

789.  N.A. "Tokyo's Round Mound of Sound." *Ebony,* October 1976, 113.

Details the dissemination of African American music by an Air Force sergeant in Tokyo who developed a wide following by playing disco, rhythm and blues, and soul music on his radio show.

790.  N.A. "Soul Explosion Rocks Land of Rising Sun." *Ebony,* July 1975, 42.

Covers American soul music artists who have toured Japan (e.g. The Three Degrees, The Four Tops, the Stylistics) and local groups like The Finger Five and the Soul Mates who have been influenced by American soul music.

791.  Browne, Kimasi Lionel John. "'Soul or Nothing': The Formation of Cultural Identity on the British Northern Soul Scene." PhD dissertation, University of California, Los Angeles, 2005.

Research focuses on a working-class British subculture that has adopted African American cultural products as their own cultural expression. Documents obscure African American soul music from Motown and other record labels and its affective work in forming emotional, social, economic and cultural identity in the predominantly male, white and working-class Northern Soul scene in England from 1967 to around 2005. Fieldwork was conducted in these "underground" communities in England, Wales and the Republic of Ireland.

792.  Garland, Phyl. "Soul to Soul." *Ebony,* June 1971, 79.

Touted as a return to the roots of African American music, the Soul to Soul concert was held in Accra, Ghana in 1971. The cultural exchange (featuring Roberta Flack, Eddie Harris, Les McCann and Wilson Pickett) was a huge success; the concert was also filmed.

793. Nowell, David. *Too Darn Soulful: The Story of Northern Soul.* London: Robson Books, 2001.

A thorough discussion of the British dance scene. The book is permeated with interviews and facts, and describes the social context that spawned the British love of African American popular music from the 1960s to 2001. The interviews cover the fans' love of artists from the Motown era to contemporary artists like Fatboy Slim.

794. Wright II, Jeffrey Marsh. "'Russia's Greatest Live Machine': Disco, Exoticism, and Subversion." Masters thesis, University of North Carolina, Chapel Hill, 2007.

In 1978 European disco group Boney M gave ten concerts in Moscow. Despite being the guests of the government, the group was censored because they performed "Rasputin," one of their biggest hits, a signifier of "Russianness" (rather than "Sovietness"). The government deemed the song unacceptable for performance or release. The author's musical analysis coupled with the Soviet rejection of the song revealed a confluence of musical signification, exoticism, and the relationship of music and politics.

## PHOTOGRAPHY

795. Edwards, A. and G. Wohl. *Picture Life of Stevie Wonder.* New York: Avon Publishers, 2006.

A collection of numerous captioned photographs that capture his early years to his musical success. The photographs cover his early years, associations with other musicians, social interests and more.

796. Gould, Philip, photography and Jason Berry, text. *Louisiana Faces: Images From A Renaissance.* Baton Rouge: Louisiana State University Press, 2000.

Gould's images, taken from a wide variety of perspectives, represent the French Quarter, Mardi Gras, the Mississippi River, and musical and political figures like David Duke, Huey Long, Fats Domino, Clifton Chenier, Aaron Neville, Barry Jean Ancelet, Pearly Toliver and others. Berry's essays that accompany the photos are drawn from interviews, anecdotes and history of this "exotic" environment, woven together with his own commentary. Includes 135 color photos.

797. Govenar, Alan. *The Early Years of Rhythm and Blues: Focus on Houston.* Houston: Rice University Press, 1990.

Numerous photographs of 1950s R&B stars taken by Benny Joseph, who was hired by Don Robey in the 1950s to photograph the rising stars of Duke and Peacock record labels. The photographs cover musicians like Johnny Ace, Bobby "Blue" Bland, Clarence "Gatemouth" Brown and Junior Parker, and other important icons like Muhammad Ali and Martin Luther King, Jr. The photographs depict high school dances, weddings and Civil Rights-related events. Limited text. [See also item 798.]

798. Govenar, Alan B. and Benny Joseph. *The Early Years of Rhythm and Blues.* New York: Schiffer Publishing, 2004.

The collection of more than 120 black-and-white photographs by Joseph A. Houston depicts many rhythm and blues artists. Govenar identifies and captions many of the images. [See also item 797.]

799. Hearn, Marcus. *The Jimi Hendrix Experience.* Rex Collection. London: Reynolds and Hearn, 2005.

A collection of photographs of Hendrix and bandmates Mitch Mitchell and Noel Redding taken in 1967. Includes publicity shots, backstage shots, shots of Hendrix in the studio, and photographs of Hendrix with Eric Clapton and Peter Townsend.

# III

# Hip hop and rap resources

## GENERAL TOPICS: AESTHETICS, CULTURE, EDUCATION, IDENTITY, RESISTANCE AND OTHER PERSPECTIVES

800. Akintunde, Omowale Achbe. "The Effect of Using Rapping to Teach Selected Musical Forms to Urban African-American Middle School Students." PhD dissertation, University of Missouri, 1996.

A study to determine the effects of a pedagogical approach of using rap music on the learning of musical forms, and to determine whether differential effects exist among students of different levels of self-esteem. Sixty-six African American students at Brittany-Woods Middle School in the urban St Louis County Public School District who were enrolled in general music classes were randomly divided into experimental and control groups. The students, in grades six through eight, were assessed according to the second edition of the *Culture-free Self-esteem Inventories* (Battle 1992) and then were divided into high, middle and low self-esteem groups. The author composed songs, used representative examples, created tests, gave explicit directions to both the experimental and control groups to ensure the reliability and validity of his conclusions.

801. Anderson, Raymond Dennis Seymour. "Black Beats for One People: Causes and Effects of Identification with Hip Hop Culture." PhD dissertation, Regent University, 2006.

The author uses Abercrombie and Longhurst's spectacle performance theory to research the influence of hip hop culture on youth.

Identification with hip hop culture was measured by using survey methodology and a questionnaire. Among the findings: it is more than likely for an African American living in an urban neighborhood to identify with hip hop culture.

802. Boyd, Todd. *Young, Black, Rich, and Famous: The Rise of the NBA, the Hip Hop Invasion and the Transformation of American Culture.* New York: Doubleday, 2003.

A provocative concise history of modern basketball and how issues of class, popular culture and race have intersected both on and off the basketball court. Describes how hip hop culture is a reflection of the world view of many contemporary college and professional basketball players, how basketball became a black sport in vibe and attitude by focusing on players like Julius "Dr. J" Erving. In addition, he connects the racial divide that existed in the Reagan era with the rivalry between Larry Bird and Magic Johnson, discusses Johnson's crossover appeal, Michael Jordan's individual style, connects the "bad boy" image of the Detroit Pistons with the rise of gangsta rap, and discusses the role and function of players like Allan Iverson as "real" and "authentic" representatives of the hip hop generation.

803. Brantley, Vanessa T. "Hip-Hop Clothing: The Meaning and Subculture Style." PhD dissertation, Florida State University, 1999.

The author uses a qualitative methodology to examine the subcultural meanings of hip hop clothing styles among African American adult male hip hoppers in the 1990s. Subcultural meanings were gleaned from exponents of hip hop subculture. Six different types of hip hop style garments were identified and the reasoning behind their adaptation was discussed.

804. Ferguson, Nakeisha Shannell. "Bling-Bling Brand Placements: Measuring the Effectiveness of Brand Mentions in Hip-Hop Music." PhD dissertation, University of Texas at Austin, 2008.

Investigates consumer behavior and marketing communication theories, specifically how the mention of brand names in music can influence memory, attitudes and purchases. Investigations of brand identification were undertaken with two groups of people through surveys and in-depth interviews. The findings indicate that mentioning brand names in music may be an effective tool to increase brand awareness.

805. Fernando, Jr, S.H. *The New Beats: Exploring the Music, Culture, and Attitudes of Hip-Hop.* New York: Doubleday, 1994.

Using a variety of interviews, the author creates a historical overview of hip hop culture. Discusses hip hop's relationship to gangs, early youth culture, graffiti art, fashions and dancing. Also discusses the role of Jamaican music in some aspects of hip hop. A list of pioneering and important recordings is provided after each chapter.

806. Hall, Tracy Denise. "A Pedagogy of Freedom: Using Hip Hop in the Classroom to Engage African American Students." EdD dissertation, University of Missouri, 2007.

A study of the impact of culturally-relevant pedagogy, like hip hop, on African American student engagement. Uses critical race theory to assess the views of students, faculty and administrators, using data collected during classroom observations, interviews and analysis of course documents. Informal interviews with faculty, students and administrators were also conducted.

807. Hess, Mickey. "Metal Faces, Rap Masks: Identity and Resistance in Hip Hop's Persona Artist." *Popular Music and Society* 28(3) (July 2005): 297–313.

Studies two examples of the rap artist persona as strategies of resistance, and uses several theories of hip hop identity and resistance to draw conclusions. Uses Tricia Rose's theory of rap as hidden transcript and Russell Potter's theory of play as resistance to argue that some hip hop acts either obscure or hide their identities to allow the artist to negotiate their own positions without regard to issues like authenticity or marketability which are often imposed upon them by others.

808. Hicks-Harper, Patricia Thandi. "Black Educators, Black Elementary School Students, and Black Rap Music Artists on Educational Entertainment Rap Music Video for Pedagogy: A Cultural and Critical Analysis." PhD dissertation, University of Maryland, 1993.

This study examines the advantages and disadvantages of using rap music videos as a pedagogical tool to ameliorate the low achievement levels of black youth. The author interviewed selected rap music artists (including Harry Allen, Chuck D, KRS One, Heavy D., Salt-N-Pepa and Professor Griff), educators and students. When teachers and students viewed rap videos during interviews, an apparent cultural divide became evident between the white Eurocentric school culture and the black Afrocentric cultural values of the students. Overall, the author concluded that the educators did not perceive the rap music videos the same way as the interviewed rappers did, and students and rappers all felt that Afrocentric educational styles are more useful to reach and teach black students.

809. Hill, Marc Lamont. "Re(negotiating) Knowledge, Power, and Identities in Hip-Hop Literature." PhD dissertation, University of Pennsylvania, 2005.

An ethnographic study that demonstrates how knowledge, power and student interpretation are negotiated and renegotiated as hip hop culture becomes a part of the curriculum in a local high school.

810. Jones, Ferdinand and Arthur C. Jones, eds. *The Triumph of the Soul: Cultural and Psychological Aspects of African American Music.* Westport, CT: Praeger Publishers, 2001.

A collection of essays by Peter R. Aschoff, Michael White, Angela M.S. Nelson, Cheryl Keyes, William Lowe, Leonard Brown, both editors, and others. The essays focus on issues of the history, gender issues, identity and representation, and the aesthetic and cultural meanings of blues, jazz, gospels, spirituals and rap.

811. Kitwana, Bakari. *Why White Kids Love Hip Hop: Wangstas, Wiggers, Wannabes, and the New Reality of Race in America.* New York: Basic Civitas, 2005.

Using the backdrop of authenticity, identity and ownership, the author researches provocative issues like why white kids love hip hop, and whether hip hop really "belongs" to black kids. The author offers thought-provoking assessments about contemporary American culture, grounded in the issues of cultural change and history. His assessments are also important because they are situated within the class, generation and racial differences that still exist in American society.

812. Lena, Jennifer Carroll. "From 'Flash' to 'Cash': Producing Rap Authenticity 1979 to 1995." PhD dissertation, Columbia University, 2003.

An investigation of the attributes, processes and structures that created the successes and failures of rap music from 1979 to 1995. She investigates artistic networks, occupations, sub-genre and sonic networks, and focuses on the connection between oligopoly and organizational structure, and the relationship between the structural and institutional production of art. The author also developed a musical innovation schemata for measuring authenticity.

813. Lynch, Krystal. "The Minstrelization of Hip Hop and Spoken Word Authenticity: Expressions of Postmodern Blackness." Masters thesis, North Carolina State University, 2005.

Deals with postmodern assessments of identity, such as blackface, feminism, manhood, minstrelization and whiteness. Also discusses hip hop and commercial music, minstrelsy and post-soul issues.

814. McFarland, Reynaldo A. "Packaging the Recording Artist: Rap Music and the Art of Commerce." Masters thesis, Long Island University, Brooklyn Center, 2007.

Focuses on the music industry's exploitation of hip hop and rap by using demographics, control, manipulation and global marketing. These phenomena are studied in regards to their respective roles and functions within the overall issue of exploitation.

815. Neal, Sandra Marjorie. "Gansta Rap Music and Its Negative Influence on Children in Urban America." Masters thesis, California State University, Dominquez Hills, 2001.

Argues that gangsta rap is detrimental to the normal development of children, and used one-on-one conversations with both teenagers and adults to support the argument.

816. Parker, Jessica Leigh. "The Hip Hop Aesthetic: A Cultural Revolution." PhD dissertation, University of Denver, 2006.

Parker uses Kristeva's theories of aesthetic revolt to examine the potential of the hip hop aesthetic to challenge dominant racial and socioeconomic structures in America. Her study also incorporates Bhabha's post-colonial theory, and theories of the diaspora from Safran and Clifford.

817. Penn, Maggie Lee Scott. "Public High School Teachers' Attitudes Toward Rap as a Strategy for Achievement and Discipline in the Classroom: A Qualitative Study." PhD dissertation, Costa Rica: Universidad de San José, 1998.

An examination of the attitudes of rural and urban public high school teachers toward using rap as a strategy for improving achievement and discipline. The author surveyed 87 certified public high school teachers, primarily African American with some Hispanics and whites, 50 from urban schools and 37 from rural areas. Her conclusions found that the most significant difference in attitudes existed not between geographically-defined groups, but between genders. All males showed a higher preference for using rap in the classroom than did females. In addition, younger, less experienced teachers favored using rap in the classroom while teachers with the highest degrees and the most seniority were less inclined to do so. All but one participant agreed that rap was not a cause of discipline problems.

818. Persaud, Elarick R. Jerry. "Hip Hop's Subversive Aesthetics." PhD dissertation, Toronto, Canada: York University, 2005.

Examines hip hop culture, and identifies the ghetto as a primal scene for this musical culture. He is concerned with the aesthetic value of rap music and the hip hop culture that birthed it. His premise is that the ghetto is a register of both past and present in the national construction and discourse of space and race.

819. Ramsey, Guthrie. *Race Music: Black Cultures from Bebop to Hip-Hop.* Berkeley: University of California Press, 2003.

Focuses on music as racial discourse and practice. Characterizes several post-World War II musical genres (e.g. blues, jazz, gospel, R&B) as *race* music, rather than as *black* music. The author chooses to use the term *race* because at one time in the black community, race represented positive self-identification among African Americans. Because there is no monolithic black experience, he argues that conceptualizations of blackness are the result of multiple African American cultural experiences. Music is a part of the process because it provides a real-life setting in which blackness is conceptualized, negotiated and worked out. The end result is that a "cultural memory" ensues which includes the process by which black identity is shaped.

820. Rose, Patricia. L. "Black Noise: Rap Music and Black Cultural Resistance in Contemporary American Popular Culture." PhD dissertation, Brown University, 1993.

Explores some of the complex cultural, social and political issues in rap music and hip hop culture. The author identifies central themes in the music, lyrics and visual images, and then contextualizes and links them to the sociocultural and institutional contexts within which they developed. Explores what stories rappers tell, why the stories are compelling to people from different backgrounds, and how these stories are represented in mainstream cultural criticism. Covers four basic areas of inquiry: the history of rap and hip hop in relationship to New York cultural politics; rap's musical and technological interventions; its racial politics, institutional critiques, and media and institutional responses; and its sexual politics, particularly female rapper's critiques of men and feminist debates.

821. Rosser, Eric Jay. "Education and Cultural Identity: Hip Hop Culture's Aim Toward the Re-Africanization of the Acculturated Subject." PhD dissertation, State University of New York at Buffalo, 2008.

The author uses narrative analysis to explore the transformative potential of hip hop cultural text in re-Africanizing post-Civil Rights-era African Americans who attend schools controlled by the dominant (white) cultural orientation. Focuses on blacks born between 1965 and 1975 because they were the first generation to be affected by busing policies associated with school desegregation and integration; they also suffered as youth from the political conservatism of the Reagan years. This generation was influential in the founding of hip hop culture, either as participants or as consumers.

822. Sewell, Jr, John Ike. "'Don't Believe the Hype': The Construction and Export of African American Images in Hip-Hop Culture." Masters thesis, East Tennessee State University, 2006.

Focuses on recurring motifs and personas in hip hop. Used qualitative methods to conduct and analyze a series of interviews with hip hop scholars, writers and music industry personnel. The informants were chosen based upon their insider knowledge as critics, hip hop scholars, ethnomusicologists and publicists, and their positions in the music industry. The author finds that the majority of constructed images are based on gangsta rap, and that gangsta has both alienated black culture from mainstream (white) culture and has caused rifts within the African American community.

823. Spencer, Jon Michael, ed. *The Emergency of Black and The Emergence of Rap.* A Special Issue of *Black Sacred Music: A Journal of Theomusicology* 5(1). Durham: Duke University Press, Spring 1991.

An interesting and provocative issue that covers feminist and religious issues that are related to rap music, along with more general topics. One essay, by Sonja Peterson-Lewis, addresses the feminist perspective regarding obscene lyrics; another, by Michael Eric Dyson, addresses performance, protest and prophecy. Other articles focus on the Nation of Islam and Public Enemy, the hip hop theology of Public Enemy and Kool Moe Dee, a discussion of the three waves of contemporary rap music, and more.

824. Worsley, Shawan Monique. "Cultural Misbehavior: Audience, Agency, and Identity in Black Popular Culture." PhD dissertation, University of Michigan, 2005.

Explores African American cultural products that pose competing narratives of black identities that work through the historical trauma of slavery and its legacy. Uses Louis Althusser's theory of interpolation and Stuart Hall's theories of black identity, subjectivity and popular culture to demonstrate that the representation of identity through culture is marked by continuous presentation, interpretation, contestation, and revision and reception of identity articulated by cultural product.

## REFERENCES

825. Bynoe, Yvonne. *Encyclopedia of Rap and Hip-Hop Culture.* Westport, CT: Greenwood Press, 2005.

Comprehensive, thorough listings of artists, producers and topics related to hip hop and rap culture and music. The entries include both famous and lesser-known artists, information on regional rap styles and more.

826. Eure, Joseph D. *Nation Conscious Rap: The Hip Hop Vision.* Afro Americanization of Knowledge Series 3, ed. James G. Spady. New York: PC International, 1991.

An important reference. The editors interviewed several important rap artists like Chuck D., Big Daddy Kane, KRS-One and Q-Tip, who represent the insider perspective. These interviews are important because the artists willingly shared intimate details of their personal and professional lives with editors they trusted. Rooted in Afrocentric perspectives, the interviews separate fact from fiction and are permeated with information on difficulties that artists have encountered.

827. Forman, Murray and Mark Anthony Neal, eds. *That's the Joint: The Hip-Hop Studies Reader.* New York: Routledge, 2004.

A definitive and comprehensive collection of articles, commentaries, criticisms, essays and selected writings of journalists. More than forty contributions, spanning twenty-five years, on aesthetics, gender issues, the history of hip hop, the role of hip hop in politics, and more. The collection is thorough, well researched, well written, and fills an important void in the scholarly literature on the subject.

828. Green, Jared, ed. *Examining Pop Culture-Rap and Hip Hop.* San Diego: Greenhaven Press, 2002.

In this collection of articles and essays, the authors examine the musical and social history of hip hop culture and rap music, and explore some of the controversies that are often associated with the culture and music. Contributions from Marlene Charnizon, Murray Foreman, Daryl Grabarek, Trevelyn Jones, Jeanne Larkins and Luann Toth cover the roots of rap and hip hop, the rise of hip hop culture, a discussion of rap, sex and violence, and Eminem and gay bashing. Much attention is devoted to the assertion that rap music glorifies gang life and violence and to media reports that rap is homophobic, sexist, racist and anti-Semitic. The four-chapter case study of Eminem focuses on his provocative lyrics in the context of American cultural values, homophobia and popular music.

829. Hoffmann, Frank W. and J. Albin, III. *Rhythm and Blues, Rap and Hip Hop.* New York: Checkmark Books, 2007.

This reference book covers numerous artists, topics and styles. The entries, arranged alphabetically, range from one or two paragraphs to several pages. Glossary and bibliography.

830. Jenkins, Sacha, Elliot Wilson, Chairman Mao, Gabriel Alvarez and Brent Rollins. *Ego Trip's Book of Rap Lists.* New York: Ego Trip, 1999.

   Lists of fashion styles, lyrics, movies, people and performances associated with rap music and culture, compiled by historians and journalists, including the authors.

831. McCoy, Judy. *Rap Music in the 1980s: A Reference Guide.* Metuchen, NJ: Scarecrow Press, 1992.

   This annotated bibliography lists over 1,000 articles, books and reviews about rap artists, culture, music and politics published between 1980 and 1990. The concise entries were taken from *Billboard, Melody Maker, Newsweek, Rolling Stone, Village Voice* and *Spin.* They are divided into two broad sections: "A Guide to the Literature" and "A Selected Discography," arranged by artist, of seventy-six recordings that contributed to the evolution, development or popularity of the genre. Annotations include information on hit singles, awards and controversies regarding the recording. The indices are arranged by date, artist and title.

832. Mitchell, Kevin. *Hip-Hop Rhyming Dictionary.* New York: Firebrands Music, 2003.

   Contains several thousand hip hop and slang terms that are designed to help create rhymes. The dictionary also contains writing tips for creative lyrics, a concise history of rap and information on important artists.

833. Nelson, Havelock and Michael Gonzales. *Bring the Noise: A Guide to Rap Music and Hip-Hop Culture.* New York: Harmony, 1991.

   A typical reference book with information on major events and rap-inspired activities before 1991. Numerous biographical sketches of hip hop artists (male and female) and a guide to important rap recordings.

834. Perkins, William Eric, ed. *Droppin' Science: Critical Essays on Rap Music and Hip Hop Culture.* Philadelphia: Temple University Press, 1996.

   The eleven essays focus on topics either omitted or poorly documented in most publications that deal with the history and evolution of rap music in America. Among the often overlooked topics covered is the role and function of Black Nationalism in rap, Latino contribution, and the contribution of women. The essays are enhanced by the photographs of Ernie Paniccioli and others.

835. Price, Emmett G. *Hip Hop Culture.* Santa Barbara: ABC CLIO, 2006.

Written by an ethnomusicologist and blues-gospel-jazz pianist and scholar, this is one of a select group of publications that combines scholarship and reference works. Includes a narrative of hip hop history, an excellent annotated bibliography, a listing of associations, organizations, magazines and journals, and programs dedicated to hip hop culture, and more. Investigates the founders, innovators and legends of the genre, and hip hop as a global phenomenon. Presents numerous biographical profiles, and discusses the people who transformed hip hop into a billion-dollar music and fashion business. A very important addition to the scholarly study and research of hip hop culture.

836. Sexton, Adam, ed. *Rap on Rap: Straight-Up Talk on Hip-Hop Culture.* New York: Dell Books, 1995.

A collection of essays on rap and hip hop topics ranging from message and power to urgency. The diverse authors, including Pat Buchanan, Ice-T, Tricia Rose and Greg Tate, come from the academic, entertainment and political worlds. Their opinions range from support to rejection.

837. Shabazz, Jamel. *Back in the Days.* New York: Powerhouse, 2001.

A diverse collection of attitudes and expressions from individuals involved in the early hip hop scene. Issues of economic access, political equality and racial injustice are addressed. Of particular note are the essays by noted hip hop scholar Ernie Paniccioli. Illustrated with Paniccioli's photos of the era, its fashions, and important people and locations, taken during the beginning of hip hop in the early 1980s.

838. Shapiro, Peter. *The Rough Guide to Hip-Hop.* New York: Viking Penguin, 2001.

A collection of pertinent information on a wide variety of hip hop artists and others associated with the culture, including B-boys and B-girls, DJs, MCs, graffiti artists, producers and more. An extensive discography; many photographs.

839. Spady, James G., Charles G. Lee and H. Samy Alim, eds. *Street Conscious Rap.* Philadelphia: Black History Museum Umum Loh Publishers, 1999.

A collection of essays, interviews, illustrations and photographs on a myriad of hip hop-related topics: the relationship between hip hop and business, importance of education, issues related to the family, hip hop and technology, and more. The perspectives are important because they present the views of pioneering artists like Eve, Chuck D., Common, Queen Latifah, Tupac Shakur and many more.

840. Stancell, Steven. *Rap Whoz Who: The World of Rap Music, Performers and Promoters.* New York: Schirmer, 1996.

A comprehensive and thorough collection of information on rap artists and social issues often connected to rap music and its practitioners. The biographical profiles contain information on their lives, influences, and social and political messages. Stancell discusses issues like rap and the music business, rap and violence, and the relationship between rap and Islam.

841. Tate, Greg, ed. *Everything but the Burden.* New York: Broadway Books, 2003.

This collection of essays from writers like Beth Coleman, Melvin Gibbs, Robin Kelley, Tony Green and the author deconstruct the title *Everything but the Burden* from a myriad of perspectives. Gibbs' provocative essay "Thug Gods: Spiritual Darkness and Hip-Hop" is permeated with insights regarding the role and function of hip hop in African American culture and in the greater American culture.

842. Taylor, Barbara, Frank Grubb and Michael Peterson, eds. *The National Rap Directory.* Atlanta: Rising Star Music, 1996.

More than 1,000 entries with contact information for numerous music labels and publishers who were active from the 1980s to the mid-1990s. Each entry contains an address, fax and phone number, and where possible the name of a contact person. The book was updated each year (until 1995). Also contains the perceptions and advice of selected music industry professionals. Although now out of date, it is still an important reference for contact information on independent rap and hip hop music labels and publishers not generally known to scholars and fans.

843. Westbrook, Alonzo. *Hip Hoptionary: The Dictionary of Hip-Hop Terminology.* New York: Harlem Moon, 2002.

The author is a New York City journalist whose objective is to create a work that captures the language and preserves the culture of hip hop. The roughly 2,500 terms are divided into three large sections: a slang-to-standard English dictionary, a standard English-to-slang dictionary, and a list of hip hop artists. Also included are famous MCs, lists of fashion lines, online dictionaries and reference materials. While informative and comprehensive, the book contains spelling errors and includes terms like copyright, cronies, hot flashes and wallflower with definitions that can be found in any standard dictionary.

## AUTOBIOGRAPHIES AND BIOGRAPHIES

### *Afrika Bambaataa*

844. Chin, Brian. "Do The Do." *Village Voice*, 3 January 1984, 37.

A concise essay that was written in the early days of Bambaataa's rise to fame. The author focuses on why Bambaataa is well liked, respected and admired for his personal and creative abilities.

845. Fricke, David. "The Renegade." *Melody Maker*, 14 April 1984, 12.

In this interview, Bambaataa discusses his diverse musical tastes and provides insight into his ability to produce successful recordings. Also expresses his belief that music should not promote divisions, and criticizes the media's penchant to use music to perpetuate divisions.

846. Hager, Steven. "Afrika Bambaataa's Hip Hop." *Village Voice*, 21 September 1982, 69.

Using New York breakdancing and rap as backdrops, Bambaataa presents a comprehensive account of his life, beginnings of rap, and his transformation from gang member to hip hop artist. Discusses the role of graffiti in hip hop culture, and the impact of hip hop on 1980s cultural expressions.

847. Jardin, Gary. "The Great Facilitator." *Village Voice*, 2 October 1984, 63–64.

This interview places Bambaataa within the social context of the Bronx, New York, and accentuates his special and respected role in the history and development of hip hop. He is profiled not as the most talented of his hip hop peers, but as a respected spiritual leader and a person with multiple talents, attributes that have made Bambaataa a significant figure in early hip hop culture.

848. ———. "Perfection." *Village Voice*, 25 January 1983, 75.

A profile of two producers and writers (Arthur Baker and John Robie) who are credited with developing the sounds of both Afrika Bambaataa and the Soulsonic Force and are lauded as forward-looking creative giants.

849. Lynden, Barbara. "Play it Again, Bam." *Melody Maker*, 20 October 1984, 10.

Thorough interview focusing on Bambaataa's roles as a rap star, bandleader and former gang member; his association with James Brown; and his influential recordings. Information on his life and music, his collaboration with James Brown on the album *Unity*, and comments on his recordings *Planet Rock* and *Looking for the Perfect Beat*.

850. Oldfield, Paul. "Edge of Darkness." *Melody Maker*, 27 February 1988, 27.

In this interview, Bambaataa updates his fans on his current activities, including his new album project *The Light*. The album features a variety of dance songs, a reflection of Bambaataa's philosophy that dance exerts a kind of freedom and can function as a vehicle for revolution.

851. Owen, Frank. "Freshers' Ball." *Melody Maker*, 19 July 1986, 24.

This concise article profiles artists scheduled to appear at the UK Fresh '86 rapfest, like Afrika Bambaataa, Grandmaster Flash, Hashim Lovebug Star-Ski, The Real Roxanne and Roxanne Shanté. Profiles their hit recordings and contributions to hip hop, and includes comments from interviews.

852. Pye, Ian. "Zulu Dawn." *Melody Maker*, 11 June 1983, 8.

Pye's interview with Bambaataa focuses on his life and the impact he has made as the counselor of Zulu Nation. He describes Zulu Nation as a black consciousness raising and community involvement organization. He comments on misconceptions about the ghetto, gives his reasons for fusing hard rock with other musical genres, and provides insight into the meanings of his recordings *Plant Rock* and *Looking for the Perfect Beat*.

## The Beastie Boys

853. Carnegie, Joanne. "Beauty and the Beastie Boys." *Creem*, September 1985, 18.

A profile of the Beastie Boys' history. Discusses how they became a group, and their move from heavy metal to rap. Also discusses some of their recent activities, such as opening for Madonna, and forthcoming projects.

854. De Curtis. Anthony. "Young, Loud, and Snotty." *Rolling Stone*, 12 February 1987, 18–19.

Covers the Beastie Boys' background, their behavior, use of humor and difficulties in achieving success. Also includes a discussion of the history behind the recording of *Licensed to Ill* and previews future projects.

855. Eddy, Chuck. "The Beastie Boys Take Over." *Creem*, May 1987, 6.

A concise portrayal is concerned with the character of the group. Specifically, Eddy views the group as immature, self-centered and spoiled. He views their behavior as reflective of many self-indulgent young people of the time, hence their popularity.

856. La Pointe, Kirk. "Beastie Boys: An Ugly Cinderella Story." *Musician*, September 1985, 36–37.

Profiles their background, how they came together as a group, road to success, and their association with producer Rick Rubin. He also includes some of their provocative lyrics and information on their sampling sources.

857. Mico, Ted. "Beastie Boys: Excess All Areas." *Melody Maker*, 21 March 1987, 24.

Covers their penchant for having fun, using humor, and reasons why they engage in outlandish escapades. The interview was conducted during their 1987 concert tour in the southern United States.

858. Moleski, Linda. "Boos Turn Into Bravos for the Beastie Boys." *Billboard*, 17 January 1987, 20.

Moleski discusses the importance of the Beastie Boys' tour with Run DMC and the role of Russell Simmons in exposing them to the hip hop community. She traces their career from the time they were booed while touring with Madonna to their eventual success.

859. Sutherland, Steve. "The Brat Pack." *Melody Maker*, 13 September 1986, 25.

Discusses their music, some of their attention-getting antics, and their responsibility to their fans. They also discuss their *Raising Hell* tour, giving their views on the violence that took place during their Long Beach, California, concert, and concert violence in general.

## Notorious B.I.G. (a.k.a. Biggie Smalls)

860. Brown, Jake. *Ready to Die: The Story of Biggie Smalls, Notorious B.I.G.* Phoenix: Amber Communications, 2005.

In addition to discussing Smalls' life, musical contributions and legacy, Brown covers his roots, loyalties and the growth of Bad Boy Entertainment. He also discusses Sean "Puffy" Combs, Faith Evans, Lil' Kim, Junior Mafia and Tupac Shakur.

861. Marcovitz, Hal. *Notorious B.I.G.* Broomall, PA: Mason Crest, 2006.

Covers Jamaican-American Christopher George Latrobe Wallace's life and musical career, from the time he was known as Biggie Smalls, Big Poppa and Frank White, to his success as rapper Notorious B.I.G. Mentions dealing drugs as a teen, his 1994 debut album *Ready to Die*, his role in the east coast–west coast rap feud, and his unsolved death on March 9, 1997.

862. Scott, Cathy. *The Murder of Biggie Smalls.* New York: St Martin's Press, 2000.

The author discusses the friendship between Smalls and Shakur, and the perception by some that Smalls and his friends might have been responsible for Shakur's murder. The east coast–west coast gangsta rap feud, Tupac Shakur, Sean "Puffy" Combs, Death Row Records head Suge Knight, and facts surrounding Smalls' death are also discussed.

863. Wallace, Voletta, with Faith Evans (Foreword) and Tremell McKenzie (contributor). *Biggie: Voletta Wallace Remembers Her Son, Christopher Wallace, aka Notorious B.I.G.* New York: Atria, 2005.

Voletta Wallace, B.I.G.'s mother, discusses how she tried to raise her son and to shield him from trouble, their early years in Brooklyn, memories of the night he was shot, the treacherous nature of the music industry, her personal life, and more.

## Black Eyed Peas

864. Sanna, E. J. *Black Eyed Peas.* Broomall, PA: Mason Crest, 2007.

The history of the Los Angeles group Black Eyed Peas. Discusses their debut album *Elephunk* in 2003, their name change to Black Eyed Peas and their pop/dance style of hip hop. The founders, William James Adams, Jr, Allan Pineda, Mookie Mook, Dante Santiago and DJ Motiv8, were influenced by the Red Hot Chili Peppers. They were one of the first hip hop groups to perform with a live band, and they adopted musical and clothing styles that differed from their gangsta rap peers.

## Mary J. Blige

865. Brown, Terrell. *Mary J. Blige.* Broomall, PA: Mason Crest, 2006.

A concise account of her life from the hardships of her early years, her decision to drop out of high school, meeting Sean "Puffy" Combs and developing a recording career with his help, and her eventual rise to stardom.

866. Torres, Jennifer. *Mary J. Blige.* Blue Banner Biographies. Hockessin, DE: Mitchell Lane, 2007.

   Traces her life from her early years singing in church. The high school drop-out made a demo tape at a mall recording studio, signed her first record contract at age eighteen, and collaborated with Sean "Puffy" Combs on several hit albums. By 2007 Blige's music had sold over 34 million units and earned a Grammy Award.

## Lil' Bow Wow

867. Bankston, John. *Bow Wow: Hip Hop Superstars.* Hockessin, DE: Mitchell Lane, 2004.

   For younger readers. The article discusses how Shad Moss (Bow Wow) got hooked on hip hop when he was six years old, after his mother took him to a Snoop Dogg concert. From his encounter with Snoop, who nicknamed him Lil' Bow Wow, Moss launched his successful career. Thirty-two pages.

## Soulja Boy

868. Wells, Peggysue. *Soulja Boy Tell Em.* Hockessin, DE: Mitchell Lane, 2006.

   Tells the story of the life of DeAndre Cortez-Way, known as Soulja Boy, and his rise to fame as a business man, entertainer, producer, hit maker and rapper. His musical career began in high school, and once he achieved fame he designed his own clothes and created original songs and dance moves. He used the internet to sell millions of singles and ring tones.

## 2 Live Crew (Luther Campbell)

869. Benarde, Scott. "Much More Than Nasty." *Rolling Stone,* 8 March 1990, 62–63.

   Comments on *As Nasty As They Wanna Be,* Luther Campbell's background, work ethic and contributions to African American education. Campbell discusses the numerous controversies that surround his work, and provides insight into his signing of Professor Griff (formerly of *Public Enemy*) to his record label.

870. Dyson, Michael Eric. "Rights and Responsibilities: 2 Live Crew and Rap's Moral Vision." *Sacred Music of the Secular City: From Blues*

*to Rap*, ed. Jon Michael Spencer, pp. 274–82. A special edition of *Black Sacred Music: A Journal of Theomusicology* 6(1) (Spring 1992), Durham: Duke University Press, 1992.

Discusses the truism that sex, race and class are intricately intertwined and have caused tensions among groups who compete for limited forms of cultural legitimacy, visibility and support. Provides insights into the rights and responsibilities of rap, including a critique of 2 Live Crew that states, "2 Live Crew controversy surfaces repressed American cultural attitudes toward black male sexuality" (p. 276), and "2 Live Crew symbolizes the black male phallus out of control, respecting no sexual territory as sacred" (ibid.), and more.

871. Haring, Bruce. "Crew Readies Release of 'Banned' Album July 4." *Billboard*, 30 June 1990, 36.

Luther Campbell is interviewed about the forthcoming release of his CD *Banned in The U.S.A.* He comments on the album's provocative lyrics and his issues with the law (apart from the obscenity cases).

872. ———. "Crew's Nasty Ruled Obscene in Florida." *Billboard*, 16 June 1990, 5.

An account of the judicial ruling that the group's album *As Nasty as They Wanna Be* is obscene. Haring also discusses the implications of the ruling and what led to the decision; quotes the opinions of several individuals with an interest in the case.

873. Owen, Frank. "Fear of a Black Penis." *Spin*, September 1990, 35–36.

This article outlines new developments in a legal dispute between Luther Campbell and John Lucas. Also includes back-to-back interviews in a point/counterpoint-style debate regarding the legal issue between Luther Campbell and Jack Thompson.

874. Ressner, Jeffrey. "On the Road With Rap's Outlaw Posse." *Rolling Stone*, 9 August 1990, 19.

The author's impressions about accompanying 2 Live Crew on tour. Discusses audience reaction, constant hassles from a variety of sources, and promotional activities. Also discusses Jack Thompson's vendetta against 2 Live Crew, and Thompson's response to the charges.

875. Russell, Lisa. "2 Live Crew's Luke Campbell Is Keen for Green, Not the Obscene." *People's Weekly*, 5 November 1990, 71.

A profile of Campbell designed to dispel the myths and misconceptions about him as a person and as a business man. Presents Campbell as a wealthy conservative who enjoys an affluent lifestyle. He is also portrayed as an astute business man who is focused more on what sells than on producing music with obscene lyrics.

## 50 Cent

876. Boone, Mary. *50 Cent*. Hockessin, DE: Mitchell Lane, 2006.

For younger readers. Covers the life and musical accomplishments of rapper 50 Cent (Curtis James Jackson III). Discusses his New York roots, issues with the law, discovery by Eminem and eventual success.

877. Marcovitz, Hal. *50 Cent*. Broomall, PA: Mason Crest, 2007.

Discusses the life and musical accomplishments of Curtis James Jackson III, from his drug-dealing days in Queens, New York, to his success as a rap singer. His discovery, his contract with Interscope Records, efforts by Eminem to get 50 Cent an acting career, the fact that he was shot nine times in 2000, and feuds with other hip hoppers are also mentioned.

## Sean "Puffy" Combs

878. Ro, Ronin. *Bad Boy: The Influence of Sean "Puffy" Combs on the Music Industry*. New York: Atria, 2001.

Examines the triumphs and the problems of actor, producer, singer and rap mogul Sean "Puffy" Combs, how he built Bad Boy Entertainment, his bad decisions, street credit, projects, rap feuds, trial and more.

879. Torres, John A. *P. Diddy*. Hockessin, DE: Mitchell Lane, 2004.

For younger readers. This concise biography for grades nine to twelve discusses Sean Combs, the various names that he has adopted over the years, his influence on hip hop/rap, his role as record producer, Grammy Awards, acting jobs and more.

## Ice Cube

880. N.A. "Ice Cube." *Melody Maker*, 27 January 1990, 5.

Presents background information on Ice Cube's split with N.W.A. and asserts that he left the group because of a dispute over royalties. Also discusses his new solo career and his recording contract with Priority Records.

881. Blackwell, Mark. "Ain't That a Bitch." *Spin*, October 1990, 24.

A discussion of Ice Cube's negative portrayal of women in his raps, using quotes from lyrics of some of his songs to illustrate the point. The article also includes Ice Cube's response to the charges of misogyny leveled against him.

882. Orr, Tawara. *Ice Cube.* Hockessin, DE: Mitchell Lane, 2006.

Covers his life from his humble beginnings to his success as a business man, record producer and rapper. This concise coverage also mentions his role in N.W.A., why he left the group, and his successful solo career as a rapper.

883. Sager, Mike. "Cube: The World According to AmeriKKKa's Most Wanted Rapper." *Rolling Stone,* 4 October 1990, 78–79.

This in-depth profile of the artist includes background and musical information. Chronicles his early childhood and eventual interest in rap, his association with N.W.A., and his version of their split. His close friends, business associates and plans for the future are also discussed.

884. Tate, Greg. "Manchild at Large: One on One With Ice Cube, Hip Hop's Most Wanted." *Village Voice,* 11 September 1990, 77.

Describes his childhood years, his association with Yo-Yo and their recording of "It's a Man's World" on *AmeriKKKa's Most Wanted.* Cube discusses his controversial lyrics, his parents, growing up and many other issues.

## Chuck D and Public Enemy

885. N.A. "Beyond the Terrordome." *Spin,* February 1990, 18.

An insightful interview with Chuck D presents his views on the use of religious and racial lyrics on Public Enemy's *Welcome to the Terrordome* single.

886. N.A.. "Rockbeat: Bumrush the Ivy League." *Village Voice,* 5 June 1990, 73.

Chronicles Chuck D's speaking engagement at Harvard as a panelist addressing Afrocentric issues, his radio interview and press conference. Concludes that his message might be more effective if it were disseminated at concerts and on albums.

887. N.A. "Public Enemy Facing New Charge of Anti-Semitism." *Variety,* 3 January 1990, 49.

The article discusses the Anti-Defamation League's letter to CBS records accusing Public Enemy's song *Welcome to the Terrordome* of being anti-Semitic. A similar letter was sent to Geffen records regarding the Guns N' Roses song "One in a Million." Presents the ADL's belief that the music industry is not concerned with hate lyrics, only with whether the record sells.

888. Cole, Lewis. "Loose Cannon Guns Down Public Enemy." *Rolling Stone*, 10 August 1989, 24.

Cole discusses the endemic announcements, contradictions and confusion that resulted as a result of Professor Griff's interview about racism, stereotypes and charges of anti-Semitism in the *Washington Times*. This essential article is an attempt at damage control and summarizes the lasting effect that the interview had on the group.

889. ——. "Def or Dumb?" *Rolling Stone*, 19 October 1989, 47–48.

Covers the group's ascent to fame and fortune, and their artistic and commercial development. Also included is a discussion of individual roles within the group, fallout from Professor Griff's interview in the *Washington Times*, and the aftermath of the interview.

890. D, Chuck. *Fight the Power: Rap, Race, and Reality*. New York: Delacorte, 1997.

A penetrating assessment of issues within the music industry that denigrate rap and hip hop. In this provocative book, Chuck D discusses the use of drugs, the negative portrayal of blacks in film and television, and the schism between the East and west coast rap communities. Of particular note is his discussion of the obstacles that hinder progress toward peace and unity, and his honest and sincere plea for respect and unity between people of different ideologies and identities.

891. DJ Red Alert and David Lee. "Public Enemy." *Interview*, September 1990, 104.

Covers the roles of Chuck D and Flavor Flav as part of Public Enemy. The brief interview discusses how their respective roles evolved as the group achieved more and more success.

892. Eiswerth, Jr, Joseph Paul. "Rap Music as Protest: A Rhetorical Analysis of Public Enemy's Lyrics." Masters thesis, University of Nevada, Las Vegas, 1996.

The author defines rap music as protest rhetoric, provides a history as an extension of African and African American oral traditions, analyzes the lyrics of Public Enemy, and argues that their discourse is a form of social protest without being part of a social movement.

893. Kohn, Marek. "The Enemy Outside." *New Statesman and Society*, 15 September 1989, 41.

Another discussion of the fallout that occurred from Professor Griff's interview with the *Washington Times*. In addition, Kohn discusses Public Enemy's image and includes an interpretation of their lyrics.

894. Leland, John. "Armageddon in Effect." *Spin*, September 1988, 46.

In this interview, Chuck D asserts that rap music is a positive force in black children's lives, discusses some of Professor Griff's controversial statements, and presents his opinions on a variety of political and racial issues from a black nationalist perspective.

895. Malone, Bonz. "Public Enemy." *Spin*, April 1990, 46.

This article was one of several devoted to important musical influences of the eighties. Malone acknowledges Public Enemy's creative and innovative use of media and message. They also extended and perfected musical accompaniment for rap. The author believes the rappers are the voice of black anger in the United States.

896. Odell, Mike and David Stubbs. "Public Enemy: A Question of Color." *Melody Maker*, 31 March 1990, 31.

Griff (interviewed by Odell) discusses his controversial interview in the *Washington Times*, his break with Public Enemy, his new solo career and other issues. Chuck D spoke to Stubbs about Griff's break with Public Enemy, and offers his perspective on lyrics that alluded to sociopolitical issues.

897. Owen, Frank. "Hip Hop Wig Out 87." *Melody Maker*, 21 March 1987, 30.

Profiles Public Enemy, chronicles Chuck D's background and political orientation, and covers the state of New York hip hop after the release of *Yo! Bum Rush the Show*. An interesting and provocative discussion of how hip hop evolved from an urban to suburban phenomenon.

898. ———. "Public Service." *Spin*, March 1990, 57.

Chuck D discusses the release and impact of *Fear of a Black Planet*. He quotes and deconstructs the lyrics of several tracks, presents his views regarding racial issues and discusses Professor Griff's issues with the media. He also discusses a recent meeting that he had with Nation of Islam leader Louis Farrakhan.

899. Reynolds, Simon. "Strength to Strength." *Melody Maker*, 17 October 1987, 14.

In this interview both Chuck D and Professor Griff voice their philosophies on several issues. Chuck D offers his opinion on the history and education of blacks in America, and on racial and sexual themes. Professor Griff adds his philosophical views on specific issues.

900. Santoro, Gene. "Music: Public Enemy." *The Nation*, 25 June 1990, 902–03.

Although the article profiles Public Enemy and their music, the primary focus is on the anti-Semitism debate. The author comments on Jerry Adler's article in *Newsweek* (19 March 1990) with a special emphasis on racial bias.

901. Sinker, Mark. "Enemy of the People." *New Statesman and Society*, 23 February 1990, 39.

Covers both their influence and ability to bring black and white audiences together. Also discusses the group's ability to speak for a silent and under-represented minority in hard, straightforward lyrics. A significant portion of the article is devoted to Professor Griff's interview with the *Washington Times* and the ensuing fallout.

902. Walser, Robert. "Rhythm, Rhyme, and Rhetoric in the Music of Public Enemy." *Ethnomusicology* 39(2) (Spring/Summer 1995): 193–219.

Walser builds upon the ethnographic work of scholars like Cheryl Keyes and Tricia Rose for a deeper analysis of hip hop. He uses the music of Public Enemy to corroborate and amplify the arguments of ethnographic scholars. Also discusses whether rap is music, mapping the groove, mapping rapping, and rhythm and sensibility; he supports his conclusions with a musical transcription of "Fight the Power."

903. Wyman, Bill. "20 Questions: Chuck D." *Playboy*, November 1990, 135.

Chuck D responded to twenty questions covering a myriad of issues, personal and professional, including what music he listened to as a child. Several questions focused on Professor Griff and Public Enemy, groupies, and why Arsenio Hall had not invited him to appear on his show.

## Heavy D and the Boyz

904. McAdams, Janine. "Heavy D Does the Right Thing." *Billboard*, 2 September 1989, 18.

A biographical profile of Heavy D and the group after the popularity of their CD *Big Tyme*. Examines the album as a whole, and specifically the hit recording, "We Got Our Own Thang." Also comments on their attempts to get a record contract and other issues.

905. Mehno, Scott. "Who Do You Think You Are." *Spin*, February 1987, 14.

Concise coverage of Heavy D and the group that focuses on their new hit recording. Some attention is devoted to the difficulties they experienced in getting their first demo accepted and in securing a record contract.

906. Sullivan, Caroline. "Just Weight and See." *Melody Maker*, 30 January 1988, 10.

This brief commentary has little or no scholarly value; however, it presents a side of Heavy D that is rarely seen in the press. He comments on his weight, performances that are devoid of raw language and metaphor, and the fact that he will not demean other rappers.

## Kool Moe Dee

907. Dee, Kool Moe. *There's a God on the Mic: The True 50 Greatest MCs*. New York: Thunder Mouth Press, 2003.

The author devises his own rating system to ascertain the fifty greatest rap MCs of all time. Among the seventeen categories he uses to rate MCs are flow, freestyle ability, lyricism, live performance ability, originality and vocabulary. After combining the scores of each category, he gave each artist a cumulative score, and thereafter a rating strength of his system is that he provides an explanation for each rating.

## Snoop Dogg

908. Dogg, Snoop and David Seay. *Tha Doggfather: The Times, Trials and Hardcore Truth of Snoop Dogg*. New York: William Morrow Co., 2001.

Filled with insights into Snoop Dogg's family, early years, drug activity, gang affiliations and eventual transformation to hip hop. Contains important information on his relationship with Suge Knight, Death Row Records and Dr. Dre.

## Dr. Dre

909. Brown, Jackie. *Dr. Dre in the Studio: From Compton, Death Row, Snoop Dogg, Eminem, 50 Cent, the Game and Mad Money and the*

*Lifetimes, and Aftermath of the Notorious Producer.* New York: Colossus Books, 2006.

Discusses Dr. Dre's prowess as a record producer and includes quotes from his 2001 co-producer Mel-Man. The latter addresses questions regarding Dr. Dre stealing credit from other producers and Dre's activities in the studio. Both Mel-Man and Scott Storch offer clues about Dr. Dre's upcoming release of *Detox*, a solo work (scheduled to be released in 2009).

910. Ro, Ronin. *Dr. Dre: The Biography.* New York: Thunder Mouth Press, 2007.

Covers his life in Compton, California, days and his group N.W.A. (Niggaz With Attitude). Focuses on his contributions as a pivotal figure in developments, feuds and trends in rap, and as a mentor to artists like Busta Rhymes, Rakim, 50 Cent, Eminem and Snoop Dogg. Also discussed, his role in the release of *Straight Outta Compton* in 1988 and the establishment of Death Row Records.

### Eminem

911. Bozza, Anthony. *Whatever You Say I Am: The Life and Times of Eminem.* New York: Three Rivers Press, 2003.

The author explores the trials and tribulations of Eminem and offers an important glimpse into the life experiences that shaped him. Also discusses the relationship between Eminem and Dr. Dre. Bozza was given unprecedented access to Eminem and was able to mold personal reminiscences into broader discussions about life, the Detroit rap scene, popular culture and his rise to fame.

912. Fernandes, Denise. "The New 'Role Model' for the Hip Hop Generation: Dissecting The Hype to Locate Eminem, Slim Shady, and Marshall Mathers Through Race Relations, Black Cool, Media Coverage, and the Search for Hip Hop Celebrity." Masters thesis, Montreal, Canada: McGill University, 2005.

Presents a case study of Eminem and explores black and white theories of belonging within American society, using the premise that identity is constructed along racial stereotypes. Discusses how Eminem employs hip hop cultural forms, styles and traits to create his rap image, and how he uses parody, play and persona to illuminate his views of American life.

913. Hasted, Nick. *The Dark Story of Eminem.* London and New York: Omnibus Press, 2003.

Traces the evolution of Marshall Mathers from his associations, schools and work places in Detroit, Michigan, to global stardom as Eminem. Chronicles his adversarial relationship with his mother, his teenage friend Kim Scott, and Dr. Dre and the Bass brothers, who guided him from the age of fourteen. Also contains information on his influence on artists like The Pet Shop Boys and Tori Amos, and his film debut in the autobiographical *8 Mile*.

914. Mattern, Joanne. *Eminem*. Broomall, PA: Mason Crest, 2006.

For younger readers. The story of Marshall Bruce Mathers III. From obscurity in Detroit to hip hop success in the 1990s, his success is traced from the debut of his album *Slim Shady*, to the release of *Marshall Mathers*, to his several Grammy Awards, acting career and other successes. His discovery and signing of 50 Cent, and issues of homophobia, misogyny and violence are also mentioned.

915. Shaffer, Tani Graham. "The Shady Side of Hip-Hop: A Jungian and Eriksonian Interpretation of Eminem's 'Explicit Content.'" PhD dissertation, Palo Alto, CA: Pacific Graduate School of Psychology, 2005.

The author uses ethnography and grounded theory to investigate ways in which rap music and Eminem's "explicit content" is perceived by fans of his music. Five themes were identified and investigated to determine meaning from individual perspectives: emotional catharsis, empowerment, authenticity, storytelling and ecstatic passion. The study is important because it allows clinical psychologists a unique perspective of their patients, whether they agree or disagree with their viewpoint.

916. Watts, Eric King. "Bordering, Patrolling and 'Passing' in Eminem's 8 Mile." *Critical Studies in Media Communication* 22(3) (August 2005): 187–201.

The author argues that the semi-biographical film *8 Mile* portrays Eminem as a racially distinctive artist with commercial appeal. In the film he was portrayed as "white trash," a white enigma of Euro-American ethnicity. He was subjected to struggles of race and gender in his career, and as a result has been authenticated by his acceptance into and negotiation of grass-roots hip hop culture. The confluence of his experiences and authentication makes him marketable as a symbol of black hip hop culture.

917. Weaver, Ryan J. "Will the Real Marshall Mathers Please Stand Up: Challenging Mathers 'White Negro' Realizing Hipsterphilia/Phobia, and Rethinking Hip Hop Music." Masters thesis, University of Kansas, 2006.

Uses rhetorical methods to study the story that popular and academic audiences tell about Mathers. He advocates that Mathers, better known as Eminem, is an interesting case study for many reasons, including the tension between his race and hip hop success. Authenticity is used as an initial point of discussion and he argues that focusing solely on the narrative that Mathers tells about himself offers a limited view of his authenticity.

## Faith Evans

918. Evans, Faith. *Keep the Faith: A Memoir.* New York: Grand Central, 2008.

An introspective look at Evans' life before and after the death of her husband Biggie Smalls. She describes herself as more than just the wife of Smalls; before her marriage, she had a successful career as a songwriter for artists like Mary J. Blige, Hi-Five, Usher, Pebbles, Al. B. Sure and others. Her career also includes collaborations with Babyface, Whitney Houston and Sting.

## Five Percent Nation

919. Miyakawa, Felicia M. "God Hop: The Music and Message of Five Percent Rap." PhD dissertation, Indiana University Press, 2003.

The dissertation covers the music and message of Five Percent Nation, an offshoot of the Nation of Islam, who use rap to spread their message. Sketches Five Percent Nation's cultural and spiritual history from Bobble Drew Ali's Moorish Science Temple, influenced by W.D. Fard, Elijah Muhammad, Malcolm X, Clarence 13X and Louis Farrakhan. Depicts the group as proponents of clean living, trying to elevate their community and promote their belief that modern African Americans are descendants of an advanced Moorish civilization. Examines the widely diverse and creative compositions of God Hop Music, and concludes that the group's style is difficult to categorize. Explains that the group's name is derived from the theory that five percent of the world's people are "the poor righteous teachers" who extol the "Black Man of Asia" as the "Living God(s)." Thoroughly researched.

## Grandmaster Flash

920. Christgau, Robert. "Magnificent Seven." *Village Voice*, 2 November 1982, 59.

The essays profiles Grandmaster Flash and the Furious Five, providing both background and musical information. Includes details of the group's concerts and compares their approach to rap with other styles.

921. George, Nelson. "The New Street Art." *Village Voice*, 6 May 1981, 75.

Reviews of "Grandmaster Flash On The Wheels of Steel" and "8th Wonder," by Flash and the Furious Five and Sugarhill Gang, respectively. Focuses on the record's innovative aural images and sounds, and the creative techniques Flash used to achieve them. George portrays Flash as a unique and creative artist in this new and emerging genre.

922. Hedges, Don. "Together, Wherever They Go." *Musician*, June 1988, 14.

This concise article focuses on the reunion of Grandmaster Flash and the Furious Five to record a new album entitled *On The Strength*. Also covers their past disagreements, their view on the fusion of rock and rap, and their determination to stay together as a group.

923. Nelson, Havelock. "Flash and 5 Back Together for Gold." *Billboard*, 26 March 1988, 24.

This article is devoted to the reunion of Flash and the Furious Five for their new album *On The Strength* and new single "Gold." Includes comments on their early works, why they disbanded, how the separation worked against them, their reunion as a group, and their collaboration with Steppenwolf on a cover of "Magic Carpet Ride."

924. Owen, Frank. "4th World Funk: The Return of Grandmaster Flash." *Melody Maker*, 24 May 1986, 12.

In this interview Flash discusses his current album, *The Source*, current trends on the New York hip hop scene, and comments on violence and the *Krush Groove* movie. He also expands on his belief that rap is an experimental music and that artists should continue to forge new and creative ideas in rap.

925. Pye, Ian. "Christmas Rapping with Grandmaster Flash." *Melody Maker*, 18 December 1982, 11.

In this interview, Flash and the Furious Five discuss their beginnings, success, their innovations, and their influence on rap music aesthetics, art and performance concepts. Of special note is their discussion of the message in rap and the emergence of issue-oriented rap.

926. Strauss, Duncan. "Grandmaster Flash's Spin Act." *Trouser Press*, October 1983, 31.

A special interview covers not only his background and how he became involved in rap, but also discusses how he developed his turntable technique. He also discusses the impact of the message in hip hop music, current projects and hopes for future success.

## M.C. Hammer

927. Billingham, Alf. "M.C. Hammer Cleaning Up Rap's Image." *Melody Maker*, 2 June 1990, 17.

Presents Hammer's perception of why he is successful, and why his approach to rap differs from others. Also includes his response to rappers who criticize him, and his forecast for the future direction of rap.

928. Blackwell, Mark. "M.C. Hammer." *Spin*, December 1990, 47.

Profiles Hammer as somewhat different from hard-core rappers and represents him as a good role model for youth. Blackwell shows Hammer to be a very popular rapper who has a strong focused personality and a positive image.

929. ———. "Murder Report." *Spin*, May 1990, 22.

This article articulates the schism that developed between Hammer and other rappers. Hammer is upset about the criticism that 3rd Bass directed at his hit song, "Turn This Motha Out."

930. Harvey, Scott. "M.C. Hammer." *Cash Box*, 2 June 1990, 3.

Unlike the many articles on Hammer and other rappers which concentrate on their background, music, influences and other issues, this one focuses on nonmusical issues. Specifically, the author is enamored with Hammer's implementation of projects to help children, and is impressed by his knowledge of the business end of rap.

931. Hochman, Steve. "Hammerin' Out The Hits." *Rolling Stone*, 12 July 1990, 29.

The profile is concerned with two broad issues, Hammer's business sophistication and the criticism leveled at him by some of his rivals. Hochman discusses his business holdings, the diverse projects with which he is involved, and his future goals. Also discusses the charge that Hammer's popularity is based upon his showmanship rather than rapping skills.

932. Long, Bob. "Hammer Forms Bustin' Records." *Cash Box*, 7 July 1990, 14.

A concise item in the "rhythm and blues" column provides details of the merger of Hammer's independent label with Columbia Records. Long describes the responsibilities of each party and identifies upper management of the new company. Hammer identifies artists associated with the company, and provides insight into the future goals and directions of the company.

933. ———. "Hammer—Total Entertainer." *Cash Box*, 2 June 1990, 12.

Concerned with Hammer's overall talent and his ability to defy classification. Hammer is represented as a very talented entertainer who is cognizant of public tastes and what is necessary to market and sell a product. The author also discusses the variety of styles represented on Hammer's album *Please Hammer Don't Hurt Em*.

934. Nelson, George. "Hammer Hits Hard with New Jack Moves." *Billboard*, 25 February 1989, 24.

This "rhythm and blues section" column attests to Hammer's popularity and discusses how he differed from other rappers of the time. The author praises Hammer's dancing and believes his approach represents a new standard for live rap shows.

935. Ressner, Jeffrey. "Hammer Time." *Rolling Stone*, 6 September 1990, 6.

This in-depth profile is full of biographical and personal information. Contains information on the controversial working conditions that he imposes upon his crew, and a continuing discussion of the schism that exists between his style of rap and that of hard-core rappers.

936. Waldron, Clarence. "M.C. Hammer Says He is More Than Just Another Rapper." *Jet*, 17 September 1990, 54.

Published in a popular magazine that represents African American culture, this article identifies the ways in which Hammer differs from other rappers: positive messages and his ability as an entertainer, including dancing, that helps him connect with his audience.

937. Williams, Joe. "M.C. Hammer: Man in Motion." *Cash Box*, 27 May 1989, 9.

Published in a special edition of the magazine which focused on rap, this article is concerned with Hammer's talents as both an entertainer and producer. A good overview of his artistic, business and philanthropic activities, and his belief that rap should encompass eclectic approaches.

## Jerry Heller

938. Heller, Jerry and Gil Reavill. *Ruthless: A Memoir.* New York: Simon Spotlight Entertainment, 2007.

    Written by Jerry Heller, a long-time artist representative and co-founder of Ruthless Records, the home to N.W.A, Bone Thugs-N-Harmony, and his partner and label co-founder Easy-E (Eric Wright). He discusses the anti-Semitic rap lyrics directed at him, pays homage to Easy-E, talks about his work with rap artists, and covers the impact of drugs, guns, bodyguards and grudges in the music business.

## L.L. Cool J

939. N.A. "Chief L.L. Cool J." *Jet*, December 1988, 55.

    Covers the artist's growing reputation and his concern for the poor. This brief article recounts L.L. Cool J being named the chief of a village in the Ivory Coast. After he was installed, he performed a concert to a sold-out audience and donated the proceeds to the village orphanage.

940. Coleman, Mark. "The Cool Life: Rapper L.L. Cool J Is Def but Not Dumb." *Rolling Stone*, 8 October 1987, 16–17.

    Reveals intimate details of his life before and after he became involved with rap. He discusses his middle-class upbringing, values and current lifestyle. He also reveals his desire to make music that people can enjoy, rather than focusing on songs with social and political messages.

941. Dougherty, Steve. "L.L. Cool J Raps to the Beat of His Box While His LP Does Better Than Dow Jones Stocks." *People Weekly*, 21 April 1986, 58.

    Another discussion of his middle-class background and his system of values. This profile is informative because in addition to his early life, he provides insight into how he became interested and developed his talent in rap. The author characterizes him as hard working, focused and determined to succeed in rap.

942. L.L. Cool J. *I Make My Own Rules.* New York: St Martin's Press, 1997.

    A penetrating account of his early life and rise to fame. The rap star and actor reveals the hardships of his childhood, how he achieved success in his career and his spiritual life. Provides an insider perspective on the world of rap.

943. McKinney, Rhoda E. "Bigger, Deffer, and Richer." *Ebony,* January 1988, 108.

   Presents an overview of L.L. Cool J's life and family influence, and his rise from obscurity to world renown as a rap artist. Also contains a discussion of his musical development, eventual success and plans for the future.

944. Owen, Frank. "Top of the World." *Melody Maker,* 13 June 1987, 24.

   Uses Umberto Eco's views on American obsession with bigger and better things to discuss L.L. Cool J's new album entitled *Bigger and Deffer.* The author views the artist as a personification of "bigger" and more dogmatic, a contradiction to rap's focus on the evils of affluence, wealth and power.

945. Reynolds, Simon. "Hell Raiser." *Melody Maker,* 7 November 1987, 24.

   The interview was conducted to ascertain the identity of the "real" L.L. Cool J. The author seems surprised to find L.L. Cool J a humble and cautious person, well spoken and anxious to not be misrepresented in the media.

946. The Stud Brothers. "The Harder They Come." *Melody Maker,* 27 September 1986, 28.

   L.L. Cool J discusses his attitudes about musical categories, and whether rap should be an entertainment vehicle. In addition, he discusses what rappers should do to communicate with their audience, what he does to maintain contact with the street, and what rappers should do to remain popular.

947. ———. "L.L. Cool J: The Power Game." *Melody Maker,* 24 June 1989, 48.

   Portrays L.L. Cool J as a workaholic who is never satisfied with his image or music. He is never satisfied with his success, instead wanting more and more. The artist comments on his heroes and on rappers who have criticized him.

948. Trakin, Roy. "Float Like a Butterfly, Sting Like a Beat Box." *Creem,* August 1986, 68.

   Depicts L.L. Cool J as a new innovative leader on rap with a plan for future success. His penchant for a more austere aesthetic ("less is more"), his contributions to soundtracks, and ambitions and vision for the future are also discussed.

949. Young, Jon. "L.L. Cool J Takes the Rap, Beats the Rap, Raps it Up, Raps Around the Clock, Encourages Bad Puns." *Creem,* October 1987, 38.

Depicts L.L. Cool J as an amenable, creative, serious and very private person. A limited amount of personal information is included along with his account of his split with Rick Rubin. The profile also comments on the strong points of his new album *Bigger and Deffer*.

## DJ Jazzy Jeff and the Fresh Prince

950. N.A. "Jazzy Jeff and Fresh Prince, Rap's More Mild Than Wild Guys." *People Weekly*, 3 October 1988, 81.

A brief introduction to the duo, their personal backgrounds, how they met and formed their group, their musical style, the meaning of some of their lyrics, and their hopes and aspirations for the future.

951. Corrigan, Jim. *Will Smith*. Broomall, PA: Mason Crest, 2006.

Traces Smith's career from his West Philadelphia roots to his success in the 1980s as the MC of the DJ Jazzy Jeff and The Fresh Prince duet and as a television and movie personality. He was the first actor to have eight consecutive films gross over $100 million each at the box office.

952. Levy, J. Allen. "Hip Hop for Beginners: D.J. Jazzy Jeff and the Fresh Prince Get Stupid." *Spin*, October 1988, 44.

This interview was conducted during the duo's *Run's House* tour and depicts their off-stage personas as fun-loving young men who enjoy each other's company. They are also serious artists who can separate their performances from their personal lives. They discuss their crossover appeal and other issues.

953. Push. "King Jazzy." *Melody Maker*, 9 January 1988, 13.

This brief interview is permeated with information on Jazzy Jeff's awards, and how he teamed up with the Fresh Prince and Rock-C. Also discusses their image compared with hardcore rappers, and the effect that recording in the UK has had on their career.

## Marion "Suge" Knight

954. Ro, Ronin. *Have Gun Will Travel*. New York: Main Street Books, 1999.

This is the story of rap label Death Row Records and its CEO Marion "Suge" Knight and his rise from football player and bodyguard to global success. Discusses the methods that Knight used to control the market, the use of drug money, and the murders of Tupac Shakur and Notorious B.I.G.

## KRS-One

955. Parmar, Priya. "KRS-One Going Against the Grain: A Critical Study of Rap Music as a Postmodern Text." PhD dissertation, Pennsylvania State University, 2002.

An argument for studying and interpreting postmodern texts by using a cultural studies and critical theory approach in today's curricula. Analyzes and critiques rap as a postmodern text, and illustrates how rap as an emancipatory pedagogy exposes power relations between oppressed groups in nearly all facets of society. KRS-One was chosen as the subject of this case study because his raps focus on issues of class, race and power. The author concludes that the use of rap legitimizes and validates the student's race, experiences, knowledge, history and voice. Educators who used critical methods enabled the students to analyze such issues, dispel myths and question stereotypes.

## Queen Latifah

956. N.A. "Queen Latifah: Soul Mother Extraordinary." *Melody Maker*, 14 April 1986, 12.

Profiles Latifah's background and her belief that rap is a socially responsible genre. She discusses her debut album, the musicians on the album, sampling sources, and the historical musical setting and social context of her songs.

957. Ehrlich, Dimitri. "The Queen of Hip-Hop." *Interview*, May 1990, 58.

Presents a profile of Latifah in conjunction with the release of her debut recording and discusses the stars who appeared on it. Covers several issues from the female perspective, including the use of drugs and prostitution as quick ways to obtain money, use of sampling, and the role of sexism in rap.

958. Haring, Bruce. "Latifah Rules on New Album." *Billboard*, 6 January 1990, 35.

Discusses the album *All Hail The Queen*, and compares Latifah's rap vocal style to the powerful soul singing of Aretha Franklin. Also includes information on her musical background, how she began rapping and her personal life.

959. Light, Alan. "Queen Latifah." *Rolling Stone*, 22 February 1990, 30–31.

Covers the wide acclaim for her album *All Hail The Queen*. Mentions a future appearance on the David Bowie show. Also contains a good discussion of her background, musical style and other female rappers.

960. Rose, Tricia. "One Queen, One Tribe, One Destiny." *Rock and Roll Quarterly* 10(27) (March 1989): 10.

Discusses her energy and strong focus, the source of her convictions, and her belief that she will continue to succeed in the future. Covers her childhood, initial interest in rap, and her goals for her raps.

961. Tracy, Kathleen. *Queen Latifah.* Hockessin, DE: Mitchell Lane, 2005.

A concise discussion of her life, introduction to and involvement in rap, belief that rap is socially responsible, and her transformation to acting in films and television.

## Ludacris

962. Scott, Celicia. *Ludicrous.* Broomall, PA: Mason Crest, 2007.

The story of Christopher Bridges (aka Ludacris) from Champaign, Illinois, his rise to success as a rapper and actor, and his three Grammy Awards. Discusses his debut album, *Back for the First Time* (2000), his foundation (formed with his manager Chaka Zulu), his dispute with conservative commentator Bill O'Reilly, and more.

## Percy Miller (Master P.)

963. Chappell, Kevin. "Master P. Raps About His Rapper Son, His $500 Million Empire And Why He Cleaned Up His Act." *Ebony,* June 2002, 56–60.

Discusses the early life and rise to success of New Orleans-born Percy Miller, better known as Master P. He turned a $10,000 inheritance into a multimillion-dollar entertainment empire. Discusses his years in Baton Rouge introducing southern rap to the world, and his eventual move with his wife and six kids to Beverly Hills. The article also details his role as adviser, business manager and parent to his son, Percy Miller, Jr, better known as Lil' Romeo.

## Joan Morgan

964. Morgan, Joan. *When Chickenheads Come Home to Roost: My Life as a Hip-Hop Feminist.* New York: Simon and Schuster, 1999.

Morgan's witty expose is written in the "sister friendly" and Ebonics-spiced prose characteristic of her contributions to *Essence, The Village Voice* and *Vibe.* The author describes herself as a woman without a college education whose interests and tastes differ from those of better-educated black feminists. She argues that many of these women have not joined their academic counterparts in present-day dogma and movements because they believe that black academic feminists have not adequately addressed the gender wars. The title is drawn from a statement made by Malcolm X that used a derogatory term from hip hop culture ("chickenhead") that denotes a woman who uses sex as her ticket to the kept life.

**Priest da Nomad**

965. Smith, William Earl. "Hip Hop as Performance and Ritual: A Biographical and Ethnomusicological Construction of a Washington, D.C. Hip Hop Artist Named Priest da Nomad." PhD dissertation, University of Maryland, 2003.

Integrates the study of one individual musician (Priest da Nomad) with a discussion of the culture itself. Analyzes the MC's rhythmic style, personal aesthetics and rhythmic structure to illuminate the artist's mechanics of innovation. Hypothesizes that Priest's style of rhyme is more fluid rhythmically and features more developed subject matter than earlier styles of hip hop lyricism, and that a connection can be drawn between hip hop performance and spirit rituals of Ifa-based communities. Uses the concept of quantum holography to scientifically explain how one individual can embody many facets of culture.

**N.W.A.**

966. Fab 5 Freddy (Frederick Brathwaite). "N.W.A. is Niggers With Attitude." *Interview*, March 1990, 132.

The author interviews Eazy-E, Ice Cube and M.C. Ren. Each artist connected his life's challenges with his music, and expressed a strong desire to use rap to produce positive change in people's lives. They discuss the meanings of their lyrics, and comment on censorship and their song "The Police."

967. Hitchens, Christopher. "N.W.A. Cops an Attitude." *Rolling Stone*, 29 June 1989, 24.

A commentary on the success and popularity of the group, especially the popularity of their forthcoming album *Straight Outta Compton.* The album became popular despite a lack of airplay.

968. Lambert, Stu. "Dr. Beat." *Melody Maker*, 16 June 1990, 47.

An interesting and informative interview with Dr. Dre reveals how he started Ruthless records and what he did to bring N.W.A. together as a group. Of special note is his discussion of his equipment, technique and the various projects that he was producing.

969. O'Dell, Michael. "Niggers With Attitude." *Melody Maker*, 19 May 1990, 29.

An interview of the group immediately before their first live concert in the UK. Discusses their lives before forming the group, how they came together as a group, and several controversies regarding their songs.

970. Push. "N.W.A.: Shot by Both Sides." *Melody Maker*, 4 November 1989, 33.

Addresses criticisms of N.W.A. from Kool Moe Dee and the Congress of Racial Equality, issues with the police, and a letter from the FBI. Profiles their lives in Compton, mentions victims and perpetrators of violence, discusses meanings of their lyrics and outlines their aspirations for the future.

971. ———. "Niggers With Attitude." *Melody Maker*, 5 August 1989, 42.

Another interview in which N.W.A. describe their music and identities. They see themselves as reporters of the real life experiences of their peers, especially those who live in Compton. Unlike many in the media and the entertainment industry, they do not see themselves as political, instead preferring to impart raw life experiences as they have witnessed them.

## Outkast

972. Simone, Jacquelyn. *Outkast*. Broomall, PA: Mason Crest, 2006.

Discusses the origins and success of Outkast (Andre "Andre 300" Benjamin and Natwan "Big Boi" Patton) from their beginnings in Georgia when they were known as OKB (Outkast Brothers). Concise discussion of their Dirty South Style and mixture with other genres, their six Grammy Awards and their musical philosophy.

## Derrick Parker

973. Parker, Derrick. *Notorious C.O.P.: The Inside Story of The Tupac, Biggie, and Jam Master Jay Investigations*. New York: St Martin's Press, 2006.

Parker, a career officer with the NYPD from 1982 to 2002, investigated many of the hip hop-related shootings, which gives his book some credibility. He names a CRIP gang member whom he believes was the trigger man in the Tupac Shakur murder, and another he believes to be a candidate for the murder of Notorious B.I.G. He cites gang involvement and rivalries as probable motives for both murders.

## Busta Rhymes

974. Hamilton, Toby. *Busta Rhymes.* Broomall, PA: Mason Crest, 2006.

Trevor George Smith, Jr, actor and musician of Jamaican descent, was discovered by Chuck D of Public Enemy, who nicknamed him Busta Rhymes. Traces his early years with Leaders of the New School and the launching of his solo career in 1996. Also mentions his association with Native Tongue Posse and A Tribe Called Quest, and his acting roles in *Shaft* (2000) and *Full Clip* (2004) with Xzibit.

## Ja Rule

975. Hughes, Zondra. "Ja Rule: Rap Star Rules Hearts and Charts." *Ebony*, April 2002, 138, 140 and 142.

Discusses Jeffrey Atkins' life and musical career before the release of his debut album *Venni Vetti Vecci* ("I came, I saw, I conquered") in 1999. Covers the release of *Rule 3:36* (2000), which was influenced by the biblical verse John 3:16. The influence of his mother, his marriage to Aisha Murray Atkins and family life are also discussed.

## Run-DMC

976. Adler, Bill. *Tougher Than Leather: The Authorized Biography of Run D.M.C.* New York: New American Library, 1987.

Profiles the lives and backgrounds of the members of Run-DMC prior to the release of their film *Rougher Than Leather.* He also covers Run-DMC's role in the early history and development of rap.

977. Blauner, Peter. "The Rap on Run-D.M.C: The Kids from Hollis Strike Gold." *New York*, 17 November 1986, 62.

Covers the group's backgrounds, early interest in rap and career development through the mid 1980s. Blauner raises the issue of violence at their concerts, and the group members offer their perspective on the issue.

978. Cummings, Sue. "Burning the Kingdom." *Spin*, July 1986, 57.

Most of the article deals with the trials and tribulations of the rock group Aerosmith, but it also contains information on Run-DMC's collaboration with Aerosmith on the remake of "Walk This Way."

979. Fricke, David. "Armour Plated Rap." *Melody Maker*, 23 March 1985, 10.

Discusses the group's fusion of hard rock and metal with rap and its effect on their popularity and street credibility. Concludes that the fusion did not effect their street credibility.

980. Goldstein, Toby. "Tear Down the Walls, Pack Out The Halls: On The (Hard) Beat With Run-D.M.C." *Creem*, December 1986, 30.

The group defends their music and message and discusses the violence that occurs at their concerts. Goldstein includes information on their backgrounds and comments on their cover of "Walk This Way," their extensive use of heavy metal samples, their future movie projects, and more.

981. Kiersh, Ed. "Beating the Rap." *Rolling Stone*, 4 December 1986, 59.

Emphasizes Run-DMC's clean image and middle-class background, and their deep commitment to social issues and their positive raps. Defends the group's music against critics who associate it with violence, and presents an introspective discussion of the group's street credibility.

982. Mehno, Scott and John Leland. "The Years of Living Dangerously." *Spin*, May 1988, 40.

Run-DMC reveal their inner feelings about what makes them happy and what frustrates them. The interview focused on the difficulties that they had experienced, and they present their views on things that transpired in the last year.

983. Owen, Frank. "Homeboys Home Truths." *Melody Maker*, 23 May 1987, 24.

Summarizes Run-DMC's work in schools and discusses the violence that occurred on their *Tougher Than Leather* tour. The group shares their philosophy that silence is masculine. In addition, Owen situates the group within rap history.

984. Ro, Ronin. *Raising Hell: The Reign, Run, and Redemption of Run-D. M.C. and Jam Master Jay.* New York: Amistad (HarperCollins), 2005.

An interesting and provocative story of Darryl McDaniels' transformation into DMC, his association with Joseph Simmons, and his union with Jason "Jam Master Jay" Mizell to form Run-DMC. Traces their rise to success via the management of Russell Simmons, Joseph Simmons' brother.

985. Rosenbluth, Jean. "Run-D.M.C. Seeks Profits Boost With New Album." *Billboard*, 21 May 1988, 46.

Praises Run-DMC's *Tougher Than Leather* while questioning the group's ability to achieve sales commensurate with their *Raising Hell* CD. In this case, Rosenblatt believes the new album does not have a crossover track with high potential popularity appeal. Another interesting point is that the group was criticized because they wore beepers (pagers) on the cover photo, which, in the author's view, contradicts their anti-drug message.

## Tupac Shakur

986. Alexander, Frank and Heidi Sigmund Cuda. *Got Your Back: Protecting Tupac in the World of Gangsta Rap.* New York: St Martin's Griffin, 2000.

Recollections by Tupac's bodyguard during the last year of his life. Covers Tupac's celebrity, but offers little insight on how and why Tupac continued to impact hip hop and rap music and culture until his death. Discusses the confrontation with Suge Knight, his own confusion and guilt about the death of Tupac, and the aftermath of Tupac's death. The last three chapters are an emotional discourse on his relationship with Tupac and contain the details of an intimate conversation between Alexander and Afeni Shakur, Tupac's mother.

987. Ardis, Angela. *Inside a Thug's Heart.* New York: Kensington, 2004.

An account of Shakur's life by his girlfriend offers an intimate perspective of the man and his character. She uses his letters and poems to her to craft her account, and includes his gentle and introspective feelings as well as his resentment and rage against injustice.

988. Aziz, Shahzad. *In The Land of the Ayatollahs Tupac Shakur is King: Reflections From Iran and the Arab World.* Springer, Netherlands: Amai Press, 2007.

Several Middle Eastern cities serve as the backdrop for a discussion of issues that exist between the Arab World and the West, including the adoption of Western popular culture (with a focus on Tupac Shakur), the war on terror, the Arab–Israeli conflict, the position of women in Islam, and more.

989. Bastfield, Darrin Keith. *Back in the Day: My Life and Times With Tupac Shakur.* New York: Da Capo, 2003.

An intimate portrait by a man who knew Shakur, and who mourns him as a personal and lost friend. He discusses their teenage years, Tupac's charisma and development as an artist, and his tendency to attract negative attention because of his intelligence, skill and sensitivity. The author also discusses their shared experiences, and provides additional insight into the man, his music and legacy.

990. Datcher, Michael and Kwame Alexander, eds. *Tough Love: Cultural Criticism and Familial Observations on the Life and Death of Tupac Shakur.* Washington, DC: Blackwords, 1996.

Essays from more than twenty African American writers present their insightful and critical assessments of the life and death of Tupac Shakur. Discussions of his early life, issues with drugs and the law, his concern with social and political issues, musical contributions, impact, legacy and more. Illustrated. Introduction by Kierna Dawsey; special epilogue by Mutula Shakur.

991. Doe, John. *Dead or Alive: The Mystery of Tupac Shakur, The Alive Theories.* Bloomington, IN: Author House, 2004.

The author uses a variety of theories and documentation to debate the validity of claims that Shakur is alive. He discusses the mystery surrounding his death, and the fact that no one has been convicted for his murder.

992. Dyson, Michael Eric. *Holler if You Hear Me: Searching for Tupac Shakur.* New York: Basic Civitas Books, 2006.

Profiles the life and music of Tupac Amaru Shakur (1971–96) as a microcosm of African American life and culture. He places gangsta rap in historical and social context, and uses Shakur's music and videos to discuss issues like machismo, the simultaneous contempt and adoration of black women, black-on-black crime, the unsolved murder of Shakur, and more. Also debates whether hip hop harms the people who listen to it since it espouses hedonism and materialism, and includes offensive language. Very insightful and provocative.

993. Gee, Alex and John E. Teter. *Jesus and the Hip-Hop Prophets: Spiritual Insights from Lauryn Hill and Tupac Shakur.* New York: Inner Varsity Press, 2003.

Offers insight into the lyrics of Hill and Shakur with special emphasis on the spiritual content. The book separates hip hop and standard English but is illuminating on the connection between urban life and the prophetic warnings of the two artists.

994. Golus, Carrie. *Tupac Shakur.* Just the Facts Biographies. Minneapolis: Lerner Publications, 2006.

For younger readers. A concise discussion geared toward ages 9–12; covers what the author calls his "thug life," problems with the law, drugs, Death Row records, musical success and his untimely death.

995. Hodge, Daniel W. "Baptized in Dirty Water: The Missiological Gospel of Tupac Amaru Shakur." PhD dissertation, Fuller Theological Seminary, 2007.

Studies Tupac's life history and musical message within the social context of hip hop, postmodernism and urban culture. Examines the missiological and theological message of Shakur and deconstructs his lyrical, poetic and spiritual message to ascertain how Shakur reached out to hip hop youth. Mentions his Gospel message, an overview of narrative, and offers suggestions for mission action.

996. Hoye, Jacob and Karolyn Ali, eds. *Tupac: Resurrection 1971–1996.* New York: Atria, 2006.

Attempts to dispel some misrepresentations about Shakur, and to paint a true picture of the man, his vision, musical contributions and humanity. This account of the man and his contributions was endorsed by Afeni Shakur, Tupac's mother.

997. Legg, Barnaby, James McCarthy and Flameboy (illustrator). *Death Rap Tupac Shakur.* Malvern, Australia: Omnibus Press, 2006.

Documents the series of events that led to the death of Shakur. Discusses his triumphs and tragedies, and portrays him as a charismatic and creative artist who defined African American culture in the United States.

998. Mills, Clifford. *Tupac Shakur.* New York: Checkmark Books, 2007.

For younger readers. Presents a balanced view of the man, his music, and death. Written for ninth- to twelfth-grade students, the concise account contains information on his contributions, legacy and impact. The book contains sidebars and other interesting features.

999. Monjauze, Molly, ed., Gloria Cox and Staci Robinson, contribs. *Tupac Remembered.* New York: Chronicle Books, 2008.

Candid and cherished memories of Shakur from a variety of actors, political leaders, rappers and others. Snoop Dogg, Eminem, Common, E40, Jada Pinkett-Smith, Nikki Giovanni, Sonia Sanchez and others made contributions.

1000. Potash, John. *The FBI War on Tupac Shakur and Black Leaders.* New York: Progressive Left Press, 2008.

Details the FBI's use of counterintelligence tactics against a generation of rap artists and African American leaders. The book is thorough, based on 100 interviews, twelve years of research, information gleaned from the Freedom of Information release of CIA and FBI documents, court transcripts and mainstream media outlets.

1001. Robinson, Heather. "'Keepin' It Hyperreal': Tupac Shakur and the Struggle for Authenticity." Masters thesis, Utah State University, 2006.

The life and influence of Shakur are used to study black cultural expression and to critique authenticity and concrete identity within 1990s American cultural thought. Incorporates Henry Louis Gates, Jr's theory of black literature, Antonio Gramsci's concepts of hegemony and wars of position, and James Davison Hunter's cultural wars of the 1990s to discuss Shakur as a pedagogical figure for diverse communities.

1002. Sandy, Candace and Dawn Marie Daniels. *How Long Will They Mourn Me?: The Life and Legacy of Tupac Shakur.* New York: One World/Ballantine, 2006.

Celebrates his life and rise to fame, and discusses involvement with drugs, sex and violence. Also covers his legacy and impact as an actor, poet and rapper.

1003. Scott, Cathy. *The Killing of Tupac Shakur.* Las Vegas: Huntington Press, 2005.

Investigates why the police had no real suspects or reliable leads in Shakur's murder. Reveals a subculture permeated with loyalty, money, power and violence. Her investigation raised several provocative questions regarding Shakur's murder and its aftermath.

1004. Shakur, Gobi and Afeni Shakur. *Thru My Eyes: Thoughts On Tupac Shakur in Pictures and Words.* New York: Atria, 2005.

The author, a professional photographer and music video director, describes Shakur as a lover of life and sex, who liked to play with his kids.

1005. Shakur, Tupac. *The Rose That Grew From the Concrete.* New York: MTV, 2009.

A collection of Shakur's poetry written between 1989 and 1991. Many poems are in his original handwriting, and feature his unique spellings, ideographs, scratch outs and corrections. Most of the poetry is accompanied by text. Foreword by Nikki Giovanni and preface by Tupac's mother, Afeni Shakur.

1006. ——. *The Tupac Shakur Collection.* Van Nuys, CA: Alfred Publishing, 2002.

A collection of his most successful compositions, spanning his entire career, from his eight Platinum records or No. 1 singles. Includes songs like "Brenda's Got A Baby," "California Love," "Changes," "Dear Mama," "Me Against the World," "To Live and Die in L.A," and several more.

1007. Sullivan, Randall. *Labyrinth: A Detective Investigates the Murders of Tupac Shakur and Notorious B.I.G., the Implication of Death Row Records' Suge Knight, and the Origins of the Los Angeles Police Scandal.* New York: Grove Press, 2003.

Explores the world of gangsta rap, money, guns, drugs, racial issues, Death Row Records, and the unresolved murders of Tupac Shakur and Notorious B.I.G. Coverage also includes a discussion of the music industry, management, the east coast–west coast feud, the roles of Suge Knight and Sean "Puffy" Combs, and more.

1008. Uschan, Michael V. *Tupac Shakur.* Minneapolis: Lucent Books, 2006.

For younger readers. A concise account of the life and music of Shakur, geared toward grades nine to twelve. Among the topics covered are his early years, the east coast–west coast rap feud, his musical contributions, legal issues and legacy.

1009. Vibe Magazine. *Tupac Shakur.* Medford, NJ: Plexus Publishing Ltd, 1998.

A collection of articles previously published in *Vibe Magazine*, beginning in 1994, which deconstruct Shakur's life and music. The portraits, based on extensive interviews with Shakur, are balanced and cover topics like his early impoverished life, involvement with drugs and legal issues, musical contributions, legacy and more. Includes a chronology, discography and filmography.

1010. White, Armond and S.H. Fernando. *Rebel for The Hell of It: The Life of Tupac Shakur.* New York: Da Capo Press, 2002.

Connects Shakur's life with the African American experience over the last three decades. Begins with an overview of his birth to an absentee father and a mother who was a member of the Black Panther Party, their moves from city to city, and his early interest in drama. Discusses his incarceration at Riker's Island and his untimely death. Draws connections between Shakur and Public Enemy, Notorious B.I.G., Dr. Dre, Ice Cube and Sister Soulja.

## Russell Simmons and Rick Rubin

1011. N.A. "Russell Simmons' Rush Represents Rappers." *Billboard*, 15 September 1984, 50.

Covers Simmons' background, introduction to rap, and creative vision which led to his successful business representing rap artists. Includes an overview of Rush Productions and Thai artists he represents. Also includes a synopsis of the current rap scene and predictions for the future.

1012. Bruce, Caryn. "Def Jam Cities Capitol Offense in Suit Over Beastie Boys." *Billboard*, 5 August 1989, 92.

Reports on a lawsuit brought by Def Jam against Capitol records for distributing *Paul's Boutique* by the Beastie Boys while they were under contract with Def Jam. Covers Def Jam's relationship with Capitol records and issues they had with the Beastie Boys.

1013. George, Nelson. "Rappin' With Russell: Eddie-Murphying the Flak Catchers." *Village Voice*, 30 April 1985, 42.

A generic profile of rap music and people involved in the creation and production of the music. The focus is on Russell Simmons and Rush productions, and the role of record labels in making and disseminating the music. Also includes a concise history of rap.

1014. ——. "Russell Simmons: King of Rap." *Essence*, March 1988, 61.

Discusses Simmons' current projects and position as a highly respected mogul and supporter of rap. Covers the history of Def Jam and some of its artists. Briefly addresses rap as contemporary African American street culture, and raises some of the issues associated with it.

1015. Light, Alan. "Kings of Rap." *Rolling Stone*, November 1990, 106.

A profile of Def Jam records and its founders Rick Rubin and Russell Simmons. Provides insight into the musical intangibles that make its artists successful, and comments on the consistency and success of their acts.

1016. McAdams, Janine. "Simmons Links With Columbia for His Growing Rush Roster." *Billboard*, 31 March 1990, 6.

Chronicles the growing collaborations between independent record labels and major labels, specifically the new deal between Russell Simmons' Def Jam and Rush labels and Columbia Records. Provides details of the deal and the future that Simmons envisions for his company.

1017. Newman, Melinda. "Def Jam Sues Over Beasties." *Billboard*, 21 January 1989, 10.

An account of the lawsuit leveled against Capitol Records by Def Jam regarding signing the Beastie Boys while they were still under contract to Def Jam. Gives readers an idea of the legal issues involved with collaborations between record labels.

1018. Ogg, Alex. *The Men Behind Def Jam: The Radical Rise of Russell Simmons and Rick Rubin*. London: Omnibus Books, 2002.

The book covers rap history, criticism and the role of Simmons and Rubin in the rise of Def Jam. Discusses recordings, executives and producers, and provides a detailed history of Def Jam recordings including a comprehensive discography of its recordings.

1019. Owen, Frank. "Paid in Full." *Spin*, October 1989, 35.

Details of the legal issues that ensued when the Beastie Boys defected from Def Jam and signed with Capitol records. Owens incorporates quotes from both sides expressing anger and betrayal and explaining their points of view.

1020. Walters, Barry. "The King of Rap: Rick Rubin Makes the Music Industry Walk His Way." *Village Voice*, 4 November 1986, 19–20.

Profiles Rubin, co-owner of Def Jam Records, at age 23, the same age Phil Spector was when he was in charge of a multimillion-dollar record business. Walters covers his early life, the influence of his parents, importance of education, and his ability to recognize a new and innovative direction in music. Discusses the various Def Jam acts and Rubin's relationship with the label's artists.

## Ice-T

1021. N.A. "Death on the Ice." *Melody Maker*, 3 February 1990, 4.

A short news item regarding some of Cube's recent activities, including his involvement with Quincy Jones' recording of *Back on the Block* (along with other rappers), and a possible collaboration between Ice-T and Megadeth.

1022. Davis, Eric. "Fuck Dick Cunt Suicide." *Village Voice*, 31 July 1990, 78–79.

The article grew out of the "Beyond Censorship" panel held at the New Music Seminar. Explores the contradictions between those who claim they are against censorship but enforce it when it suits their needs (e.g. the censorship of Guns N' Roses, Audio Two and comedian Sam Kinison). Of particular note, the panel credits Ice-T for advocating that dialogue, not suppression, effects ideological change.

1023. Farber, Jim. "Ice-T, Chet Baker: Hip Hop, Cool Jazz." *Rolling Stone*, 8 February 1990, 108.

A good review of Ice-T's video *The Iceberg*. Discusses his ability to connect gangsta lyrics and moral messages. Describes him as a fiery but articulate rapper who can impart a message without preaching to his audience.

1024. Forman, Bill. "Hollywood Chilling." *Melody Maker*, 9 January 1988, 10.

Gives background on Ice-T and discusses his approach to music and related issues. Discusses parents' attempts to control the content of rap lyrics since they cannot prevent their children from listening to it. Of special note is the discussion of the messages in rap, Ice-T's musical influences, and the meaning and purpose of his raps.

1025. Light, Alan. "Ice-T." *Rolling Stone*, 15 November 1990, 23.

An up-to-date overview of Ice-T's recent projects, including collaborations with Guns N' Roses, Jane's Addiction and Megadeth.

1026. Loder, Kurt. "Ice-T Speaks." *Cash Box*, 30 December 1989, 20.

In this interview, Ice-T gives his opinions on a variety of issues: his perspective on the bad press that he has received, the chaos and confusion surrounding his music, and his views on education and success. Mentions that *The Iceberg/Freedom of Speech* is his favorite album.

1027. McIver, Peter. *Attitude*. London: Sanctuary, 2003.

Covers Ice-T's humble beginnings, his early rap associations, and his eventual rise to movie and TV stardom.

1028. O'Dair, Barbara. "Ice-T and No Sympathy." *Spin*, August 1988, 18.

Ice-T responds to charges that he is homophobic, sexist and violent. He also reacts to the criticism about the movie *Colors*, and discusses his new album *Rhyme Pays*.

1029. The Stud Brothers. "Fear and Loathing in L.A." *Melody Maker*, 3 February 1990, 46.

Ice-T describes his previous life as a criminal and gang member and comments on how those experiences influence his raps. He also expresses his opinion about the goodness of his work, addresses charges of sexism, and discusses the PMRC and Tipper Gore.

1030. ———. "Ice-T: Rhyme Pays." *Melody Maker*, 18 February 1989, 27.

Profiles how he disconnected from his criminal past after being discovered rapping in a club as a hobby. He believes he is successful because his raps, like him, are real. He also comments on the lives of his old friends and provides insight into how they helped him to pursue his rap career.

## Q-Tip

1031. Lee, Charles. "A Solo Quest." *Los Angeles Times* Arts and Music Calendar. 13 July 2008, F1, F9.

An article about the return of Q-Tip to the hip hop world. Details his hiatus since his last recording in 1999 when his last album, *Amplified* rose to No. 4 on the US hip hop/R&B chart. Highlights his second solo CD which features the single "Shaka," which incorporates Barak Obama's soaring voice intoning his message of change and hope over a heavy background beat. Mentions Q-Tip's release of *The Renaissance*, a rebirth of the "hip hop cool" he helped to create. Discusses the reunion of A Tribe Called Quest for ten concert dates around the country. Provides a thorough overview of the artist's musical activities since 1999.

## Kanye West

1032. Simons, Rae. *Kanye West*. Broomall, PA: Mason Crest, 2008.

For younger readers. Traces the life and career of Kanye Omair West from his roots in Atlanta. The ten-time Grammy Award-winning rapper, producer and singer discusses his career, his debut album *The College Dropout* (2004), his brief encounter with higher education, the role and influence of his mother, and his success as a producer.

## Vincent Wilson

1033. Wilson, Vincent. *The Father of Hip Hop*. Bloomington, IN: iUniverse. com, 2008.

The author, born in Kingston, Jamaica, is a significant figure in the development of hip hop. He developed a hook that is widely used in hip hop, reggae, R&B and other musical genres, which he describes as repetitious, functioning like a chorus. Available as an ebook or paperback.

**Wu-Tang Clan**

1034. Rockworth, Janice. *Wu-Tang Clan.* Broomall, PA: Mason Crest, 2007.

Traces the origins and musical accomplishments of this New York City hip hop collective. Mentions the expertise of its members, how the group got its name, their musical philosophy, and the fact that several successful hip hop artists—musicians, producers and promoters—began their careers with the group.

**Jay-Z**

1035. Barnes, Geoff. *Jay-Z.* Broomall, PA: Mason Crest, 2007.

Covers his life from his humble roots, interest in hip hop, and his creative and business acuity in hip hop culture. Barnes also discusses his musical influences, and his meeting Beyoncé Knowles, his wife.

1036. Brown, Jackie. *Jay-Z—And the Roc-a-Fella Dynasty.* New York: Amber Books, 2005.

Covers his road to success and his legacy in the New York rap scene. Discusses how Shawn Carter became Jay-Z, the birth of Roc-a-Fella records, and the role that two Brooklyn icons, Jay-Z and Biggie Smalls, have played in hip hop.

## COLLECTIVE BIOGRAPHIES

1037. N.A. "Ebony's Surprising Music Poll: The Best Singers and Rappers and the Best Black Song Ever." *Ebony,* June 2002, 70–78.

The poll covers best male and female singers, favorite female and male rap and hip hop artist, greatest pop and R&B songs of all time, the greatest gospel song, and many more. Mary J. Blige and Tupac Shakur won the best female and male rap awards, "What's Goin' On" won the greatest pop/R&B song award, and "Precious Lord Take My Hand" won the gospel award. Luther Vandross won the best male singer of all time award, and Aretha Franklin won the best pop/soul award of all time.

1038. Chappell, Kevin. "The CEOs of Hip-Hop and the Billion Dollar Jackpot." *Ebony,* January 2001, 116–22.

Discusses the success of Sean "Puffy" Combs, Percy "Master P" Miller and Russell Simmons as CEOs in the hip hop industry. The author covers their entry into business, lists their investments and their overall economic worth, discusses their involvements outside the hip hop world and their plans for future success.

1039. Howard, Stephanie (Asabi). "One Voice/One Mic ... Remixing and Rhyming the Sacred and the Secular: A Comparative Study of Traditional Spirituals and Gangsta Rap in the African-American Oral Tradition." PhD dissertation, Virginia Beach, VA: Regent University, 2006.

The dissertation uses historical, descriptive and textual analysis to conduct a cross-cultural and cross-generation investigation of slaves and members of the hip hop culture. The focus is on the lyrics of rappers Tupac Shakur and DMX; includes a comparison of twelve spirituals with twelve rap songs.

1040. Oliver, Richard. *Hip-Hop, Inc.: Success Strategies of the Rap Moguls.* New York: Da Capo Press, 2006.

A look at the business of rap, rather than the music. Praises the entrepreneurship of moguls (specifically Sean "Puffy" Combs, Percy "Master P" Miller and Russell Simmons), their marketing abilities and their accumulation of stock options.

1041. Quinn, Eithne. *Nuthin' but a "G" Thang: The Culture and Commerce of Gangsta Rap.* New York: Columbia University Press, 2004.

A study of rap's musical and cultural roots to antebellum days through a discussion of toasting; legends of the badman, the trickster, and the black cultural debates; neoconservative politics; and subculture formations of the music industry. The author demonstrates that gangsta rap was a logical progression in the development of urban music by exposing its artists, fans and meaning within the black community. Provides concise insights into the lives and contributions of artists like Ice Cube, Dr. Dre and Snoop Dogg, with a final chapter on Tupac Shakur.

1042. Reeves, Marcus. *Somebody Scream!: Rap Music's Rise to Prominence in the Aftershock of Black Power.* London and New York: Faber and Faber, 2001.

A collection of essays that examine the rise of ten distinct hip hop movements, and connect tracks and rhymes to social struggles. The author applies his theory to artists like Afrika Bambaataa, Kool Herc, Grandmaster Flash, Jay-Z, Salt-N-Pepa and Run-DMC.

1043. Small, Michael. *Break It Down: The Inside Story from the New Leaders of Rap.* New York: Citadel, 1992.

Contains a wealth of biographical information on 1980s rappers like L.L. Cool J, KRS-One and Salt-n-Pepa. The interviews are provocative because they provide insight into issues other than music, including crime, negative representations of rap in the media, racism and violence.

1044. White, Russell Christopher. "Construction of Identity and Community in Hip-Hop Nationalism With Specific Reference to Public Enemy and Wu-Tang Clan." PhD dissertation, UK: University of Southampton, 2002.

This study focuses on the role of groups like Brand Nubian, X-Clan, Public Enemy and Wu-Tang Clan in the re-emergence of black nationalist thought into black popular culture. Focuses on the importance of Public Enemy and Wu-Tang Clan's "sampling strategies" on black nationalism and the formation of black communities in hip hop music and culture. He also compares African American and black British cultural criticism, strategies used, hip hop nationalists, and more.

## B-BOYING/B-GIRLING

1045. Johnson, Imani. "Dark Matter in B-Boying Cyphers: Hip Hop Dance Circles as a Model of Cross-racial Collaboration." PhD dissertation, University of Southern California, 2008.

This multi-sited, interdisciplinary study analyzes breakdancing culture, which is known as cyphering. Uses cyphering as a transformative space to examine cross-racial activities in Boston, Los Angeles, London, New York and other sites from 2005 to 2008. Reviews fifty dancers and research sites.

## CINEMA, JOURNALISM AND MEDIA

1046. Boyd, Todd. "It's a Black 'Thang': The Articulation of African-American Cultural Discourse." PhD dissertation, University of Iowa, 1991.

The author's premise is that the discourse of African American culture expresses itself across a number of mass media venues. He focuses on three cultural areas to explore African American identity within an Afrocentric perspective: religion, music and African American cinema. In the discussion of religion, the author uses the words of Minister Louis Farrakhan of the Nation of Islam; the music he examines is rap music; and he focuses on Spike Lee's *Do The Right Thing* as representative of African American film.

1047. Capeda, Raquel, ed. *And It Don't Stop: The Best American Hip-Hop Journalism of the Last 25 Years.* New York: Faber and Faber, 2004.

A collection of twenty-nine essays that trace the growth of hip hop music and journalism. Begins with hip hop's history, divided by decade: early attempts to report on hip hop in the 1980s, critical analysis in the 1990s, and the 2000s when hip hop images permeated everything from TV jingles to fashion and language. Issues include the role of the writers in popularizing hip hop music and culture, the strained relationship between writers and artists, and issues that deal with crossover. Includes contributions from a variety of writers, including Nelson George (who also wrote the foreword), Cheo Hodari Coker, Joan Morgan, Greg Tate, Toure and others.

1048. Edwards, Timothy. "Lyrics to the Rhythm: The Uses and Gratifications of Rap Music for African American Teenagers." PhD dissertation, University of Kentucky, 1998.

Examines the uses of rap music among African American teenagers, and researches both the gratification of listeners and the negative impact that it has on its listeners, especially youngsters. A questionnaire and qualitative interviews were the primary methods of data gathering. Concludes that teenagers have a variety of reasons for listening to rap music, including their love of the beat, its creative lyrics, the ability to affect mood, issues of personal identity, and danceability.

1049. Gautier, Alba. "Producing a Popular Music: The Emergence and Development of Rap as an Industry." Masters thesis, McGill University, 2003.

Focuses on the evolution of the rap market from its emergence in the Bronx, New York, to its development into a nationwide industry in 1990. The motivations of the producers and mechanisms that led to the current status are analyzed, as is the division of labor between production and distribution.

1050. Rutherford, Marc Allen. "Mass Media Framing Hip-Hop Artists and Culture." Masters thesis, West Virginia University, 2001.

He situates his research within the framework that media coverage is influenced by a reporter's background, experience, time constraints and other factors. Argues that media coverage of hip hop culture and the artists has been decidedly negative in the twelve years prior to his study. He postulates that the works of artists like Jazzy Jeff and the Fresh Prince, Tupac Shakur, Notorious B.I.G. and Eminem have been framed as "bad boy" music, produced by criminals and derelicts, and analyzes the causes for such framing.

1051. Samuels, Jamiyl. "Although the Portrayal of Black Fathers as 'Deadbeat Dads' is Prevalent in the U.S. Media, Over the Last 20 Years

Some Hip Hop Artists and Hip Hop-Inspired Films Challenge the Stereotype By Showing the Young Black Father as a Responsible Adult Eager to Take Care of His Family." Masters thesis, Long Island University, Brooklyn Center, 2008.

The author investigates two areas, the unfair assessment that black fathers are "deadbeat dads" who abandon their children and responsibilities and the negative backlash toward hip hop music and the plight of the black father. He notes that some of the most visible fathers taking care of their children are from the hip hop community, and that some hip hop artists have used their talents to discuss the importance of fatherhood.

1052. Scism, Jennifer Lynn. "This is My Mic: Hip Hop and the Media, 1970s–1990s." Masters thesis, University of North Carolina, Greensboro, 2008.

An exploration of how the print media in New York City portrayed hip hop culture from the 1970s through the early 1990s. Surveys many New York newspapers and concludes that journalists did not always intentionally create a biased and negative image of hip hop, that their interpretations of the phenomenon were often ill-informed, and that at times their articles were coded in language that mirrored racial and class-based stereotypes.

1053. Watkins, Samuel Craig. *Representing: Hip Hop Culture and the Production of Black Cinema*. Chicago: University of Chicago Press, 1998.

The book explores the relationship between cinema, hip hop and the culture industry since the mid-1980s. Explores the contradictions of corporate image-making, the varied responses of African Americans to black cultural productions, and the struggles of black filmmakers to achieve financial resources and to obtain creative autonomy. Illuminates a social contradiction, specifically that while many young African Americans have been associated with crime, moral decline and welfare, simultaneously black cultural productions like fashions, lifestyles and linguistic innovations have captured the popular imagination of mainstream America. Discusses cultural production and audience reception, an African American film cycle, effects and decline of some of the African American films, and the role and function of filmmakers like Spike Lee in the success and decline of "ghetto films."

## COMMUNICATION, LANGUAGE, POETRY AND TEXT

1054. Anglesey, Zoe, ed. *Listen Up!: Spoken Word Poetry*. New York: One World/Ballantine, 2006.

Argues that rap's honesty, narrative and self-referential lyrics is evidence of a culture in conflict. Within her discussion is evidence of the polarity of lyrics and message, including hip hop's embrace of the materialistic values of the dominant society while simultaneously rebelling against its oppression, and deifying and demonizing women, which the author concludes is evidence of an American culture in conflict. Also acknowledges that hip hop is one of the most significant American cultural movements of all time.

1055. Babb, Tracie Nicole. "Rap Music's Transformation in a Postmodern World." PhD dissertation, Howard University, 2005.

Presents an analysis of the postmodern characteristics that have represented rap music over the last three decades. Songs that appeared on the weekly Billboard Top 100 R&B singles charts between 1979 and 2004 were analyzed to determine themes, messages and meaning as affected by postmodern forces. Concludes that 1970s rap lyrics speak to the new post-civil rights community.

1056. Benson, Michon Anita. "From the Ride 'n' Tie to Ryde-or-Die: A Pedagogy of Survival in Black Youth Popular Cultural Forms." PhD dissertation, Rice University, 2005.

Investigates key similarities between 19th-century slave accounts and what she terms as "hip hop captivity narratives." Identifies specific aspects of slave authors' literary strategies that urban hip hop artists have reinvented in their music or filmmaking, and positions hip hop texts as the most recent arrivals in a long series of African American traditions of instructional literature.

1057. Boyd, Todd. *Am I Black Enough For You: Culture From The Hood and Beyond.* Bloomington: Indiana University Press, 1997.

Fuses academic analysis with hip concepts and language to assess how the media, especially Hollywood, present images of African American men, and how African Americans view or define American culture. Of special note is his discussion of how rap music relates to politics and black identity within the African American community. He uses concepts of affirmative action and Reaganomics to draw conclusions and to discusses the influence of African American cultural icons like Bill Cosby, Spike Lee, gangsta rappers and African American basketball players.

1058. Brown, Sonja Monique. "Alternative Explanations: A Textual Analysis of Rap Music Lyrics." Masters thesis, California State University, Fresno, 1998.

Investigates allegations that many rap lyrics promote misogyny, racism and violence, and argues that such assertions are misrepresentations of the music. Explores some implicit messages in rap without literary valuation of its text; transcriptions and analyses of thirty rap songs support her arguments.

1059. Campbell, Kermit Ernest. *Gettin' Our Groove On: Rhetoric, Language, and Literacy for the Hip Hop Generation.* Detroit: Wayne State University, 2005.

Campbell deals with issues of representation and identity, including a defense of the black vernacular, representing rhetoric, a chronology of the gangsta ethos from Stag-O-Lee to Snoop Dogg, and the interrelationship between African American students, hip hop and literacy. Extensive bibliography and an index.

1060. Chrobak, Jill McKay. "The Rhetoric of Appropriation: How Upper Middle Class White Males Flipped the Script on Hip Hop Culture and Black Language." PhD dissertation, Michigan State University, 2007.

The study is concerned with appropriation, specifically how and why upper middle-class white males appropriate hip hop culture and black language styles as a way to better understand this phenomenon. Furthermore, the author asserts that while attempting to become a part of a culture via appropriation, they create something different than what they intended to appropriate. Uses case study interviews of thirty upper middle-class white male participants who displayed a deep interest in hip hop and who had appropriated aspects of culture and black language.

1061. Cooper, Jr, Richard M. "Kijana (Youth) Finding Their Own Voices: A Qualitative Study on the Meanings of Rap Music Lyrics for African American Male Adolescents." PhD dissertation, Temple University, 2002.

A qualitative study of the meanings that ten African American male adolescents ascribe to rap music lyrics. Two ninety-minute interviews were conducted in a detention center located in the Delaware Valley to discover the respondents' methods for understanding rap lyrics, the existence of rap role models, the impact of hard-core rap, and how rap relates to their life experiences. Gives a list of specific recommendations of ways that educators and other professionals can use hip hop culture with their students.

1062. Dimitriadis, Greg. *Performing Identity/Performing Culture: Hip Hop as Text, Pedagogy, and Lived Experience.* Intersections in Communications and Culture, Volume I. New York: Peter Lang, 2001.

This appears to be the first book-length ethnography devoted to young people and their uses of hip hop culture. The book is based on four years of fieldwork at a community center, and argues that contemporary youth often fashion notions of self and community by means that educators have often ignored. Examines the historical evolution of hip hop through the work of artists like the Sugarhill Gang, Run-DMC, Eric B and Rakim, Public Enemy, N.W.A. and the Wu-Tang Clan. Looks at the uses and functions of rap texts, how notions of a southern identity are constructed by using southern rap artists like Master P. Eightball and MJG, how history is constructed by viewing the film *Panther*, how young people dealt with the life and death of Tupac Shakur, and more.

1063. Donahue, Matthew A. "The Message Behind the Beat: Social and Political Attitudes Expressed in American Rap and Punk Rock Music of the 1980s and Early 1990s." PhD dissertation, Bowling Green State University, 2001.

An analysis of the lyrical content of rap and punk rock music through 1992. Although both genres originated in the United States, in distinctly different communities, their lyrics cover similar issues. Findings indicate that both genres addressed similar social and political issues that transpired in the United States between 1980 and 1992. Both genres were censored, and the social and political content of each became less potent after 1992.

1064. Edwards, Timothy. "Lyrics to the Rhythm: The Uses and Gratifications of Rap Music for African American Teenagers." PhD dissertation, University of Kentucky, 1998.

The author proceeds from the premise that many people do not like rap because of its perceived negative impact on listeners, especially young people. Primarily interested in what it is about rap that captures a person's attention. Examines the uses and gratifications of rap music among African American teenagers. Uses both quantitative and qualitative research methods, including a questionnaire administered to 110 African Americans, aged thirteen to nineteen. Data were categorized into nine major groups. He concluded that some people enjoy listening to and liked rap for dancing and entertainment, while others listen to be educated and informed.

1065. Elligan, Don. *Rap Therapy: A Practical Guide for Communicating With Youth and Young Adults Through Rap Music*. Dafina: Kensington, 2004.

The author, a clinical psychologist, demonstrates that as the language of hip hop culture, rap can be used as a therapeutic tool with inner-city youth. By focusing on the lyrics of respected rap artists, a therapist can influence values and provide insight into behaviors and moral beliefs. In part one of the book he describes the different styles of rap music, and in part two he explains the five steps of rap therapy. Includes a six-page list of rap songs recommended for use in therapy.

1066. Fab 5 Freddy (Frederick Brathwaite). *Fresh Fly Flavor: Words and Phrases of the Hip Hop Generation.* Stamford, CT: Longmeadow, 1992.

The work of a hip hop insider and highly respected pioneer, this is a dictionary of phrases, terms and words endemic to hip hop culture. The strength of the book is that it explains phrases and words from an insider perspective, providing clarity for those unfamiliar with hip hop jargon. Supplemented with illustrations and photographs of hip hop artists and culture.

1067. Griffin, Monica Denise. "The Rap on Rap Music: The Social Construction of African American Identity." PhD dissertation, University of Virginia, 1998.

Deals with the images portrayed in gangsta rap lyrics. The substance of the debate pertains ideologically and experimentally to the social construction of African American identity, specifically that social commentary constructs an identity of African Americans as urban, masculine and poor. Focuses on the role of rap music in the construction of African American identity, and argues that rappers and critics of rap employ a politics of identity to make claims about rap lyrics. The author samples rap videos and reviews the 1994 Congressional Hearings transcripts on rap music lyrics to ascertain thematic patterns in the construction of African American identity.

1068. Heath, Ryan Scott. "Head Theory: Hip-Hop Aestheticism, Globalized Text, and A Critique of Cultural Studies." PhD dissertation, University of Michigan, 2002.

Investigates the juxtaposition of African American literary criticism and postcolonial studies in the analysis of cultural text. Hip hop is used as a transnational, cosmopolitan text in which African Americans negotiate issues of citizenship and race in a global system of exchange. Uses advertisements, film and video footage, periodical literature, transcriptions of lyrics and other methods to illustrate nationalist community and cultural authenticity. Also, he discusses issues like "nation," "real," "underground," and "representation."

1069. Jemie, Onwuchekwa, ed. *Yo' Mama! New Raps, Toasts, Dozens, Jokes and Children's Rhymes from Urban Black America,* Philadelphia: Temple University Press, 2004.

A rich collection of African American oral literature collected primarily in metropolitan New York and Philadelphia in the late 1960s and early 1970s. The anthology includes boasts, children, rhymes, jokes, raps, signifyings, toasts and the trading of abuse. The author situates the work in a pan-African heritage where traditional stories, exaggeration and hyperbole of some oral inner-city African American culture are similar to those practiced in other African-derived cultures. A highlight of the collection is the inclusion of many different versions of the same material. Concludes that rap music is "the latest flowering of modern African American oral tradition so richly represented in this collection."

1070. Kearse, Randy. *"Mo Betta." Street Talk: Da Official Guide to Hip-Hop and Urban Slanguage*. New York: Barricade Books, 2007.

Numerous definitions of hip hop terms with examples of how the term can be used. The author distinguishes between east coast and west coast usage, southern and general slang, and old and new school interpretations of phrases.

1071. Kitwana, Bakari. *The Rap on Gangsta Rap: Who Runs It? Gangsta Rap and Visions of Black Violence*. Chicago: Third World Press, 1995.

Uses lyrics to draw conclusions on moral, political and social issues endemic to hip hop. Well-reasoned discussions of rap as an art form, media representations, the relationship of rap to drugs and violence, racism and sexism. A balanced and informative assessment.

1072. Knight, Shaldea A. "Perceptions of African American Parents Regarding the Influence of Rap Music and Hip Hop on Their Youth." Masters thesis, California State University, Long Beach, 2005.

An exploration of the perceptions and opinions of African American parents regarding their views on rap and hip hop, and the degree to which the lyrics have affected the behavior of their children. Two additional objectives were to ascertain whether rap desensitized their youth to drug abuse, sex and violence, and to determine the level of parental involvement and guidance in the lives of their children.

1073. Koonce, Richard Sheldon. "The Symbolic Rape of Representation: A Rhetorical Analysis of Black Musical Expression on Billboard's Hot 100 Charts." PhD dissertation, Bowling Green State University, 2006.

Uses rhetorical criticism to examine how blacks are depicted in the lyrics of popular music, especially hip hop music. Forty popular songs on Billboard's Hot 100 singles charts from 1999 to 2006 were analyzed using black feminist and critical theories since black males perform most hip hop songs and many songs contain misogynist messages.

1074. Kuehn, Christy Lynn. "BlackSpeare: Hip-Hop, Tricksters, and the Bard." Masters thesis, Arizona State University, 2007.

Cultural and performance theory are used to investigate the intercultural performances linking hip hop and Shakespeare. Argues that such performances subvert the duality of "highbrow" and "lowbrow" art. Researches the ways that hip hop artists navigate between this duality, enabling creative moments that go beyond adaptation or appropriation.

1075. Kulkarni, Neil. *Hip Hop: Bring the Noise; The Stories Behind the Biggest Songs.* New York: Thunder's Mouth, 2004.

An honest portrayal of the origin and meaning of some hip hop texts that provides an alternative perspective to media representations of hip hop artists. Reveals the sociopolitical underpinnings that influenced artists to create fifty of hip hop's greatest songs. The end result provides a window into issues that fueled the creative process of many hip hop artists. This volume is an expansion of the publisher's *Stories Behind the Songs* series.

1076. Logan, Jr, John Charles. "Rap, Ritual and Reality: The Effects of Rap Music on Communication." PhD dissertation, Cincinnati, OH: The Union Institute, 1997.

The author has three purposes: first, to determine the extent of student interest in African American popular music, especially rap; second, to discuss the political ramifications surrounding rap; and third, to explore the impact of technology on the study of rap music and popular culture. Discusses interdisciplinary issues of technological advances in music distribution, the fact that telecommunications have not kept pace with technology, and minority ownership and participation in media outlets. Concludes that parental interaction with the child about their heritage is a significant factor in the student's understanding of gangsta rap.

1077. Low, Bronwen Elizabeth. "Spoken Word: Exploring the Language and Poetics of the Hip Hop Popular." PhD dissertation, Toronto: York University, 2001.

The author argues that language and communicative practices are evolving in a world of rapid cultural and technological change, and that popular youth cultures both drive and reflect that change. She uses a post-structural theory to examine spoken word forms, the changing relationships youth establish with language, and how these relationships affect communication and poetics, culturally, formally and socially. This research creates a critical space in which both teachers and students can explore their imaginations with words. She also believes that the strengths and limitations of contemporary youth cultures may allow one to find pedagogical resonance with future needs and requests for multi-modal literacies.

1078. Neal, Mark Anthony, Davey D., Jared Bell and Hadji Williams. "Words, Beats, Life." *Global Journal of Hip Hop Culture* 2(1) (2006): 20–32.

This issue features essays by some of the best-known writers on the genre, including Jared Bell, Mark Anthony Neal, Brian Coleman, China N. Okasi, Ron Herd and others. They discuss a myriad of issues and topics germane to understanding the history and evolution of hip hop culture.

1079. Nicholson, Sara Warburton. "Beyond Quotation: Intertexuality in Popular Music Since 1990." PhD dissertation, University of Rochester, Eastman School of Music, 2006.

The author applies the literary and philosophical theories of Julia Kristeva and Ronald Barthes to four popular music subgenres: electronica, hip hop, mainstream rock and riot grrrl. Hermeneutic analysis of two songs in each genre categorizes the subgenres' intertextuality, from the particular to the general. The final chapter examines the relationship between the subgenres and how they inform musical intertextuality at large.

1080. Ogg, Alex. *Rap Lyrics: From the Sugarhill Gang to Eminem.* London: Wise Publications with Omnibus Press, 2002.

The author cites and categorizes numerous rap texts from popular and lesser-known artists, past and present.

1081. Robinson, Ellington Rudi. "Underneath the Music." Masters thesis, University of Maryland, College Park, 2008.

A study is centered on using the influences of the past as guides to survival. Those influences and tragedies are translated into motifs used to create forms of communication. In turn, these motifs can tell a story that is layered with the history of the Civil Rights movement, hip hop culture, drugs and music.

1082. Sitimer, Alan and Michael Cirelli. *Hip-Hop Poetry and Classes.* Beverly Hills: Milk Mug, 2004.

Provides a deep understanding of the bridges that connect poets of the past to contemporary poets. Connects Robert Frost, Langston

Hughes, Rudyard Kipling, Edgar Allan Poe and William Shakespeare to hip hop artists Eminem, Public Enemy, Tupac Shakur, KRS-One and the Notorious B.I.G. Explores poetic devices, writing techniques and the creative process that was used to make the poetry.

1083. Stavsky, Lois, I.E. Morrison and Dani Reyes. *A–Z: The Book of Rap and Hip-Hop Slang.* New York: Boulevard Books, 1995.

This collection of 1,000+ rap and hip hop terms provides useful definitions and insights into their uses. Includes generic, regional and local terms; their definitions enable outsiders to understand how they are used in a specific sociocultural context.

1084. Tummons, Jonathan P. "Cultural Assimilation, Appropriation and Commercialization: Authenticity in Rap Music." Masters thesis, West Virginia University, 2008.

Examines the changes in authenticity in rap lyrics between 1997 and 2004. In the last twenty years, rap has been commercialized and appropriated by capitalistic industries and primarily white audiences with the result being the assimilation of black cultural expression into white culture. Authenticity is applied across time and, the author argues, by extension, "blackness" becomes synonymous with a single dimension.

1085. Tyree, Tia Camille Matthews. "The Pursuit of 'Movie Money': A Textual Analysis of Rap Artists as Actors in Hollywood Films." PhD dissertation, Howard University, 2007.

Explores the emergence of rappers in the film industry. Investigating links between movements in rap and the appearances of rappers in Hollywood films, and the connection between the rappers' musical personalities and the characters they play. Media sources are analyzed using semiotics and textual analysis to determine the factors that influence rappers to accept movie roles, and to discover how newspapers reports frame rappers who appear in Hollywood films. Findings indicate that gangsta, hardcore and party rappers with strong personalities or popular gimmicks were most frequently cast in movies.

1086. Williams, Frank Douglas. "Rap Music in Society." PhD dissertation, University of Florida, 1995.

A discussion of rap music as a recent linguistic form in African American oral culture. The author uses rap's openness of language, constant movement, and forceful, politically charged messages to prove his thesis. Uses the concept of signifying to discuss the roots of rap and to compare rap with other African American cultural forms. Includes a discussion of issues dealing with the emergence of rap music in American society, sampling, rap in the mass media market place, and more. Findings indicate that rap's orality—signifying—results in presence and recognition for those responsible for the creation and audibility of the music.

1087. Yasin, Jon. A. "In Yo Face! Rappin 'Beats Comin' at You: A Study of How Language is Mapped onto Musical Beats in Rap Music." EdD dissertation, Columbia University Teachers College, 1997.

Traces the phenomenon of *talk* in African American music back to the eighteenth century, and postulates that talk in the prose-speaking voice foregrounds language, with music serving as background. His study focuses on the language used by young African American rapper from New Jersey to create the lyrics of "We Lackin'." The author mapped the lyrics onto the musical meter, analyzing how each syllable is pronounced in time (over multiple beats, a single beat, or a fraction of a beat). He concludes that the interaction between repetition, alliteration and assonance are stylistic features within which rap lyrics are composed, and that the interaction between these elements, the musical beat and rap lyrics are distinctive features of the musical talk known as rap.

## DISCOGRAPHIES AND LISTENING GUIDES

1088. Bogdanov, Vladimir. *All Music Guide to Hip-Hop: The Definitive Guide to Rap and Hip-Hop.* San Francisco: Backbeat Books, 2003.

A comprehensive and thorough reference that contains both biographical and discographical information. The 1,200 bio-musical profiles cover east and west coast artists, including some who are all but forgotten. Equally impressive is the information on more than 3,000 recordings, including multi-platinum and out-of-print releases.

1089. Wang, Oliver. *Classic Material: The Hip Hop Album Guide.* Toronto: Canada: ECW Press, 2003.

Critiques of more than sixty albums that the author considers to be among the most influential in hip hop. An important feature of the essays and reviews is the emphasis on providing critical assessments on the artists and albums. Among the many recordings covered are those of Run-DMC, Public Enemy, Tupac Shakur, Ice-T, Jay-Z and many more.

## DJING AND MCING

1090. Ahearn, Charlie. "White Emcees Are No Suckers." *Interview*, April 1990, 44.

An interview of 3rd Bass and their description of their interest in rap. The interview also contains their opinion on a variety of philosophical and racial issues.

1091. Azard, Marc Gabriel. "'Freestyle, A True M.C.'s Trait and Then You Do It Ill, Niggas Respect It as Great': The Study of Freestyle as a Creditable Discourse." Masters thesis, Tarleton State University, 2005.

The purpose is to survey freestyle as it functions within the hip hop community. Traces freestyle's relationship to African rhetoric and the bard/caller archetype to the concept of Nommo as its own discourse, community, practice and system of classification. Also discusses freestyle's acceptance and international recognition.

1092. Brewster, Bill and Frank Broughton. *Last Night a Disc Jockey Saved My Life: The History of the Disc Jockey.* New York: Grove, 2000.

Based on interviews with critics, musicians and music industry officials, the authors provide an insider perspective of the role of the DJ in popularizing musical genres like hip hop and techno. Illustrates that a genre's popularity is often the result of the recording, the marketing and the selling ability of the DJ.

1093. George, Nelson. "Rappin Deejays," *Musician*, April–May 1980, 22.

An important essay on the history and evolution of DJing, an art form traced back to pre-"Rappers Delight" times. Discusses pioneering rappers and their influences, the use of slang, and pop culture. Predicts that all future DJs will need to become familiar with and use rap language and style to remain effective in the profession.

1094. Reighley, Kur B. *Looking for the Perfect Beat: The Art and Culture of the DJ.* New York: Pocket Books, 2000.

Focuses on the influence of DJs on popular music genres like hip hop, house music, rock and techno. Introduces some of the great DJs and provides insight into their lives, contributions and legacies. Gives practical advice about the equipment and techniques that one should use to DJ.

1095. Schloss, Joseph G. *Making Beats: The Art of Sampling-Based Hip-Hop.* Middletown, CT: Wesleyan University Press, 2004.

Discusses sampling as an art form that has evolved concurrently with technology. Explores the importance of the cutting-edge sampling used by many artists and discusses what techniques, sampling processes and procedures are used and why. Based on the author's dissertation.

1096. Souvignier, Todd. *The World of DJs and the Turntable Culture.* Milwaukee: Hal Leonard, 2003.

The author combines the history of DJing with practical advice about equipment, techniques and instruction on DJing skills. His data and conclusions are drawn from interviews with many prominent DJs, and from the author's own firsthand knowledge of the topic.

1097. Yapondjian, Maria Arshalouis. "Using the Four Elements of Hip-Hop as a Form of Self-Expression in Urban Adolescents." PhD dissertation, University of Hartford, 2005.

The author argues that DJing, MCing, breakdancing and graffiti art can be used as a form of self-expression when working with urban youth. She compiled twenty educational modules that utilized the four elements and addressed some of the issues confronting urban students.

## GENDER

1098. N.A. "Ladies First." *Rolling Stone*, 13 December 1990, 81.

The focus is on current and past female rappers as viewed from a new rap feminism. The article signals the growing importance and significance of female rappers around 1990, and that fact that new feminine rap identities are emerging.

1099. Anderson, Darnell. "The Portrayal of African American Women in Rap Music Video." PhD dissertation, Wayne State University, 1999.

The study is concerned with the portrayal of sexual stereotypes of African American women in African American-dominated videos. Using content analysis, the author categorized six character types, including mammy, matriarch, welfare queen, jezebel, mulatta and sapphire. His findings reveal that in approximately 90% of the sampled rap videos, African American women are portrayed through negative sexual characterizations.

1100. Barnes, Michael Paul. "Redefining the Real: Race, Gender and Place in the Construction of Hip-Hop Authenticity." PhD dissertation, University of California, Berkeley, 2007.

Examines the construction and negotiation of authenticity in hip hop culture. The author interviewed fifty-five informants in and around Atlanta, Georgia and the San Francisco Bay Area to ascertain the ways that race, gender and place affect the construction and performance of authenticity by hip hop DJs. Since hip hop is associated primarily with African American males, non-black men and all women were often disadvantaged because they lack "face-value authenticity." However Asian DJs in the Bay Area were an exception, primarily because of their long-standing connection to Bay Area hip hop.

1101. Beatty, Angie Collette. "What is This Gangstressism in Popular Culture: Reading Rap Music as a Legitimate Hustle and Analyzing the Role of Agency in Intrafemale Aggression." PhD dissertation, University of Michigan, 2001.

Explores the roles of agency, autonomy and historical context in black female rappers' practice of gangstressism and the perceptions that it produces regarding black-on-black female violence. Also examines how constraints on women's agency affect female rap lyrics, using the author's coding scheme to quantify agency.

1102. Biferie, Michelle Joanne. "Gender, Race, Class and the Problem of Meaning: Black Female Rappers as a Site for Resistance." Masters thesis, Florida Atlantic University, 1993.

The author asserts that it is primarily through language that social customs, beliefs and practices are normalized and viewed as "common sense" by the people engaged in it. Additionally, she argues the fact that black female rappers resist the hegemonic modes that construct and control the human subject.

1103. Burton, Nsenga K. "Traveling Without Moving: Hypervisibility and Black Female Rappers." PhD dissertation, University of Southern California, 2005.

The author defines hypervisibility as the omnipresence of African American women in the media who satisfy dominant ideologies about class, gender and race that reflect past stereotypical visual representations in media and society. She uses black female rappers as case studies, and situates her theoretical perspective within the historical subjugation of the black female body.

1104. Celious, Aaron Kabir. "Blaxploitation Blues: How Black Women Identify With and Are Empowered by Female Performers of Hip Hop Music." PhD dissertation, University of Michigan Press, 2002.

Concerned with how black women consume and interpret hip hop music. Explores how black women interpret lyrics in hip hop and determines the extent to which the interpretation of lyrics are either empowering or destructive to black women. Interprets their roles as facilitators of social change, whether rationalizing women's discontent or contributing to women's subjugation. The results show that people interpret words differently, and that the process of interpretation involves more than what is being said; it also involves the interaction between audience member and speaker.

1105. Cheney, Charise L. *Brothers Gonna Work it Out: Sexual Politics in the Golden Age of Rap Nationalism.* New York: New York University Press, 2005.

The author begins with introductory thoughts regarding rap music, black nationalism, and the golden age of rap nationalism. Among the issues discussed are mas(k)ulinity and the gender politics of black nationalism, the popular/political culture of rap music, defining manhood in the golden age of rap nationalism, masculinity and the use of the Bible in rap music, and the politics and practices of the hip hop nation.

1106. ———. "Phallic/ies and Hi(s)tories: Masculinity and the Black Nationalist Tradition, From Slave Spirituals to Rap Music." PhD dissertation, University of Illinois, 1999.

Explores the black nationalist tradition as embodied social politics by focusing on how the politics of gender and race have influenced its discourse. Covers cultural politics of slave spirituals and the political culture of the "Golden Age" of black nationalism, as well as postmodern manifestations of black nationalist thought in rap music. Through an analysis of lyrics and text, the author traces the survival and transmission of a nineteenth-century black male literary tradition into a politicized form of an oral expression invented by male members of a late twentieth-century urban black underclass.

1107. Choslad, Lynn. "Hip Hop Music and the Identity and Self-Esteem of Adolescent Girls." PsyD dissertation, San Francisco: Alliant International University, 2008.

A qualitative focus group study of twenty-three white and African American girls between the ages of fourteen and sixteen who attended a south-eastern Massachusetts public high school and were fans of hip hop music. Examines how adolescents girls hear and react to negative messages in popular hip hop music. Among her findings were that socioeconomic status was a more salient factor than race or ethnicity in determining how the girls heard and reacted to the music. Class status was a factor because working-class girls had been listening to hip hop longer than the middle-class participants.

1108. Cooper, Carol. "Girls Ain't Nothing but Trouble." *Essence,* April 1989, 80.

This article is concerned with female hip hop acts. The author notes that female rappers have trouble receiving proper credit for their writing and production work. She also believes rap is the only forum that enables one to address the real issues that are confronting the African American community.

1109. Davies, Alastair P.C. "Sex Wars: Evolved Psychological Sex Differences and Sexual Conflict in the Context of Infidelity, Persuasion, and Hip-Hop Song Lyrics." PhD dissertation, Florida Atlantic University, 2008.

The author researches issues related to the determination of behavioral sex differences. Originating from divergent evolution selection pressures, these differences lead to conflict between the sexes. Deals with asexual infidelity concept known as "human poaching," use of physical attractiveness as a tactic to persuade opposite-sex individuals, and sex differences and sexual conflict in the lyrics of hip hop songs.

1110. Desnoyers-Colas, Elizabeth Frances. "Sista MC Droppin' Rhymes With a Beat: A Fantasy Theme Analysis of Songs Performed by African American Female Rap Artists." PhD dissertation, Virginia Beach, VA: Regent University, 2003.

The study looks at how rap is used as a platform for young disenfranchised African American women from all socioeconomic backgrounds. The author details the challenges that African American women have faced historically in establishing and sustaining a voice in their community. Surveys 260 songs (all performed between 1988 and 2002) by Missy Elliot, Eve, Lauryn Hill, Lil Kim and Queen Latifah, and identifies forty major themes, 165 coded fantasy types and 216 rhetorical visions. The survey found that 261 of the 300 African American female respondents understood and related to the songs' messages, realized that not all female rappers spoke for young African American females, and felt that only artists with positive and uplifting messages were deemed spokeswomen for young African American women.

1111. Dino, Angela Lea Thieman. "Making Fun: How Urban Black Girls Craft Identity." PhD dissertation, University of Colorado, 2007.

This is a girl-centered research project that explores identity and agency in girls' own terms, and in contexts that are relatively unstructured by adults. The study focused on urban African American middle school girls who participated in a social group called Millennium's Finest Girls Club (MFGC). Among her findings (contradicting other studies) is that the MFGC girls externalized adversity and project self-confidence in their own values.

1112. DiPrima, Dominique. "Beat The Rap." *Mother Jones*, September/October 1990, 32.

Showcases the messages of strong and positive female rappers, including the author. She presents some interesting viewpoints about sexism in rap music. The article also includes interviews by Lisa Kennedy.

1113. Durham, Aisha S. "Homegirl Going Home: Hip Hop Feminism and the Representational Politics of Location." PhD dissertation, University of Illinois, 2007.

An exploration of the representation and lived experience of black women of the hip hop generation, the post-Civil Rights generation of 1965–84. She uses autoethnography, textual analyses and a focus group of five women from a Virginia public housing community. Addresses hip hop feminism as it relates to hip hop culture, media studies and third-wave feminism.

1114. Fitts, Mako. "The Political Economy of Hip Hop and the Cultural Production of Racialized and Gendered Images." PhD dissertation, Arizona State University, 2005.

A black feminist approach is used to study critical political economy and to determine contemporary power relations among entertainment industries that produce, market and distribute rap music. Also addresses an urban sensibility that influences popular culture in the United States. A variety of methods are used to explain the expansion of hip hop into mainstream culture, and to demonstrate its negotiation of issues of gender, ideologies, race and sexuality.

1115. Gallo, Susanne. "Music Preference With an Emphasis on Gangsta Rap: Female Adolescent Identity, Beliefs, and Behavior." PsyD dissertation, San Francisco: California Institute of Integral Studies, 2003.

The author used a correctional design to explore the relationship between music preference and female adolescent identity, beliefs and behavior. Two levels of musical preference were used. One included gangsta rap, hard rock, heavy metal and hardcore punk rock, and the other comprised underground rap and other music. No relationship was found between musical preference and self-esteem, resiliency, childhood sexual abuse, or between ethnicity and self-esteem and resiliency.

1116. Gosa, Travis Lars. "Oppositional Culture, Hip-Hop, and the Schooling of Black Youth." PhD dissertation, Johns Hopkins University, 2008.

Builds on previous research to explain how hip hop music reconstructs racial and gender identities in opposition to formal education. Investigates the claim that hip hop music is anti-intellectual, and that oppositional messages encourage black youth to turn away from formal education by establishing what notions of schooling, identity and success are embedded in hip hop music.

1117. Guillory, Nichole Ann. "Hip Hop Pedagogies of Black Women Rappers." PhD dissertation, Louisiana State University, 2005.

Textual analysis within a black feminist theoretical framework examines the intersections of class, gender, race and sexuality in black female rappers' representations of black women identities. Conclusions are based upon an examination of the lyrics of Missy "Misdemeanor" Elliot, Eve, Lil Kim, Foxy Brown, Trina, Mia X, Da Brat and Queen Pen.

1118. Harvey, Bonita Michelle. "Perceptions of Young African-American Males About Rap Music and Its Impact on Their Attitudes About Women." EdD dissertation, University of Massachusetts, 1999.

An investigation of African American male attitudes toward women and rap music. The author surveyed 100 males, aged thirteen to twenty-five. Upon completion of the survey, five young men were randomly chosen to be interviewed. Each was asked four questions regarding how they responded to the images of women in rap music, how they perceived manhood and heterosexual relationships, and how rap music affected their relationships with women. Her findings include a personal view of manhood that included violence against women, a strong view of women as "gold diggers," and a rejection of rap music as a form of control. Views rap as a form of entertainment that allows African Americans to express themselves.

1119. Horton-Stallings, LaMonda. "Trickster-Troping on Black Culture: Revised Readings of Gender and Sexuality." PhD dissertation, Michigan State University, 2002.

An exploration of how the hermeneutics of hip hop, black literature, folk and oral studies complicate issues of class, gender and sexuality. Issues like goddesses, trickster figures and matrilineal folk figures are used to discuss gender and sexuality beyond the Eurocentric lens.

1120. Jeffries, Michael. "Thug Life: Race, Gender, and the Meaning of Hip-Hop." PhD dissertation, Harvard University, 2008.

Given that whites control the vast amount of decision-making regarding the commodification and distribution of hip hop, the author researches how one should interpret objectionable themes performed by black male hip hop artists. Investigates whether black listeners interpret and rearticulate hip hop performances differently than white listeners, and how discourses of race, class and gender interact with hip hop. He employs textual, semiotic and interview-driven data analyses throughout the study.

1121. Jenkins, Mercilee Macintyre. "Stories That Women Tell: An Ethnographic Study of Personal Experience Stories in a Women's Rap Group." PhD dissertation, University of Illinois, 1983.

An exploration of communication in a female rap group that focuses on storytelling. Uses a symbolic interactionist approach to analyze storytelling as a linguistic and social interactional phenomenon. Supplements the theoretical approach with interviews of each group member, and includes members' response to an episode of *talk*.

1122. Kopano, Baruti Namdi. "An Historical and Contextual Analysis of the Use of the Black Rhetorical Form of Signifying in the Performances of Black Male Personality Radio Disc Jockeys and Rap Musicians." PhD dissertation, Indiana University of Pennsylvania, 2002.

Examines the relationship between African American male disc jockeys, rap musicians, and others to determine if they used signifying in their performances. He researched radio air checks from six disc jockeys, the lyrics from thirty-six different artists (including two who presented nine different raps). The signifying was divided into three major categories: indirection, loud talking and understatement. The findings demonstrated commonality in the use of language including rapping and rhyming, and that overall African American disc jockeys and rap musicians tapped into the black rhetorical tradition, especially signifying, in their respective performances.

1123. McFarland, Pancho. *Chicano Rap: Gender and Violence in the Post-industrial Barrio.* Austin: University of Texas Press, 2008.

A discussion of the author's introduction to and initiation into rap while growing up in Colorado Springs, Colorado. He was introduced to Sugarhill Gang, cumbias, rancheras and African American funk before becoming involved with hip hop. He chronicles Chicano/a participation in hip hop culture and rap music as a vehicle for uncovering how racial, cultural, economic and political environments of the late twentieth century shaped the identity of many Chicano/a youth.

1124. Merriday, Jodi. "Hip Hop Herstory: Women in Hip Hop Cultural Production and Music From Margins to Equity." PhD dissertation, Temple University, 2006.

Traces the contributions of women in the production of hip hop culture and music, and their resistance to misogyny, objectification, racism and social marginalization. Argues that African American women in hip hop have sustained legacies of resistance, resilience and protest. Concludes that African American women co-created hip hop, and that they have sustained agency as activists and artists negotiating urban terrain.

1125. Muhammad, Fatimah Nadiyah. "Hip-Hop Culture's Impact on Young, Black Women's Identity." PhD dissertation, Northwestern University, 2003.

A study of the dynamics of media and individual identity that focuses on patterns of interaction between hip hop culture and black women. The author investigates how black women are incorporated into hip hop, which of their identity issues are most affected by mass media culture, and how they use hip hop logic to define themselves and to view society. Concludes that young black women do incorporate hip hop cultural ideals and values into their own attitudes, and they use its cultural forms and styles to indicate their degree of identification with black racial issues and youth culture. Fieldwork was conducted in the Chicago area.

1126. Nichols, Jason. "The Realest Nigga: Construction of Black Masculinity Within Rap Music." Masters thesis, University of Maryland, 2000.

The author raises questions regarding black masculinity and hip hop. In his interviews with several rap artists, he ascertained that issues of performance and gender authenticity are central to black masculinity. He also asserts that when describing "a real man," the rappers nearly always use the same words they used in describing their own everyday personas.

1127. Pemberton, Jennifer M. "'Now I Ain't Sayin' She's A Gold Digger': African American Femininities in Rap Music Lyrics." PhD dissertation, Florida State University, 2008.

This dissertation looks at representations of black women, sexuality and gender relations in rap music lyrics. Explores the extent to which rap music lyrics either reproduce or challenge gender, racial and sexual stereotypes of African American women. Additionally, investigates how rap music lyrics construct a relationship between black masculinity and femininity. Her study used 450 songs randomly selected from a database that she created from platinum albums released between 1984 through 2000. Demonstrated that many male rappers depict black women as promiscuous sexual "freaks" and "bitches" and that female rappers also reproduce gender and racial stereotypes.

1128. Phillips, Layli, Kerri Reddick-Morgan and Dionne Patrick Stephens. "Oppositional Consciousness Within An Oppositional Realm: The

Case of Feminism and Womanism in Rap and Hip Hop." *The Journal of African American History* 90(3) (2005): 253–78.

A feminist analysis of female rappers and their lyrics that reconsiders traditional ways of assessing women's empowerment. Presents a historical overview of feminist ideas in the songs of female rappers, and demonstrates how black female ideas about themselves and their relationships with men are packaged and expressed. Furthermore, the authors assert that female rappers offer a street interpretation of the realities that confront black women, and reject the premise that black female rappers only reinforce the negative stereotypes about black women.

1129. Pough, Gwendolyn D. *Check it While I Wreck It: Black Womanhood, Hip Hop Culture, and the Public Sphere.* Boston: Northeastern University Press, 2004.

Explores the relationship between black women, hip hop and feminism. Researches the rhetoric of black women "bringing wreck" (explaining, deconstructing, commenting on, etc.) by using rap and other musical genres, novels, spoken word poetry, hip hop cinema and hip hop soul music. Illustrates that black female rappers like Missy Elliot, Lil Kim and Queen Latifah are continuing the legacy of earlier black women like Sojourner Truth and sisters of the Black Power and Civil Rights movements. In addition, she discusses how young black women are struggling against the negative stereotypical language of the past, including the use of terms like bitch, chickenhead, ho and mammy. She also discusses how the denigrating language used by men has been appropriated by black female rappers as a way to empower their own lyrics.

1130. Pough, Gwendolyn D., Elaine Richardson, Aisha Durham and Rachel Raimist, eds. *Home Girl Make Some Noise! Hip-Hop Feminism Anthology.* New York: Parker, 2007.

Deconstructs the belief that hip hop is a male space by identifying the women who were always involved in the culture. The authors explore hip hop as a world view, an epistemology, and as a cultural site for recreating identity and sexual politics. The authors use interviews, published essays, fiction, narratives, poetry and more to draw their conclusions. Foreword by Marc Anthony Neal; afterword by Joan Morgan.

1131. Richardson, Elaine. "She Was Workin' Like Foreal: Critical Literacy and Discourse Practices of African American Females in the Age of Hip Hop." *Discourse and Society* 18(6) (2007): 789–809.

Examines how young black women negotiate the stereotypical and hegemonic representation of black men and women as sexual images in mass media. Investigates how these women read rap texts in relation to their own experiences as black women.

1132. Schoenstein, Ralph. "Rap Renegade Roxanne Shanté Makes Feminism Rhyme with Success." *Mademoiselle*, April 1990, 132.

An exposé on Shanté's life with a focus on her ability to juggle several challenges into a successful career. Shanté discusses how she is raising a child, developing and managing a career, pursuing a college degree, and still has been able to record a new album, *Bad Sister*. She is characterized as ambitious, focused and independent.

1133. Sharpley-Whiting, T. Denean. *Pimps Up, Ho's Down: Hip Hop's Hold on Young Black Women*. New York: New York University Press, 2007.

The book is an in-depth provocative account of how hip hop has affected young black females. Written for B-girls who embrace Lil Kim and the pro-feminism of Lauryn Hill. Combines scholarly discourse and research with perspectives gleaned from personal observations and interviews to address this important topic. Documents the complexity of attitudes and feelings regarding the engagement that young African American women share with hip hop musical subculture. Discusses issues like light-skinned black females getting more exposure in hip hop videos, female participation in the sexualizing of black America, and unreported sexual abuse in the black community.

1134. Shaw, Redelia A. "African American Women in Rap Music Videos: A Visual Female Analysis." Masters thesis, Georgia State University, 2004.

An examination of how African American women are presented as "jezebel stereotypes" in rap music videos where the lead artists are African American males. Specifically, she explores the acting, costuming and framing of African American women in six rap videos that were made between 1999 and 2004.

1135. Smith-Cooper, T. L. "Contradictions in a Hip Hop World: An Ethnographic Study of Black Women Hip Hop Fans in Washington, D.C." PhD dissertation, Ohio University, 2002.

The author ponders why, given the abundance of misogynistic images and obscene lyrics in hip hop, black women continue to support and participate in hip hop culture. She conducted her research in Washington, DC's hip hop culture and discovered parallels with go-go, a local underground musical culture that fuses funk with hip hop.

1136. Trapp, Erin. "The Push and Pull of Hip-Hop: A Social Movement Analysis." *The American Behavioral Scientist* 48(11) (July 2005): 1,482–96.

Explores how hip hop can be both the engine and mirror of a social movement. Uses new social theory and political opportunity theory and the work of W.E.B. DuBois to examine the portrayal of women in rap. Concludes that artists who attempt to represent and influence reality often carry the mantle of leadership.

1137. Turner, Jr, Albert Uriah Anthony. "Bad Niggers, Real Niggas, and the Shaping of African American Counterpublic Discourses." PhD dissertation, University of Massachusetts, 2004.

He uses the counterpublic discourses inherent in African American folklore, literature, film and popular music to investigate ways in which African American males react to the negative masculine identities imposed upon them. He discusses the oppositional divide, and elucidates the circumstances that must arise for these images to become less culturally and rhetorically relevant.

1138. Ward, Christa Janel. "African American Girls Rap Music, and the Negotiation of Identity: An Analysis of Gender, Race, and Class in Relation to Rap Music Videos." PhD dissertation, University of Iowa, 2003.

An ethnographic investigation of the role of rap music videos among a group of middle-class African American females. The data were collected from diaries, in-depth interviews and group observation interviews. Discovered that the girls' interpretations of the videos were based on their understandings of their cultural norms. They were critical of the limited range of bodies represented in the videos, compared their bodies with those idealized as "perfect" in the videos, and recognized that most rappers in the study were reifying stereotypical notions about both African American female sexuality and African American male-female relationships. The respondents seem to favor what they describe as the "ghetto" mentality in rap music videos over their own middle-class lives.

1139. White, Miles. "We Some Killaz: Affect, Representation and the Performance of Black Masculinity in Hip-Hop Music." PhD dissertation, University of Washington, 2005.

The author focuses on five issues: hip hop as the black body in performance; the hybridity and shifting nature of racial attitudes; the construction, appropriation and performance of tropes of black masculinity by non-black actors; the contradictory stance of hip hop as both a reflection of personal and social identity and as cultural commodity; and the continuing ambivalence surrounding issues of race and the black body in American culture. His presentation is thorough and sheds new light on the issues.

1140. Williams, Melinda Elizabeth. "The Relationship Between Womanism, Black Women's Body Image, and Their Attitudes Towards the Depiction of Black Women in Pop Music Videos." Masters thesis, Howard University, 2006.

A survey of the attitudes of sixty-nine black females attending Howard University, a historically black university. The research focused on the degradation and sexualization of black women in black rap videos, and the belief that these representations may serve as behavioral models for black female adolescents.

1141. Zichermann, Sandra Claire. "You'se a HO! Mo-Fos!: The Effects of Hip Hop/Rap on Young Women in Academia." EdD dissertation, University of Toronto, 2008.

Investigates the rise of hip hop and rap as it proliferates its positions and wealth. Concerned with hip hop and rap as a subculture, and the effect of the music and culture on the behavior of young women enrolled in interdisciplinary programs (especially critical race and gender studies) who enjoy hip hop music.

## HISTORIES AND SURVEYS

1142. Aldridge, Daniel and James B. Stewart. "Introduction: Hip Hop in History; Past, Present, and Future." *The Journal of African American History* 90(3) (2005): 190–96.

Advocates that hip hop must be taken seriously as a cultural, economic, intellectual and political way and means of expressing oneself. The authors also believe that hip hop should be given the same scholarly status and attention that has been given to blues, jazz, the New Negro Renaissance, Civil Rights, the Black Power movement and the Black Arts Movement. An important component of the essay is a critique of several books that are devoted to the serious study of hip hop.

1143. Ayazi-Hashjin, Sherry and Sule G. Wilson. *Rap and Hip Hop: The Voice of a Generation.* New York: Rosen, 1999.

The authors trace the history and evolution of rap music and hip hop culture from its African roots, through the slave trade, to contemporary realization. They discuss the importance of the drum in African American culture and the evolution of black music in

America. Although their information is not new, the article is useful as an introduction.

1144. Baker, Soren. *The Music Library—The History of Rap and Hip Hop.* New York: Lucent Books, 2006.

Discusses the chronological development of rap and hip hop. The primary emphasis is on rap music, but also includes information on rapping, DJing, B-boying, graffiti art and breakdancing.

1145. Birnbaum, Larry. "Hip Hop: A Schoolboy's Primer." *Ear,* No. 2 (1988), 6.

Clarifies the differences between hip hop purists and those who see their product as entertainment. Includes information on the role of technology in the creation of hip hop. Chronicles the history and evolution of hip hop with a focus on breaking, scratching and sampling.

1146. Chang, Jeff. *Can't Stop Won't Stop: A History of the Hip-Hop Generation.* New York: St Martin's, 2005.

Chang uses black nationalism, monumental recordings, major events and the concept of rap as activism to situate the thirty-year history of rap. He interviewed gang members, hip hop producers, and pioneering artists like Afrika Bambaataa and DJ Kool Herc to chronicle the rise of rap to world prominence. Comprehensive, thorough and based on fieldwork.

1147. Conyers, James L., ed. *African American Jazz and Rap: Social and Philosophical Examinations of Black Expressive Behavior.* Charlotte: McFarland, 2001.

Conyers' theme is that jazz and rap are indigenous American folk musics whose unique innovative uses of melody and rhythm make them great art forms. The essays cover jazz history, unsung performers and their instruments, jazz culture in America and abroad, and the economic and political significance of jazz in American history. The author argues that both jazz and rap have had to confront the demands of both art and commerce, and both are struggling to maintain their artistic and political integrity in light of public tastes and the demands of the marketplace.

1148. Dagbovie, Pedro. "Of All Our Studies, History is Best Qualified to Reward Our Research: Black History's Relevance to the Hip Hop Generation." *Journal of African American History* 90(3) (2005): 299–323.

Examines the relationship between the hip hop generation and African American history, the concept of the hip hop generation, the history of black cultural consciousness and nationalism, and the pointed ideas first introduced by Harold Cruse in *Crisis of the Negro Intellectual* (1967). Challenges the hip hop generation to study African and African history to enhance their understanding of the role of hip hop in black history.

1149. Forman, Murray and Mark Anthony Neal. *That's The Joint: The Hip-Hop Studies Reader.* New York: Routledge, 2004.

Covers a variety of topics related to the beginning of hip hop culture and music. The topics include the forefathers, relating gang culture to hip hop, origin of the MC, commercialization of the music, role of women, and the globalization of hip hop culture. The Bronx, New York, is the primary locus for research. A major strength is the substantial number of interviews conducted by the authors with artists like Afrika Bambaataa, Fab 5 Freddy, Grand Master Flash and Grandwizard Theodore; their discussions of DJ Kool Herc's parties and Sugarhill Gang's recording of "Rapper's Delight" in 1979; and more. Introduction by Nelson George.

1150. George, Nelson. "Rap Breaks Through to the Majors." *Billboard*, 20 February 1988, 1.

This historically important article discusses deals between independent and major record labels. Argues that the deals are mutually beneficial because some acts' sales increased after they became associated with major record labels. Given the collaborations, the author believes that radio stations will begin to program more rap.

1151. Greenberg, Keith. *Rap.* New York: Lerner, 1988.

A superficial assessment of rap, loosely organized into six concise chapters. Lacks the depth and scholarship of studies based on fieldwork and analysis. There are no lyrics, few comments from the rap artists that he discusses, and the bibliography lacks depth.

1152. Haskins, James. *One Nation Under a Groove: Rap Music and Its Roots.* New York: Hyperion, 2000.

For younger readers. Geared to grades four to nine, this book focuses on rap roots and evolution and argues that rap is part of a long tradition of African American social commentary through art. Also discusses the place of women in rap and rap as a global phenomenon. Includes many quotes; uses selected rap lyrics to make his point.

1153. Hatch, Thomas. *A History of Hip-Hop: The Roots of Rap.* New York: Brick Learning, 2005.

A concise discussion of the history and evolution of the music from its Bronx roots. Including contributions of the west coast gangsta rappers to the music and related hip hop culture.

1154. Havelock, Nelson. *Bring the Noise: A Guide to Rap Music and Hip Hop Culture.* New York: Three Rivers Press, 1991.

Covers the history and evolution of hip hop culture, and the people who created and popularized it. Begins with its early history in the Bronx. Also includes the contributions of Compton, California, artists.

1155. Hess, Mickey. *Is Hip Hop Dead? The Past, Present, and Future of America's Most Wanted Music.* Westport, CT: Praeger Publishers, 2007.

The book focuses on how artists use claims of authenticity and outlaw status in critiques of the music industry. Also included is a discussion of how authenticity and outlaw status is used to co-op hip hop.

1156. Johnson, Christopher Keith. "On The Grind: Hip Hop and the Legacy of the African-American Work Song in the Postindustrial United States." PhD dissertation, Temple University, 2006.

Discusses the relationship between postindustrial economic realities for the African American worker, and the impact these conditions have had on their musical expressions. Three broad areas of hip hop are explored: the traditional economy, work performed in the music business, and work performed in the underground or illegal economy.

1157. Jones, Maurice. *Say it Loud: The Story of Rap Music.* Brookfield, CT: Millbrook, 1994.

For younger readers. The book is geared toward grades seven to twelve and presents the history of rap from its African roots to the early 1990s. Discusses the importance of the Bronx, list the names of some pioneers, and covers the steady climb of rap's popularity to its current international status.

1158. Light, Alan, ed. *The Vibe History of Hip Hop.* New York: Three Rivers Press, 1999.

More than fifty contributors focus on hip hop artists, scenes and movements from its beginnings until 1999. The essays tell the history and evolution of rap but do not cover some important individuals and groups (e.g. Gang Starr, Naughty By Nature, Heavy D., Kool Moe Dee and the Mighty EPMD). The essays include concise discographies. Includes comprehensive discographies; 200+ photos.

1159. Lommel, Cookie. *The History of Rap Music.* New York: Chelsea House, 2001.

The author includes numerous references to rap artists and a chapter on rap artists who have become moguls by overseeing business empires that market clothing to mainstream America. Contains several quotes from academics regarding rap as a manifestation of social problems. This book does not break new ground; much of the information is available elsewhere.

1160. Marshall, Wayne Glenn. "Routes, Rap, Reggae: Hearing the Histories of Hip-Hop and Reggae Together." PhD dissertation, University of Wisconsin, Madison, 2007.

The author examines the translocal interplay of hip hop and reggae, focusing on their interactions during the late twentieth century as an embodiment of the flow of social and cultural politics in and between Jamaica and the United States. Acknowledges the global circulation of both genres while focusing on their local historically contingent meanings in Kingston, Jamaica, and New York City. Uses a chronological social and cultural paradigm to reflect on and to challenge the forms of representation that have characterized the telling of hip hop's and reggae's stories.

1161. McKinney, Rhoda E. "What's Behind the Rise of Rap?" *Ebony*, January 1989, 66.

A concise summary of rap styles and profiles some of its most significant exponents to the late 1980s. Categorizes the groups by specific styles, and also probes several issues related to the rise and popularity of rap.

1162. McQuillar, Tayannah Lee. *When Rap Music Had a Conscience: The Artists Organizations and Historical Events that Inspired and Influenced the Golden Age of Hip-Hop From 1987 to 1996*. New York: Da Capo Press, 2007.

A reflection on contemporary urban youths' reluctance to reflect on the world around them, their obsession with inaction (except partying), and their determination not to deal with the past. In addition, she is concerned that many young African Americans are not conversant with the politically motivated rap of artists like Arrested Development, A Tribe Called Quest, Public Enemy and X-Clan. She also discusses selected films like *Boyz in the Hood*. Foreword by Brother J of X-Clan.

1163. Mook, Richard. *Rap Music and Hip Hop Culture: A Critical Reader.* Dubuque, IA: Kendall Hunt, 2007.

Covers topics related to the role of hip hop and rap in contemporary culture. Among the issues covered are hip hop and rap in the academy, its history, theory and impact.

1164. Norfleet, Dawn M. "Hip-Hop and Rap." In *African American Music: An Introduction*, eds Mellonee V. Burnim and Portia Maultsby, pp. 353–91. New York: Routledge, 2006.

This overview of the history, music and popularity of hip hop and rap includes a discussion of a myriad of issues, including cultural roots, the 1970s era of DJs, rap's entrance into the mainstream (1979–85), hip hop and the corporate world, the gangsta rap controversy, the east–west coast feud, women and hip hop, and much more. The essay is very thorough and well researched.

1165. Ogg, Alex and David Upshal. *The Hip Hop Years: A History of Rap.* New York: Fromm International, 2001.

This history and evolution of rap music and MCing begins in the Bronx and covers events, activities and people associated with its ascent to global popularity. The strength of the book is the 100+ interviews conducted with the original movers and shakers of rap and hip hop culture: Wu-Tang Clan, Eminem, Grandmaster Flash, DJ Kool Herc, Ice-T and many more. It is important to note the author's thorough understanding of the evolution of rap and hip hop culture.

1166. Rollins-Haynes, Levern. "Empowerment and Enslavement: Rap in the Context of African-American Cultural Memory." PhD dissertation, Florida State University, 2006.

Investigates the interconnections between African American music of the past and contemporary rap. Uses cultural memory as a catalyst for cultural retention and recollection, and to ascertain whether it is manifested into rap, theoretically and culturally.

1167. Stewart, James B. "Message in the Music: Political Commentary in Black Popular Music From Rhythm and Blues to Early Hip Hop." *The Journal of African American History* 90(3) (2005): 185–90.

The author challenges the misconception that R&B failed to engage the community and social issues of the 1970s. He uses the ideas of W.E.B. DuBois, Zora Neale Hurston and Alaine Locke to theorize that a myriad of political messages and ideas have always been inherent in R&B. He also covers the roots of hip hop.

1168. Tanz, Jason. *Other People's Property: A Shadow History of Hip Hop in White America.* New York: Bloomsbury, 2007.

Discusses the racial and cultural obstacles that separate consumers and producers of rap. The author interviews Chuck D and presents case histories of white rappers who attempted to emulate Eminem. He also discusses pumpsta, marketing and commercialization, and white appropriation of hip hop culture.

1169. Toop, David. *Rap Attack 3: African Rap to Global Hip-Hop.* London: Serpent's Tail, 2000.

In the third edition of his book, the author uses hip hop culture as the primary focus of his investigation of African American rap in its various forms. His discussion begins with African roots and proceeds to global acceptance, from artists like Slim Gaillard, James Brown and Willie Jackson to original rappers like Grandmaster Flash, Afrika Bambaataa, and to contemporary artists/groups like Roxanne Shanté, Run-DMC, Public Enemy, De La Soul, N.W.A., M.C. Hammer and Vanilla Ice. He also discusses the crisis of identity that ensued after the deaths of Tupac Shakur and Notorious B.I.G. and the nostalgia for old school hip hop. [See also items 1170 and 1171.]

1170.  ———. *Rap Attack 2: African Rap to Global Hip Hop.* London: Serpent's Tail, 1991.

An update of the 1991 material adds several hip hop pioneers, producers and entrepreneurs like Arthur Baker, Paul Winley and Bobby Robinson. In this edition, he also covers both the 1980s and the rise of The Beastie Boys, L.L. Cool J, De La Soul and Run-DMC. [See also items 1169 and 1171.]

1171.  ———. *Rap Attack: African Jive to New York Hip Hop.* Boston: South End, 1984.

One of the earliest attempts to chronicle the history and evolution of hip hop as a heavily African-influenced phenomenon. Includes interviews of prominent pioneers like Afrika Bambaataa, Grandmaster Flash, Spoonie Gee, Double Trouble and others. Of note is the author's ability to collect, analyze and create a historical chronology and timeline for the development of hip hop. [See also items 1169 and 1170.]

1172.  Wheeler, Jamar Montez. "Rap Music and Hegemony: A Historical Analysis of Rap's Narratives." Masters thesis, University of Louisville, 2006.

A historical analysis of the narratives of rap music and their relationship to hegemony. The study focuses on whether rap music's relationship to hegemony has changed and, if so, how.

## Regional studies

1173.  Adler, Bill. "The South Bronx Was Getting A Bad Rap Until a Club Called Disco Fever Came Along." *People Weekly*, 16 May 1983, 42.

Describes the club's role in the life and culture of the South Bronx and its importance to the development and support of rap artists. A brief comment on the club's social and fund-raising activities is also included.

1174. Baker, Jr, Houston. *Black Studies, Rap, and the Academy.* Chicago: University of Chicago Press, 1993.

A history of rap with special emphasis on how the music began in New York City in the mid-1970s. Baker espouses that the music deserves serious attention. Illustrates how groups such as Run-DMC, Public Enemy and KRS-One echo the feelings of people who are often viewed as either criminals or criminal suspects by the larger society, and concludes that rap represents the thinking of a generation of African Americans who feel both discriminated against and misunderstood. He uses the case of the Central Park to illustrate the disconnect between African American and white perspectives in interpreting events. The author shifts between lyrics that sound like the verse of a rapper and straightforward prose passages that criticize postmodernist conceptions. One of his most provocative conclusions is that rap is an "absolute prerequisite" for classroom teaching in the 1990s.

1175. Blakely, Preston A. "The Decision-Making Process for Two Urban Mainstream (Hip Hop) Radio Stations." PhD dissertation, Michigan State University, 2001.

Investigates the decision-making processes of two commercial radio stations in Georgia regarding management, personnel, policy, sales and programming. The managements of both stations feel that they are meeting the needs of their listeners without regulation. Both followed a standard decision-making process and adjustments were made when necessary. Both disapprove of low-power radio stations because they represent competition and broadcast interference.

1176. Clemons, Kawachi Ahmon. "Hip Hop as a Cultural Genre of the African American Tradition: A Critical Race Theory Analysis of Hip Hop's Pioneers' Experiences." PhD dissertation, University of North Carolina, Chapel Hill, 2008.

Examines hip hop in its historical and cultural context, and chronicles the genre through the eyes of those who contributed to its creation and development. Presents a plausible approach for using hip hop in a culturally responsive pedagogical framework. The study is an outgrowth of the hip hop initiative developed at North Carolina Central University.

1177. Costello, Mark and David Foster Wallace. *Signifying Rappers: Rap and Race in the Urban Present.* New York: Ecco Press, 1997.

A good discussion of the influence and impact of rap on popular culture and society. Covers rap's influence on popular music and the life styles of late 1990s youth, money and power, the role of racial

politics in rap culture and music, and the use and function of language in rap music. Explain why the genre has achieved and retained
its popularity in North Dorchester, Massachusetts.

1178. Cross, Brian. *It's Not About Salary: Rap, Race, and Resistance in
Los Angeles.* London and New York: Verso, 1993.

This is the first book to document the rich, varied and influential Los
Angeles hip hop scene. Introduces and examines artists like Nefertiti,
a black Muslim woman; an Irish American group called the House
of Pain; a Mexican American rapper named Kid Frost; a Samoan
American family group known as Boo Yaa Tribe, and a Jewish rap
group called Blood of Abraham. A comprehensive history of rap in
Los Angeles, including the local development of the music and its
connection to New York. Includes several interviews of musicians,
producers and promoters, including obscure artists like T-Love,
established rappers like Ice-T and Ice Cube, the Watts Prophets, and
Roy Porter, who reminisced about the bebop scene along Central
Avenue in Los Angeles. Rapper T-Love explains the importance of
freestyle rapping, and R. Kelly discusses the development of Chicano
hip hop against the background of *pachucos*, lowriders and the linguistic style of Calo or *Spanglish*. The book is well researched, well
written and permeated with information regarding the diversity of
the hip hop and rap scene in Los Angeles.

1179. Cutler, Cecilia Anne. "Brooklyn Style: Hip-Hop Markers and
Racial Affiliation Among European Immigrants in New York City."
*International Journal of Bilingualism*, 1 March 2008, 20–31.

The author interviewed teenage immigrants to the United States from
countries like Armenia, Bulgaria, Russia and the Ukraine, many of
whom were surprised at being labeled "white", to ascertain the depth
of their affiliation with and enjoyment of hip hop. Argues that hip
hop and African American culture are more attractive models of
identity formation for immigrants than the white mainstream culture
of Brooklyn and Queens.

1180. ———. "Crossing Over: White Youth, Hip-Hop and African-American
English." PhD dissertation, New York University, 2002.

Investigates the speech of white middle-class students in the New York
City area who use elements of hip hop language (HHL) to signal
their connection or affiliation to hip hop culture. Data, collected over a
two-year period from selected public and private schools, include
interviews, several hours of music, spoken word performances and
discussions focused on hip hop. Concludes that a shift is transpiring
in the way that young people are constructing their identities, and

challenges traditional sociolinguistic assumptions about language and identity.

1181. Evans, Latiera Brunson. "The Influence of Images in Hip Hop Culture on Academic Identity and Schooling Experiences of Students at Kennedy Junior High." PhD dissertation, University of Cincinnati, 2007.

An investigation of how images of youth in hip hop culture influenced the academic identities and experiences of twenty-eight eighth-grade students of different genders and races in a midwestern junior high school, using one-on-one interviews, focus groups (with eleven additional participants), and field observations. Among the findings were that boys of color felt teachers were ascribing radicalized identities that reinforced negative stereotypes of them as threats, but regardless of ethnicity, girls did not emphasize race as a factor in their views of hip hop images.

1182. Feezel, Jessica Timpani. "Stereotype: The Influence of Music Preference on Political Attitudes and Behavior." PhD dissertation, University of California, Santa Barbara, 2008.

An examination of a theory which links music preference and political attitudes. Researches the feasibility of predicting political attitudes based upon musical preferences. Findings show associations between key political attitudes and country music, R&B, rap and hip hop; the author concludes that music is an effective and influential form of political communication, and that political norms are constructed and encouraged among particular political genres of music.

1183. Gause, Charles Phillip. "How African American Educators 'Make Sense' of Hip Hop Culture and Its Influence on Public Schools: A Case Study." PhD dissertation, Miami University, 2001.

A study to determine the issues and concerns negotiated by African American educators when teaching African American students in a suburban midwestern junior-senior high school. Concludes that educational organizations and school districts must recognize that schooling is a political act in which cultural politics in the areas of class, gender and race are at work, and that culturally relevant ways of knowing through African American "first person" narratives can be utilized to ferment social transformation.

1184. Gillen, Sarah. "Hip Hop According to the Adolescents of the Inland Empire." Masters thesis, California State University, Fullerton, 2007.

Examines hip hop culture among adolescents in the Inland Empire (a large region east of Los Angeles) and seeks to understand the perceptions of hip hop music and culture in this geographical area. Uses ethnographic methods to ascertain the attitudes of students at one area high school to elicit their definitions of hip hop culture and music, trace the history and evolution of hip hop, determine hip hop culture in the Inland Empire, and discuss the current state and future of hip hop in the area.

1185. Ginwright, Shawn A. *Black in School: Afrocentric Reform, Urban Youth, and the Promise of Hip-Hop Culture.* New York: Teachers College Press, 2004.

The book is based on fieldwork and research conducted in Oakland, California by the author. The primary focus is to implement multicultural educational reform in an impoverished urban community. Traces the history of Afrocentrism as an approach to teaching and focuses on the economic and social factors that led to the implementation and eventual failure of the Afrocentric curriculum at McClymonds High School. Researches his belief that Afrocentrism does not adequately address the social ills that plague many urban schools and communities, deconstructs the process that led to the adoption of the curriculum, and explores how an Afrocentric reform might better respond to the needs of low-income and working-class youth. He believes the community is best suited to diagnose and solve the issue, and that educational reformers would be more effective if they included the opinions of youth as part of an intergenerational and multidimensional approach.

1186. Gutierrez, Eric. *Disciples of the Street: The Promise of a Hip Hop Church.* New York: Seabury Books, 2008.

When the author's 150-year-old South Bronx church began offering hip hop services, he was prompted to reassess the nature of rap, religion and community. He discusses the role of the preacher, crew of rappers and religious leaders through their religious and personal struggles to the evolution of the new church service.

1187. Harrison, Anthony Kwame. *Hip Hop Underground: The Integrity and Ethics of Racial Identification.* Philadelphia: Temple University Press, 2008.

Using hip hop as a medium, Harrison discusses the relationship between hip hop culture, demographic change, ethnic and racial identities and relations. The book is an outgrowth of research conducted in the San Francisco Bay Area for his doctoral dissertation. He concludes that the notion that hip hop culture in the San Francisco Bay Area is color blind is contrary to his findings.

1188. ——. "'Every Emcee's a Fan, Every Fan's an Emcee:' Authenticity, Identity, and Power Within Bay Area Underground Hip Hop." PhD dissertation, Syracuse University, 2003.

Researches whether oppositional subcultures pose a threat or offer a legitimate alternative to institutions of power. Specifically focuses on west coast underground hip hop as practiced in the San Francisco Bay Area. Characterizes Bay Area hip hop as a "do it yourself" (DIY) ethos, which undermines the distinction between hip hop producers and consumers. This research is a by-product of a participant-observer model which included the author's experiences as a recognized artist within this subculture scene.

1189. Hebdige, Dick. *Cut 'n' Mix: Culture, Identity and Caribbean Music.* New York: Methuen, 1987.

Although primarily concerned with Caribbean musical traditions, Hebdige includes a provocative chapter that focuses on their incorporation into South Bronx hip hop: "Rap and Hip Hop: The New York Connection" (pp. 136–48). The author focuses on DJ Kool Herc as a conduit through which Caribbean cultural practices were transmitted, transformed and implemented into hip hop in New York. The chapter is well researched, informative and insightful.

1190. Hopkinson, Natalie Adele. "Go-go Live: Washington, D.C.'s Cultural Information Network, Drumming the News, Knitting Communities, and Guarding a Black Public Sphere." PhD dissertation, University of Maryland, College Park, 2007.

Uses Habermas' theory to argue that go-go, a Washington DC funk-based musical genre, functions as a unique public sphere. Go-go is defined as a powerful counter-discourse to hip hop. The author asserts that both genres originally functioned as a medium for news and culture within specific black communities. Concludes that through a network of entrepreneurs and businesses, go-go has protected the sanctity of this public sphere and continues to build via a variety of media.

1191. Johnson, Amber Lauren. "'We Don't Write Just to Write: We Write to be Free': A Rhetorical Ethnography of Spoken Word in Los Angeles." PhD dissertation, Pennsylvania State University, 2006.

Examines the interdependence among the study of identity, counter-publicity and performance. Explores the spoken word as a counter-public collective that engages in oppositional discourse, and uses ethnographic observation, interviews, focus groups and rhetorical analysis to analyze the performance of collective identity and membership. Also examines the ways in which the Spoken Word Counterpublic Collective attempts to confront oppression.

1192. Kelley, Robin. *Race Rebels: Culture, Politics, and the Black Working Class.* New York: Free Press; Toronto: Maxwell Macmillan Canada; New York: Maxwell Macmillan International, 1994.

Focused primarily on issues relevant to the African American working class: history, the black poor, civil rights, African American
communists and roles in the Spanish Civil War, and rap. One chapter
addresses the role and meaning of gangsta rap in postindustrial Los
Angeles.

1193. Keyes, Cheryl. *Rap Music and Street Consciousness.* Urbana: University
of Illinois Press, 2002.

Keyes uses theoretical paradigms from cultural studies, ethnomusicology and folklore to present a comprehensive assessment of the
urban youth movement that emerged in the South Bronx in the late
1970s. Examines breakdancing, graffiti art, DJing and MCing. Building on the distinction provided by KRS-One between rap and hip
hop, the author argues that rap is a cohesive arts movement which
provides disenfranchised youth a vehicle for self-expression. Traces
rap's origins back to the West African bard tradition, and espouses
that "the dozens," field hollers, and exchanging insults are all ante-
cedents of rap. In addition, she argues that "toasting," a Jamaican
dancehall tradition, is also an antecedent of rap. Includes a discussion of Afrika Bambaataa, gangsta rap and sexism; presents rap as a
positive impact on urban youth.

1194. ——. "Rappin' to the Beat: Rap Music's Street Culture Among
African-Americans." PhD dissertation, Indiana University, 1991.

Rap music is presented and analyzed as street culture among African
Americans. Based on fieldwork conducted in New York City, the
dissertation explores the philosophy and aesthetic ideology, examines
rap as a form of communication, and situates rap within a continuum
of black expression. Findings indicate that rap is a display of cultural
values and aesthetics; it is an expressive form, an agent for social
control and social cohesiveness, a political forum, and a symbol of
ethnicity. It is also a means of socioeconomic mobility for African
American youth within mainstream America.

1195. Kline, Christopher. "Represent: Hip-Hop and the Self-Aesthetic
Relation." PhD dissertation, Indiana University, 2007.

Uses philosophy and critical ethnography to uncover the deep connections between philosophy and hip hop culture. Uses ethnography of
underground hip hop artists in Chicago to address questions about
the construction and maintenance of self through hip hop aesthetics.

1196. Leland, John. "Singles." *Spin*, July 1989, 122.

Written by a prolific scholar of rap, this concise column is devoted to
the style and musical approach of east coast rappers (2 Live Crew,

M.C. Hammer, Ice-T, Tone-Loc and N.W.A.) and their respective influences and relationship to Los Angeles.

1197. Marlowe, Duff. "L.A. Rap; Go West, Young B-Boy." *Cash Box*, 27 May 1989, 10.

A concise but important article about the history, evolution and, most importantly, distinctive aesthetic features of west coast rap. The author profiles some of the popular individuals and groups, and discusses the difficulties that some groups have experienced in getting rap gigs and gaining acceptance.

1198. ——. "Miami Rap: This is Bass." *Cash Box*, 27 May 1989, 11.

This article from the "Cityscapes" section of *Cash Box* highlights the strong Caribbean and Miami influence on rap music. The author acknowledges that rap is indebted to both, and notes the Miami groups' heavy use of the drum machine rather than the synth bass. He profiles Luther Campbell and his record company, and mentions other Miami groups.

1199. ——. "Seattle Rap: Nastymix Rocks." *Cash Box*, 27 May 1989, 11.

Another "Cityscapes" column from the *Cash Box* special edition on rap music. Profiles Sir Mix-a-Lot, his hits, and his appreciation for Seattle. Includes attitudes about ego and the belief that rap groups should remain close to the streets.

1200. Marquez, John David. "From Bebop to Hip Hop: A Comparative Analysis of Cultural Resistance in Mexican-American and African-American Communities' Adolescents, 1940–96." Masters thesis, University of Texas, El Paso, 1998.

The author, who grew up in a culturally diverse environment, explores "authentic" Mexican American culture, investigates the fluidity of cultural exchange, and illuminates multicultural exchanges and adaptations that have transpired among ethnic groups that have experienced similar historical experiences, such as Mexican Americans and African Americans.

1201. McAdams, Janine. "A Message of Peace Outta Compton: Rappers Unite for Anti-Violence Project." *Billboard*, 5 May 1990, 26.

Discusses a collection of west coast rappers who united to create a single and video entitled "We're All in the Same Gang." Among the artists are Michael Conception and Eban Kelly. The article alludes to the anti-violence movement as a diverse philosophy shared by most west coast rappers. Proceeds from the project were to be donated to Project Build.

1202. Mendez, Jason Cory. "The BX Chronicles: Exploring the Complexities of Life in the South Bronx." PhD dissertation, University of North Carolina, Chapel Hill, 2008.

An exploration of the complexities of life in the South Bronx, from a Puerto Rican perspective. He uses détournement, critical race theory, lived experience and representation to counteract distorted representations of life in the South Bronx. Discusses the life of a hip hop pioneer and hip hop as a lived experience, and examines the origins, evolutions and objectification of hip hop.

1203. Morgan, Marcyliena. *The Real Hiphop: Battling for Knowledge, Power, and Respect in the LA Underground.* Durham: Duke University Press, 2009.

The research begins at Project Blowed in 1994, followed by the Good Life, and thereafter at the KAOS Network in the Leimert Park area, all in Los Angeles. The author explores the cultural meaning, language and artistic practices of the artists, and infuses her ethnographic analysis with personal observations, excerpts from interviews and transcriptions of freestyle lyrics to determine the meaning of language, what is emphasized, wordplay, attributes of MCs, evaluation, competition and more.

1204. Morin, Matthew McNamara. "Facilitating Paraxial Music Education at the East Boston Youth Center." Masters thesis, Tufts University, 2008.

Examines the relevance of music education pedagogy to the field of ethnomusicology to demonstrate how Praxis-oriented music education facilitates community and personal growth for youth across ethnic and racial lines. Zumix, a small non-profit organization located in a low-income area of East Boston, offers after-school music programs that range from hip hop beat making and songwriting to four-part harmony, and more.

1205. Neff, Ali Colleen. "Let the World Listen Right: Freestyle Hip-Hop at the Contemporary Crossroads of the Mississippi Delta." Masters thesis, University of North Carolina, Chapel Hill, 2007.

Collaborative ethnographic work with Mississippi Delta hip hop artists and in the surrounding community is used to investigate interaction of diasporic aesthetic practice, local cultural tradition and global networks, and how they influence the form and function of expressive culture of the area. Draws a parallel between freestyle hip hop and blues, and concludes that Delta hip hop continues many of the stylistic traits, performance techniques and functions of Mississippi Delta blues.

1206. Norfleet, Dawn Michelle. "Hip-hop Culture in New York City: The Role of Verbal Musical Performance in Defining a Community." PhD dissertation, Columbia University, 1997.

Focuses on the verbal musical expression of rap music. The author discusses the paradoxical relationship that characterizes many hip hoppers: trying to maintain social and ideological ties with their communities while reaping the economic benefits of a successful commercial career. Fieldwork was conducted in New York City between 1992 and 1996, among hip hoppers (amateurs and professionals), and published materials were reviewed. The author suggests is that dichotomization may be a useful tool for understanding human practices; however, these practices are also subject to cultural processes of defining, refining and redefining.

1207. Palmer, Tamara. *Country Fried Soul: Adventures in Dirty South Hip-Hop.* New York: Backbeat Books, 2005.

Details how the south is leading the way in the hip hop global movement. Discusses the origins of Dirty South hip hop, where it is headed, and the hopes, frustrations and struggles of performers and producers. Provides a list of the best southern hip hop on CD and DVD, in magazines and on the web.

1208. Patacsil, N. Judy. "Kapwa—Embracing Our Shared Identity: The Influence of Role Models on Being Filipino American." PsyD dissertation, San Diego: Alliant International University, 2007.

An examination of the influence of Filipino American role models on thirty-five Filipino American college students (twenty-one females and fourteen males, aged eighteen to twenty-eight). Influential Filipinos included teachers, grandparents, siblings and a well-known hip hop DJ. Data were collected from essays written by the participants and were analyzed for meaning and themes. The students expressed pride in being Filipino or Filipino American and discussed the process of blending two cultures and experiences of discrimination and racism by whites and other groups of color.

1209. Pulido, Isaura Betzabe. "Knowledge—The Fifth Element of Hip Hop Music: Mexican and Puerto Rican Youth Engagement of Hip Hop as Critically Rac(ed) Education Discourse." PhD dissertation, University of Illinois, 2008.

An investigation of the interrelationships among Mexican and Puerto Rican youth in Chicago schooling and the use of hip hop as critical pedagogy. The author uses critical race and Latino critical race theories to analyze student narratives from twenty Mexican and Puerto

Rican youth in Chicago about the influence of culture, ethnicity and race in their everyday lives, power relations in their communities, and their assessment of education by using hip hop culture and music. Concludes that educational researchers, policy-makers and educators would benefit by understanding how race, ethnicity and culture operate for youth of color because they have bearing on how students respond to their education.

1210. Ramjattan, Radha. "The Intervention of Hip-Hop Music to Promote HIV Prevention: A Comparative Study Among Students in a Middle School in Miami-Dade, Florida." PhD dissertation, Minneapolis: Walden University, 2007.

This study was conducted in a Miami-Dade county public school to determine if hip hop music, as an advocate of HIV prevention, would be more effective than traditional methods of increasing the awareness about HIV risk behaviors, reception of information about HIV, motivation to engage in preventative behaviors, and more. The author concluded that the use of age-appropriate hip hop or other culturally sensitive music as a teaching tool could create social change in HIV awareness among America's adolescent population.

1211. Reynolds, Simon. "Hip Hop Wag Out 87: The Big Chill." *Melody Maker*, 28 March 1987, 32.

In this article on New York hip hop artists, the author profiles Skinny Boys, KRS-One and Scott LaRock regarding Skinny Boys, their mundane family-oriented lives, and raw music. Focuses on KRS-One's background and rise to musical prominence. Discusses neighborhood feuds between the Bronx, Brooklyn and Queens regarding which is the true cradle of rap. Alludes to the rapper as a reporter of urban African American life.

1212. Rivera, Raquel Zoraya. *New York Ricans from the Hip Hop Zone.* New York: Palgrave Macmillan, 2002.

An outgrowth of author's dissertation, in which she pays tribute to Puerto Ricans who made contributions to hip hop music since the 1970s. Explains the significance of New York Puerto Rican (Nuyorican) and Latino influences in hip hop history, credits African Americans and Puerto Ricans for collaborating to create hip hop in the early 1970s, expresses concern about some Latino stereotypes, and provides insight into the contributions of Fat Joe, Angie Martinez and the Big Punisher.

1213. ——. "New York Ricans From the Hip Hop Zone: Between Blackness and Latinidad." PhD dissertation, City University of New York, 2000.

Explores the ways in which New York Puerto Ricans (Nuyoricans) have navigated ethno-racial identification within the hip hop scene, the consequences of their strategies, how they perceive their Puerto Rican identity within the context of pan-ethnic Latino labeling constructed Puerto Ricanness in tandem with or in contradiction to African Americanness. The author believes that the meanings given to blackness and *latinidad* are complex among older African Americans, Puerto Ricans and in mass media representations of these racial identities. Concludes that hip hoppers partly deconstruct and reconstruct ethnic and racial categories, while simultaneously influenced by the dominant construction of identities.

1214. Ro, Ronin. *Gangsta: Merchandising the Rhymes of Violence.* New York: St Martin's Press, 1996.

A collection of Ro's non-fiction articles for *Rolling Stone* and *The Source* (1992–95) about rap culture and its implications in the 1990s. Presents an overview of gangsta rap and the cocaine traffic, combined with a discussion of artists like Luther Campbell, Kid Frost, N.W.A., Scarface and Too Short. The focus is on the Los Angeles and New York rap scenes. He argues that the commercialism of gangsta rap has contributed to the growth of the gang culture that the music glorifies. Although provocative and well written, the articles do not demonstrate conclusively the effect of gangsta rap on the demoralization of youth, its connection to the growth of the gun culture, or the exploitation of sexism in mainstream American culture.

1215. Rowe-Adjiborgoun, Jill. "The Impact of Structural Constraints on the Quality of Life for African American Males in Lima, Ohio: A Community History." PhD dissertation, Michigan State University, 2004.

The study is based upon the lives and identities of African American males in Lima, Ohio. Using ethnographic and historical theories, the author researches the changing identities of African American males, structural constraints that have contributed to the normalization of violence, and historical events and structural features that have shaped their current identities.

1216. Samuels, Allison. *Off the Record: A Reporter Unveils the Celebrity Worlds of Hollywood, Hip-Hop and Sports.* New York: Amistad, 2007.

This is not a scholarly discourse; rather it is a series of funny anecdotes about the entertainers and sports celebrities that the author covered as a journalist for *Newsweek* magazine. In addition to entertainers like Bill Cosby, Whitney Houston and Eddie Murphy, she also includes perceptions and stories about Bone Thugs-N-Harmony, Dr. Dre, Eminem, Snoop Dogg, Suge Knight, Death Row Records and Tupac Shakur. The book is permeated with insider stories that have never been published.

1217. Sandow, Gregory. "L.A. Rap: Gettin' Hard in Cali." *Village Voice*, 4 April 1989, 12.

He profiles the musical careers of gangsta rappers Easy-E, Ice-T and N.W.A., and comments briefly on the Los Angeles roots of 2 Live Crew and the popularity of Tone-Loc and other Los Angeles groups.

1218. Sarig, Roni. *Third Coast: Outkast, Timbaland, and How Hip Hop Became a Southern Thing*. New York: Da Capo Press, 2007.

Recounts the story and history of the evolution of southern rap with a special focus on Pharrell Williams, Jermaine Dupri, Outkast and Timbaland. Also distinguishes between the different approaches to and styles of rap.

1219. Schipper, Henry. "Long Beach Center to Curtail Concerts Following Rap Riots." *Variety*, 20 August 1986, 78.

Report on a new ban enacted against acts considered to attract violence (especially heavy metal and rap), although no artist or genre was mentioned. In addition to comments on the violence that occurred at a recent concert, the author acknowledges the anti-drugs and anti-crime message found in some rap.

1220. Sharma, Nitasha Tamar. "Claiming Space, Making Race: Second-generation South Asian-American Hip-Hop Artists." PhD dissertation, University of California, Santa Barbara, 2004.

Focuses on the contemporary relationship between African Americans and South Asian Americans and how Asian immigrants insert themselves into existing racial hierarchies and in the process develop new discourses of race. She reveals how South Asians Americans (Indians, Indo-Fijians, Nepalis, Pakistanis, Sri Lankans and others) develop new models of immigrant identity that challenge the identity politics of ethnicity. Uses a multi-sited ethnographic model to investigate these issues in selected northern California cities. Concludes that racial consciousness expressed by hip hop artists facilitates the development of coalitions that cross boundaries. Her analysis contradicts the assimilationist views of those predicting "downward mobility" for second-generation youth who imitate blacks and black culture.

1221. Shaw, William. *Westside: The Coast to Coast Explosion in Hip Hop*. New York: Cooper Square Press, 2000.

A discussion of the cultural diffusion of hip hop and its appeal. Contains information on east coast and west coast styles and the divergent social, economic and political issues that characterize each. Discusses the approaches and world views of Dr. Dre, Eminem, Ice Cube, Jay-Z and Tupac Shakur. [See also item 1222.]

1222. ———. *Westside: Young Men and Hip Hop in L.A.* New York: Simon and Schuster, 2000.

This is the American release of a British book entitled *Westside: Stories of Boys in the Hood*, set in South Central Los Angeles during the late 1980s. Focuses on the life-challenges and hardships of seven young men who hope to use their respective talents and experiences to imitate the success of artists like Dr. Dre, Snoop Dogg and Tupac Shakur, and to use music as a vehicle to escape their drug-infested and crime-ridden neighborhoods. [See also item 1221.]

1223. Smith-Cooper, Tina. L. "Contradictions in a Hip-Hop World: An Ethnographic Study of Women Hip-Hop Fans in Washington, D.C." PhD dissertation, Ohio University, 2002.

With messages of empowerment and political agency being drowned out by consistent misogyny and obscene lyrics, the author questions why black women continue to participate in a culture that degrades and devalues them. Uses ethnography to ascertain the spaces of contradiction in Washington, DC, hip hop culture. Using this approach, she was able to determine how black women contest misogyny and sexism and simultaneously create spaces of pleasure.

1224. Weber, Laura C. "Welcome to Detroit." Masters thesis, University of Southern California, 2008.

A study of Northern Lights, dubbed "Shoes House" on Tuesday nights, as an open campus for self-taught hip hop academics. Describes the place as a comfort zone for those familiar with Detroit hip hop, and a place where one could become a participant in dances known to all who frequent the place.

1225. Wegner, Kyle David. "Children of Aztlan: Mexican American Popular Culture and the Post-Chicano Aesthetic." PhD dissertation, State University of New York at Buffalo, 2006.

Researches the premise that issues of popular culture and the construction of Chicano identity cannot be separated from issues of citizenship, class, labor, language, nationality and political economy. Discusses power relations embedded in different forms of popular culture and how Chicano popular culture is shaped by the economic and social matrices from which it emerges. Argues that historically

Chicanos have played an important role in all aspects of hip hop culture but their contributions have been largely invisible within both popular culture and academic discourse.

## Global studies

1226. Alim, H. Samy, Awad Ibrahim and Alastair Pennycook. *Global Linguistic Flows: Hip Hop Cultures, Youth Identities, and the Politics of Language.* New York: Routledge, 2008.

The subject matter is situated between sociolinguistics and hip hop scholarship, and explores hip hop cultures in Africa, Asia, Australia, North annd South America, and the European Union, specifically the Brazilian *favelas*, Lagos, Nigeria, Dar es Salaam, Tanzania, Germany's Mannheim district of Weststadt, and selected "hoods" of the San Francisco Bay Area. Their discussion focuses on issues like cultural flow, diaspora and transnationalism to expand theoretical approaches to language agency, choice, speech style, stylization, code switching, language mixing, crossing and more.

1227. Alook, Angele. "An Ethnographic Study of the Edmonton Hip Hop Community: Anti-Racist Cultural Identities." Masters thesis, Edmonton: University of Alberta, 2005.

Examines the cultural practice of hip hop and the hybrid nature of the culture. This ethnographic study of the Edmonton hip hop community includes interviews of fifteen local artists from diverse cultural backgrounds. Attempts to determine how community occurs within the context of Canadian multiculturalism, and the radicalization and racism toward ethnic minorities.

1228. Baker, Geoffrey. "Hip Hop Revolucion!: Nationalizing Rap in Cuba." *Ethnomusicology* 49(3) (2005): 368–403.

Given the negative history of rap in Cuba because of its roots in North America, the author was amazed to hear a Cuban state official promoting it. Examines how and why the Cuban Government has become amenable to rap music and looks at strategies used by officials like Alpidio Alonso to promote its acceptance in Cuba.

1229. Barnwell, Lisa A. "The Multiple Performances of Identity Through Hip Hop Culture Relevance for Black Youth in the Canadian Context." Masters thesis, University of Toronto, 2004.

Investigates the ways in which African Canadian youth who participate in hip hop culture gain meaning from its numerous geographical and ideological contexts. Focused on a group consisting of eight young people (four boys, four girls) to ascertain whether parallels exist between African American and African Canadian uses of hip hop culture.

1230. Bere, Wonderful G. "Urban Grooves: The Performance of Politics in Zimbabwe's Hip Hop Music." PhD dissertation, New York University, 2007.

Focuses on the theorization of artistic practice, especially performance's oppositional potential, as a political force. In Zimbabwe music lends itself to be used as a tool of oppression, so the author researched two issues: whether urban groovers have deconstructed the state's deception of artists by fronting support for the industry while the state uses the artists to drum up support for its political agenda, and whether artists are deceiving the state by accepting its support while simultaneously subverting the state's narrative.

1231. Buffam, H.V. Bonar. "Becoming Part of Inner City Space: A Critical Ethnography of Racialized Youth." Masters thesis, University of Alberta, 2006.

A discussion of the ambivalent ways that inner city youth experience colonial processes of subjugation to criminalized, impoverished social spaces. The fieldwork was conducted at an inner city recreation center in Edmonton. Examines how youth negotiate stereotypes of age, race and space. Additionally, discusses how middle-class notions of these same concepts mesh with efforts to create a space that values hip hop experiences. The center's hip hop program demonstrates how indigenous youth subvert colonial racism through performance.

1232. Caudeiron, Daniel. "Conducting a Rap Symphony." *Canadian Composer*. Spring 1990: 8.

The article profiles Canadian rapper Maestro Fresh-Wes, describes his early interest and success in rap, difficulties in securing a record contract, and his most recent success. Of particular note is his view of the differences between the Canadian and American rap scenes.

1233. ———. "Can Con Hip Hop." *Canadian Composer*. November 1989: 30, 32, 34.

Comments on the state of the Canadian hip hop nation, and the difficulties of promoting a cutting-edge genre in a musically conservative environment, including too little air play and too few labels willing to sign new artists creating new music. In spite of these obstacles, the author is optimistic about the future of Canadian rap.

1234. Chaudhuri, Arun Kumar. "Culture, Community, and Identity in the 'Sampled Word': South Asian Urban/Electronic Music in Toronto." Masters thesis, Toronto: York University, 2005.

An ethnographic study of a "scene" of South Asian urban/electronic musicians in Toronto which engages concepts of culture, community and identity in their respective complexity and fluidity. The author uses critical social theory, anthropology, cultural studies and post-colonial theory to analyze the "scene," which includes musical styles that range from hip hop to abstract electronic music.

1235. Chennault, Schyler B. "Je vis donc je vois, donc je dis: Banlieue Violence in French Rap." Masters thesis, Brigham Young University, 2007.

French rap has become very popular and controversial since its inception two decades ago. The author explains the French MC's role as representative and reporter of France's suburbs (la banlieue), and uses French rap lyrics to determine both the conditions and causes of the violence, and to gauge the rappers' perception of it.

1236. Clark, Andrew. "Hip-Hop Rules." *Maclean's*, November 1999, 42–46.

Covers the popularity of hip hop in Canada. Includes comments by Daniel Caudeiron (founder of the Black Music Association of Canada), an estimate of hip hop album sales, history of the musical style, identification of selected Canadian hip hop artists, and a comparison of Canadian hip hoppers with their American counterparts.

1237. Codrington, Raymond George. "Sessions from the Big Smoke: Rap, Race and Class in London." PhD dissertation, City University of New York, 2001.

A study of how race and class are incorporated into the lyrics of rap music among London's black and other working-class groups. He is concerned with how race and class are treated in rap, and with the changes that have occurred in the class and race composition of the rap community since its introduction to London in the mid-1980s. Investigates how members of the rap community negotiate the construction of cultural and racial difference, and how popular culture, class and race are linked to issues of choice and power.

1238. Condry, Ian. *Hip-Hop Japan: Rap and the Paths of Cultural Globalization*. Durham: Duke University Press, 2006.

A study of gender, prosody and race in Japanese hip hop. He interviewed several Japanese artists and traces the history and evolution of Japanese hip hop from its origins to around 2006.

1239. ———. "Japanese Rap Music: An Ethnography of Globalization in Popular Culture." PhD dissertation, Yale University, 1999.

The study is concerned with the shifting winds of capitalism, and what sociopolitical issues give rise to transnational popular culture. Investigates how globalizing forces spread pop culture around the world, given the localizing tendencies of Japanese consumers and artists in appropriating such products and practices. Explores the intersection of culture and commerce in Tokyo, 1995–97, and assesses the issue from three perspectives: as a business, as a community of musicians and fans, and as a media-generated phenomenon. The study was framed by theories of consumption and globalization; argues that globally-available popular culture is becoming accessible to larger audiences and, simultaneously, smaller hip hop scenes like Japan's are becoming deeper and more widely connected than before.

1240. Dennis, Christopher Charles. "Afro-Colombian Hip-Hop: Globalization, Popular Music and Ethnic Identities." PhD dissertation, Ohio State University, 2006.

The author approaches Afro-Colombian hip hop as a form of testimonial revealing what young black Colombians perceive about the challenges of globalization. Various factors that interpolate Afro-Colombian ethnic identities constructed through music and its practices are also researched. Finds that globalization and neoliberal reforms have aggravated sociopolitical issues through intensified warfare, poverty, income inequalities, massive displacement, violence and other aspects of life. Also concludes that we cannot understand Afro-Colombian hip hop without understanding its history and culture, and how they are affected by global processes.

1241. Dominello, Zachariah. "Keepin' it Real Mate: A Study of Identity in Australian Hip Hop." *Griffith University Working Papers in Pragmatics and Intercultural Communication* 1(1) (2008): 40–47, Brisbane, Qld, Australia: Griffith University.

Explores areas of identity formation in the United States and Australia. Examined phonological differences between Australian hip hop artists' performance speech and regular speech. His primary focus was to determine how artists represent their Australian-ness.

1242. Durand, Alain-Philippe, ed. *Black, Banc, Beur: Rap Music and Hip-Hop Culture in the Francophone World.* Lantham, MD: Scarecrow Press, 2002.

This is the first book-length work on French rap music and hip hop culture written in English. The scholarly contributions include Andre

J.M. Prevos' discussion of French rap production since the 1980s; Jean-Marie Jacono's musicological analysis of rhythm, sampling and speech flow in IAM; Gaf Larage's illumination of parallels between stylistic diversity and the spatial and sociological landscapes of Marseilles; Anthony Pecqueux's study of artistic-audience reactions during concerts; and Michelle Auzabbeau's discussion of the linguistic meaning of rap in Gabon. The central theme is how rap revolves around conceptions of authenticity and identity. Because the essays are not full of theoretical jargon, the book is understandable for students and others interested in the diffusion of rap and hip hop culture outside of the United States.

1243.  Easton, Paul and Sean Ross. "Rap Gets Freer Rein on U.K. Radio." *Billboard*, 24 November 1990, 12.

A comparison between the amount of airplay given to rap in the United States and in the UK. Also discusses differences in movement of singles on the rap charts in the UK and the United States.

1244.  Fenn III, John Bennett. "Rap and Ragga Musical Cultures, Lifestyles, and Performance in Malawi." PhD dissertation, Indiana University, 2004.

Ethnographic fieldwork was conducted over a two-year period to ascertain how youths in Malawi engage with rap and ragga musical genres in their daily social life. Using performance as a central thesis, the author presents three case studies on the consumption and production of rap and ragga. The first study is situated in the rural district of Nkhta Bay, the second in the urban center of Bintyre, and the third followed the cosmopolitan orientations of Malawi youth who move between the urban centers of Blantyre or Lilongwe and various locations in the United States, United Kingdom and South Africa. The performance contexts included rap and ragga competitions, recording studios, soccer fields, school grounds and patios. Findings show that in each context, performance comprises social practices informed by musical ethos, ideas and material culture in a variety of ways.

1245.  Ferrigno, Emily Daus. "Technologies of Emotion: Creating and Performing Drum 'n' Bass." PhD dissertation, Wesleyan University, 2008.

Drum 'n' bass emerged as a genre of electronic dance music in London in the early 1990s. This study focuses on the contemporary drum 'n' bass scene typically found at raves in the United States, presenting the practices, artistic philosophies, and stylistic preferences of producers and DJs. Examines the relationship between affect and sound to study the creative processes behind drum 'n' bass production, while simultaneously viewing the genre as a musical expression of its cultural context.

1246. Fischer, Dawn-Elissa Tive Ighosotu. "'Kobushi Ageroo! (Pump Ya Fist!)': Blackness, 'Race' and Politics in Japanese Hip Hop." PhD dissertation, University of Florida, 1997.

Researches how specific communities of Japanese hip hoppers translate their political identities within an imaginary black diaspora. Also focuses on the performance of "blackness" by using black English, hip hop language, ideology and other aspects of hip hop aesthetics in ways that reflect the intersection of racialized, gendered and sexualized identifications. Another objective was to understand the discursive qualities of "race" as an organizing principle of social order when its existence cannot be reduced to origins, histories, or biology.

1247. Flores, Juan. *From Bomba to Hip-Hop: Puerto Rican Culture and Latino Identity.* New York: Columbia University Press, 2000.

At the core of this book is a challenge to the notion that hip hop culture is solely created by African Americans, and a need to document Puerto Ricans' contributions to the phenomenon. Anecdotal and historical evidence demonstrates Puerto Rican creativity and involvement in shaping hip hop throughout the years. The book is important because, to my knowledge, it is the first book to contextualize the Puerto Rican involvement in hip hop culture from its earliest days.

1248. Green, Alecia. "Whose Revolution is Televised?: Young African Nova Scotian Women Respond to Sexual Politics in Hip Hop Culture and Everyday Life." Masters thesis, Halifax, NS: Saint Mary's University, 2007.

Researches responses of young African Nova Scotian women to images of black female bodies depicted in three popular hip hop videos. Grounded in black feminist theory, she elicits the opinions of five university students and concludes that factors such as academic achievement, spirituality and communal affiliation acted as bases for the counter-hegemonic viewing of the images, and that the participants describe black female beauty as a quality that emanates from the inside.

1249. Halasa, Malu. "London Calling: Brit Hip Hop Heats Up." *Cash Box,* 27 May 1989, 12.

This article, in a special edition on rap, presents a historical overview of British hip hop. Discusses popular rap acts, the difficulties historically experienced by rap groups in getting live gigs, and the close relationship between rap and dance music.

1250.  Henderson, April K. "Gifted Flows: Engaging Narratives of Hip Hop and Samoan Diaspora." PhD dissertation, University of California, Santa Cruz, 2007.

An exploration of Samoan involvement with hip hop culture, with special focus on Aotearoa, New Zealand. The author examines Samoan artists' articulations of sameness and difference, and belonging and not belonging, by using discourses of authenticity that are central to both Samoan and hip hop cultures.

1251.  Hochman, Steve. "Hispanic Rappers Stake Out New Turf." *Rolling Stone*, 15 November 1990, 36–37.

Discusses the contributions, growing influence and popularity of Hispanic rappers. The author notes that Hispanics have been involved since the beginnings of rap, and focuses on the successful albums of Kid Frost and Mellow Man Ace. He also mentions other Chicano rappers, discusses the effect that rap has had on Chicano youth, and how the dominance of African American rappers has affected Hispanic rap.

1252.  Ibrahim, Awad el Karim Mohamed. "Hey, Whassup Homeboy? Becoming Black; Race, Language, Culture, and the Politics of Identity; African Students in a Franco-Ontarian High School." PhD dissertation, University of Toronto, 1998.

Looks at African youth in a French-language high school in Toronto, how and where they form and perform their social identities, and their process of learning a language. Using ethnography of performance as a methodology, he investigates the process of identity formation as a creolization, translation and negotiation phenomenon. In addition, he offers an alternative anti-racism scheme to determine what works and does not work for the students.

1253.  Jabbaar-Gyambrah, Tara Aminah (Ama Sika). "Hip-Hop, Hip-Life: Global Sistahs." PhD dissertation, State University of New York at Buffalo, 2007.

The study examines African American and Ghanaian women's roles and representations in hip hop and hip life. Discusses the history and origins of hip hop in the South Bronx, and hip hop life in Ghana. Research methods included interviews, participant-observation, ethnography, data collection, audio and video recordings, and subject and cultural analyses. Focuses on themes of gender, resistance and a legacy of place. Argues that women's roles are connected through resistance, sociocultural historical experiences, and the transmission of culture and ideologies.

1254. Jeffs, Nick. "Counting the Beatz: Hip Hop Culture, Commercialisation and the State in Aotearoa, New Zealand." Masters thesis, Auckland University of Technology (AUT), 2006.

Explores the interplay between hip hop culture, music, and the state and commercial entities in New Zealand. Analyzes the relationship between those who embrace hip hop as a phenomenon capable of creating a public good and organizations which exploit this culture as a musical form, and the role of the state in mediating between public good and private consumption.

1255. Kelley, Robin D.G., ed. *The Vinyl Ain't Final: Hip-Hop and the Globalisation of Black Popular Culture.* New York: Pluto Press, 2006.

An exploration of hip hop as both culture and commodity from a variety of perspectives. The articles explore the gap between American-oriented hip hop and its global dissemination. Perspectives from the UK, Cuba, Germany, Hawaii, Japan, Samoa, South Africa and the United States provide insights into local and global implications of hip hop. Issues like cultural politics and cultural production are also discussed.

1256. Keyes, Cheryl. "At The Crossroads: Rap Music and Its African Nexus." *Ethnomusicology* 40(2) (Spring/Summer 1996): 223–49.

Explores Africanisms in rap through fieldwork conducted in Detroit, Los Angeles and New York City. Discusses the interdependence between sociocultural and musical change, black language, rhetorical style, music-making practices and non-musica-lingual practices. Transcriptions from Grandmaster Flash and the Furious Five, Chuck D and Public Enemy, and the theoretical paradigms of Henry Louis Gates, Jr and others support her claims.

1257. Krims, Adam. *Rap Music and the Poetics of Identity.* New Perspectives in Music History and Criticism. Cambridge, UK: Cambridge University Press, 2000.

Krims acknowledges the limitations of his study, that he is a middle-class white academic "examining vernacular culture." Discusses the musical poetics of rap and how poetics can be used as a mapping of social mediation. The strands of mediation include audience reflection, geography and style. He deconstructs the flow, musical style and topics of Bohemian rap, Mack rap, jazz/party rap and reality rap. He credits the west coast style of Dr. Dre and Snoop Dogg for using live instrumentation with heavy bass and keyboard, and presents a clear distinction between the Cleveland and New York styles of MCing. Chapter four presents a somewhat controversial use of

W.E.B. DuBois' theory of "double consciousness" to discuss "The Souls of Rap Folk" in reconciling their urban and rural identities. A highlight of the book is his discussion of selected rap groups outside the United States, including the Dutch rappers Osdorp Posse and the Spookriders, and Bannock and the Cree of Alberta, Canada.

1258. LaPointe, Kirk. "Nasty Rap Reaches Canada." *Billboard*, 3 November 1990, 90.

A concise account of a London, Ontario, record retailer being charged for violating obscenity laws because he sold *As Nasty As They Wanna Be*, the classic by 2 Live Crew.

1259. ———. "Rapper Maestro Fresh-Wes Teaches Canadian A&R Execs a Lesson." *Billboard*, 12 May 1990, 31.

Covers the success of rapper Maestro Fresh-Wes, his effect on Canadian rap, and the difficulties he experienced trying to secure a record contract. Also compares the Canadian and American rap scenes.

1260. Laurie, Shoshanna Kira. "Funk and Hip-hop Transculture in the 'Divided' Brazilian City." PhD dissertation, Stanford University, 2000.

Discusses the changing racial and spatial identifications that are rooted in the globalization of African American cultural forms and their respective ideologies. The author uses theories of globalization of culture to discuss consensus-building through culture and engages this with issues of lyrical content, dance, journalism, media and interviews. Situates her discussion within the racial polarization and social disparities of Brazil, and argues that the new Brazilian identities are forming which contradict identities formed by colonialism and post colonialism entities and issues.

1261. Malinowski, Stuart. "Race, Resistance and Rap Music." Masters thesis, University of Alberta, 1995.

Explores the relationship between black youth and rap music, especially when rap is perceived and used as a form of resistance. Interviews with sixteen black Canadians (nine males, seven females) demonstrated that they did perceive the music as a form of resistance.

1262. Mapuranga, Tapiwa Praise. *Gangsters for Christ: Youth Identity in Gospel, Rap and Hip-Hop Music in Harae.* Harae: University of Zimbabwe, 2006.

An interesting and provocative study of the impact that gangster rappers have had on the singing of gospel music in Harae. Focuses on the construction of identity, and whether society views them as real Christians singing for God, and more.

1263. Maxwell, Ian. *Phat Beats, Dope Rhymes: Hip Hop Down Under Comin' Upper*. Middletown, CT: Wesleyan University Press, 2003.

The author uses anthropological and musical analyses to present a post-modern cultural critique of the presence of hip hop in Sydney, Australia, between 1992 to 1994. His scholarly approach is concerned with the formation of identity, creation of a hip hop community in Sydney, and the relationship of Sydney hip hop to the global hip hop community. Incorporated within his discussion is the impact of hip hop on Australia, and reasons why hip hop has gained a foothold in Sydney, Australia.

1264. McDonald, David A. "My Voice is My Weapon: Music, Nationalism, and the Poetics of Palestinian Resistance." PhD dissertation, University of Illinois Press, 2006.

The focus is on the dynamics of music, nationalism and resistance as realized through performance among Palestinians in Israel, the Occupied Territories and Jordan. Three interrelated sites of performance were studied—Amman, Jordan; Ramallah, West Bank; and Tel Aviv, Israel—along with three repertoires of Palestinian resistance music (indigenous Palestinian folk songs, protest songs, and popular hip hop and rap. Examines the Palestinian hip hop movement as a new direction in resistance music.

1265. Mitchell, Tony, ed. *Global Noise: Rap and Hip-Hop Music Outside the USA*. Middletown, CT: Wesleyan University Press, 2001.

A collection of essays that detail the history, status and style of rap music in the global community. Each essay covers a different country; almost equally divided between Asia and Europe, they cover Australia, Bulgaria, Canada, Germany, Italy, Japan, the UK, South Korea and New Zealand, plus the Basque and Maori ethnicities. Illustrates that rap is used for distinct and different purposes by different cultures and communities. The essays are well researched and consistent with the theme of rap's distinct social, cultural and expressive purposes in different nations. However, a possible drawback is that many of the performers cited in the essays are unknown to the average American hip hop and rap fan.

1266. Mulholland, Mary-Lee. *Annotated Bibliography of Canadian Theses and Dissertations on Diversity*. Toronto: York University, 2001.

Contains over 1,500 entries on diversity topics completed at Canadian Universities. The emphasis is on ethnocultural, racial, religious, linguistic and immigrant issues. Contains some entries on hip hop.

1267. Neale, Patrick. *Where You're At: Noises From the Frontline of a Hip-Hop Planet*. New York: Riverhead, 2004.

A well-written and well researched narrative by a British novelist who crafted this account after visits to Johannesburg, New York, Rio de Janeiro and Tokyo. The strength of this assessment is the author's ability to conceptualize and compare the different approaches to hip hop. His unique ability to recognize the different cultural approaches is complemented by his ability to conceptualize and discern generic phenomenon in global hip hop.

1268. Okumura, Kozo. "Far East Coast is in da House: Examination of Hip Hop Culture in Japan." Masters thesis, Michigan State University, 1998.

The thesis accompanies a thirty-two-minute documentary video on hip hop culture in Japan. Provides background data on hip hop culture and art forms and discusses the schism between it and traditional Japanese values. The video demonstrates Japanese hip hop street culture.

1269. Osumare, Halifu. *The Africanist Aesthetic in Global Hip-Hop: Power Moves.* New York: Palgrave Macmillan, 2008.

Presents two major reasons for the proliferation of hip hop throughout the world: the global centrality of African American popular culture and the transnational pop culture industry of record companies and entertainment conglomerates, and "connective marginalities" that are extant social inequalities of an underground network of hip hop communities.

1270. ———. "African Aesthetics, American Culture: Hip Hop in the Global Era." PhD dissertation, University of Honolulu, 2002.

Explores the four artistic components of hip hop—rap, B-boying and B-girling, aerosol art (graffiti art), and DJing—as part of a global pop culture. Research is based on internet and library research, fieldwork and analysis of lyrics. Focuses on issues like the cultural synthesis, hip hop history, creative principles steeped in an Africanist aesthetic, and the effect of economics and media in the creation and dissemination of hip hop. Concludes that hip hop culture embodies a methodology that can foster a self-reflexive improvisatory stance that can ameliorate postmodern pressures for a younger generation.

1271. Pardue, Derek Parkman. "Brazilian Hip-Hop Material and Ideology: A Case of Cultural Design." *Image and Narrative* 10 (March 2005): 23–31.

The author developed a theory called "Cultural Design," which incorporates the critical and generative aspects of graphic arts and social science. His major premise is that people order the world into meaningful environments through orchestrations of text, image movements and sound. He also espouses the importance of individual or group occupations. Research was conducted in San Paulo, Brazil, for the author's dissertation. [See also item 1272.]

1272. ——. "Blackness and Periphery: A Retelling of Marginality in Hip Hop Culture of Sao Paulo, Brazil." PhD dissertation, University of Illinois, 2004.

He addresses the two main concepts used by Brazilian hip hoppers in the construction of meaning: the processes and technologies by which practitioners perform and produce hip hop, and how hip hoppers mediate articulations between themselves and society. Argues that Brazilian hip hop constructs arenas for citizenship debates, educational debates, economic development, and more. Based upon four years of fieldwork in Sao Paulo, Brazil. [See also item 1271.]

1273. ——. "Writing in the Margins: Brazilian Hip-Hop as an Educational Project." *Anthropology and Education* 35(4) (2004): 411–32.

Pardue is one of the first scholars to document hip hop's connection to educational practices. The study, based on fieldwork conducted in a Sao Paulo, Brazil, youth correctional facility in 1999 and 2002, aimed to ascertain how state institutional practices mediated hip hop educational practices in the aforementioned correctional facility.

1274. Perry, Marc D. "Los Raperos: Rap, Race, Ethnicity, and the Performance of Diasporic Identities." PhD dissertation, University of Texas, 2004.

An exploration of the emergent *Movimiento de Hip Hop* (Cuban hip hop movement) as a critical site in which to examine the interplay of race and social transformation in contemporary Cuba. Focuses on ways that young Cubans use rap to fashion a new black identity, and rap as a race-based social critique. Argues that rap and hip hop represent an active social agent within the shifting transnational race formation that is transpiring in contemporary Cuba.

1275. Perullo, Alex. "Hooligans and Heroes: Youth Identity and Hip-Hop in Dar es Salaam." *Africa Today* 51(4) (Summer 2005): 74–103.

A discussion of the rise of hip hop culture in Tanzania in the 1990s, and the increased public scrutiny that occurred as a result. The news media labeled the youth as disruptive, hostile and violent *wahuni* (hooligans). As a result, youth sought to combat these negative stereotypes by using music to portray themselves as creative and empowered individuals in society. The author examines the ways that youth used music to confront the negative stereotypes, and to broadcast their political and social relevant messages to a wider audience. Argues that youth have used rap to impart their message of social empowerment, thereby creating a sense of community among other urban youth.

1276. Poteet, Morgan B. "Cultural Identity and Identity Performance Among Latin American Youths in Toronto." Masters thesis, Toronto: York University, 2005.

The study focuses on Latin American youth in Toronto. The author approaches identity as performance and demonstrates that youths are involved in the transformation of their identities and in the representation of their communities. Findings reveal that hip hop provides the resources necessary to assert an idealized identity in a social context of racism and marginalization.

1277. Potts, Kerry L. "'Music is the Weapon': Music as an Anti-Colonial Tool for Aboriginal People in Toronto." Masters thesis, University of Toronto, 2006.

The author is concerned with how music as a public medium can transcend dominant racist narratives to create avenues through which Aboriginal identity can be articulated and experienced. Argues that music can be used by Aboriginals as a tool to decolonialize themselves and their nation. Includes interviews with musicians (e.g. Lucie Idlout, Leela Gilday, Derek Miller, Elaine Bomberry of Rez Bluez), traditional singers (e.g. The Eagle Heart Singers, Red Spirit Singers, Morning Star River and Spirit Wind), and music industry people who were involved with the Aboriginal community of Toronto. Author notes that blues and hip hop are being used to foster relationships between the black and Aboriginal communities of Toronto.

1278. Quinn, Eithne. "Black British Cultural Studies and The Rap on Gangsta." *Black Music Research Journal* 20(2) (Fall 2000): 195–217.

A theoretical and provocative essay that draws upon theories by British scholars like Stuart Hall, Kobena Mercer and Paul Gilroy, and American scholars like Houston Baker, Henry Louis Gates, Jr, and George Lipsitz to discuss gangsta rap within the complex issue of representation. Uses the theme of racial uplift and the music of artists like Easy E and Dr. Dre to view gangsta rap through the prism of selected British cultural studies scholars.

1279. Rahfaldt, Michal J. "Music-Based Radio and Youth Education in South Africa." PhD dissertation, University of Michigan, 2007.

His argument is centered on the theory that music-based radio is a primary reference point for social relations around which South

African youth position themselves. The primary focus is on youth relationships with music-based radio stations, presenters and content, and investigates the issues that are endemic to these social dynamics. Research methodologies includes field notes, interviews, focus groups, radio production workshops and a listener-centric approach.

1280. Raphael-Hernandez, Heike, ed. *The Blackening of Europe: The African American Presence.* New York: Routledge, 2004.

Covers the influence and impact of black contact in Europe (e.g. Josephine Baker, jazz, blues, rap and hip hop), issues of identity, and much more. Of special importance to scholars of hip hop are the numerous essays that deal with the acceptance, impact and transformation of African American musical forms in different European cultures (UK, France, Germany, Romania, Russia and Spain). The book is divided into three sections: "Creating a Foundation," "Accompanying Europe into the Twenty-first Century," and "Turning into a Theory for Europe." Foreword by Paul Gilroy.

1281. Rivière, Melisa. "Son Dos Alas: The Cultural Diffusion of Hip-Hop in Cuba and Puerto Rico." PhD dissertation, University of Minnesota, 2005.

Based on fieldwork in Cuba and Puerto Rico, the author documents the cultural diffusion of the four elements of hip hop (rap, B-boying and B-girling, graffiti art, and breakdancing) in both countries. She also produced songs with artists from each location and created a musical dialogue between them.

1282. Ross, Sean. "In Canada, Hunt is On for Rap, Dance Talent." *Billboard,* 31 March 1990, 1.

Article covers the first Canadian rap hit by Maestro Fresh-Wes entitled "Let Your Backbone Slide." Details the impact of the hit on signing other Canadian dance and rap artists, and focuses on the role of Canadian demographics on record label attitudes toward African American music.

1283. Sackeyfio, Christina N.T. "Hip-Hop Cultural Identities: A Review of the Literature and its Implications for the Schooling of African-Canadian Youth." Masters thesis, University of Toronto, 2006.

Examines the impact of hip hop on black cultural identity formation and development in African Canadian youth. Uses existing literature on hip hop and the Canadian context to address its pedagogical potential. The author is concerned with ways that hip hop can be used in classroom teaching, specifically with the relationship between identity and schooling, the pedagogical relevance of hip hop culture, and how the aforementioned ideas intersect and contribute to the debate on alternative schooling.

1284. Saleh-Hanna, Viviane. "Lyrical Passages Through Crime: An Afrobeat, Hip Hop and Reggae Production, Featuring Black Criminology." PhD dissertation, Indiana University, 2007.

Analyzes black oppression produced through the lyrics of black musicians who create socially conscious black liberation musicianship. Following the geography of the European cross-Atlantic slave trade, the author documents black musicians' ideologies in the lyrics of Afrobeat in Nigeria, reggae in Jamaica and hip hop in the United States. The research tries to desegregate academic scholarship on blackness from the analyses and knowledge present in black musicianship.

1285. Sneed, Paul Michael. "Machine Gun Voices: Bandits, Favelas, and Utopia in Brazilian Funk." PhD dissertation, University of Wisconsin, 2003.

In Brazil, funk is a form of popular culture from the *favelas*, the hillside slums of Rio De Janeiro. The author's methodology combines cultural and literary theory to examine irony, complex masking, and subversive messages and practices inherent in funk. In addition, he discusses drug abuse, the social and economic organization of the Rocinha community, ideologies of criminal factions, and funk as both a form of entertainment and as a black Atlantic culture.

1286. Templeton, Inez H. "What's So German About It? Cultural Identity in the Berlin Hip Hop Scene." PhD dissertation, Scotland, UK: University of Stirling, 2005–06.

Attempts to determine whether local interpretation of hip hop in Berlin, Germany, is still reliant on its African American origins. The author uses a theoretical approach to move beyond globalization. Focuses on the meanings that young Berliners assign to the hip hop practices within their cultural context, and in the ways in which Berlin spaces and places shape the cultural practices found there. Based on field work on the Berlin hip hop scene.

1287. Thompson, Robert Ferris. "Hip-Hop 101." *Rolling Stone*, 27 March 1986, 95–100

Written by a highly respected scholar of African and African American culture, one who has long espoused African retentions in African American culture. This is one of the earliest essays to lend credibility to African influence in rap music. Traces the roots of rap to Africa, and asserts that rap is the continuation of numerous African-derived and influenced cultural characteristics that are present in

North American African American culture. Well reasoned and well researched.

1288. Tiongson, Jr, Antonio T. "Filipino Youth Cultural Politics and DJ Culture." PhD dissertation, University of California, San Diego, 2006.

He investigates an emergent form of expression that is associated with Filipino youth identities, especially notions of ethnicity, gender, generational issues, and race and what they mean to Filipinos in the United States and in the Filipino diaspora. Interviewed Filipino DJs and researched existing periodical literature to develop insights into the ways that Filipino youth contest their placement within the racial hierarchies and economic structures of the United States, and the way that identities can be imagined that both challenge and accommodate the boundaries assigned to them.

1289. Valdes, Alberto Domingo Gonzalez. "Rapeando en el 'Periodo Especial': Espectro integrativo de la cultura Hip-Hop en Cuba." PhD dissertation, University of Connecticut, 2006.

He explores the Cuban hip hop movement 1990 as a critical site in which to examine cultural and social relations within contemporary Cuba. Encompasses the aesthetic, compositional, and interpretative dimensions of Cuban hip hop. Uses textual analysis, rhythmic analysis, and literary and cultural values to draw conclusions. In addition, he examines the impact of Cuban hip hop as a subversion of cultural identity, and the resultant impact that this movement has had within and outside state institutions. In English.

1290. Walcott, Renaldo Wayne. "Performing the Postmodern: Black Atlantic Rap and Identity in North America." PhD dissertation, University of Toronto, 1996.

The author addresses the dialectics of black cultural politics and hip hop culture by discussing representation and performativity, and by positioning them within both black cultural studies and postmodernism. Argues that understanding blackness as performative is crucial in the deconstruction of the complex and shifting identities of black Atlantic expressive cultures, and for non-blacks who wish to be politically important players in black cultural politics as exemplified in hip hop. Uses rap music and hip hop culture to demonstrate how a postmodern black subjectivity is evident in cultural politics, how black Atlantic memory and dialogues produce a multiplicity of identities, and how black expressive culture can be used to locate and read black cultural practices and identifications.

1291. Walker, Tahombe. "The Hip-Hop Worldview: An Afrocentric Analysis." PhD dissertation, Temple University, 1998.

Rather than studying a specific culture outside the United States, this research presents a perspective that the author feels is missing from hip hop scholarship of that time, specifically that Eurocentric critics and scholars have failed to acknowledge that the rap music industry is a clearinghouse for American popular culture. The Afrocentric perspective adds another facet to the dominant Eurocentric analyses and perspectives of the time. Research is based on twenty interviews of hip hop practitioners that focus on hip hop as an art form, lifestyle and world view. The work is significant because it is one of the few studies from this period to advocate an African-centered perspective when analyzing or discussing hip hop, and because it reinforced cultural agency by encouraging the artists to discuss hip hop in their own terms.

1292. Warikoo, Natasha Kumar. "The Cultural Worlds of Second-Generation Teenagers in London and New York." PhD dissertation, Harvard University, 2005.

Analyzes the cultural worlds of children of immigrants to determine the utility of theories of oppositional culture and downward assimilation for the second generation. The author collected data via a random survey and interviews of students aged fourteen to seventeen, in multi-ethnic working-class schools in London and New York City: 120 interviews with Afro-Caribbean and Indian youth in both cities, Indo-Caribbeans in New York City, and white English youth in London. Her findings indicated that the downward assimilation theory does not hold, that the youth emphasize hip hop musical preferences.

1293. Warner, Remi. "Battles Over Borders: Hiphop and the Politics and Poetics of Race and Place in the New South Africa." PhD dissertation, Toronto: York University, 2007.

This is an exploration of the diverse ways that South African youth— in Cape Town, Johannesburg and the surrounding townships— appropriate, translate and perform global hip hop musical-cultural forms as a means to negotiate identities and social positions of race, class, ethnicity and gender in post-apartheid South Africa. The author concludes that a global hip hop "grammar of blackness" is prompting a timely meditation of identity and community in the post-apartheid era.

1294. Whiteley, Sheila, Andy Bennett and Stan Hawkins. *Music, Space, and Place: Popular Music and Cultural Identity.* Burlington, VT: Ashgate, 2004.

The book examines the urban and rural spaces in which music is experienced, produced and consumed. The central thesis is that music takes place within a particular space and place, and is shaped by specific musical practices and by economic and political pressures. A particular focus is on rap that has shaped identities of socially marginalized groups in Cuba, France, Italy, New Zealand and South Africa. Issues of authorship, creativity, musical texts and gender politics are discussed, and are combined with community and identity, race, vernaculars, power, performance and production.

## PHOTOGRAPHY

1295. Cooper, Martha (photographer), Akim Walta, Charlie Ahearn, Patti Astor, FABEL and ZEPHYR. *Hip Hop Files: Photographs, 1979–1984*. New York: Powerhouse, 2004.

A collection of photographs of New York hip hop culture in the early 1980s. Text by Charlie Ahearn, FABEL and ZEPHYR accompanies photographs of pioneers like Afrika Bambaataa, Rock Steady Crew and Fab 5 Freddy, plus numerous graffiti artists, B-boys and B-girls, DJs and MCs.

1296. Hager, Steven. *Hip Hop: The Illustrated History of Break Dancing*. New York: St Martin's, 1984.

This is one of the first attempts to chronicle an important component of hip hop culture: breakdancing. Hager provides a glimpse into the development of early Bronx-based hip hop. His assessments are concise and easy to understand; the text is enhanced by numerous photographs.

1297. Kenner, Rob and George Pitts. *VX: 10 Years of Vibe Photography*. New York: Vibe, 2003.

This is a collection of photographs published in *Vibe* magazine between 1993 and 2003, plus some not previously published. Also contains a collection of candid photographs and additional images from David LaChapelle, Baron Claiborne, Melodie McDaniels, Ellen Von Unwerth, Albert Watson and many more. Foreword by *Vibe* founder Quincy Jones.

1298. Malone, Bonz and Nicole Beattle. *Hip Hop Immortals: The Remix*. New York: Thunder's Mouth Press; New York: Da Capo Press, 2003.

Photographs by David LaChapelle, Jesse Frohman, Nitin Vadukul and Christian Witkin are supplemented with text by Bonz Malone. The candid photographs (black and white and color) depict provocative images of hip hop pioneers like Dr. Dre, Notorious B.I.G.,

Kurtis Blow, Lil' Kim, DJ Kool Herc, Public Enemy, Ice-T, Run-DMC and others.

1299. Paniccioli, Ernie. *Who Shot Ya? Three Decades of Hip Hop Photographs.* New York: Amistad, 2002.

This collection by the renowned hip hop photographer contains more than 200 images of many hip hop greats, including Notorious B.I.G., Kurtis Blow, Grandmaster Flash, DJ Kool Herc, Queen Latifah, Tupac Shakur and Will Smith. Paniccioli's collection is important because of its scope, following the history and evolution of hip hop since its origins in the early 1980s.

1300. Powell, Ricky. *Oh Snap! The Rap Photography of Rick Powell.* New York: St Martin's Griffin, 1998.

Images from ads, publicity shots and rap. The more than eighty images, captioned by the author, include the likenesses of artists like Public Enemy, Run-DMC, L.L. Cool J, Cypress Hill, Method Man and others.

## POLITICS

1301. Alridge, Daniel. "From Civil Rights to Hip Hop: Toward A Nexus of Ideas." *The Journal of African American History* 90(3) (2005): 226–53.

The author addresses the schism between hip hoppers and the Civil Rights generation, and argues that they share common ideas and ideologies with the Civil Rights, Black Power and other struggles for black freedom. He finds common ground for the two sides to forge collaborations and coalitions to continue the ongoing struggle for the liberation of blacks and other oppressed peoples.

1302. Asante, Jr, M.K. *It's Bigger Than Hip Hop: The Rise of the Post-Hip-Hop Generation.* New York: St Martin's Griffin, 2009.

Portrays hip hop as a vehicle for a larger discussion about social and political issues affecting the post-hip hop generation. Theorizes a new group of youth which is seeking an understanding of itself outside of the commodified, self-destructive image of the corporate hip hop monopoly.

1303. Boyd, Todd. *The New H.N.I.C. (Head Niggas in Charge): The Death of Civil Rights and the Reign of Hip Hop.* New York: New York University Press, 2002.

Boyd's primary thesis is cited in the title: "the death of civil rights" and "the reign of hip hop." Summarizes the relationship when he asserts that "hip hop has rejected and now replaced the pious, sanctimonious nature of civil rights as the defining moment of blackness" (p. xxi). Clearly elucidates the difference between rap and hip hop, and distinctions between hip hop genres (e.g. gangsta rap, conscious hip hop), and provides a glossary of hip hop and rap terms. Argues that hip hop has brought about substantive economic, social and political change and underlines hip hoppers' contributions to that change. Because of the author's insider status and experiences with the hip hop community, this is an important addition to the literature.

1304. Bynoe, Yvonne. *Stand and Deliver: Political Activism, Leadership, and Hip Hop Culture.* Brooklyn, NY: Soft Skull Press, 2004.

Bynoe advocates replacing black charismatic but ineffectual leaders with "citizen–leaders" who are engaged in a policy-centered relationship with the white power structure. She demonstrates how hip hoppers can create a more sophisticated dialogue about what constitutes leadership, politics and political action. Asserts that leadership evolves from influence, and that influence is an outgrowth of the ability to deliver or to deny money, votes, or both to a politician or political party. Presents a detailed overview of black activism since the 1970s, including the Black Panthers' ten-point plan, interviews with figures like Clarence Lusane, Kate Rhee, Newark City Councilman (now mayor) Cory Booker, and hip hop entrepreneur Sean "Puffy" Combs.

1305. Daniels, Lee S. *The State of Black America, 2001.* Washington, DC: National Urban League, 2001.

An annual national assessment of the breath and depth of the cultural, educational, economic and political issues confronting the well-being of African Americans. Also covers issues like black Americans and the internet, home ownership and housing, male and female identities, and the socioeconomic divide that exists among African Americans under the age of thirty-five. The two articles on rap, by Yvonne Bynoe and David W. Brown, offer insights into the roots of the music and thoughts on rap music as representative of hip hop culture.

1306. Evans, Derek James. "It's Bigger Than Hip Hop: Popular Rap Music and the Politics of the Hip Hop Generation." Masters thesis, University of Missouri, 2007.

Begins with the premise that rap music could serve as the next vehicle of the Civil Rights movement. Yet the extent to which rap music has addressed post-Civil Rights political issues has not been researched. The author's primary purpose is to determine the political issues most important to African Americans, and to analyze the extent to which the most popular rap songs address the issues.

1307. Eyerman, Ron and Andrew Jamison. *Music and Social Movements: Mobilizing Traditions in the Twentieth Century.* Cambridge: Cambridge University Press, 1998.

The authors use a meso-level approach to centralize the importance of cultural forms and practices, and to provide a cognitive approach to social movements. They argue that music is both knowledge and action and part of the frameworks of interpretation and representation produced within social movements. They believe that the civil rights movement imbued soul music with a special intensity and responsibility. They include the sociomusical contributions of Arrested Development in their discussion of rap.

1308. Forman, Murray Webster. *The 'Hood' Comes First: Race, Space, and Place in Rap and Hip-Hop Musical Culture.* Middletown, CT: Wesleyan University Press, 2002.

Forman's primary objective is to examine the "spatial dimensions" of rap music and hip hop culture. He situates his argument within the social construction of space which has always been a significant factor in the creation and evolution of rap and hip hop. First, he frames hip hop within the urban experience and thereafter deconstructs its spatial dimensions into discursive space, textual space, industrial or organizational space, and the material spaces of the "real." He uses a variety of theoretical approaches, including the ideas of Houston Baker, Paul Gilroy and Henri Lefebvre to assign meanings to hip hop practices absent the exponents of rap or hip hop. Although the book is deeply indebted to interpretative theory, the first two chapters ("Hip Hop and the Spatial Perspective" and a review of the literature on spatial discourse) are both informative for those not conversant with rap or hip hop.

1309. ———. "The Hood Comes First: Race, Space, and Place in Rap Music and Hip Hop, 1978–96." PhD dissertation, Montreal: McGill University, 1996.

The dissertations covers the evolution of rap music and hip hop culture from two spatial modalities. First, he introduces the theoretical construct of a geographic scale and sociospatial values as a method to examine rap and hip hop's geo-cultural expansions from their beginnings in urban African American communities. He also analyses the processes and structuring logic of how rap has been integrated into localized musical scenes and transnational music and media industries. In addition, issues regarding the dynamics between race, social space and youth are assessed. The author concludes that emphasizing the "hood" is a significant element of the genre; researches the "hood" as an important factor in the reproduction of spatial sensibilities in hip hop culture.

1310. George, Nelson. *Hip Hop America*. New York: Viking Press, 1998.

A thorough discussion of the business, culture and politics of hip hop. Outlines the history of the movement from its beginnings in urban communities to its status as a multi-million-dollar international business. Addresses the concerns of academics who complain that publications by some of their colleagues are an attempt to change their disciplines because they are writing about subjects that they know little about. Others believe that hip hop is one-dimensional thuggery and does not deserve the attention of a scholar.

1311. Hendershott, Heidi A. "The Politics and Pedagogies of Rap Music." PhD dissertation, Pennsylvania State University, 2004.

The author explores the pedagogical implications of rap music, especially the ideologies that work to find the public pedagogy of rap, how rap music has changed throughout its history, and the social, political and economic issues that have influenced the production of rap music over the last three decades. Researches rap music as a pedagogical tool in education curricula, and how it can be used to address questions of gender, inequality, power, race and representation.

1312. Hill, Marc Lamont. *(Re)negotiating Knowledge, Power, and Identities in Hip-Hop Literature*. Philadelphia: University of Pennsylvania Press, 2005.

This ethnographic study demonstrates how knowledge, power and student interpretations are negotiated and renegotiated as hip hop culture becomes an acceptable and official part of their curriculum of Howard High School. Focuses on the student-teacher relationship and how relationships reconfigured roles of students, teachers and researchers within the classroom.

1313. Hoch, Danny. *Jails, Hospitals, and Hip-Hop and Some People*. New York: Villard, 1998.

A unique commentary on the power of hip hop to influence people outside of the African American community. The author's interest stems from hip hop's ability to heal and he provides numerous accounts of this (including a white teenager who wanted to become a gangsta rapper and a Puerto Rican on crutches who wanted to become a dancer).

1314. Kitwana, Bakari. *The Hip Hop Generation: Young Blacks and the Crisis in African American Culture*. New York: Basic Civitas, 2002.

Concerned with finding solutions to some of the social issues and challenges faced by African American youth who embrace hip hop attitudes and values. He defines the hip hop generation as individuals born between 1969 and 1984, and presents possible solutions, but has little proof that his recommendations are adaptable to hip hop youth.

1315. Maher, George Ciccariello. "Brechtian Hip-Hop: Didactics and Self-Production in Post-Gangsta Political Mixtapes." *Journal of Black Studies* 36(1) (September 2005): 129–39.

This article uses the theories of Bertolt Brecht (1898–1956) to understand current issues and developments in political rap. The author focuses on the theory of self-production and didactics to determine meaning in the mixtapes of Dead Perez. He also situates Dead Perez between N.W.A. and Public Enemy, and concludes that their style is a fusion of the ghetto-centric and Afrocentric elements of the larger black culture.

1316. Ntarangwi, Mwenda. *East Africa Hip Hop: Youth Culture and Globalization*. Urbana: University of Illinois Press, 2001.

The author combines local popular musical traditions with American and Jamaican styles of rap to analyze how young exponents in Kenya, Uganda and Tanzania deal with both the challenges and opportunities posed by the globilization of the music. Hip hop is also used as a medium to discuss East African economic, political and social conditions, and to vocalize identity, issues related to education, HIV, AIDS and poverty. The book is based on extensive fieldwork, interviews with artists and the analysis of 140 songs to conclude that the music offers East African youth a platform for cultural and social commentary.

1317. Ogbar, Jeffrey. *Hip-Hop Revolution: The Cultural Politics of Rap*. Lawrence, KS: University of Kansas Press, 2007.

Celebrates hip hop and discusses the culture of authenticity that determines the character of the music. He specifies authenticity as how performers talk, walk and express themselves while keeping everything real. Ogbar also discusses how hip hop negotiates its own sense of identity (especially in the lyrical world), black images, the hip hop social milieu, and the historical and political awareness of artists like Mos Def.

1318. Perkinson, James W. *Shamanism, Racism, and Hip Hop Culture: Essays on White Supremacy and Black Subversion*. New York: Palgrave Macmillan, 2005.

A provocative and in-depth collection of essays that explore the 500-year history of white Christian hegemony that has shaped American society. The author explores the idea that collective American identity and history are informed and shaped by an interweaving of white privilege and entitlement with black disenfranchisement that strangles other forms of cultural identity.

1319. Perry, Imani. *Prophets of the Hood: Poetics and Politics in Hip Hop.* Durham: Duke University Press, 2004.

Perry uses an intertextual approach to reveal the music's origin in African American culture and to expose the hybrid nature of the music itself. Explores different dimensions of hip hop, its origins, the ethics of love and authenticity, constructions of masculinity and femininity, and mass production and global consumption. Researched three issues: how to fairly judge hip hop's aesthetic value, the political issues that obscure perception of its aesthetical value, and whether its aesthetic will survive commercialism. The author believes that the blackness of hip hop has precluded it from receiving an appropriate analysis of its aesthetic, and its political image has made it a scapegoat for both the social ills of the African American community and the moral decay of American society.

1320. Potter, Russell A. *Spectacular Vernaculars: Hip-Hop and the Politics of Postmodernism.* SUNY Series in Postmodern Culture. Albany: State University of New York, 1995.

The author argues that the historical experience of slavery forced African Americans to create postmodernism before French theorists conceived of it. Among the many provocative issues discussed is his belief that rap has enabled whites to evoke a "double consciousness," a burden usually shouldered by African Americans. Argues that academics should not be satisfied with their respective positions outside of the rap world, and that if academics do not understand the music it might be because they are not listening. Also states that academics are paying more attention to rap as it becomes more commercial, and illustrates how racial lines can be crossed by identifying with rap. Because rap is ever changing, Potter argues that any critic who attempts to make either a definitive or final claim about rap is attempting the impossible.

1321. Rahn, Janice and Michael Campbell. *Painting Without Permission: Hip-Hop Graffiti Subculture.* Westport, CT: Bergin and Garvey (Greenwood Press), 2002.

The author evokes the truism that students are required to study the social context of youth culture to understand and elicit a meaningful understanding of another culture. States that there is a need to bridge the gap between theory and practice when addressing the critical issues that confront the education of today's youth. She uses hip hop graffiti to achieve this goal, and provides an understanding of the signs, symbols and reasons that youth use graffiti to impart social and political messages.

1322. Sampson, Coretta. "Black Voices, Black Souls: Black Music as a Means of Voice, Resistance, and Social Transformation." Masters thesis, University of Toronto, 2004.

She addresses the ways that African American musical genres like blues, spirituals, gospels, rap and hip hop have created a powerful venue in which African Americans can express their opinions about discrimination and society. Also covers the origins of the genres, and discusses how they serve as means of resistance, voice and transformation.

1323. Shomari, Hashim A. (William A. Lee III). *From the Underground: Hip Hop Culture as an Agent of Social Change.* Fanwood, NJ: X-Factor, 1995.

The author addresses three important interconnected points in hip hop culture: first, he establishes that hip hop culture is inclusive of more than rap music; second, he discusses the sociopolitical possibilities and possible downfall of hip hop culture; third, he addresses media representations of hip hop culture to the general public.

1324. Watkins, Samuel Craig. *Hip Hop Matters: Politics, Pop Culture, and the Struggle for the Soul of a Movement.* Boston: Beacon Press, 2005.

He focuses on the fierce battle being waged in academia, politics and pop culture to control the hip hop movement. Among the representative individuals discussed are Detroit ex-mayor Kwame Kilpatrick, Chuck D, and several young rappers who are perceived to represent contemporary world views. He also discusses issues like corporate control, popularity in American colleges and universities, and the rampant misogyny that underlines the movements' progressive claims.

## RELIGION

1325. Davlatzai, Solail. "Prophets of Rage: Race, Nation, Islam and the Cultural Politics of Identity." PhD dissertation, University of Southern California, 2003.

Focuses on the debated surrounding globalization, the nation-state, immigration, multi-culturalism and the anti-racism struggle in the United States and Europe in the post 9/11 era. Researches the role of culture (cinema, TV, hip hop culture, and sports) in the relationship between cultural identity, nation, race and Islam.

1326. Dyson, Michael Eric. *Between God and Gangsta Rap: Bearing Witness to Black Culture.* New York: Oxford University Press, 1997.

This book is about race and identity and what is needed to heal the American cultural and racial divide. The book contains several essays, divided into three categories: "testimonials" focuses on the lives of contemporary black men; "lessons" covers politics from the Black Panthers to the late 1990s US Congress; and "songs of celebration" runs the musical gamut from gospel to pop to gangsta rap. He also discusses the impact of the O.J. Simpson case, and covers the influence of both politics and religion on the lives of African Americans from the Civil Rights movement to the late 1990s.

1327. ———. "Rap Culture, The Church, and American Society." *Sacred Music of the Secular City: From Blues to Rap,* ed. Jon Michael Spencer, pp. 268–74. A special edition of *Black Sacred Music: A Journal of Theomusicology* 6(1) (Spring 1992). Durham: Duke University Press, 1992.

Dyson describes his essay as being concerned with the expanding repertoire of created selves that invites him to interrogate the values and visions of rap culture, to perceive the force of its trenchant criticism of racism, historical amnesia and classism, and to gauge its capitulation to American traditions of sexism, consumerism and violence. His discussion of values and visions contains references to black religious themes.

1328. Garovich, Lori Ann. "Lest We Forget: Sacred and Secular Responses to Rock and Rap Concert Violence." PhD dissertation, Ohio: University of Akron, 1994.

An investigation of patterns of violence at rock and rap concerts and the sacred and secular responses to that violence. Jeffrey C. Alexander's early 1990s theoretical model of the five phases that a society experiences after a crisis—with a sixth element added from Scarisbrick-Hauser's solution-centered sociological theories regarding attitudes, activities and social events—was applied to four case studies of concerts where deaths occurred (concerts by The Who, AC/DC and Public Enemy). The author used a qualitative approach to assess data (interviews, participant-observation, photographs, video tapes and official documents) and focus on the myriad reasons why violence takes place at some rap and rock concerts.

1329. Johnson, Patricia. "The Impact of Hip-Hop Ministries on Post Traumatic Slavery Disorder." PhD dissertation, New York: Union Theological Seminary, 2006.

The primary objective was to assess the impact of rotating hip hop ministries on Post Traumatic Slavery Disorder. The author used questionnaires, surveys, interviews, and audio and video recordings as data gathering tools. Thai hip hop ministry congregants acknowledged that the hip hop ministry services assisted in their healing processes.

1330. Nelson, Angela Marie Spence. "A Theomusicological Approach to Rap: A Model for the Study of African American Popular and Folk Musics." PhD dissertation, Bowling Green State University, 1992.

This study demonstrates that a theology enmeshed in the contemporary black experience is both implicit and explicit in African American folk and popular musical traditions, especially rap music. Examines the importance of rhythm and rhyme, percussion and percussiveness, and call-and-response organizational concepts. Discusses rap from three perspectives: 1) the theology of the texts (value of truth, faith, hope, self-affirmation, knowledge and education, and social and political liberation); 2) the theodicy of the texts (including "white supremacy" and "slave mentality" theodicies); and 3) the mythology of the texts (e.g. representative mythoforms of historic, folk and legendary heroes like Shine, Stagolee and Harriet Tubman). In addition, she divides the lyric context into cultural, and social, economic and political divisions. The author constructs a philosophy of African American music through analysis of 200 rap lyrics (from both female and male perspectives). Includes a cursory consideration of soul music, spirituals and work songs, 1979–91.

1331. Pinn, Anthony B., ed. *Noise and Spirit: The Religious and Spiritual Sensibilities of Rap Music.* New York: New York University Press, 2003.

The four essays in the first section of this book, Rap and Religious Traditions, present an in-depth assessment of rap music's connection to and impact on Christianity, Islam and secular humanism. Of special note is the essay "Jihad of Words: The Evolution of African American Islam and Contemporary Hip Hop" by Juan M. Floyd-Thomas, which suggests that many hip hop artists are disillusioned with other African Americans' obsession with the materialistic goods of the white "American Dream." Suggests that they have created a lyrical jihad by regenerating their songs to include the teachings of Malcolm X and Louis Farrakhan. The second section, Rap and Issues of "Spirit" and "Spirituality," presents an overview of rap's lyric content. Here, the article "Bringing Noise: Conjuring Spirit: Rap as Spiritual Practice" by Mark Lewis Taylor espouses that music has been used historically to impart a people's attitudes, beliefs and world view. In the final section, Rap and the Art of

Theologizing, William C. Banfield acknowledges the global influence of rap, especially in the African diaspora, in his article "The Rub: Markets, Morals, and the Theologizing of Music."

1332. Utley, Ebony A. "Transcendence: The Rhetorical Functions of Gangsta Rapper's God." PhD dissertation, Northwestern University, 2006.

This study draws attention to the introspective characteristics of gangsta rap that include contemplation of divine figures. Uses textual analyses of Tupac Shakur's "Blasphemy," Lady of Rage's rap "Confessions," and Snoop Dogg's mini-feature "Murder Was the Case" to discuss the relationship between the hardness of gangsta rap and the sacredness of divine figures through the lens of suffering, especially suffering until death.

## SAMPLING

1333. Birnbaum, Larry. "Hip Hop—A Schoolboy's Primer." *Ear*, No. 2, 1988, 6.

Traces the history of hip hop through a discussion of breakdancing, scratching and sampling. He also discusses the emerging technology used in the hip hop and the differences between real and synthetic hip hop.

1334. Considine, J.D. "Larcenous Art?" *Rolling Stone*, 14 June 1990, 107.

An honest and critical look of the artistic and ethical issue of sampling. The author criticizes the use of sampling to augment live performances, believes sampling is changing music from live art to studio art, and presents his viewpoint regarding art and theft.

1335. Demers, Joanna Teresa. "Sampling as Lineage in Hip-Hop." PhD dissertation, Princeton University, 2002.

Focuses on sampling as one of the most distinctive features of hip hop. Acknowledges the importance of sampling and the fact that it can be recontextualized in ways that can be described as humorous, ironic, or respectful. Traces the uses of sampling and the impact of legal issues, and concludes that sampling is a way to recycle black images in music. When combined with fashion and blaxploitation cinema, hip hop constructs an authentic African American identity, and sampling is one effective means of self-assertion.

1336. Hodges Persley, Nicole. "Sampling Blackness: Performing African Americaness in Hip Hop Theater and Performances." PhD dissertation, University of Southern California, 2007.

The author uses a comparative approach in ethnic studies to examine how the global diffusion of African American articulations of blackness in hip hop music impacts performance practices of non-African American artists. She imagines sampling as an improvisational process of meaning to challenge dominant narratives about racial differences as it creates new possibilities to envision bodies and the cultural products they engender as public texts.

1337. Mitchell, Stephan and Melinda Newman. "Turtles' Flo & Eddie Sue De La Soul Over Sampling." *Billboard*, 26 August 1989, 10.

The article focuses on the conflicting opinions regarding copyright, fair use and length of a De La Soul sample taken from a Turtles' song. He provides documentation to support the various positions and mentions a Beastie Boys court case.

1338. Owen, Frank. "Bite This." *Spin*, November 1989, 33.

A discussion of the cultural, ethical, historical and musical issues surrounding the uses of sampling. A reference is made to the lawsuit filed against De La Soul for sampling the Turtles' hit "You Showed Me."

1339. Peaslee, Dave. "Rappers Spur James Brown Revival." *Billboard*, 27 September 1987, 29.

Chronicles the heavy influence of James Brown's samples in rap music. Discusses rap artists who use James Brown samples, and some of the ethical and legal issues of using sampling.

1340. Phillips, Chuck. "Digital Sampling: The Battle Over Borrowed Beats." *Cash Box*, 27 May 1989, 5.

The article appeared in a special issue on rap, and discusses selected creative, ethical and legal issues of using sampling. The article is important because it presents a wide variety of viewpoints, including those of artists, industry officials and producers.

1341. Ressner, Jeffrey. "Sampling Amok?" *Rolling Stone*, 14 June 1990, 103.

A provocative discourse on sampling; the author surveys the viewpoints of those sampling and those who are being sampled. Focuses on aesthetic, ethical and legal implications of sampling.

1342. Schloss, Joseph G. "Making Beats: The Art of Sample-Based Hip-Hop." PhD dissertation, University of Washington, 2000.

While many have written about hip hop's origins, historical evolution and biographical information of artists, the community that produces hip hop has been largely neglected. This article explores the ways in which vocal elements of hip hop are conceived by producers, and how conceptualizations are informed by a variety of artistic, social and practical concerns. Addresses the specific ways that sample-based hip hop is produced, the relationship between aesthetics and technology, steps that one must take to produce a finished product, and how legal and moral issues are resolved.

1343. Schmuckler, Eric. "D St. Builds From Scratch." *Village Voice*, 25 December 1984, 93.

Grandmixer D St. discusses his technique of scratching. He believes he is the most creative scratcher of the time, and mentions the samples and techniques that he used on several successful records (e.g. Herbie Hancock's "Rockit," which catapulted him to fame).

1344. Zimmerman, Kevin. "Old is New Again in World of Sampling." *Variety*, 1 August 1990, 69.

This article adds to previous discussions on sampling. Examines the various economical and legal issues that engulfed rap in the 1990s. Implies that the resistance to sampling was generated by both those artists whose works were sampled and their record companies.

# IV

# Appendices

## APPENDIX A: SELECTED BLUES WEB SOURCES, MAGAZINES AND PERIODICALS

The most important criterion for inclusion in this appendix is the website's content, first and foremost. Websites included here contain the most outstanding or compelling content that I found—historically rich or detailed, well-referenced, well-structured and organized, technologically current or innovative (i.e. RSS feeds, podcasts, downloads, audio and visual examples, interactivity), with archival or biographical depth. In some cases the site of a well-known individual artist is included if it was exceptional. Alternatively, a site may have been included because it was somehow useful or interestingly unique. Website design was of secondary importance unless it proved detrimental to accessing the information. Many websites are better in one aspect than in another. In those cases they were included if the "good" outweighed the "bad." The list is selected, but obviously cannot be comprehensive because of the nature of the internet.

The websites of many foundations and societies are focused on local and regional current events and venues or may be focused on a stated mission (for example, sponsoring local students in educational endeavors) rather than the publishing of substantive material. There are many such organizations in every state and around the world. Often, though they may have good intentions, their published content is limited in scope or depth. These sites have not been included. On the other hand, if a local or regional site has particularly unique content or innovative interactivity they have been included.

## General web sources for blues

A1. www.blues.org
The Blues Foundation, 49 Union Avenue, Memphis, TN 38103.

References to The Blues Foundation (a nonprofit corporation head-quartered in Memphis, Tennessee) are ubiquitous on the web. It has over 165 affiliated blues organizations and memberships around the world. Founded in 1980, its primary mission is the preservation of blues history. It sponsors The Blues Hall of Fame and carries out annual inductions of pioneers. It also pays tribute to legendary artists with its Lifetime Achievement Award, historically presented in Los Angeles. There are other several traditional programs conducted by the organization including Blues in the Schools.

A2. www.barrelhouseblues.com
Barrelhouse Blues, Boston, MA.

This site is well-organized and easily navigated. They accept music submissions (send a CD/DVD of your original blues music for their online audio showcase "Sound Impressions"). They publish reviews and maintain a video gallery. Their resource links are plentiful and useful. They feature a subsection titled "Route 66 Blues Across America" that spotlights artists from across America and beyond.

A3. www.pbs.org/theblues
PBS, 2100 Crystal Drive, Arlington, VA 22202.

This web location is a subsection of the Public Broadcasting Service website. It is based around Martin Scorcese's seven-part film series *The Blues* and is dedicated to raising awareness about the blues and its contribution to American culture. Internal sections include "About the Film Series," "Songs and the Artists," "Blues Road Trip," "Blues Classroom," and "Partners and Resources." Blues discographies and biographies are available.

A4. thebluehighway.com
Curtis Hewston, 7794 Country Place, Winter Park, FL 32792.

The site is one of the oldest blues sites on the web but it still contains some interesting and diverse links, information on blues events, and a chronology of past blues awards. Links include some outside the United States. The site was a recipient of The Blues Foundation's 1998 "Keeping the Blues Alive" Award for Blues on the Internet and was also named by *Yahoo! Internet Life* magazine as one of the 100 best sites for the year 2000.

A5. www.bluesworld.com
Joel Slotnikoff, Box 21652, St Louis, MO 63109.

This award-winning site contains links to a variety of blues resources including magazines, interviews with and essays by individual scholars, and regional music websites. Examples of the site's variety include a link to an archivist's page titled *Vintage 78 rpm Era American Record Company Sleeves* containing images and contact information and a link to a book titled *American Hoboes and Their Songs* with publication information and reviews (including an endorsement by black music scholar Samuel Floyd).

A6. afgen.com/bluslink.html
Smith/McIver, *African Genesis*.

This site on African American music is a subsection of the *African Genesis* website. It provides history, genre information and, most interestingly, artists' quotes and biographical sketches.

A7. www.cathead.biz
Cat Head Delta Blues & Folk Art, Inc., 252 Delta Avenue, Clarksdale, MS 38614-4213.

Cat Head Delta Blues & Folk Art, Inc., located in Clarksdale, Mississippi, is a noted retail outlet for all things blues. It carries a full selection of blues CDs, videos, DVDs, books and other collectibles, including folk art. Merchandise cannot be purchased online; purchase inquiries must be made by phone or email.

A8. www.theboogiereport.net
Mason Media Services, 5430 Executive Place, Jackson, MS 39206.

The blues of the southern United States is the focus. This site has an unusually large number of web pages but they are not arranged in any particularly clear categories. The sheer variety of materials (some better quality than others) makes for a measure of interest. Radio stations, individual artists, music charts, links, a newsletter, retail distributors, artist managers, "music pools," "club and street reports," product reviews, and much more. It features a potpourri of subjects that may reveal some interesting local music information. The site is "rough around the edges" and can load slowly.

A9. www.blueslinks.nl
Oost-souburg, Zeeland, The Netherlands.

This website originates in the Netherlands and calls itself "the mother of all blues links collections." The links are certainly extensive, diverse and the coverage is worldwide. At the time of this annotation the site claimed 5,587 links. Categories include bands, CDs/DVDs, forums, lyrics, museums, photography, radio, clubs, festivals, record labels, magazines, worldwide calendars, weblogs and podcasts. Visitors can embed the site's banner on the webpage of their choice and can also sign up for a mailing list. Streaming radio originating from around the globe can be accessed.

A10. www.bluesnet.hub.org/gorgen
Blues Bibliographic Database

A comprehensive listing of information related to all areas of blues research and performance, including autobiographies, biographies, history, styles and more.

A11. www.bluesworld.com/BluesLinks.html
Blues World Blues Links

Posted by blues researcher and scholar, John Broven, this site is important because it contains information on a myriad of topics related to blues history and practices. The site contains links to Chicago, Louisiana, Memphis and St Louis blues, artists, booking agencies, books and magazines, festivals, guitar and harmonica information, internet radio, photography, record collecting, and societies. In addition, each link contains sublinks which, in turn, provide additional information on the specific subject. This site is an important resource for both blues enthusiasts and scholars.

A12. doddcenter.uconn.edu/findaids/charters/MSS20000105.html
Samuel and Ann Charters Archives of Blues and Vernacular African American Musical Culture, Thomas Dodd Research Center, University of Connecticut, Storrs, CT 06269-1205.

In addition to African American spirituals and the Ragtime music of Scott Joplin, the archive contains a wealth of materials on blues. The collection contains thousands of hours of recorded music on LPs, 45 RPM and 78 RPM records and compact discs, and the complete catalog of music produced by Arhoolie records. Among the special features of the collection are the materials on artists like B.B. King and Robert Johnson, the many Ragtime recordings hosted by the Maple Leaf Club, and information on later African American musical genres and artists like Snoop Dogg.

A13. www.chipublib.org/branch/details/library/harold-washington/p/Vpablues
Chicago Blues Archives, Harold Washington Library Center, 400 S. State Street, Chicago, IL 60605, tel. 312-747-4300.

Established in 1981, the archive holds an extensive collection of recordings – commercial and non-commercial – from 78s to compact discs. The collection also includes recordings from WXRT's Blues Breaker Specials featuring artists like Willie Dixon, Buddy Guy, John Lee Hooker, Taji Mahal and Johnny Winter performing in Chicago clubs. The archive has an extensive video and audio collection, including tapes from the Soundstage performances, WTTW's live public television performances from the 1970s, including the famous Muddy Waters episode. The video and audio tapes include the Speaking of the Blues Series of interviews and performances by local blues artists held in the Harold Washington Library.

A14.   www.olemiss.edu/depts/general_library/archives/blues
       The Blues Archive, University of Mississippi Libraries, Archives and Special Collections, Greg Johnson, Blues Curator, University, MS 38677, tel. 662-915-7753, fax 662-915-5734, gj@olemiss.edu.

A premier blues archive that contains over 60,000 sound recordings, 20,000 photoraphs, 1,000 videos, 6,000 books, and numerous manuscripts, periodicals, newsletters, and more. It is one of the most comprehensive collections of blues and blues related materials (African American Studies, and Southern Culture) in the world. Included in the collection is B.B. King's personal record collection, the Jim O'Neal and Amy Von Singel Living Blues collection, the Trumpet Records collection, the Sheldon Harris Collection, the John Richbourg collection, and the Percy Mayfield collection. Establiished in 1984, this non-circulating collection is housed in the John Davis Williams Library.

A15.   www.memphis.edu/libraries
       University of Memphis Library, Anna Neal, Head of Music Library, University of Memphis, Memphis, TN 38152, tel. 901-678-4412, abneal@memphis.edu.

Within its collection of around 44,000 books, scores and bound periodicals, 16,500 recordings, 11 pieces of microform, and other holdings are substantial materials on blues and other southern vernacular musical genres. The collection supplements research for a PhD in musicology with a focus on southern regional studies, and a speciality in the vernacular musics of the southern United States. The program is led by Dr David Evans, an eminent blues scholar, performer and researcher.

**Blues museums, foundations and societies web sources**

A16.   www.deltabluesmuseum.org
       The Delta Blues Museum, 1 Blues Alley, Clarksdale, MS 38614.

This is a quality regional site. Of particular interest is The Delta Blues Museum's Uncensored Blues Podcast that looks at the early history of recorded blues in the United States. The podcasts include a series of rare pre-war blues tracks accompanied by discussion of those songs.

A17. bbkingmuseum.org
B.B. King Museum and Delta Interpretive Center, 101 S Sunflower Avenue, # B, Indianola, MS 38751.

This is the official website for the B.B. King Museum Foundation in Indianola, Mississippi. The Museum's mission represents the values of B.B. King in an endeavor to preserve the musical heritage of the Mississippi Delta region. The site has an interesting aesthetic and contains original drawings of the building's spaces. The physical edifice in Indianola is built on the location of the last brick cotton gin in Mississippi.

A18. www.robertjohnsonbluesfoundation.org
Robert Johnson Blues Foundation, PO Box 1005, Crystal Springs, MS 39059.

The mission of the Robert Johnson Blues Foundation, founded in 2005, is to preserve the art and legacy of Mississippi Blues legend Robert Johnson. The foundation is headed by Claud and Steven Johnson, son and grandson of Robert Johnson. As of this writing, the site featured a newly discovered photo of the artist taken alongside another fellow musician of the era.

A19. www.chicagobluesfoundation.org
Chicago Blues Foundation, Inc., Chicago, IL.

The foundation's mission is the archiving and restoration of Chicago Urban Blues materials from the 1960s and 1970s. The foundation also houses selected master tapes recorded at Chess and other Chicago studios by independent producers. They display their holdings periodically in museum settings and make the materials available to scholars and historians by request. They also display the collection at the annual Chicago Blues Festival.

A20. www.msjohnhurtmuseum.com
The Mississippi John Hurt Blues Foundation, Route 109, Avalon, MS.

The Mississippi John Hurt Blues Foundation was established by Mary Frances Hurt Wright in 1999. Its goal is to preserve the musical history of Mississippi John Hurt and to offer educational opportunities in the area of folk/blues music to under-served urban and rural children. They maintain a museum site and sponsor a festival.

A21.  www.bayareabluessociety.net
      Bay Area Blues Society, 408 13th Street, Suite 512, Oakland, CA 94612.

      The Bay Area Blues Society (BABS) was established twenty-two years
      ago in order to preserve the "west coast blues" tradition. It reaches
      into the communities of Oakland, Hayward-Russell City, Pittsburg,
      Richmond, and Vallejo—all communities that the site describes as
      having deep roots in the blues idiom. Blues events, education and a
      hall of fame are all endeavors of BABS. A page on the site is titled
      "The Music They Played on 7th Street" discusses the west coast
      blues tradition as it was performed in venues such as Slim Jenkins
      Supper Club. It highlights such musicians as Saunders Samuel King
      and acknowledges the Reed Record Shop and Bob Geddins who was
      the first African American in the area to own a record plant and
      recording studio. There are no formal citations, but names and places
      are tools for further research.

A22.  www.ihobf.org
      The International House of Blues Foundation, 6255 Sunset Boulevard,
      18th Floor, West Hollywood, CA 90028.

      The goal of the International House of Blues Foundation (IHOBF)
      is to bring arts to schools and communities by increasing public
      awareness of African American contributions to American culture.
      The site features a PDF file on blues education that is prepared for
      classroom instruction.

A23.  www.brbluesfoundation.org
      Baton Rouge Blues Foundation, 639 Main Street, Baton Rouge, LA
      70802.

      The Baton Rouge Blues Foundation was founded in 2002 and sponsors
      a Music in the Schools Program as well as the Baton Rouge Blues
      Foundation Awards and Baton Rouge Blues Week. The site is well
      organized.

A24.  www.southernroseproductions.net
      North Mississippi Hill Country Blues Association, Southern Rose
      Productions, 1070 County Road, Ripley, MS 38663.

      One of the highlights of this site is its link to the documentary *M for
      Mississippi*. The film highlights the still-thriving blues tradition in
      Mississippi. The site posts a calendar of regional blues events and
      publishes a newsletter.

A25.  www.deltablues.org//MACE
      Mississippi Action for Community Education, Inc., 119 Theobald
      Street, Greenville, MS 38701.

Mississippi Delta Blues and Heritage Festival sponsors several programs besides mounting a yearly festival. It also conducts a periodic blues conference.

A26. blusd.org

Blues Lovers United of San Diego, PO Box 34077, San Diego, CA 92163.

This non-profit regional organization is affiliated with The Blues Foundation of Memphis, Tennessee. They promote blues music in the Southern California area, publish the website and newsletter, produce blues events in the San Diego area, and conduct a Blues in the Schools educational program for primary and secondary school students.

A27. www.sacblues.com/whoweare.php

The Sacramento Blues Society, PO Box 60580, Sacramento, CA 95860-0580.

This organization claims to be one of the oldest blues societies in California, founded 1979. It is based in the Sacramento area where it promotes live blues events. It, like many other regional blues societies is a member of the umbrella organization, The Blues Foundation. They also conduct the Blues in the Schools program for youth. The newsletter, *Blue Notes*, is published bi-monthly. The website has a fairly extensive list of blues bands in the area; other blues societies in California, and a report on the Blues in the Schools activities.

## Individual artist websites

A28. www.bbking.com

A well-designed site with comprehensive biographical, product, audio and video, and event information. Interactivity is high-end; includes many links to the artist's other web presences: MySpace, YouTube, Facebook, Yahoo, Wikipedia, iTunes, and RSS feeds.

A29. resources.glos.ac.uk/departments/Lis/archives/collections/paul-oliver.cfm

The Paul Oliver Collection (Blues), archives@glos.ac.uk, tel. (1242) 714815 (UK)

The collection includes information on blues, and disciplines such as American and African American history, American studies, anthropology, cultural studies, popular music and transatlantic studies. Also known as the Paul Oliver Archive or Blues Collection, it contains numerous books, papers, recordings, visual materials and other artifacts. The collection is held on a custodial basis by both Paul Oliver and the European Blues Association.

**Web radio for blues**

A30.  www.live365.com/cgi-bin/directory.cgi?genre=blues
      Live365, Inc., 950 Tower Lane, Suite 1550 Foster City, CA 94404.

      An award-winning internet radio site launched in 1999 that offers
      listening by genre. It carries 203 blues online blues stations and is an
      officially licensed ASCAP, BMI and SESAC site.

A31.  www.slacker.com
      Slacker, Inc., 16935 W Bernardo Drive, Suite 270, San Diego, CA
      92127.

      Founded in 2004, Slacker is an interactive internet radio service.
      Stations offer pre-programmed traditional genre, specialty and artist
      stations. Stations are customizable, allowing users to build playlists
      and send them to portable devices. Slacker is cutting edge in terms of
      interactivity and contains over 2 million songs. It is affiliated with
      both major and independent record labels.

A32.  americanbluesnetwork.com
      The American Blues Network, PO Box 6216, Gulfport, MS 39506.

      The American Blues Network describes itself as the only twenty-
      four-hour globally accessible blues format via satellite.

**Blues record companies**

A33.  www.alligatorrecords.com
      Alligator Records, PO Box 60234, Chicago, IL.

      This record label is focused on contemporary blues and was started
      in 1971 by Bruce Iglauer, a twenty-three-year-old blues fan. Music,
      video, photos, posters, books and apparel are all available online.
      Streaming radio is featured as well as a "jukebox" where music can
      be previewed before purchase.

A34.  www.biograph.com
      Biograph Records, 2042-A Armacost Avenue, Los Angeles, CA 90025.

      Biograph was established in 1967, and claims to be the first to record
      and release piano rolls and to have restored and released the field
      recordings of legendary bluesman Son House. The company has
      obtained master tapes from jazz and blues including Dawn, Regal
      and Melodeon. The website is particularly slick and easily navigated.
      The Biograph catalogue is extensive and includes the music of Scott
      Joplin and Fats Waller.

A35.  www.blindpigrecords.com/index.cfm
Blind Pig Records, PO Box 2344, San Francisco, CA 94126.

Blind Pig Records was established in 1977 in Ann Arbor, Michigan. Artists include Bonnie Raitt, Eddie Taylor, Otis Rush and Hound Dog Taylor. Video clips and free downloads are offered on their website. DVDs may be purchased online.

A36.  www.delmark.com
Delmark Records, 4121 N Rockwell, Chicago, IL 60618.

Delmark Records was established in 1953, making it one of the oldest independent record labels in the United States. The label focuses on traditional blues and jazz. Bob Koester, its founder, is a noted blues archivist.

A37.  www.earwigmusic.com
Earwig Music Company, Inc., 2054 W Farwell Avenue, Garden Unit, Chicago, IL 60645.

Earwig Music Company, started in 1978, is also known as Earwig Records. It is an independent blues music record label and produces new recordings and reissues traditional and contemporary blues. Videos, artist bios, tour dates and more are offered on their website.

A38.  www.fatpossum.com
Fat Possum Records, PO Box 1923, Oxford, MS 38655.

This is a simple commerce site. The record label operates out of Oxford, Mississippi. Starting out, Fat Possum focused primarily on more obscure Mississippi blues artists (for the most part from Oxford or Holly Springs, Mississippi). More recently, Fat Possum has signed younger rock acts to its roster.

A39.  www.musicmaker.org
Music Maker Relief Foundation, Eno Valley Station, PO Box 72222, Durham, NC 27722-2222.

This record label was created by the Music Maker Relief Foundation to help elderly blues artists. The Music Maker Relief Foundation has built a noted catalog of traditional blues. The site features a "juke box," videos, a photo gallery, news and reviews. Music can be searched by derivative idioms within the blues genre, e.g. "electric blues," "Piedmont blues," "one man band," etc.

A40.  www.rounder.com
Rounder Records, One Rounder Way, Burlington, MA 01803.

Rounder Records is an independent record label specializing in roots music. Founded in 1970, it is now one of the largest independent record labels in the United States. It has several specialized projects, one of which is the Alan Lomax Collection, featuring the work of the pioneering ethnomusicologist and scholar of the blues.

A41.  stackhouse-bluesoterica.blogspot.com
Stackhouse Recording, 232A Sunflower Avenue, Clarksdale, MS 38614.

Formerly Rooster Blues, the company was sold in 1999 and now operates under the name Stackhouse Recording Company with its head-quarters in Clarksdale, Mississippi. Stackhouse and its sister company BluEsoterica are dedicated to the appreciation of the blues. The company buys, sells and trades in blues music. Owner Jim O'Neal is a contributor to *Living Blues* magazine and an author on blues topics.

A42.  www.yazoorecords.com
Shanachie Entertainment, 37 E Clinton Street, Newton, NJ 07860.

Yazoo Records is a record label founded in the late 1960s by Nick Perls. It specializes in early American blues, early country, jazz, and other rural American genres (collectively referred to as "roots" music). Yazoo's sister label Blue Goose, founded in 1970, records black blues artists and younger blues and jazz performers. In 1989 Yazoo was acquired by Shanachie Records.

**Journals, magazines and periodicals**

A43.  *Living Blues*, PO Box 1848, 1111 Jackson Avenue West, University, MS 38677.
www.livingblues.com

*Living Blues* is one of the oldest blues publications in the United States (1970). Back issues are available through online ordering. Issue contents are posted online with annotations. Content features interviews with blues artists and product reviews.

A44.  *Southern Spaces*, Robert W. Woodruff Library, Emory University, 540 Asbury Circle, Atlanta, GA 30322-2870.
www.southernspaces.org.

An interdisciplinary online journal with a solid music component. It features scholarly essays on roots musics of the southern United States and includes a calendar of performances, events and con-ferences. It is under the auspices of the Robert W. Woodruff Library of Emory University.

A45.  *Black Music Research Journal*, 600 Michigan Avenue, Chicago, IL 60605.

www.colum.edu/CBMR/CBMR_Publications/Black_Music_Research_
Journal.php

This biannual peer-reviewed academic journal founded in 1980 covers
a variety of black music genres from classical composers to blues
artists. For example, Vol. 8, no. 2 (Fall 1998) focuses on country
blues performances. It includes articles about the philosophy, aesthetics, history and criticism of black music. It is published by The
Center for Black Music Research at Chicago's Columbia College.

A46. *Blues Access*, Boulder, CO.
www.bluesaccess.com

This publication, discontinued in 2002, was a respected quarterly for
its coverage of both contemporary and traditional blues. Back issues
are available through the website and include articles on the blues
genre, interviews and record reviews.

A47. *Big City Blues* (formerly *Detroit Blues*), Big City Blues Magazine,
PO Box 1805, Royal Oak, MI 48068.
www.bigcitybluesmag.com

*Big City Blues* is a quarterly that covers the local and blues scenes in
Detroit and Chicago. Back issues and artist profiles are available
online.

A48. *Sing Out!*, PO Box 5460, Bethlehem, PA 18015-0460.
www.singout.org

*Sing Out!* is the publication for the not-for-profit corporation of the
same name. The stated mission is to preserve and support traditional
and contemporary folk musics. Blues is one of their focus idioms.
The magazine is distinguished by its inclusion of the lyrics and music
of selected songs and, since 2001, an accompanying CD. The publication carries in-depth articles profiling musicians and musical traditions
as well reviews of recordings and other print publications. It also
features comprehensive festival and camp listings, and columns covering
songwriting, storytelling, children's music and the folk process.

A49. *Jefferson Blues Magazine*
www.jeffersonbluesmag.com

*Jefferson Blues Magazine*, named for bluesman Blind Lemon Jefferson.
The Swedish publication, founded in 1968, claims to be the world's
oldest blues magazine. Its focus is primarily African American blues.
The magazine's writers, photographers and editors travel regularly to
the United States. It carries the work of American writers such as
Dick Shurman, who writes about the blues scene around Chicago

and the west coast. It lists the winners of the Keeping the Blues Alive Awards 2008 (sponsored by The Blues Foundation), in every category and offers profiles on each of the winners.

A50. *Blues Magazine* Selective Index
www.aliveandpicking.com/bluesmag.html

An index of the essays that have appeared in the magazine.

A51. *Blues World*, 22 Manor Crescent, Knutsford, Cheshire, WA16 8DL, United Kingdom.
www.bluesworld.com

This site contains a listing of the essays that have appeared in the journal *Blues World* and a list of other research published by them as well as references to bibliographies or information on scholars.

### Additional blues magazines and periodicals

The journals and magazines listed below are devoted wholly or occasionally to blues research. In addition to my research, additional listings were taken from Robert Ford's *A Blues Bibliography* (2007).

A52. *Arhoolie Occasional* (USA)

A53. *BBR Boogie* (British Blues Review, UK)

A54. *Black Music/Black Music and Jazz Review* (UK)

A55. *Black Music Research Journal* (USA)

A56. *The Black Perspective in Music* (USA)

A57. *Blueprint/Blues in Britain* (UK)

A58. *Blues Access* (USA)

A59. *Blues and Rhythm* (UK)

A60. *Blues and Soul* (UK)

A61. *Blues Bag* (UK)

A62. *Blues: Bimestrel International Blues and Jazz* (Belgium)

A63. *Blues Collection* (UK)

A64. *Blues et Jazz* (Belgium)

A65. *Blues, etc.* (later retitled *Blues Magazine*) (France)

A66. *Blues Forever Magazine* (UK)

A67. *Blues Forum* (Germany)

A68. *Blues Gazette* (Belgium)

A69. *Il Blues Trimestrale di Cultura Musicale* (Italy)

A70. *Blues Life* (Austria)

A71. *Blues-Link* (UK)

A72. *Blues Magazine* (Canada)

A73. *Blues Magazine* (formerly known as *Blues, etc.*) (France)

A74. *Blues Matters* (UK)

A75. *Blues News* (*Das Deutsche Bluesmagazin*) (Germany)

A76. *Blues News* (Finland)

A77. *Blues Notes* (Germany)

A78. *Blues Power* (Italy)

A79. *Blues Power Magazine* (Germany)

A80. *Blues Research* (USA)

A81. *Blues Review Quarterly/Blues Review* (USA)

A82. *Blues Statistics* (UK)

A83. *Blues Unlimited* (UK)

A84. *Blues World* (UK)

A85. *Boogie Woogie and Blues Collector* (The Netherlands)

A86. *Bulletin du Hot Club de France* (France)

A87. *Cadence* (USA)

A88. *Coda* (Canada)

A89. *Crawdaddy* (USA)

A90. *Crazy Music: The Journal of the Australian Blues Society* (Australia)

A91. *Cream* (UK and USA)

A92. *Crescendo* (UK)

A93. *Detour: Country Folk and Blues Magazine* (UK)

A94. *Detroit Blues* (USA)

A95. *Dirty Linen* (USA)

A96. *Discographical Forum* (UK)

A97. *Downbeat* (USA)

A98. *Ebony* (USA)

A99. *Folk Roots* (UK)

A100. *German Blues Circle Info* (Germany)

A101. *The Guitar Magazine* (UK)

A102. *Guitar Player* (USA)

A103. *Guitar World* (USA)

A104. *The History of Rock* (UK)

A105. *Jazz and Blues* (UK)

A106. *Jazz, Blues and Co.* (France)

A107. *John Edwards Memorial Foundation Newsletter and Quarterly* (USA)

A108. *Living Blues: A Journal of the Black American Blues Tradition* (USA)

A109. *Magi Blues* (USA)

A110. *Mojo* (UK)

A111. *Mr. Blues* (The Netherlands)

A112. *Solo Blues* (Spain)

A113. *Talking Blues* (UK)

A114. *West Coast Blues* (later retitled *Real Blues*, USA)

## APPENDIX B: SELECTED FUNK, RHYTHM AND BLUES, AND SOUL MUSIC WEB SOURCES, MAGAZINES AND PERIODICALS

A great deal of information on rhythm and blues and soul (whether online or in print) originates outside of the United States, particularly in the UK. In many cases the information is well researched and organized. I have included the best and most ubiquitous of these sources while balancing the entries most heavily toward US-based entities and those produced by culture bearers. Physical addresses are not always available for websites, but I have included them where possible.

### General web sources for funk, rhythm and blues, and soul music

B1. www.soulmusic.com
Soul Music.com, PO Box 10722, Silver Spring, MD 20914.

This site is a resource for profiles and the purchase of rhythm and blues and soul music artists. Subcategories include Soul Music Global, an interactive community; Soul Talking, articles and interviews with rhythm and blues/soul artists; selections from David Nathan's radio show "Dedicated to Soul"; a posting of R&B events; and an archive of rare rhythm and blues and soul music from the 1960s, 1970s and 1980s (e.g. The Complete Motown Singles, Vol. 10: 1970 can be reviewed). Site map offers links to products and information about particular artists and global resources, including podcasts and file sharing.

B2. www.soul-patrol.com/soul
Soul-Patrol, 798 Woodlane Road, Suite 10264, Mount Holly, NJ 08060.

Soul Patrol.com breaks down R&B and soul into its sub-idioms (e.g. funk, doo-wop, classic soul, etc.). A radio station is offered and there is a page for books and book reviews. Music events are posted and RSS feeds, a newsletter and chat room are available.

B3. www.soultracks.com
SoulTracks, LLC, 201 S Main Street, Ann Arbor, MI 48104.

The SoulTracks website was established in 2003 and includes an extensive index of artists and their profiles as well as a national CD and record store directory. It also offers downloadable music. Interviews, reviews, news, events, RSS feeds, an online store, a discussion forum, and a "Where are they now?" section. The site is thorough and easily navigated. The publisher, editor and writers have solid standing in blues scholarship.

B4. www.justsoul.net

This website features artist profiles, new releases, interviews, reviews and a discussion forum. Periodic contests are featured and winners receive signed CDs, DVDs, advance promos, tickets, T-shirts and exclusive gadgets from international R&B and soul acts.

B5 industrysoul.com

Industrysoul.com is a video blog site of R&B/soul music. They feature a radio show called "Soul Conversations" that airs Friday Nights, 11:00 pm–1:00 am EST (online: wpfw.org).

B6. hiphoprnbsoul.com

HiphopRnbSoul.com describes itself as a "venue that allows new and upcoming artists free exposure." New artists can post their biographies, stream their music content, upload photos and direct users to other external links. The site publishes an online newsletter, maintains archives, and they have recently become a blog site.

B7.  www.honeysoul.com
     V. Woods, PO Box 554, Fresno, TX 77545.

The site was established by soul music aficionado and radio show host Vonnie "Honey" Woods. The site now claims visitors from more than fifteen countries and is ranked highly among soul music internet searches. From the realm of R&B and soul it offers news, reviews, interviews, underground artists' profiles, audio, videos, a discussion board, a blog and an archive. The site claims references and/or acknowledgements from Prince's official website, Vibe.com, Eurweb.com, Capital Records, AOL Black Voices and *Philadelphia Weekly.*

B8.  www.soul-sides.com
     oliverwang@gmail.com, facebook.com/owing
     Oliver Wang, Assistant Professor of Sociology California State University, Long Beach, CA.

Soul Sides is an audio blogspot giving users the opportunity to upload music, connect to other audio blogs and view videos (Soul Sights). Oliver Wang, the site author, says that "the point of an audioblog is to provide 'edutainment'." There is a downloadable playlist of songs, a selection of compilations, and recommended reading. Wang is an assistant professor of sociology at CSU-Long Beach and teaches courses in popular culture, social issues, and race/class/gender. Wang offers a guide for users who are interested in starting their own audioblog.

B9.  www.southernsoulrnb.com
     Southern Soul RnB.com LLC, PO Box 19574, Boulder, CO 80308.

Daddy B Nice's Southern Soul RnB.com is not a slick website but it profiles a large selection of R&B artists from the southern United States. Biographical information and links to examples are offered in a "down-to-earth" style. Southern soul, the "Chittlin Circuit," southern soul songwriters and more are discussed.

B10.  www.rnbhaven.com

Rhythm and blues artists from the 1990s are featured on this site. Reviews, news, interviews, videos and a discussion board are among the inclusions. The site features a poll for viewers to express their opinions of the music and the artists. Videos and, notably, song lyrics are posted.

B11.  www.blastro.com
      Blastro Networks, 609 W 18th Street, Suite C, Austin, TX 78701.

A primarily free video site offering a large selection of R&B videos (hip hop, pop and dance videos are also featured). Interactivity is excellent, featuring email, bookmarks, playlists, MySpace, Facebook, comments and much more. Numerous artists are indexed and profiled. This is a great site for video viewing.

B12.  www.blackmusicamerica.com
Black Music America (BMA), Urban Mass Media Group, MN.

Black Music America Digital Network produces audio, video and online urban entertainment and other content for programming. It operates two twenty-four-hour cable music and video channels on its website.

B13.  www.last.fm
Last.fm, Shoreditch, London, UK.

Last.fm is an internet radio and music community website based in the UK. It was founded in 2002 and claims over 21 million active users in more than 200 countries. Rhythm and blues and hip hop are among the categories of music that are offered. The site builds a detailed profile of each user's musical taste by recording details of all the songs to which the user listens, either on the streamed radio stations or on the user's computer or some portable music devices. Users can create custom radio stations and playlists from any of the audio tracks in Last.fm's music library; they can also listen to or download individual tracks on demand. Visitors must register to create a profile but listening to radio stations is open to all. The site also offers social networking features.

B14.  www.pandora.com
Pandora Media Inc., 360 22nd Street, Suite 440, Oakland, CA 94612.

Pandora is an "automated music recommendation and internet radio service" and was created by the Music Genome Project in 2000. Users enter a favorite song or artist and the station creates a custom radio station based on that choice. Users can give feedback on the music provided which further guides Pandora in providing more suitable music to that user in the future. Users are given access to purchase through Amazon mp3, Amazon.com (for CDs), or the iTunes Store. The Pandora media player allows for cross-platform portability.

B15.  rhythmflow.net
RHYTHMflow Enterprises, PO Box 130, Bronx, NY 10467.

RHYTHMflow.net calls itself an "e-zine." It features a radio station, downloads, RSS feeds (both entries and comments), festivals and video. It also functions as an audio blog.

B16.   www.rhythmandtheblues.org.uk

The site profiles a substantial number of **R&B** artists from the 1950s, 1960s and 1970s. It features an extended essay on the history of rhythm and blues, a suggested reading list, and profiles of some of the best known **R&B** record labels including Atlantic, Chess and Stax. It includes a "Shades of **R&B**" primer—twenty CDs for purchase touted as a good foundation for experiencing **R&B** music. **R&B** postcards (e-cards) can be sent to an email account of the user's choice. The site also has an RSS feed and blogspot.

B17.   soul45.com / www.soul45.net
Bolruptstrasse 19, 6900 Bregenz, Austria.

This website is a soul music mail order outlet called Voices from the Shadows. It specializes in 7-inch and 12-inch recordings, LPs and CDs dating from the late 1960s. They claim a stock of nearly 500,000 titles. By signing up for their newsletter the user will receive information on the newest additions to their collection.

## Museums and foundations web sources

B18.   www.rhythm-n-blues.org
Rhythm & Blues Foundation, 100 S Broad Street, Suite 620, Philadelphia, PA 19110.

The Rhythm & Blues Foundation, Inc., located in Philadelphia, was founded in 1988. It is "dedicated to the historical and cultural preservation of Rhythm & Blues music, and recognition of contributions of its participants to our musical heritage." The Foundation serves to give financial and medical assistance, educational outreach, performance opportunities and archival activities to those in need among the rhythm and blues community. The website features news, testimonials and an outline of its programs. Donations may be made online.

B19.   www.soulsvilleusa.com
Stax Museum of American Soul Music, 926 E McLemore Avenue, Memphis, TN 38106.

The website for the Stax Music Museum allows the visitor to take a virtual tour of the museum including featured exhibits and past exhibits. It also has a Teacher's Corner that offers lesson plans for K-12 students. The lessons can be viewed online or the CD-ROM can be ordered. There is an online museum shop offering CDs and books. The affiliated Soulville Foundation sponsors the Stax Music Academy and Soulville Charter School. The site also features a blog spot.

**Journals, magazines and periodicals**

B20. *BRE Magazine*, 15030 Ventura Boulevard, Suite 864, Sherman Oaks, CA 91403.
www.bremagazine.com

After thirty years of being published as the magazine *Black Radio Exclusive (BRE)*, as of 2008, the acronym will stand for *Black Renaissance Exclusive*. The monthly journal reports on the black urban entertainment industry. The website and the journal are partnered. The website features the following categories: radio spotlight, music spotlight, features, daily news, big shots, multimedia. Back issues are available.

B21. *Blues & Soul Ltd*, 153 Praed Street, London W2 1RL, UK.
www.bluesandsoul.com

Published bi-monthly, *Blues & Soul* magazine and its online counterpart cover current urban music including rhythm and blues, soul, funk, hip hop, rap and reggae. It was first published in the UK in 1966 and covers music charts, reviews, events and clubs, in-depth interviews and editorial articles. It offers back issues and has representatives in New York and Los Angeles. It is circulated internationally and has featured articles on the histories of Atlantic, Chess and Motown records as well as in-depth profiles of rhythm and blues and soul artists.

B22. *Blues & Rhythm*, 82 Quenby Way, Bromham, Bedfordshire, MK43 8QP.
www.bluesandrhythm.co.uk

*Blues & Rhythm*, first published in July 1984, is published ten times a year. It contains in-depth articles, interviews, discographies, feature columns, and reviews of CD, DVDs and books. It also includes coverage of pre- and post-war blues, rhythm and blues, doo-wop vocal groups, soul, gospel and the contemporary blues scene.

B23. *Soul Society of Finland*
www.soulexpress.net

Print copies of *Soul Express* can be ordered on the site. Content includes discographies, interviews, reviews, feature articles and columns. Music is ranked in their "charts" category and can be purchased online.

*Additional journals, magazines and periodicals*

The listings are devoted wholly or occasionally to research on R&B and soul music.

B24. *Black Music Research Journal* (USA)

B25. *The Black Perspective in Music* (USA)

B26. *Blues and Rhythm* (UK)

B27. *Blues Unlimited* (UK)

B28. *B.M.I. The Many Worlds of Music* (USA)

B29. *Ebony* (USA)

B30. *Hot Buttered Soul* (UK)

B31. *Popular Music* (UK)

B32. *Popular Music and Society* (USA)

B33. *R and B Collector* (retitled *R and B Magazine*) (USA)

B34. *R and B Monthly* (UK)

B35. *R&B Scene* (UK)

B36. *Rhythm and Blues: Covering the Blues and Jazz Scene* (USA)

B37. *Rhythm and Blues Panorama* (Belgium)

B38. *Sepia* (USA)

B39. *Soul Music/Soul Music Monthly* (UK)

B40. *Soul: The magazine for the R&B collector* (UK)

B41. *Soul* (USA)

B42. *Soul Bag* (France)

## APPENDIX C: SELECTED HIP HOP AND RAP WEB SOURCES, MAGAZINES AND PERIODICALS

### General web sources for hip hop and rap

C1. www.mrwiggles.biz
Divine Rhythm Productions, 250 W 50th Street, 12S, New York, NY 10019.

Created by "Mr. Wiggles," a Puerto Rican raised in the South Bronx, the site has a pull-down "knowledge" menu containing several categories. The "timeline" category is a chronicle of hip hop history that interestingly begins from 1925 (identifying stylistic similarities in historical performance traits, e.g. "Snake Hips" Earl Tucker) to 2006. Other categories include: Hip hop dance; MC facts; "poppin lessons"; ghetto slang—a "glossary"; misconceptions; history—this section includes an essay by the site's author describing the Bronx scene of early hip hop from his personal perspective; "Graff" Facts (graffiti writing); and resources—books on the topic. The site is colored with the creator's personal irony and humor.

C2. www.rapindustry.com

The site is a comprehensive source for new music, videos, radio, fashion, magazines, industry news and more. It streams rap music and features interviews with rap artists.

C3. www.rapscene.com

The site offers new videos, new music, reviews and interviews. Live performances can be accessed with a click. R&B, Latino and rock categories are included. Movies that contain hip hop culture references are promoted. There is also a chat room.

C4. www.hiphop-elements.com

The site features RSS feeds for hip hop news and videos featuring new music videos, hip hop interviews, concerts and freestyles.

C5. therapup.uproxx.com

This a hip hop and rap audio blog that is networked with similar blogs, including Real Talk NY, the Smoking Section, Fatlace Mag and Buzzcuts.

C6. www.wydublog.com

Authored in the US, this audioblog has writers from Luxembourg, Sweden, Croatia, Germany and Australia. It has a long list of affiliate audio blogs, which are in turn networked with others. Extensive resources.

C7. www.hiphop-directory.com

An online resource directing the user to hip hop-related sites.

C8. www.realrap.net

Artist reviews and biographies are offered here. Artists are categorized by region or hip hop style, e.g. West Coast, East Coast, foreign, gangsta, Latin, Midwest, political, underground and more.

C9. www.centralcali.com

This site is about the hip hop scene in Central California. It features message boards, reviews and news about local events.

C10.  www.youthhiphop.com

This is a directory site linking to urban hip hop, music industry and hip hop dance class categories. There are links to DJ sites as well as to "jungle" and "drum and bass" electronica sites.

C11.  www.westcoast2k.net/interviews.htm

The site features downloadable freestyle raps. It also includes interviews and reviews.

C12.  www.bet.com/music
Black Entertainment Television, 1235 West Street NE, Washington, DC 20018.

This site is part of the Black Entertainment Television Corporation. Hip hop videos, new music, blogs and a wide range of music news, including a "newswire" are featured. The site is slick and well designed.

C13.  www.globalartistscoalition.org
Hip Hop Culture Center In Harlem, Magic Johnson Theater, 2309 Frederick Douglass Boulevard, 2nd Floor, Harlem, NY 10027.

Sponsored by the Global Artists Coalition, dedicated to helping "young adults in underserved communities to pursue successful, sustainable careers in the arts, communication and entertainment industries." The non-profit organization sponsors a hip hop exhibition at its Hip Hop Culture Center housed in the Magic Johnson Theater in Harlem. The site discusses the exhibition. It also includes an "edutainment" page providing video that describes their educational program that uses the hip hop musical genre to educate youth. The program travels and has scheduled events in venues such as Columbia University and Medgar Evers College in Brooklyn.

C14.  www.triciarose.com

This is the website for Tricia Rose, a noted scholar of hip hop culture. The site lists her upcoming lectures and information about her publications.

C15.  www.hiphop-network.com
Hip Hop Network, 177 Stillman Street, San Francisco, CA 94107.

Founded in 1982, this site describes itself as a resource for hip hop, not rap. The founders (unnamed) claim that they were motivated to establish the site because of their dissatisfaction with the way that hip hop was represented in the mainstream media. They stress streaming videos as an important tool in communicating the characteristics of this "very animated and visual" genre. The site uses a graffiti-influenced graphic look. There are webcasts of hip hop shows; a "culture" page featuring video exposés on DJ/turntablists, MCs/ rappers, graffiti art, B-boys/breakers, and rappers/MCs. The site also features downloadable images, a radio station, videos, articles on hip hop topics, a store, news and other resources.

C16. unitedhiphop.ning.com

An online hip hop community that features "United Hip Hop TV." It includes photos, videos and blogs.

C17. www.undergroundhiphop.com

The site features a large inventory of hip hop and rap music for sale online and reviews of new music. The site also includes old school hip hop videos and hip hop fashion (the T-shirt collection is varied and the artwork interesting). There is sizable list of underground hip hop and rap record labels. The site sells graffiti art magazines, books and vinyl LPs/EP records. Toys and "free stuff" are offered.

C18. www.hiphopsite.com

This is a slick site with a downloadable music catalog. News, reviews, interviews and an online forum are offered. Digital singles (Digi-12s) can be purchased and downloaded here. Music can also be previewed before purchasing via the online shopping cart.

C19. thehiphopmusic.blogspot.com

This is a comprehensive hip hop audio, video and hip hop culture blogspot. "On the set" provides photo galleries of hip hop artists at work and a "magazine" page offers titles and images of magazines that feature hip hop and other contemporary urban culture themes. Live performance videos and a substantial list of mix tapes are also featured. The navigation is a bit odd (the opening page is a bridge to each category page).

C20. www.harlemhiphoptours.com
Harlem Hip-Hop Tours, 69 W. 106th Street, Suite 5B, New York, NY 10025.

Harlem Hip-Hop Tours (H3 Tours) offers tours of Harlem and New York City's hip hop industry. Because of hip hop's New York origins, the company seeks to benefit from the city's tourists. The company was founded in 2005 by Columbia Business School graduates and includes artist profiles, a history of Harlem, a store and a blog.

C21. www.defjam.com
The Island Def Jam Group, Worldwide Plaza, 825 8th Avenue, 28th Floor, New York, NY 10019.

Def Jam Recordings is a pioneering hip hop recording label, now owned by Universal Music Group. Its first officially catalogued recordings were released in 1984. Jay-Z, Ludacris, L.L. Cool J, Nas and Rihanna are among its noted hip hop and rap performers.

C22. www.npr.org/templates/story/story.php?storyId=4823817
National Public Radio, 635 Massachusetts Avenue NW, Washington, DC.

The History of Hip Hop is a subsite of NPR online. It includes interviews with noted personalities in hip hop history. Grandmaster Flash & the Furious Five, Russell Simmons, L.L. Cool J, Queen Latifah and Will Smith are featured.

C23. www.b-boys.com
B-Boys (Don't Blink Media, Inc.), 400 E Pine Street, Suite 301, Seattle, WA 98122.

The B-Boys website is primarily a communication/discussion forum for hip hop music, news and politics. It features free participation in busy hip hop forums and rap battles. Its "Hip Hop Community" allows the participant to set up a personal profile and meet other hip hop aficionados, read news, explore new music and set up a blog.

C24. www.africanhiphop.com

The Africanhiphop.com site (formerly called Rumba-Kali Home of Hip Hop) is based in Amsterdam, Holland. It provides a forum for hip hop artists from all over the continent of Africa. The site has collected information about the development of hip hop in Africa since the early 1990s and was initiated in 1997. Features news about African hip hop "crews," a news archive, and links and resources (including a newly added clickable map that takes the visitor to hip hop and rap information in the chosen geographical region).

C25. www.oldschoolhiphop.com

The site features music, films and books, along with videos of shows and concerts from hip hop and rap's "old school" period (approximately 1979–84). There are old school battles, radio and an online store. Anyone can post relevant interviews and reviews.

C26. www.daveyd.com

Davey D is a self-described "hip hop historian, journalist, deejay and community activist," who was raised in the Bronx, where much of early hip hop was produced. He later became a co-founder of the Bay Area Hip Hop Coalition (BAHHC) and a member of the Bay Area Black Journalist Association (BABJA). He is the webmaster for what claims to be one of the oldest and largest hip hop sites on the web. There is a decidedly journalistic tone in the site's offerings. It carries extensive articles, news on hip hop culture, and "politics."

C27. www.hiphoplinguistics.com

HHL describes itself as an "underground" hip hop website and online hip hop magazine. It features reviews, news, events, a forum, blog and articles, and offers an "interpretation" of hip-hop lyrics.

C28. hiphopruckus.com

This site includes music, videos, news and audio interviews. "Meet The Block" is a podcast interviewing independent and unsigned artists from New York City and other smaller hip hop communities around the United States. It is free and available on iTunes, Google and Yahoo podcast. It is also syndicated through other podcast locations. The language of the site is street vernacular and there is a measure of "raw" language in a section called "Macking 101." Visitors can subscribe to an RSS feed.

C29. www.itstherub.comradio.htm

This Brooklyn-based site presents a serialized broadcast of the history of hip hop that can be downloaded in mp3 format.

C30. www.zulunation.com

The site expounds a "Universal Zulu Nation" philosophy, based on ideas espoused by New York hip hop artist Afrika Bambaataa. The site has a diverse set of categories, including the standards like hip hop history (with profiles of the early hip hop artists) and more unusual categories such as "Nuwaubian knowledge," "UFOlogy," "world music," and "books for the mind."

C31. www.hiphopmusic.com

The website features news in both text and video format that may be of interest to hip hop audiences. Many of the offerings are politically motivated performances, both serious and humorous. For example, a video titled "West Philly Emcees for Barack Obama" was posted; also posted are the video and lyrics of *Saturday Night Live's* October hip hop spoof about former vice-Presidential candidate Sarah Palin (with Palin on screen as *SNL* cast member Amy Poehler raps the song). An archive is maintained.

C32. www.mtv.com/music/hiphop

This is MTV's online hip hop publication. It includes message boards and a music video search.

C33. www.hiphopdx.com

This is an online journal featuring news features, columns, editorials, blogs, message board, chat room, audio, visual, mix tapes, features and more.

C34. www.24hourhiphop.com

Reviews, video, music and current hip hop news are featured, as well as "rumours," interviews and an online radio station. The site is comparatively sophisticated and comprehensive.

C35. www.hiphophavoc.com

Featured videos photos, news clips, a newsletter and podcasts. The site is part of a group of regional websites called HIPHOPHAVOC NETWORK SITES (Video HAVOC, Dirty South HAVOC, West Coast HAVOC, Midwest HAVOC, and East Coast HAVOC). It is a blog site and registered members can participate in photo battles. It also offers a classified section for those seeking jobs in the hip hop world (e.g. rappers needing jobs or employers needing DJs).

C36. www.hiphopmusicdotcom.com

This is a slick site with audio, including mix tapes, freestyles, interviews, downloads, music videos and live performances.

C37. www.allhiphop.com

A valuable resource for hip hop on the internet that features daily news, interviews, reviews, multimedia and other interesting content.

C38. www.hiphopgame.com

Features exclusive interviews and in-depth reviews of the people and music impacting the urban streets of America. Unfortunately, the site is permeated with advertisements, pop-ups and flashing ads.

C39. www.hiphopportal.net
Hip Hop Research Portal

A database which provides bibliographic access to published resources about hip hop culture, including MCs, DJs, break dancing and graffiti art.

C40. www.pbs.org/newshour/infocus/fashion/hiphop.html
Hip Hop Style: What is Cool

This is an online documentary that details the evolution of hip hop's influence on fashion over the past twenty years.

C41. www.empsfm.org/exhibitions/index.asp?article/d=664
Experience Music Project's Hip Hop Timeline

The Experience Music Project is a Seattle Museum. It offers an interactive timeline covering the first two decades of hip hop from its Bronx (1970s–92).

C42. www.africanhiphop.com
Pan-African Hip Hop

This site, formerly known as Rumba-Kali and Motherland Funk, contains news and archival articles on hip hop music in Africa, reviews of hip hop artists, interviews with prominent members of the music community, and a calendar of events. The site covers hip hop scenes from Tanzania to South Africa and Liberia, and provides a link to Rumba-Kali radio.

C43. www.rapstation.com

The site is dedicated to news and discussions about rap music. It includes its own television station, music videos and streaming radio, interviews with artists, concert information, editorial essays, information on the music industry and aspiring artists, and mp3s available for downloading. Regularly updated.

C44. www.sohh.com

Judged the best hip hop site by *Rolling Stone Magazine*, it provides daily news and features on performers and record labels. The site is often slow to load.

C45. urb1.com

This is the first hip hop fashion website to appear online. It provides the latest news, rumors, and interviews within the hip hop fashion world.

## Journals, magazines and periodicals

C46. *Hip Hop Connection*, The Bunker of Funk, Infamous Ink Ltd, PO Box 392, Cambridge, CB1 3WH, United Kingdom. www.hhcmagazine.com

*Hip Hop Connection*, the oldest monthly periodical dedicated to hip hop culture, was established in 1988. Its first issue was published six months before *The Source* magazine began in newsletter form. It is a UK-based journal and subscriptions are available online. It has been described as being in a position to offer a more open critique of hip hop music than US-based magazines because it is not as subject to US record company approval.

C47. *The Source: The Magazine of Hip-Hop Music, Culture & Politics*, Source Publications, Inc., 11 Broadway, Suite 315 New York, NY 10004. www.thesource.com

After *Hip Hop Connection, The Source* is the second-oldest rap periodical. It was founded as a newsletter in 1988 and has since become highly influential in hip hop culture. Sometimes called "The Bible of Hip-Hop." Digital subscriptions are available online. The company also publishes *Source Latino, Source France*, and *Source Japan.*

C48.   *VIBE*, 120 Wall Street, New York, NY 10005.
       www.vibe.com

*Vibe* magazine describes itself as the "definitive voice of urban culture, influencing global music, life, and style for more than eight million readers around the world." The award-winning publication reports on the many aspects of urban culture with a focus on hip hop culture. *VIBE* magazine was founded in 1993 by renowned artist and producer, Quincy Jones.

C49.   *Wax Poetics*, 45 Main Street, # 224, Brooklyn, NY 11201.
       www.waxpoeticsmagazine.com

*Wax Poetics* was established in New York in 2002. A substantial measure of the journal's focus is black music forms, particularly hip hop. It is known for in-depth interviews with music artists. Its companion website (digital.waxpoetics.com) features over 1,000 hip hop titles that can be previewed and purchased online.

C50.   *Words, Beats and Life*, 1525 Newton Street NW, Washington, DC 20010.
       www.wblinc.org/Journal.htm

The goal of *Words, Beats and Life, Inc.: Global Hip Hop Journal, from the Streets to the University,* is to feature scholarly, as well as alternative and creative perspectives on the culture of hip hop. Among the peer reviewers listed are Dr Mark Anthony Neal (Duke University), Scott Heath (Georgetown University) and Dr Clyde Woods (University of California, Santa Barbara). Founded in 2002, inspired by the Words Beats & Life (WBL) Hip-Hop Conference at the University of Maryland. The philosophy is that the owners, producers and scholars of hip hop culture should be instrumental in determining "meaning, value and relevance" for the genre. The Cipher, also discussed on this site, is a non-profit program developed by WBL to support hip hop nonprofit and for-profit ventures. This appears to be a comprehensive and promising venture.

C51.   *XXL*, Harris Publications, Inc., 1115 Broadway, New York, NY 10010.
       www.xxlmag.com

*XXL* is a hip hop magazine published by Harris Publications, founded in 1997. It carries a wide variety of articles on hip hop topics.

C52. The Hiphop Archive at Harvard, W.E.B. DuBois Institute for African and African American Research, Dr Marcyliena Morgan, Director, tel. 617-496-0352, fax 617-496-2871, mmorgan@fas.harvard.edu; Benjamin Carter 111, Program Coordinator, tel. 617-496-8885 or 617-495-9366, abcarter@fas.harvard.edu.
www.dubois.fas.harvard.edu/hiphop-archive-harvard-university

The Hiphop Archive at Harvard was established by Professor Marcyliena Morgan in 2002, and since 2008 has been housed in the W.E.B. DuBois Institute for African and African American Research. The digital archive's primary objective is to "facilitate and encourage the pursuit of knowledge, art, culture, and responsible leadership through Hiphop." The Archive aims to "sponsor and facilitate projects, events, and numerous other activities." In addition, it publishes a newsletter six times a year, and its Hiphop University provides digital links to bibliography, courses offered throughout the United States, conferences, events and more. For information about the archive's activities, projects and function as a resource "for those interested in knowing, developing, building, maintaining and representing Hiphop," one can contact the Director and Program Coordinator.

## APPENDIX D: SELECTED AFRICAN AMERICAN MUSIC WEB SOURCES

D1. www.indiana.edu/~aaamc
Archives of African American Music and Culture (AAAMC)
School of Music, Indiana University, 2805 E Tenth Street, Suite 180-181, Bloomington, IN 47408-2601, tel. 812-855-8547, fax 812-856-0333, aaamc@indiana.edu.

Established in 1991, this is one of the oldest and most distinguished archives devoted to the serious study and research of African American music. The archives are "a repository of materials covering a range of African American musical idioms and cultural expressions from the post-World War II era." The collection covers popular, religious and classical musical traditions, is a resource for students, Indiana faculty scholars like David Baker, Portia Maultsby and Mellonee Burnim, as well as external scholars of African American music. In addition to extensive holdings on blues, R&B, rap, gospel music, jazz and other genres, the AAAMC provides "access to oral histories, photographs, musical and print manuscripts, audio and video recordings, educational broadcast programs, and the papers of individuals and organizations concerned with black music." In addition, AAACM houses numerous materials related to black radio, provides public events, print and online publications, and more.

D2.  www.colum.edu/cbmr
The Center for Black Music Research (CBMR)
Columbia College Chicago, Dr Monica L. Hairston Executive Director,
600 S Michigan Avenue, Chicago, IL 60605-1996, tel. 312-369-7559,
mhairston@colum.edu.

The Center's mission is to collect, document, desseminate and preserve information about the common roots and parallel histories of
black music throughout the African diaspora. In addition to extensive
holdings (books, monograms, recordings) in blues, R&B and rap, the
Center also houses numerous research materials and recordings on
other African American musical traditions, including Euro-American
art music, and on African diaspora musical traditions. The Center
publishes a newsletter, a scholarly journal, presents conferences and
symposia, performances, and provides links to African American
cultural activities throughout the United States.

D3.  The Cornell University Library Hip Hop Collection, Circa 1975-1985.
Division of Rare and Manuscript Collections
Katherine Regan, Curator, 2B Carl A. Kroch Library, Cornell University, Ithaca, New York 14853, tel. 607-255-3530, fax 607-255-9524,
rarereF@cornell.edu.
http://rmc.library.cornell.edu
http://rmc.library.cornell.edu/hiphop/resources.html.

A collection of hip hop recordings, memorabilia, posters, and other
printed materials that were donated to Cornell University in 2008.
The collection covers the 1975-85 period, the early days of the movement, and includes materials on the pioneering DJ's who scratched
records, and the street parties that drew rappers, street dancers, and
graffiti artists. Specifically, the collection contains1, 000 recordings,
mostly LPs, the photographs of Joe Conzo, jr., books and magazines,
textile art, and more than 500 original party and club flyers that were
designed by Buddy Esquire and others. The collection is important
because it contains information on the origins of hip-hop as a community, cultural, and musical phenomenon that evolved in the Bronx, New
York in the early 1970s.The collection is also important because it
contains information on the global influence of hip hop, rap musicians,
break dancers, disc jockeys, street art, rap music, and more.

D4.  Rock and Roll Hall of Fame and Museum
Cleveland, Ohio, tel. 216-515-8425.
www.rockhall.com

The Rock and Roll Hall of Fame and Museum (RRHFM) is located
in downtown Cleveland, Ohio, and is dedicated to recording the

history of artists, producers, and music industry officials who impacted the history and evolution of Rock Music. Although its primary mission is to sponsor events and exhibitions, both are important because they often contain information that is useful to serious scholars of Blues, Funk, Rhythm and Blues, Soul, Hip Hop and Rap. In addition, the events and exhibits are important because of the roots relationship between the aforementioned musical genres and rock music, a relationship that RRHFM has acknowledged and recognized since its founding on April 20, 1983. To this end, since its first inductions in 1986, the RRHFM has inducted Chuck Berry, James Brown, Ray Charles, Sam Cooke, Fats Domino, Run D.M.C, Grandmaster Flash and the Furious Five, Kenny Gamble and Leon Huff, Buddy Guy, Michael Jackson, The Jackson Five, Gladys Knight and the Pips, Little Richard, Little Walter, Bobby Womack and many other artists, composers, producers, and music industry officials associated with the musical genres contained in this book.

The museum contains several floors, which in turn, feature permanent exhibits. Among the most interesting permanent exhibits is the history of audio technology, outfits of famous past and present performers, and an exhibit of music scenes representing Memphis in the 1950s, Detroit, Liverpool, and San Francisco in the 1960s, Los Angeles, New York City, and London in the 1970s, and 1980s, and Seattle in the 1990s. In addition, the museum features permanent collections on Chuck Berry, Fats Domino, The Everly Brothers, Janis Joplin, and The Who.

# Index of authors and artists

The main bibliography is indexed by section numbers; appendices are indexed by page numbers, indicated in bold.

# Index of titles, organizations and places

The main bibliography is indexed by section numbers; appendices are indexed by page numbers, indicated in bold.